DATE DUE

DE 8 '98			
MY 25 99			
DE 10 00			

DEMCO 38-296

As If Jesus Walked on Earth

As If Jesus Walked on Earth

Cardenismo, Sonora, and the Mexican Revolution

Adrian A. Bantjes

A Scholarly Resources Inc. Imprint
Wilmington, Delaware

Scholarly Resources Inc.
104 Greenhill Avenue
Wilmington, DE 19805-1897

Library of Congress Cataloging-in-Publication Data

Bantjes, Adrian A., 1959–
    As if Jesus walked on Earth : Cardenismo, Sonora, and the
    Mexican Revolution / Adrian A. Bantjes.
        p.   cm. — (Latin American silhouettes : studies in history
    and culture)
        Includes bibliographical references (p.   -   ) and index.
        ISBN 0-8420-2653-3 (cloth : alk. paper)
        1. Sonora (Mexico : State)—Politics and government.
    2. Sonora (Mexico : State)—Social policy. 3. Sonora (Mexico :
    State)—Economic policy. 4. Mexico—Politics and government—
    1910–1946. 5. Cárdenas, Lázaro, 1895–1970. I. Title. II. Series:
    Latin American silhouettes.
    F1346.B37   1997
    972'.17—dc21   97-12365
                                                                  CIP

⊗The paper used in this publication meets the minimum require-
ments of the American National Standard for permanence of paper
for printed library materials, Z39.48, 1984.

Acknowledgments

I have incurred many debts during the lengthy trajectory of this project. My first introduction to Mexican culture and history occurred during a wonderful year at El Colegio de México. There, and later at the University of Texas at Austin, I learned much from colleagues, professors, and friends. During my numerous research trips I received invaluable aid from archivists and librarians, notably, in Mexico City at the Archivo General de la Nación, the Archivos Plutarco Elías Calles y Fernando Torreblanca (where director Norma Mereles de Ogarrio and her *superequipo* were particularly helpful), and the Secretaría de Educación Pública; in Hermosillo at the Archivo del Gobierno del Estado de Sonora (especially from Dr. Rosario Arias and his *muchachos*—I fondly remember our pleasant excursions to the Ures and Yaqui valleys), the Museo de Sonora, and the libraries of El Colegio de Sonora and the Centro Regional del Noroeste of the Instituto Nacional de Antropología e Historia; and in Jiquilpán from Héctor Madrid at the Archivo Francisco J. Múgica. In the United States I received expert service at the Benson Latin American Collection of the University of Texas at Austin, the National Archives in Washington, DC, the Arizona State Historical Society, the Arizona State Museum, and Coe Library at the University of Wyoming.

In Hermosillo I enjoyed the hospitality of the History Department of the Universidad de Sonora, the Centro Regional of INAH, and, especially, of El Colegio de Sonora, where *rectores* Gerardo Cornejo Murrieta and Jorge Luis Ibarra Mendívil and their colleagues were extremely supportive of my research and provided me with special facilities and a stimulating intellectual environment. In Mexico City the Departamento de Ciencias Sociales of UNAM and El Colegio de México granted me research privileges, while the inhabitants of the Residencia Universitaria Panamericana introduced me to a variety of Mexican cultural expressions, including the *norteño* mentality.

This project was financed by generous grants from the Netherlands-Mexican Cultural Exchange Program, the Institute of Latin American Studies and the History Department of the University of Texas at Austin, and the College of Arts and Sciences and the History Department of the University of Wyoming.

My work was built on the foundations laid by a number of historians. I am particularly indebted to the pioneering work on Sonora in the 1930s by José Carlos Ramírez, Cristina Martínez, and Rocío Guadarrama, who all collaborated on the monumental *Historia General de Sonora*, which should be a starting point for anyone interested in Sonoran history. I must specifically thank Gabriela González Barragán, Samuel León, Carlos Macías, Juan Ortiz, José Carlos Ramírez, and Victor Manuel Reynoso for their interest in my research and their generous help during my stays in Hermosillo and Mexico City. I also benefited immensely from the insights and support of Ignacio Almada Bay (whose excellent dissertation on Yocupicio complements my findings), Bernabé Arana León, Ariane Baroni, Gilberto Escobosa Gámez, Leopoldo García, Guillermo García Zamacona, Juan José Gracida Romo, Professor Amadeo Hernández Coronado, the late Padre Ernesto López Yescas, Cristina Martínez, Sergio Peña Medina, Cynthia Radding, Ernesto Robles, Juan Manuel Romero Gil, Carlos Salas Plasencia, Leopoldo Santos Ramírez, Friedrich E. Schuler, and Maren von der Borch.

An early version of this study was read by the late Nettie Lee Benson, Jonathan Brown, Susan Deans-Smith, Aline Helg, and Bryan Roberts. I am particularly grateful to Alan Knight, my dissertation supervisor at Texas, for his assistance, encouragement, and profound insights. A later version was read by William Beezley, Cynthia Radding, Cheryl Martin, Mary Henning, Evelyn Hu-DeHart, and several anonymous readers, who all provided helpful suggestions. Obviously, any remaining errors are mine. I am also grateful for the tireless help of Rick Hopper, Michelle Slavin, and many others at Scholarly Resources, and especially for Bill Beezley's constant encouragement and enthusiasm.

Finally, I would like to thank my parents for their enduring support and, last but not least, my wife Mary for her patience, love, and unflagging optimism. These are just a few of the individuals without whom this project would never have been completed. I wish I could thank every one of them here.

Contents

IV The Politics of Cardenista Reform and the Reform of Politics, or the Demise of Cardenismo, 1938–1940

Acronyms

CAAES	Confederación de Asociaciones Agrícolas del Estado de Sonora
CESU	Centro de Estudios sobre la Universidad
CGT	Confederación General de Trabajadores
CNC	Confederación Nacional Campesina
CNTE	Confederación Nacional de Trabajadores de la Enseñanza
CROM	Confederación Regional Obrera Mexicana
CTM	Confederación de Trabajadores de México
CTS	Confederación de Trabajadores de Sonora
EPL	Ejército Popular Libertador
FEMSS	Federación Estatal de Maestros Socialistas Sonorenses
FMTE	Federación Mexicana de Trabajadores de la Enseñanza
FOCH	Federación Obrero-Campesina de Hermosillo
FOCSS	Federación Obrera y Campesina del Sur de Sonora
FROC	Federación Regional de Obreros y Campesinos
FSTSE	Federación de Sindicatos de Trabajadores al Servicio del Estado
FTP	Federación de Trabajadores de Puebla
FTS	Federación de Trabajadores de Sonora
LCASC	Liga de Comunidades Agrarias y Sindicatos Campesinos
PDS	Partido Democrático Sonorense
PNR	Partido Nacional Revolucionario
PP	Partido Popular
PRI	Partido Revolucionario Institucional
PRM	Partido de la Revolución Mexicana
SIPS	Sindicato Industrial Progresista Sonorense
SITMMSRM	Sindicato Industrial de Trabajadores Mineros, Metalúrgicos y Similares de la República Mexicana

SNCOP	Sindicato Nacional de Carreteras y Obras Públicas
SNTE	Sindicato Nacional de Trabajadores de la Educación
SRE	Secretaría de Relaciones Exteriores
STERM	Sindicato de Trabajadores de la Enseñanza de la República Mexicana
STFRM	Sindicato de Trabajadores Ferrocarrileros de la República Mexicana
SUTEP	Sindicato Unico de Trabajadores de la Educación de Puebla
SUTES	Sindicato Unico de Trabajadores de la Enseñanza de Sonora
SUTSEMS	Sindicato Unico de Trabajadores al Servicio del Estado y de los Municipios de Sonora
UGOCM	Unión General de Obreros y Campesinos de México
UMM	Unión de Mecánicos Mexicanos
UMM	Unión Minera Mexicana
UNVR	Unión Nacional de Veteranos de la Revolución

Introduction*

" When [Lázaro Cárdenas] was president even the birds sang cheerfully. . . . In those days . . . it seemed as if Jesus Christ walked on Earth. All the campesinos had their livestock and sowed and made a living from this, all were smallholders who could sow a little piece of land and no one bothered them."[1] A Sonoran campesino wrote these words to Mexican presidential candidate Cuauhtémoc Cárdenas, the son of Lázaro Cárdenas, in 1988. They powerfully express the persisting strength of the Cardenista mystique. Nearly a half-century after the legendary leader Lázaro Cárdenas left the presidency, peasants tearfully recall how "tata Lázaro" restored their lands to them, thereby fulfilling the promises of the Mexican Revolution of 1910–1920. Cárdenas indeed has become a "revolutionary symbol . . . virtually deified by the masses."[2] Thus, it is impossible to interpret the revolution and the postrevolutionary society it spawned without a clear understanding of the nature, meaning, and impact of Cardenismo.

The persistence of Cardenista utopianism, however, has clouded our understanding of Mexico's past. The image of Cárdenas may be more popular today than it was during his presidency (1934–1940).[3] It is extremely difficult to break through the Cardenista myth and reconstruct the contours of Mexican history during the crucial 1930s. Even historians have perpetuated a hagiographic view of Cardenismo, depicting it as the culmination of the revolutionary process. According to this interpretation, it was Cárdenas who finally addressed the deep-rooted popular grievances that sparked the revolution. He created a powerful alliance with the peasantry and organized labor. The campesinos benefited from the largest agrarian reform program in Mexican history, which destroyed the Porfirian haciendas and redistributed eighteen million hectares to

*Sections of the introduction appear in Adrian A. Bantjes, "Cardenismo: Interpretations," in *Encyclopedia of Mexico: History, Society and Culture*, edited by Michael Werner (Chicago: Fitzroy Dearborn Publishers, 1997).

some 800,000 landless peasants. A newly galvanized labor movement saw real wages increase, working conditions improve, and gained an enhanced bargaining position vis-à-vis capital. Cárdenas served the revolutionary cause of economic nationalism by triumphantly expropriating the foreign-owned petroleum sector in 1938. He created Mexico's unique, remarkably stable, corporatist political system by founding the official Partido de la Revolución Mexicana (PRM) in an effort to institutionalize the political participation of the Cardenista masses and to safeguard the achievements of reform for the future.

Hagiographies and official eulogies depict Cardenismo as the most authentic expression of the revolution. They characterize Cárdenas as the embodiment of *el pueblo* (the people). Frank Tannenbaum wrote that "it is clear that Cárdenas is deeply rooted in the Mexican soil. He is part of the earth itself, and he is timeless." Or, as Roberto Blanco Moheno stated, "Mexico and this man were the same thing."[4] Interpretations of Cárdenas mirror the diverse utopian hopes of his sympathizers. Contemporary U.S. observers portrayed the Mexican president as a New Deal democrat, a natural ally in the struggle against European facism, and compared him to Franklin D. Roosevelt.[5] Later, socialist analysts depicted Cardenismo as a Mexican version of world socialism. Adolfo Gilly classified Cardenista utopianism as an important component of the Latin American socialism represented by José Carlos Mariátegui, Antonio Guiteras, Augusto César Sandino, and José Martí.[6] However, these interpretations stretch conventional definitions of socialism. Cárdenas may have been sympathetic toward socialist ideology but never thought of it as a realistic short-term alternative for Mexican development.[7]

Recent historical analysis by Alan Knight and Nora Hamilton considers Cardenismo "a genuinely radical movement," willing to experiment with "quasi-socialist" control of the means of production.[8] Leon Trotsky, Cárdenas's guest-in-exile, saw it somewhat differently: he characterized the Mexican State as bourgeois, the president as an anti-imperialist liberal, and his regime as "sui generis bonapartism."[9]

The original hagiographic school gave way to disappointed revisionism in the wake of the 1968 Tlatelolco massacre. Cardenismo was a controversial phenomenon even during the 1930s. Conservatives branded Cárdenas an anti-Mexican communist traitor, a dangerous radical who negated the ideals of the revolution and imported exotic ideologies with the purpose of destroying private property, the family, and religion.[10] But it was the slaughter of hundreds of peacefully demonstrating students and workers by the Mexican government and military in 1968 that finally convinced many intellectuals, in particular socialists, that Mexico was just another Latin American authoritarian regime, despite its revolutionary legacy.

This revisionist school portrayed Cárdenas as a Machiavellian populist who demobilized and manipulated workers and peasants by means of a corporatist "cardenista machine."[11] Cardenismo spawned the powerful, bureaucratic authoritarian state responsible for the massacre at the Plaza de las Tres Culturas. It brought about capitalist development and the triumph of the bourgeoisie. Arnaldo Córdova described Cárdenas as the "most inspired prophet" of the "capitalist counterinsurgency," which defeated Mexico's revolutionary proletariat and created "the Leviathan which ultimately devoured all of society."[12]

The few regional studies of Cardenismo, not coincidentally mostly of Cárdenas's home state of Michoacán, offer us more harsh revisionism. According to Marjorie Becker's early work, Cárdenas, ignorant, condescending, and disdainful toward campesino culture, launched "a widespread assault on [the] grass roots traditions" of the *michoacano* peasantry in an effort to create a docile work force for dependent capitalist development. He established political hegemony through a network of repressive caciques and *pistoleros*, thus trampling on indigenous traditions of democracy, religiosity, and economic justice. Likewise, John Gledhill argues that Cárdenas, strongly distrustful of the "unprepared masses," instated an authoritarian, corrupt, clientelistic regime that harassed a resistant peasantry with an "abusive form of arbitrary power."[13] For both, the result of Cardenismo was a stronger capitalist state, the ascendancy of the bourgeoisie, and the defeat of the peasantry. These studies may explain why some Mexicans rejected the Cardenista project, but they fail to account for its widespread support and persisting appeal. Why, one wonders, did Michoacán remain loyal to the Cardenista myth after the revolution even though this loyalty has meant losing government patronage and becoming a pariah within the official political system? One-sided revisionism only answers part of the question.

Becker, however, has dramatically modified her earlier thesis and now offers a more balanced evaluation of Cardenismo that explores both official and popular cultures. She argues that Cardenismo in Michoacán, although initially oblivious to peasant

values, was a malleable movement. The interaction of the Cardenista project with campesino culture resulted in the emergence of
a new hegemonic political culture that allowed for a modicum
of peasant participation.[14] Becker's recent study is an important
step in the direction of providing a much-needed reinterpretation of Cardenismo. Future research should move beyond a two-
dimensional approach and explore the heterogeneous forces that
shaped modern Mexican society.

Historians have alternately characterized the Cárdenas administration as communist, socialist, social-democratic, liberal, bona-
partist, national reformist, corporatist, authoritarian, and populist.[15]
Cárdenas has been hailed as a Mexican democrat and viciously attacked as the creator of "that enormous concentration camp that
Mexico was becoming."[16] Obviously, both approaches are problematic. Eulogistic interpretations ignore the continuities between
Cardenismo and earlier regimes and tend to downplay the more
authoritarian aspects of Cardenista reform. Revisionism, in stressing Machiavellian populism, tends to confuse the final authoritarian outcome of Mexico's revolutionary process with the intentions
of Cárdenas. It thus makes sense to answer Gilbert Joseph's call for
a synthesis of revisionist and populist theses, combining top-down
with bottom-up analysis of peasant and worker mobilization and
militancy.[17]

This study attempts to break away from both mythology and
black legend to analyze what Cardenismo actually meant for ordi-
nary Mexicans culturally, politically, and economically as they
struggled through those difficult years of radical reform. I find that
Cardenismo has a variety of meanings. It was not a monolithic ideology and movement but an arena in which diverse political cultures clashed violently. During this chaotic era of Mexican history,
there were not only "many Mexicos" but many Cardenismos as well.
Unlike revisionists, I advocate exploring the multivocality of
Cardenismo in an effort to understand both the utopianism and
the praxis of postrevolutionary Mexican society. How was this phenomenon understood by different groups (not just labor and the
peasantry but also the bourgeoisie, the political elites, indigenous
peoples, and Catholics), and how did it operate at a practical, everyday level? The meaning of Cardenismo has been appropriated,
manipulated, and diverted from its original source. It is this fluid-
ity that explains why Cardenismo was so controversial during the
1930s, and why the Cardenista myth persists to this day.

Not only should this study enhance our understanding of Cardenismo, but it also contributes to the wider debate on the nature of the Mexican Revolution. Did the revolution constitute an autonomous, popular struggle for land and liberty, or was it a cynical ploy by an excluded, modernizing middle class to gain control of the State?[18] Reality was, of course, more complex, but the Sonoran case clearly indicates that worker and peasant agency was a major factor in Cardenista reform.

Most accounts discuss Cardenismo from a national perspective, a position that at times leads to ill-founded generalizations. The new regional historiography of the last decades has produced a spate of excellent studies on the period from 1910 to 1929 that has deepened our understanding of the revolutionary process, often debunking myths of varied political plumage. However, these studies seldom extend into the 1930s and 1940s, the crucial years during which postrevolutionary society took shape.[19] The goal of this study is to analyze the impact of Cardenismo at the regional level and, at the same time, the impact of regional developments on Cardenismo. How was Cardenista political control extended? By force, through the tentacles of the growing Leviathan state, or through informal, clientelist ties? Did Cárdenas mobilize the masses "from above" or merely ally his regime with pre-existing regional movements? How successful were the Cardenista reforms at the state level? What type of resistance to the Cardenista project developed in the provinces, and what impact did this resistance have on the implementation of Cárdenas's policies?

These questions can only be answered by closely examining Mexican history from a regional perspective while never losing sight of national-level linkages. Local and national history were articulated in a dialectics of power. One of the aims of this study is thus to examine a major phase in the process of postrevolutionary centralization by an increasingly powerful Mexican State, which by the 1930s had begun to exert a strong military, bureaucratic, political, economic, and cultural influence in the periphery. The outcome was a growing loss of local autonomy as states were exposed to the agents of revolutionary change and modernization, such as federal labor inspectors, teachers, union leaders, political emissaries, military officers, and agronomists. However, regionalism still constituted a major factor in national politics during the 1930s, and regional forces throughout Mexico combined to force the course of Cardenismo, and of the revolution, in a very different direction than that envisaged by representatives of the revolutionary state.[20] It was not the blueprint of the revolutionary elite but the interaction of local, regional, and national actors that forged postrevolutionary society. Therefore, just as this study argues that radical Cardenismo was as much the reflection of popular agency as of top-down elite planning, it also argues that regional forces, both progressive and conservative, were crucial players in the formation of a new Mexican nation.

Until the 1930s fiercely independent Sonora, one of the cradles of the Mexican Revolution, remained largely untouched by revolutionary change. Sonora produced the "Sonoran dynasty," a group of revolutionaries, including Alvaro Obregón and Plutarco Elías Calles, that dominated the national government during the 1920s and early 1930s and generated many of the ideological currents of the revolution. But despite its key role in the revolution, Sonora did not witness the dramatic attempts at socioeconomic restructuring that occurred in the "laboratories of the revolution," or the slow, piecemeal change experienced by some states. Instead, the Cárdenas reforms came as a shock.

Postrevolutionary Sonora constitutes a perfect laboratory for historical analysis because of its great diversity. The state contained both modern export-oriented mining and agricultural sectors as well as isolated serrano communities and substantial indigenous populations, thus offering the historian the possibility of examining the response to Cardenista reform of diverse social groups. True, Sonora had developed a distinct, often romanticized, *norteño* culture during the colonial era and the nineteenth century due to its isolation and the frontier, later border, nature of its society. But by the 1930s it had begun to lose some of this singularity as it was increasingly incorporated into the Mexican nation by the revolutionary state.[21] The case of Sonora during the Cárdenas era is thus representative of the rest of the nation, as far as any region can be. By dissecting the process of Cardenista reform in Sonora and comparing it with other states throughout this analysis, one can reach a deeper understanding of the general national pattern.

Sonora rose to economic and political prominence during the dictatorship of Porfirio Díaz (1876–1911). For most of the century the state had been a frontier area, characterized by small urban settlements, isolated haciendas and mines, and ethnic territories. Continuous Yaqui and Mayo resistance to mestizo encroachment, combined with frequent Apache raids and political turmoil, created an unstable environment in which the economic potential of

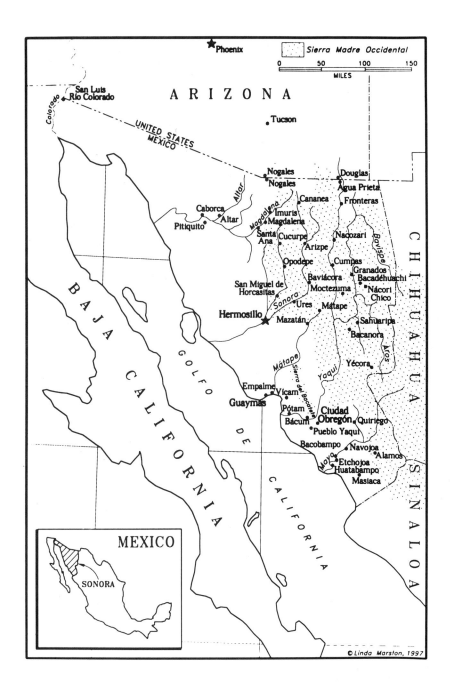

Sonora could not be fully exploited. The state's population actually declined during the nineteenth century. Sonora's isolation limited the market for the region's products. During the Díaz administration this situation changed dramatically. Economic growth accelerated due to the elimination of bottlenecks, and Apache resistance was finally broken. Railroads, especially the Guaymas-Nogales line, finished in 1882, linked the region to markets in Mexico and the United States, opened up the emerging agricultural zones in the Yaqui and Mayo Valleys, and created a string of new urban settlements. The population grew rapidly, in part due to migration, from 131,400 in 1871 to 265,400 in 1910, and 364,200 in 1940.[22] Massive investment by U.S. corporations led to a spectacular mining boom. Land-surveying companies opened up vast tracts of land in the Yaqui Valley, where agricultural entrepreneurs, many of them North Americans, established modern capitalist farming enterprises that relied on migrant wage labor. These workers formed the basis of a rapidly developing rural proletariat after the revolution. Economic expansion spawned primitive industrialization, especially in the food-processing sector. Numerous merchant houses, often owned by foreigners, benefited from the economic *hausse.* However, the price paid for "progress" was steep. The Díaz administration sought a final solution for the "Indian problem" and deported thousands of Yaquis to the henequen plantations of Yucatán, brutally repressed the labor movement (for example, at Cananea in 1906), and fostered the entrenchment of an exclusionary political elite.[23]

During the nineteenth century, politics remained the domain of elite factions, consisting of overlapping groups of landowners, merchants, and miners. On the eve of the Mexican Revolution, opposition to the Díaz regime originated with out factions comprising members of the elites and middle class. Popular resistance was largely limited to the Yaqui people, who staged a series of bloody rebellions. In Sonora the 1910 revolution led by Francisco I. Madero only resulted in an elite political realignment under José María Maytorena. However, when counter-revolutionary forces toppled Madero's regime in 1913, Sonora came to play a crucial role in the Constitutionalist movement. Young Sonorans such as Alvaro Obregón led revolutionary armies, including thousands of Yaqui troops, to the bloody battlefields of central Mexico. It was this group of Sonoran revolutionary leaders (Obregón, Calles, and others) that finally seized control of the national government in 1920, thus ending the civil war and embarking on a period of reconstruction. The

Sonorans, although increasingly disunited, dominated Mexican politics and the presidency into the 1930s. It was against this background that General Lázaro Cárdenas, a *michoacano* with close ties to the Sonorans, came to power in 1934.

After the armed phase of the revolution, Sonoran politics continued to center on the struggle for power between factions, in particular the Obregonistas and Callistas, the followers of revolutionary leaders Obregón and Calles. In 1929, in response to the assassination of Obregón, a failed national Obregonista uprising resulted in Callista hegemony in Sonora and the exclusion of Obregonistas from the political system until 1936.

Throughout the years of revolutionary strife, Sonoran society saw little social change. Factionalism continued as before, and popular mobilization was limited. It was not until the days of Lázaro Cárdenas that agents of the revolutionary state tried to transform Sonoran society dramatically, in the process galvanizing progressive local movements. This study chronicles how Sonorans responded to radical reform "from without," interacting with State projects and, in the process, reshaping Mexico's political culture. Cardenismo was embraced by some, opposed by others, compromised and refashioned beyond recognition. Regional reality, in Sonora and elsewhere, stymied the consolidation of Cardenista hegemony. Sonorans' tenacious resistance not only led to the decline of Cardenismo, but it also resulted in the demise of the Mexican Revolution. Once Cárdenas's revolutionary project had been emptied of meaning, "the Revolution" became a hollow concept, to be filled by capitalist modernization and authoritarianism. After 1940, revolutionary reform was rolled back or terminated. The impact of Cardenista reform in Sonora was short-lived and limited. But the Cardenista myth has proven more enduring and continues to inspire shaken Mexicans as a chaotic end of the century draws near.

I

Politics, Class, and Culture in Postrevolutionary Sonora

1

The Revolution Comes to Sonora

Politics and the Failed Cultural Revolution, 1929–1935

The Legacy of Callismo

It was not until the 1930s, twenty years after the outbreak of the Mexican Revolution, that revolutionary change came to Sonora.[1] The profound sociopolitical and cultural polarization in Mexico and Sonora during the Cárdenas years can be traced back to the dominance of the national revolutionary faction of Sonoran General Plutarco Elías Calles, president of Mexico from 1924 to 1928 and *jefe máximo* of the revolution from 1928 until his exile in 1936. In Sonora, Callista hegemony was represented by Governors Francisco S. Elías (1929–1931), Rodolfo Elías Calles (1931–1934), and Ramón Ramos (1934–35). Sonoran Callismo was in many ways more progressive than its national counterpart and shared much in common with radical Cardenismo, despite the rift that emerged between the two factions by 1935. Although sharing the Jacobinism[2] of Calles and his belief in agrarian capitalism, Sonoran Callistas espoused a more radical brand of populism and incorporated labor and campesino groups into a new regional coalition. They may have initiated this process with some hesitation and cynicism. But by 1935, labor had benefited in concrete ways (political power, agrarian and labor reform), while Callistas depended increasingly on labor to stay in power.

The Callista faction in Sonora, in particular Calles's son Rodolfo Elías Calles, exemplified the new modernizing political elites who had risen to power in the wake of the revolution. They stressed the development of a capitalist, export-oriented agricultural sector based on medium-sized farms operated by a dynamic agrarian bourgeoisie. Although far from advocating radical change in class relations, Sonoran Callistas envisaged an important role for organized labor and favored preemptive agrarian reform "from above," which, they believed, would lead to the absorption of new groups into capitalist agriculture. Some segments of the economic elites found this moderate position threatening. But what distinguished the Callistas from other Sonoran factions, in particular the Obregonistas, was their approach to culture. The goal of the fanatically anticlerical Callistas was to forge "new men" and a new revolutionary civil religion.

Sonoran Callismo, 1929–1935: Factional Politics and Socioeconomic Development

Despite the modernity of developmentalist ideology, Mexican politics remained the realm of traditional political culture, based on such *sociabilités traditionnelles* as personalism, kinship, clientelism, and factionalism, all of which were reinforced by revolutionary experience. These loyalties coexisted well with the developing bureaucratic structures of the postrevolutionary State.[3]

Factional strife distinguished Sonoran politics during the 1920s and 1930s. The principal contending groups were the Callistas and Obregonistas. Throughout the 1920s members of the *camarilla* of former President Alvaro Obregón, in particular Governors Alejo Bay and Fausto Topete, dominated the political arena, increasingly to the exclusion of a Callista faction. The strength of Sonoran Obregonismo was underscored by the physical presence of Don Alvaro, who retired to the rural life on his hacienda, El Naínari. The assassination of President-elect Obregón in 1928, popular suspicions concerning Plutarco Elías Calles's complicity, and the ensuing debate on the presidential succession led part of the Obregonista faction, including its Sonoran adherents, to rebel against the government in 1929. Calles's suppression of the Escobar rebellion effectively swept the Obregonistas from power. Leading rebels fled to the United States and were never to play a role in state politics again. But many lesser *renovadores*, as adherents of the rebel Plan de Hermosillo were known, formed the backbone of anti-Callista opposition during the early 1930s and would rise to power in 1936.[4]

Calles placed Francisco S. Elías, a close relative, in charge of the political reconstruction of Sonora. The Callistas purged all *renovadores* from office, including municipal councils, and constructed an effective apparatus of the official government party,

General Plutarco Elías Calles entering Guaymas in 1933, flanked by General Lázaro Cárdenas (left) and Governor Rodolfo Elías Calles (right). *Courtesy of the Fideicomiso Archivos Plutarco Elías Calles y Fernando Torreblanca*

the Partido Nacional Revolucionario (PNR). Calles committed the ultimate act of nepotism by engineering the "election" of his son Rodolfo as governor. Calles Jr., a young man educated in the United States, more experienced in agribusiness and banking than in politics, was recalled from his job as manager of his father's sugar mill at El Mante. Traumatized by the Escobar rebellion, the now quiescent Sonorans hardly resisted the imposition of this unknown leader: "He is being accepted principally out of respect and deference for his father."[5]

As Sonorans grudgingly accepted Callista supremacy as inevitable, the once fiercely independent cradle of the Sonoran dynasty experienced a period of tranquility. The opposition lacked leadership and was easily controlled by the state PNR machine. "Due to the dominance of the [PNR] in Sonora and the fact that the key positions . . . are occupied by relatives or friends of the ex-President, it is safe to say that at the present time Sonora is as strongly bound to the Federal Government as any State in Mexico."[6] Initially, Sonorans regarded Calles Jr. as a representative of Yaqui Valley agricultural interests, but he proved to be less a stooge of

rural elites or factions than a relatively independent authority with
an agenda of his own. His modernizing, populist style soon gained
him substantial popular support.[7]

However, upon coming to power, Calles Jr. faced a rapidly de-
teriorating economic situation. He sought the advice of his father
in an effort to solve the "great and very serious problems" trou-
bling Sonora, such as the collapse of mining and ranching, mass
unemployment (due to the closure of mines and the repatriation to
Sonora of 17,000 Mexican workers from the United States), and the
decline of revenue.[8] In response, the state government assumed an
interventionist and increasingly radical role. Calles implemented a
broad development program that included support for commercial agriculture and the creation of a solid infrastructure (irrigation
systems, roads, communications). The government established tight
controls on the marketing of agricultural products through the formation of compulsory producers' associations, which effectively
destroyed middlemen and antagonized sectors of the rural elites.
Calles also sought to create a "strong, organized, collectivist" Sonora
by ordering peasants and workers along protocorporatist lines.[9] He
implemented a program of limited, preemptive agrarian reform,
creating ejidos voluntarily financed by landowners as a means of
countering popular pressure for land reform. These efforts were
relatively successful in the Mayo Valley, but popular demand soon
outstripped such limited reform.

Calles's popularity was enhanced by his brutal handling of the
so-called Chinese problem, which led to the forced exodus of some
four thousand Chinese by 1931. By exploiting xenophobia, racism,
and resentment of Chinese economic success, Calles gained widespread support from most sectors of society. He even had some
trouble reining in the *comités nacionalistas*, which not only aided in
the expulsion but also plundered U.S.-owned businesses and assassinated Chinese.[10] However, the most controversial aspect of the
Callista project was the cultural campaign.

Burning Saints, Molding Minds: Iconoclasm, Civic Ritual, and the Failed Cultural Revolution in Sonora

"You remember this place before the Red Shirts came?"
"I suppose I do."
"How happy it was then."
"Was it? I didn't notice."
"They had at any rate—God."
—Graham Greene, *The Power and the Glory*[11]

The Mayo Indians still speak of that fateful day in 1934 when Juan Pacheco, head of the Mayo Valley rural police, walked into the little church at Júpare:

> At that time the church doors were never locked as they are now. He set fire to the church. It was just a little mud and cane building with one bell. It burned and fell. And he gathered up all the Little Children [saints' images in the church] and carried them away. As they came to the river and started to cross, San Juan [Bautista] jumped away from [Pacheco] and hopped into the river where the little bridge is now. [Pacheco] pulled out his gun to shoot San Juan, but the little santo ducked under the water and [Pacheco] could not harm him. That is why the cross stands under the big oak at the place where it happened. [Pacheco] went on to the place in the bush where [the Little Crosses] now stand, and there he burned up the Little Children. That is why [the Little Crosses] are in that place now. The charred bodies of the Little Children lie there. . . . Our Father . . . will burn him down for that pain. Those little bodies suffered agony. [Pacheco] and his [cause] will be destroyed by Father Sun.[12]

This event, recorded from oral tradition, is still vividly present in Mayo collective consciousness. It was not an isolated act of revolutionary vandalism but formed part of a wider cultural clash experienced throughout Mexico in the wake of the revolution.

Historians tend to view the Mexican Revolution primarily from a socioeconomic and political perspective, characterizing it as an agrarian, bourgeois, or failed socialist revolution. Cultural origins and consequences only recently have received some attention.[13] Cultural manifestations formed an integral part of the wider revolutionary project. The revolutionary elite envisaged not only a socio-political revolution but a cultural one as well. The origins of this project can be traced back to Porfirian "character education," nineteenth-century liberalism, and even the late colonial Bourbon reforms, inspired by the Enlightenment. But the cultural blueprint was transformed and radicalized in a dramatic way during the revolution and assumed a distinct, more urgent, and violent character. By the 1920s and 1930s persistent efforts were made to execute a veritable cultural revolution. The revolutionary elite sought to destroy the old Mexico and erect upon its ruins a new utopian society. Leaders such as Calles (father and son), Cárdenas, Francisco J. Múgica, Tomás Garrido Canabal, Salvador Alvarado, and Adalberto Tejeda all shared what Alan Knight has called a developmentalist ideology.[14] They believed that the only way to build a new society was by molding minds and creating "new men" who would be modern, dynamic, secular, and educated.

General Lázaro Cárdenas (center) visiting Governor Tomás Garrido Canabal (right) of Tabasco during the presidential campaign. *Courtesy of the Fideicomiso Archivos Plutarco Elías Calles y Fernando Torreblanca*

Some scholars consider this ideology to have been the product of the *frontera nómada*, a northern (largely Sonoran), petty bourgeois, secular, modern worldview generated by the harsh struggle of *norteño* ranchers against savage Indians and barren desert wastelands.[15] However, this romantic notion is problematic. True, northern society, more literate, secular, economically diverse, and "Americanized" than that of other regions of Mexico, may have been more receptive to modernizing ideology, but developmentalism was not an exclusively northern phenomenon. While principal exponents, such as Calles (father and son), Obregón, and Alvarado, were *norteños*, many others, such as Garrido, Múgica, and Cárdenas, hailed from central and southern Mexico.

It also may be misleading to view these exponents as the product of peripheral regions linked to the international market such as Sonora, Tabasco, Veracruz, and Yucatán.[16] Instead, it may be more illuminating to stress a shared political culture and education, derived from nineteenth-century developmentalist liberal ideology and revolutionary praxis. Like their liberal precursors, many revolutionaries regarded the "feudal" hacienda, the Catholic Church, and the retrograde habits and morals of traditional Mexico as obstacles in the path of progress. Their primary goal was to create a modern capitalist society dominated by a strong centralized State. To create this new Mexico, founded, as Calles Sr. put it, on "order and progress," one would have to purify or completely destroy traditional society. This cleansing implied waging war on the Catholic Church, "fanaticism," "superstition and idolatry," ignorance, vice, and poverty, all of which were seen as interrelated problems.[17]

The language of the elite clearly delineated the modernizing project. As Lynn Hunt asserts in her study of the French Revolution, revolutionary language constitutes "an instrument of political and social change, . . . a way of reconstituting the social and political world."[18] Like their French predecessors, Mexican revolutionary leaders believed it to be their sacred duty to mold *gente nueva* (new people) by means of education, civic ritual, and, if necessary, coercion. As Calles stated, "The Revolution has not ended. We must enter a new revolutionary period, which I would call the psychological revolutionary period: we must enter and take control of the consciousness of the youth, because it does and must belong to the revolution. . . . The reactionaries mislead us when they claim that the child belongs to the home, and the youth to the family; that is an egotistic doctrine, because the child and the youth belong to the community, and it is the revolution which has a compelling obligation toward the consciousness, to banish prejudice and to form the new national soul."[19]

Education was at the heart of the modernizing project. Radical governors, many of whom had been exposed to novel pedagogic currents during the Porfiriato, made education their primary concern. They adhered to so-called rationalist education with its scientific, materialist emphasis. In practice, rationalism often meant little more than anticlericalism. During the revolution, Jacobinism became the key feature of developmentalist liberalism, and religion was viewed as the main obstacle to progress.[20] In the 1920s, Calles tried to impose this creed on the people of Mexico but failed miserably, thereby plunging the nation into the Cristero rebellion (1926–1929), a bloody bout of religious civil war, which resulted in a stalemate between the State and the Catholic resistance.

From 1931 on, many states, including Sonora, experienced a second, more sophisticated attempt at effecting a cultural revolution. Coercion was supplanted by a combination of persuasion and persecution. This trend was marked in the "laboratories of the revolution"—Sonora, Tabasco, Veracruz, and Michoacán—but was directed from Mexico City and evident throughout Mexico. The elite employed an array of cultural weapons (iconoclasm, civic ritual, education, theater, language, art, poetry) in its war on fanaticism and superstition.[21] The first phase consisted of the desacralization of the old cultural order, in particular religion, through iconoclasm, satire, and religious persecution. The next step was to produce a Durkheimian "transfer of sacrality" away from Catholicism, with its religious rites and Church education, to a secular religion with civic ritual and rationalist, socialist education.

Sonoran Callistas were characterized by their fanatic anticlericalism and sought to create a revolutionary mystique, without which the revolution would not be complete. In Sonora, when Jacobin Governor Rodolfo Elías Calles failed to win the hearts and minds of the people, he was forced to resort to the same coercive methods that his father had used. The burning of saints' images, the closing of churches, and the persecution of the clergy and the faithful all reflected Callistas' impatience with a society that they were not willing to understand or accept. The "defanaticization campaign" soon degenerated into a war of symbols: red and black banners were pitted against the images of saints. The Callistas had opened Pandora's box, from which emerged the hydra of insurrection. This resistance would lead not only to the demise of the Callista faction in Sonora but also ultimately to the failure of the Mexican cultural revolution.

Iconoclasm and Cultural Revolution: The Defanaticization Campaign, 1931–1935[22]

> Maldito es el ídolo, y las manos que lo hicieron.
> —Fray Juan de Torquemada, *Monarquía indiana*[23]

The most controversial part of the Sonoran Callista project was the defanaticization campaign. Calles Jr. had inherited his father's dogmatic zeal, authoritarianism, and rabid hatred of the Catholic Church, "that confirmed enemy of progress and the Revolution."[24] Calles Sr. viewed his native Sonora as a bastion of liberalism and modernity, quite distinct from the more fanatic central and southern Mexico: "The clerical problem . . . has never been a threat in our State, because . . . there is no fanaticism in our popular masses." He strongly encouraged his son to suppress priests (*curitas*), sanctimonious women (*viejas beatas*), and "bad Catholic elements."[25] Calles Jr., influenced by the Jacobin governor, Garrido of Tabasco, embarked on a fierce antireligious crusade, including education and mass propaganda, repression of worship, expulsion of priests and ministers, closure of churches, and the extirpation of religious symbols—that is, the burning of fetishes, crucifixes, and other sacred images.

These policies were supported by President Cárdenas, who had implemented similar measures as governor of Michoacán during the early 1930s. He publicly endorsed Garrido's attempts to eradicate that "idolatrous cult that had subjugated the masses." With Calles, in 1934, Cárdenas called for the expulsion of Apostolic Delegate Leopoldo Ruiz y Flores and Archbishop Pascual Díaz. Such feelings were widespread. Since 1931, Congress had been clamoring for mass defanaticization, while the PNR exhorted state authorities to apply existing anticlerical legislation strictly.[26]

The first step toward the creation of a new society was the destruction of all religious symbols in an effort to undermine the wider system of meaning they represented. The new community was to be purged of priests, churches, and chapels, as well as the images of saints, crosses, religious literature, and other manifestations of fanaticism. In 1931–32 the Sonoran government enacted legislation to limit the number of priests and ministers, requiring clergymen to register with the authorities. Sonoran law permitted only thirteen Catholic priests and eight Protestant ministers to officiate. Calles deported several priests to the United States on charges of preaching against socialist education. The bishop of Sonora, Juan María Fortino Navarrete y Guerrero, went into hiding in 1932. Finally, on May 22, 1934, all priests were expelled.[27]

Beginning in 1931 nearly every church, from the cathedral of Hermosillo to the smallest chapel in the most remote *ranchería*, was closed and sealed. All "invariably [flew] from the steeple the Red and Black flag, the emblem of the Bolsheviki in the mind of the Mexican people."[28] Pentecostalists, Methodists, and other Protestant denominations shared a similar fate to the Catholics. These developments took place throughout Mexico, for example, in Tabasco, the Federal District, Michoacán, Veracruz, Guanajuato, and Chiapas.[29] During 1934 the authorities and teachers closed or burned most of the indigenous churches in the Mayo Valley (Tesia, Pueblo Viejo de Navojoa, San Ignacio, San Pedro, El Júpare, and Masiaca), forbade religious ceremonies, and incinerated images, much to the displeasure of the Mayo villagers, who still vividly recall the iconoclasm of the chief of rural police, Pacheco, who personally torched churches and destroyed the Little Children. After the burning, schoolteachers removed the church bells. Only at Batacosa was

Hermosillo religious college (Hermandad de la Vela), 1924. *Mexican Heritage Project, Courtesy of the Arizona Historical Society*

Pacheco unsuccessful. On his way, armed villagers forced him to return, thus saving the now particularly popular image of San Bartolo.[30] According to the Ley de Nacionalización de Bienes of 1935, expropriated church properties were to be controlled by the State. They were often handed over to unions, peasant organizations, and PNR committees and converted into offices, meeting halls, schools, cultural centers, or granaries. Dances were held in churches to emphasize their desecration. A number of churches, such as the Capilla del Carmen in Hermosillo and the church of Alamos, were looted, while others were outright destroyed.[31] Religious persecution frequently also involved the deliberate destruction of religious paraphernalia and church art, especially the images of saints, which the Jacobins called fetishes or idols (familiar terms in revolutionary France), "abracadabra" utilized by cynical clergymen to stupefy and exploit an ignorant, superstitious mass of semi-pagan peasants.[32]

Revolutionary iconoclasm was not mere vandalism but an attempt to strike at the heart of religion's symbolic structure. R. N. Bellah defines religion as a "set of symbolic forms and acts which relate [persons] to the ultimate condition of [their] existence."[33] Since symbols are at the heart of man's attempts to understand the world, it is obvious that a struggle between Weltanschauungen involves an effort to eliminate the symbols of one legitimating system and replace these with new ones or imbue them with new meaning. According to David Freedberg, iconoclasts destroy images not because they believe in their inherent magic but to break the unity between signified and signifier and to demonstrate their superiority over the power of both. The reaction to iconoclasm is profound because the symbol is part of a wider system of meaning by which individuals orient themselves. As Martin Warnke comments, "Aggression against religious symbols is [considered] as outrageous as the slaying of the innocent."[34] Not surprisingly, the religious persecution, and especially iconoclasm, still evokes strong memories. Popular iconoclasm was a rare phenomenon: a small minority of teachers, mayors, and policemen, known as *quemasantos* (saint burners), supervised the public burning of fetishes. At times, teachers played a leading role, "[giving] more importance to the defanaticization campaign . . . than to their educational tasks."[35]

The most celebrated case involved the statue of San Francisco Xavier in the church of Magdalena. This saint, believed to work miracles and cure the ill, is widely venerated, especially by the Pápago Indians but also by mestizos and Yaquis. Thousands of believers make an annual pilgrimage to the shrine on October 4 (which is actually the saint's day of Francis of Assisi), the most important religious feast of the region. They offer *milagros,* coins, and candles, and stroke and kiss the face of "El Pancho," as the saint is affectionately known. The fiesta is also an important opportunity to visit the market, meet friends, eat, and drink.[36] In 1934 teachers stormed the church and set fire to most of its images. The authorities removed the statue of San Francisco, temporarily stored it in the Governor's Palace, and finally burned it in the ovens of the Sonora Brewery. The faithful reacted immediately: "For many days there were pilgrimages of people from the different barrios of Hermosillo, who filled little paper bags and pouches with the ashes that were extracted every day from the oven, believing that these might contain some of the ashes of the Saint." In one account, the unknowing perpetrator of this desecration, a pious Yaqui stoker, went mad and died after learning what had happened. Such stories, mostly apocryphal, are common. James Griffith, for example, mentions how a teacher involved in the burning is believed to have gone insane, and that the driver who transported the image was said to have been hit by a Sonora Brewery truck. According to another legend, the statue was actually smuggled out of the church before the arrival of the *quemasantos* and hidden for years. It was either returned to Magdalena or is still being kept by the Pápagos in Rabbit Wells, Arizona.[37] As late as 1947, Catholics dared not hold the traditional processions with the new image of San Francisco Xavier "because there are so many bad people about . . . they are afraid the figure of the saint will be injured."[38] A similar fate befell the miraculous image of Nuestro Señor de Esquípulas in Aconchi, which was burned in the forge of the local smithy. Such representations were more than objects of veneration; they also functioned as symbols of the community, of its pride and history.[39]

Public burnings of religious paraphernalia became a type of iconoclastic civic ritual, often conducted in the new open-air theaters of rural schools. Teachers filled out bimonthly statistical forms on the number of fetishes burned.[40] One inspector instructed principals that at the 1934 Manifestación Socialista Revolucionaria "all teachers, peasants, and workers, children, women, and adults, must bring to the Proletarian Bonfire all saints, images, sculptures, fetishes, banners, religious vestiments, books, etc. that served the Church and the Clergy to lull the people to sleep, make a pyre of all these and set fire to them while singing the Socialist Hymn, the Labor Hymn, the Marseillaise, or the Mexican National Anthem."[41] The director of Federal Education proudly wrote his superiors that teachers had incinerated thousands of images:

> As proof of the spontaneous antireligious attitude that the children of the federal schools of the state of Sonora have assumed, I permit myself the honor of informing you of the following events: When I presented myself at the Mayo Indian village of Macoyahui to conduct my inspection, 35 children of both sexes came to meet me, declaring that they were waiting for me to burn the fetishes that were in the village church and in their houses, fetishes that had been valiantly extracted by the teacher, Miss Antonia Montes, with the aid of the Comisariado Ejidal and the Education Committee. Once the pyre had been lit, the little Indians started dancing a *pascola*, and to the gay sound of their autochtonous music, they started flinging the fetishes into the fire, one by one, until the pyre was converted into an enormous bonfire, which consumed those symbols of fanaticism and exploitation. [In Tojibampo] the Union of Mothers, the Education Committee and the Infant School Community organized an antireligious social ceremony, and . . . proceeded to incinerate their fetishes of wood, cloth and chrome. As the bonfire blazed up with these icons, the children sang the Socialist Hymn and the Mexican National

Anthem, solemnly pledging their allegiance to the revolutionary ideology currently supported by the Government of the Republic.[42]

Even sacred nomenclature had to be eradicated. The authorities of Navojoa had the San Juan Bautista sale renamed the "June sale."[43]

The State outlawed Mass, prayer, and religious feasts; ordered gatherings raided; and penalized believers with large fines or imprisonment. In 1935 workers and soldiers raided a secret Easter celebration at a house in Magdalena and arrested forty of the two hundred persons present. When the villagers of Júpare organized a fiesta to celebrate Pentecost, complete with "fireworks, *gigantes*, firecrackers, prayers, and songs," a teacher demanded an end to the celebration and had a number of "intoxicated Indians" arrested. Calles ordered the closing of a Mayo church in Navojoa during the preparations for the fiesta of San Miguel, thereby provoking a riot. In Batuc, a teacher even tried to stop a funeral procession, and violence nearly erupted.[44] Privately owned religious paraphernalia were confiscated, meticulously registered, and destroyed. After raiding a secret Mass in Magdalena, the authorities took twelve religious paintings, four statuettes, three small medallions, one small wooden crucifix, one small glass candelabrum, three candles, five candle stumps, five devotional books, and one book without a cover.[45]

The Transfer of Sacrality: Civic Ritual and Civil Religion

The Mexican elite deemed pure repression insufficient in creating the new revolutionary man. Citizens were to be molded through socialist education and civic festivals that would fill the spiritual vacuum left by the destruction of religion. This campaign to win the hearts and minds of Sonorans involved anticlerical satire, civic ritual, the formation of anticlerical organizations such as the Liga Anticlerical and the Juventudes Revolucionarias, a radical youth group comparable to Garrido's *camisas rojas* (Red Shirts) or Cárdenas's Bloque de Jovenes Revolucionarios, and a concerted effort to inculcate the youth with rationalist attitudes.[46] The ultimate goal was the creation of a revolutionary civil religion—a set of beliefs, rites, and symbols that legitimates and provides meaning and solidarity to the new social system.

Revolutionaries recognized that Catholicism had given Mexican society a degree of social cohesion and solidarity. Elsewhere in

Mexico, Luis Morones, following French revolutionary Robespierre, made pathetic and unsuccessful attempts to develop a schismatic Mexican Church. In Cardenista Michoacán, revolutionaries appropriated elements of the Catholic liturgy and ministered the "socialist sacraments."[47] The Sonoran Callistas did not seek to harness religion as a means of maintaining social solidarity. Instead, they attempted to replace religious rites with secular civic ritual, thereby creating what Governor Calles called a "Cult of the Social Revolution."[48] French revolutionary examples, familiar to the Mexican elite, may have provided inspiration. Mona Ozouf brilliantly demonstrates how, in the case of France, revolutionary festivals served as a means of filling the vacuum left by the suppression of religious ceremonies by what she refers to as a "transfer of sacrality."[49] A similar process occurred in Mexico.

In Sonora the Sunday Mass, followed by the customary visit to the cantina, was replaced by the PNR-sponsored Cultural Sunday, the Mexican equivalent of the French *fête décadaire*. Religious holidays were replaced by secular festivals. On May Day, Calles mobilized five thousand persons to listen to anticlerical speeches. Two thousand workers, eight hundred children, and two hundred athletes marched down the streets of the state capital.[50] In Huatabampo, the board of the Casa del Pueblo occupied the church, removed the altar and statues of the saints, and proceeded to "erect a little pavilion [*templete*] in which, each Sunday, they held the cultural festivals." Union members and teachers always participated in these celebrations, which were generally boycotted by wealthy citizens.[51] These efforts only managed to generate considerable resentment instead of a Durkheimian moral consensus. Official and popular perceptions of civic ceremonies differed widely, and such gatherings often served to exacerbate conflict.

A typical Cultural Sunday in Hermosillo featured the play "Death to Religion" by teacher Dolores Cortés, speeches on "Science and Religion" and "Women and the Religious Problem," and the incantation of the "Socialist Hymn." PNR-organized Labor Day festivities opened with the "Iconoclast Hymn," followed by speeches by union leaders, sports events, dances, an anticlerical play called "The Priest of Satebo," and ended, once again, with the singing of the "Socialist Hymn."[52] Anticlerical propaganda penetrated into the most remote backwaters by means of the rural teachers, who functioned as key agents of cultural dissemination. One education inspector hired a troupe of circus artists, the Compañía Fronteriza, to tour the Sahuaripa area and enact comedies featuring depraved priests and their lurid activities during confession. Some comedies, such as "El Padre Francisco," targeted children and sought to demonstrate that the Devil, the bogeyman, and witches did not exist. The authorities, aware of the power of popular festivals, used the Sahuaripa Carnival as an occasion to attack the Church: "A parade was organized (with approval of the director of education) in which participants wore masks and costumes caricaturing and ridiculing the Pope and Priests. . . . The persons dressed as Priests performed acrobatic stunts and made themselves ridiculous in every way possible. The performance was announced as a truly socialistic festival, demonstrating scientifically the lies taught by religion."[53]

In addition to such parodies, also common during the French de-Christianization, other forms of anticlerical satire emerged. In poems and plays, priests were generally depicted as lascivious, corrupt, alcoholic charlatans. Teachers and students crafted engravings representing not only images of sturdy peasants harvesting wheat, or a bourgeois corpse clad in an evening suit and dangling from a tree, but also anticlerical scenes such as a priest, loaded with sacks of alms, fleeing across the border, or a peasant atop a burning cathedral with the red and black flag flying overhead.[54]

Anticlerical rhetoric stressed the nefarious past of papism. Orators in remote mining camps spoke out against exploitation by the clergy, affirming that "Catholicism means misery, hypocrisy, and corruption" and reminding their audiences of the heinous crimes committed by the Inquisition. Just as doctors would not exist without disease, so "the Church needs a corrupt, hypocritical, and perverted humanity; otherwise, it has no meaning." Public speakers referred to the infamous role played by the Church in Mexican history, in particular its accumulation of vast wealth and treasonous collaboration with Emperor Maximilian.[55]

The language of Mexican de-Christianization bears a startling resemblance to that of the French Revolution. The historical parallels were not lost on the political elite or their foes. Priests compared Mexican anticlericalism to the scourge of 1793, and revolutionary ritual featured the "Marseillaise." When Calles Sr. lost the showdown with Cárdenas, one congressman shouted, "Calles should die like Robespierre!" Governor Calles expounded the ideals of "equality, fraternity, and humanitarianism," while even the relatively unsophisticated General Cárdenas invoked the oratorical skills of the Comte de Mirabeau.[56] A remarkable similarity exists between the eighteenth-century de-Christianization discourse and the language of Mexican defanaticization. For example, key terms such as "rationalism," "fanaticism," "superstition," "hypocrisy," and "idols," identified by Michel Vovelle as elements of this discourse, resurfaced in Mexico.[57] Such terminology, inspired by the French Revolution, formed part of a wider vocabulary of secularization and modernity.

The Molding of Minds: Education and Anticlericalism

> Que no vayan las muchachas a la escuela, enférmalas, Miguela,
> que no vayan.
> —La Choyo Prudencio, Granados[58]

Education was at the heart of the ideological conflict. It was in the classroom that the battle for control of the consciousness of a new generation would be fought. Teachers were expected to expose the fallacy and hypocrisy of religion and to stress scientific truth and rationalism. The revolutionary elite's concern with education was hardly novel but formed part of a wider modernizing ideology already prominent in the Latin American debate on barbarism versus civilization. Both nineteenth-century liberals, especially *científicos*, and the revolutionary elite considered education a panacea for Mexico's ills. In the laboratories of the revolution, Calles Jr. and other strongmen such as Garrido, Cárdenas, Múgica, and Tejeda strongly endorsed rationalist education, which they regarded as a fundamental vehicle for modernization. Calles Jr. spent more than one-third of the Sonoran budget on education.[59]

President Cárdenas supported a type of socialist education that differed little from the old rationalist, anticlerical type that he had advocated earlier as governor of Michoacán.[60] The wording of the reformed Article 3 of the Constitution showed more affinity to Jacobinism than to socialism: "State education will be socialist, and besides excluding any religious doctrine, will combat fanaticism and prejudice, to which purpose the school will organize its teaching and activities in a form that will imbue the youth with a rational and exact conception of the universe and of social life."[61] Cardenista educators saw the struggle against superstition as a key element in class struggle, arguing that "the roots of modern religion are firmly anchored in the *social oppression* of the working masses and their apparent impotence in the face of the *blind forces of capitalism.* . . . . Class struggle must be intensified by introducing among them socialist doctrine: the philosophy of historical materialism, etc."[62]

Education was to play a central role in defanaticization. Calles Jr. sought to instill in the nation's youth "a revolutionary conscience and mystique" and considered rationalist, scientific education and defanaticization to be major components of the revolutionary project: "The Revolution will be carried out by the School." Teachers were to form the vanguard. "First, the revolution was carried through in the realm of politics; it is being carried out in the economy; and now we have to bring it about in the consciousness of the *new people.* Every teacher must be a leader, and every leader must be a soldier in the vanguard battalions of workers and peasants."[63] However, before rationalist education could be implemented, religious education, considered "an instrument of the bourgeoisie against the worker, like fanaticism and alcoholism," would have to be suppressed. The state government outlawed and closed at least sixteen Catholic schools.[64]

The federal teachers, chosen to spearhead the psychological phase of the revolution, were to be purged of those tainted by fanaticism and superstition. Director General Fernando Dworak warned that he would eliminate immoral, inept, and fanatic teachers. Similar purges were executed in Michoacán under Cárdenas, in Yucatán, Aguascalientes, Guanajuato, Jalisco, Zacatecas, and Baja California.[65] Sources indicate that as many as 35 percent of all Sonoran teachers were dismissed, men and women who "due to their ideology in religious matters do not consider themselves sincerely and honestly capable of undertaking this task."[66] Many faced an unpleasant choice between betraying their beliefs or losing their jobs, and some even crossed the border to start religious schools in Arizona. In Cananea, several teachers resigned to protest government plans for sex education. In each school district, purge committees of the local chapters of the new teachers' union monitored their revolutionary zeal. Peasants' and workers' organizations also kept a watchful eye. Teachers were forced to join municipal PNR committees and participate in the Cultural Sundays or risk being fired. Like Ozouf's revolutionary festivals, these events served a repressive "sorting" purpose. The teachers also were compelled to sign an "ideological statement" pledging not to profess or practice Catholicism or any other faith, and to combat religion by all means. Those who refused, many of them women, were fired.[67]

Based on their revolutionary ideology, including participation in the defanaticization campaign, social work, and skills, teachers were evaluated according to a fifteen-point system. The purge, however, was not only limited to educators but also affected other federal and state employees, who were forced to sign a declaration of doctrinal support in 1934. Calles insisted on a "radical purge of our personnel," and in 1935 several high state officials resigned after being accused of religious sympathies.[68]

Teachers were reeducated by the Antidogmatic Doctrinary Propaganda, a secular catechism that attacked the Bible on scientific grounds and claimed to prove that primitive man knew no property, family, government, or religion: "For a long time people believed that man was a special being, created by another special being. Paleontological studies have demonstrated that primitive man was not as perfect as modern man, and thus could not have been as perfect as Adam was, as described in the Bible, one of the most error-ridden books, which has contributed to the retardation of human progress."[69] This scientific knowledge trickled down into the classroom, as shown by this description of an official school visit when the teacher, in order to show the officials how well she has taught her students, asks: "Children, who is God?" The children reply that "he is some old man with whiskers who, they say, lives in the sky (heaven)." The teacher then asks if that is true, and all the children reply in unison, "No!" She asks why it is not true, and they answer because if he did live in the sky, he would fall to Earth as do all bodies which are heavier than air.[70] Teachers also organized children in a Bloque Juvenil Revolucionario, which met after classes to discuss the revolution, defanaticization, morals, and patriotism. A fanatic, passionate atmosphere pervaded such gatherings. Avoiding such anticlerical propaganda was difficult. For example, parents who refused to send their children to school on Catholic holidays were fined by the authorities.[71]

Religion and ignorance were not the only threats to modernization. Vice was to be combated as well, both by organizing youth groups and by stimulating sports that would keep the young from centers of vice and also encourage a new competitive spirit and a desire to excel, important attributes for the new citizen. Furthermore, teachers attempted to close down the numerous *vinaterías* (liquor shops).[72] Finally, Calles's successor, Ramón Ramos, made the particularly unpopular decision of decreeing complete Prohibition in 1935.

Conclusion

The revolutionary process included a radical cultural blueprint for Mexican society, one that was not implemented until the 1920s and 1930s. Although its roots can be traced back to the Bourbon reforms and nineteenth-century liberalism, the cultural project radicalized during the revolution, in particular in its approach toward religion. While the ultimate goal—the creation of "new men"—remained the same, the methods utilized by an impatient, modernizing elite became more draconian and violent. The revolutionaries, convinced that persuasion and education alone would not suffice to create new citizens, sought the destruction of the old cultural order, specifically its symbols, rituals, beliefs, and institutions. Statue-burning and religious persecution must not be considered acts of senseless vandalism, random excesses of Jacobinism. Instead, they formed an integral part of a broad cultural pattern: the attempted desacralization of the old order to be followed by a transfer of sacrality to a new, revolutionary civil religion which would supplant Catholicism and provide postrevolutionary society with the necessary social cohesion. Just as the revolution sought to destroy the institutions of the Old Regime, it also endeavored to purge Mexico of traditional culture. In Durkheimian terms this episode forms part of the process of Western secularization which began with the Enlightenment.

The cultural revolution was implemented externally by a small revolutionary cadre consisting of politicos, campesino and labor leaders, and teachers. This top-down nature of iconoclasm does not mean that popular anticlericalism did not exist. Collaboration was strongest among workers and *agraristas*, who cooperated with the elite because of their patronage in labor and land reform.[73] But authentic popular anticlericalism was of minor importance. Revolutionary Jacobinism would soon generate sufficient opposition to pose a serious threat to Callista ascendancy in Sonora. Thus, the revolutionary cultural project of this period was unable to forge a new man and a new cultural hegemony; in fact, defanaticization hindered this process. It was not until the late 1930s, when anticlericalism was largely abandoned, that the Mexican State could move forward with its nationalist hegemonic project.

2

The Calles-Cárdenas Conflict and the Anatomy of Sonoran Politics

When Cárdenas came to power in 1934, many considered him just another stooge of General Calles. Within a year their close relationship had soured: Calles openly criticized the new president for the wave of labor unrest that beset the country. Cárdenas desperately sought allies as rumors spread of an imminent Callista coup. He courageously commenced a massive purge of Callistas from the government and the military and succeeded in remaining in power. On April 10, 1936, Calles was placed aboard a plane and sent into exile in California.

In Sonora, diverse forces lay dormant, waiting for an opportunity to topple Callista rule. This moment arrived in 1935 with the Calles-Cárdenas split. Sonoran Callismo caused strong opposition to arise in three distinct spheres. First, Calles Jr.'s rabid anticlericalism spawned widespread Catholic and ethnic resistance. Second, some economic elites resented Calles Jr.'s admittedly moderate labor and agrarian policies. Fearing a radicalization of these trends under Cárdenas, they sought a "return to normalcy." Finally, discontent was related to the primordial ebb and flow of regional factionalism. In 1935 the battered remnants of the Obregonista faction, disgraced and ostracized in the wake of the ill-fated Escobar rebellion, united with other out factions to topple Sonoran Callismo.

In Defense of Blessed Ignorance: Religion, the Catholic Church, and Socialist Education

In Sonora, popular opposition to Callismo centered on the religious issue. Until 1934, Sonorans seemed "apathetic and resigned." Inertia prevailed as disgruntled Catholics bided their time. Indeed, some sectors of society embraced Jacobinism: "Part of the lower classes do support the religious policies, dance in churches, approve of the destruction of saints and church property, [and] of the use of churches as warehouses and meeting places."[1] But, in general, popular anticlericalism was weak, limited to liberal, male, Callista workers and *agraristas* who identified anticlericalism with the broader revolutionary program and associated clerical opposition with reactionary caciques and *el capital*. Thus, popular anticlericalism must not be interpreted as antireligious sentiment but as part of the liberal, revolutionary traditions that informed popular behavior. The apparent quiet was merely the calm before the storm. Most Sonorans resented religious persecution but were afraid to speak out and were waiting for a chance to vent their anger.

The Catholic Church was a vocal dissenter against the antireligious campaign. After the Cristero rebellion (1926–1929), which pitted Catholic campesinos against the federal army, the Vatican and the Mexican prelacy accepted the Church-State modus vivendi of 1929 as a temporary recourse. After 1931, under Presidents Pascual Ortiz Rubio and Abelardo Rodríguez, persecution accelerated once again and continued after Cárdenas came to power. In 1932 the Vatican responded to "revolutionary atheism" in the strongly worded encyclical, *Acerba Animi*, which denounced socialist education. In January 1934, Mexican bishops forbade Catholics to belong to the PNR. In July the archbishop of Mexico, Mons. Pascual Díaz, appealed for a boycott of socialist education and threatened parents and teachers participating in the program with excommunication. The hierarchy was split on the issue of armed resistance. While Leopoldo Ruíz y Flores, the apostolic delegate, advised against violence, others such as the exiled bishop of Huejutla, Mons. José de Jesús Manríquez y Zárate, admonished Catholics to "defend ourselves and our children. . . . Parents must convert themselves into lions, and every home must become a bulwark of our dignity and independence. . . . None can evade this combat." Catholics were to topple "modern idols" in an apocalyptic "gigantic wave of slime and blood."[2]

Hopes that the Calles-Cárdenas split would lead to greater religious tolerance soon vanished. By September 1935 a second Cristiada seemed inevitable. In Sonora, priests spoke out from the pulpit against religious persecution and socialist education, and even engaged in subversive activities. Radio transmissions from Tucson beamed antigovernment propaganda across the border, while priests collected funds for arms purchases from as far away as Los Angeles.[3]

The crucial actor in this drama was Mons. Juan María Fortino Navarrete y Guerrero. Bishop of Sonora since 1919, Navarrete was expelled in 1932 and led an underground existence for five years. He traveled incognito throughout Sonora, staying in urban safe houses or moving through the sierra from ranch to ranch on horseback, disguised as a bearded vaquero "with leather leggings and a straw hat, mounted on a sorrel," *un hippie heroico,* as his partisans later recalled.[4] Between 1932 and 1934 the bishop used the remote ranch of Buenavista in the Sierra de Magdalena as his base of operations. He was joined by a devout band of apostles, consisting of priests and seminary and high-school students. Here, *el viejo* led a rough but arcadian existence, preaching under the mesquite trees and busying himself with farming, hunting, and the construction of a chapel and seminary. The band was plagued by tarantulas, rattlesnakes, and severe drought. Rurales who discovered the seminary tolerated it in return for having their confessions heard and receiving communion. It was difficult, however, to keep the illegal seminary a secret from local ranchers, who wondered why Buenavista's "vaqueros," whom they occasionally met for business or a baseball game, never showed up for village dances. The threat of a police raid finally forced the seminary students into a diaspora in 1934. Aided by ranchers, the Durazo brothers, Navarrete hid on a ranch in the Sierra Oriente of Santa Ana. He later reestablished the seminary among the ancient pine forests and clear mountain streams of Los Ciriales in the Sierra de Convirginia, where his followers planted a milpa and built log cabins and a library.[5] This sylvan primitive church in the mountains was a poorly kept secret.

These men were no hermits, even though they were in hiding. Idyllic descriptions of their travails fail to mention their important political role. Throughout Mexico, priests waged a propaganda campaign against socialist education. It was this activity that finally led Calles to expel the entire clergy of Sonora. Navarrete and two priests actively engaged in the dissemination of antigovernment propaganda. Printed material reached even the smallest villages, where teachers lamented its negative influence. The bishop actively lobbied in U.S. cities such as San Antonio to garner support.[6]

The antigovernment propaganda called for civic defense of Church sovereignty and of the "natural rights" of life, education, and private property. Socialist education was the main grievance, for it "leaves [the student] without feelings, without real knowledge, . . . with no resistance to vice, it abases, it degrades."[7] "The

School without God is a social crime . . . [that brutally destroys] the germs of truth and life" and would result in barbarism.[8] Blessed ignorance was preferable to degeneration: "Prefer to have ignorant, but good and saintly children, instead of imbeciles who think they are wise, but are corrupted by vice and crime."[9] The same applied to the dreaded sex education, "dangerous experiments with your children. . . . Our grandparents were educated with a blessed ignorance of sexual problems and still knew how to be men and women conscious of their human responsibility and dignity. . . . A child of twelve or thirteen is still incapable of understanding how properly to channel sexual instincts and will feel nothing but a morbid curiosity that will soon lead to abnormality and, ultimately, madness."[10] The goal of socialist education was to "prostitute [children] in the full sense of the word, making them criminal, pernicious, impious, Masonic, and malicious."[11] The Church was particularly concerned with the perceived communist tendencies of the Cárdenas government. Mexico was frequently compared with Stalinist Russia. Navarrete argued that communism, with its emphasis on free love, posed a threat to the family and to the nation.[12]

Although officially discouraged, many Catholics deemed armed resistance necessary. The Liga Nacional Defensora de la Libertad, a lay organization, summoned the faithful to take up arms.[13] Bishop Navarrete endorsed armed resistance in a barely veiled fashion: "passive resistance . . . is the minimum fulfillment of our duty. . . . If in addition to this there are those who wish to resist in another fashion . . . I judge that such action would be nothing more than the exercise of their natural, inalienable rights."[14]

Popular Responses to Religious Persecution

Catholic propaganda, combined with the daily experience of persecution, resulted in growing opposition to Callista rule. By late 1934 "quiet resignation has given place to open expression of discontent. . . . General apathy is being replaced by a mixture of resentment and ridicule."[15] As in revolutionary France, women played a dominant role. In northern Mexico, women had been the principal carriers of religious values and norms. "[They] tend to safeguard the continuity of Catholicism by insisting on the Catholic sacraments of matrimony, baptism and the last rites for all and passing on their practices to their daughters. At a youthful age, males join their fathers in the ranks of freethinkers."[16] Navarrete had successfully organized Catholic women in the Sociedad de Señoritas

Auxiliares, a lay association active in churches, schools, hospitals, and charitable organizations. A strong pro-clerical women's movement arose throughout Sonora as well as in other states, such as Michoacán and Veracruz. This group, responsible for petitions, mass demonstrations, and violent attempts to reopen churches, proliferated during 1936 and continued into the 1940s. In Guaymas, for example, a group of women, many of them wives of leading merchants, met with the mayor to discuss the desecration of churches, much to the dismay of their husbands, who preferred not to rock the boat.[17] Suzanne Desan's work on popular religion during the French Revolution suggests that religion "legitimated and even acclaimed the potential spiritual value of those without earthly power" and "simultaneously provided women with an earthly arena for collective activism, initiative, and voice in the community at large."[18]

Closed church in Hermosillo, 1930s (Capilla del Carmen). *Earl Fallis Collection, Courtesy of the Arizona Historical Society*

The state government reacted harshly. Interim Governor Corella warned the women of Santa Ana that their movement would be "energetically repressed." Government-related groups, such as the *camisas rojas de la juventud* (Red Shirts), devised childish schemes to disrupt demonstrations by releasing "mice, wasps, and all kinds of bugs" among the protesting women. The authorities finally arrested a number of female protesters, but no one less than Doña Margarita de Ramos, the governor's wife, came to their rescue by attempting to gain their release.[19]

During 1935 mass petitions from most towns and villages, often signed exclusively by women, and reminiscent of those of Catholic peasants in eighteenth-century France, protested religious persecution and socialist education and demanded the reopening of churches.[20] The villagers used an archaic and personal style when addressing the president, reminding him of perceived promises made when he traveled through Sonora as a young revolutionary. The inhabitants of Banámichi, who remembered his arrival, addressed him as *su alteza* (Your Highness): "When you honored us with a stay here, back in 1912 or 1913, . . . you asked the then authority of this town for a place to quarter, and they only found the Catholic Church, to which you replied that you professed the Catholic Religion and would never be lacking in respect to the society of this place."[21] And the *vecinos* of Pitiquito wrote Cárdenas that "the only entertainment we had was to go to Church on Sundays to pray to the Supreme Being, and now we don't even have that pleasure. In addition this Temple . . . sure has been maltreated by being closed for so long, and it's a pity it's getting to the point of collapsing as it's such an ancient building, and such admirable construction . . . at least cleaning it and taking care of it our new generations will come to know these pure works [*sic*]."[22] These letters show that the church not only functioned as a place of worship but also as a symbol of the community, lending it a sense of pride and history.

One of the many problems confronting Catholics was the unavailability of the sacraments. Before the expulsion of priests, there was a veritable run on the churches by hundreds of desperate Catholics. Afterward the underground celebration of Mass and religious feasts became common.[23] With regard to socialist education, Catholics faced the unpleasant choice between excommunication or punishment by the State. Parents feared the "school of the Devil." "People in all classes are threatening to keep their children away from school and seem to be thoroughly opposed to the idea, although probably very few have any definite notion as to what it means."[24] By late 1934 federal schools "were detested by all of society," as one inspector admitted, and attendance dropped sharply. Some parents sent their children to Catholic schools across the border in Arizona. Others kept them at home.[25]

During the summer of 1935 discontent led to violent acts of defiance. Catholics throughout Mexico (Puebla, Aguascalientes,

Veracruz) started reopening churches by force, a common sight in Sonora, especially on important religious holidays.[26] The struggle between Catholics and the revolutionary elite was often conducted in the realm of symbols. While the government eliminated idols, churches, and priests, Catholics assaulted revolutionary symbols like the red and black flag, flown from the steeples of many former churches. Schools were attacked, teachers' houses fired upon, and religious objects recovered by force. Federal teachers, the most visible disseminators of the revolution's "invisible religion" and the main perpetrators of the anticlerical campaign, occasionally fell victim to popular ire. The teachers of isolated villages, such as Yécora and Guisamopa, were physically assaulted.[27] Still, violence against teachers in Sonora was limited compared with other states, accounting for a mere fraction of the two to three hundred assassinated throughout Mexico.[28]

There are two influential interpretations of the Catholic resistance. Some view it as a "ruse to defend the established interests of landowners and caciques," yet another episode in the endemic class warfare ravaging the Mexican countryside since time immemorial. Others see it as a heroic struggle of traditional communities against the onslaught of the modern political culture propagated by a powerful revolutionary State.[29] Both interpretations, although overstated, are valid. Many Sonorans abhorred and resisted revolutionary Jacobinism and were even willing to take up arms to defend Church and religion. But popular resistance frequently combined with other elements such as factionalism and socioeconomic questions. Thus, only part of the 1935 revolt can be interpreted as a *cristiada*.

Factional Politics

Es pleito entre los mismos, hombre, de quítate tu para
ponerme yo.[30]
—Abelardo Casanova, *Pasos Perdidos*

Religious opposition was just one of the factors responsible for the Sonoran crisis of 1935. The Calles-Cárdenas conflict galvanized factional opposition to Callismo throughout Mexico. Once the president began to move against Calles, excluded regional factions maneuvered in an effort to oust dominant Callista elites. Sonoran factions still centered on the old politico-military groups of the revolution. Factional politics involved the distribution of power, jobs, and business opportunities, whether legal or illegal (for example, lucrative gambling concessions and the bootleg liquor trade).[31] While factions did adhere to distinct ideological positions, these were of secondary importance. Although Callismo had a more popular backing than the more conservative Obregonismo, membership cut across classes. All factions received financial support from the economic elites, who hoped to gain concessions from the dominant power group.

The main opposition factions in Sonora were the Obregonistas and Vasconcelistas. Historically the Obregonista faction—the followers of the late Sonoran revolutionary and president, Alvaro Obregón—was the most significant group excluded from power, although they were discredited by the failed Escobar rebellion in 1929. In the wake of this debacle many of its leaders fled to the United States, where they made a living as gas station attendants, ice cream-parlor employees, or, if lucky, Hollywood actors.[32] Much weakened, Obregonistas were forced to seek an alliance with the Vasconcelistas. *Renovadores* involved in the anti-Callista movement included former Secretary of Government Jesús G. Lizárraga, General Román Yocupicio, Enrique Fuentes Frías, and Adolfo Ibarra Seldner.[33]

Vasconcelismo was particularly strong in Sonora, where José Vasconcelos, presidential candidate of the opposition during the 1929 elections, received the highest proportion of votes in the nation. This political current formed what Victor Reynoso and Ignacio Almada call the Sonoran civic-liberal tradition, with its emphasis on anti-authoritarianism, democracy, individualism, federalism, legalism, electoral politics, and social harmony, much in the vein of Maderismo.[34] However, judging from the often less than democratic tactics employed by this group, it may be more accurate to consider it primarily an out faction. Vasconcelista politicians—such as newspaperman Israel C. González, rancher/teacher Jesús María Suárez Arvizu, and Hermosillo politicos and labor leaders Marcos "El Mocho" Coronado, a shoemaker, and José Abraham Mendívil, a carpenter—played a key role in the anti-Callista opposition movement. This group was aided by wealthy merchants from Guaymas and Navojoa. In 1935, Vasconcelos called for armed resistance, even sending agents to Sonora to line up his followers.[35] Finally, a small renegade Callista faction discreetly opposed the Calles government. Francisco S. Elías, a wealthy relative of Plutarco Elías Calles and two-time provisional governor, became alienated when bypassed for the coveted governorship by Calles's son.[36]

The opposition's goal was to avert the imposition in the 1935 gubernatorial elections of yet another Callista, Rodolfo's associate, Ramón Ramos. During the summer of 1935 numerous rallies, attended by thousands of demonstrators, primarily disgruntled Catholics, rattled the nerves of Callista authorities. Seeking to manipulate the national political crisis and to gain a measure of legitimacy, the organizers claimed to support Cárdenas. But the rank and file were clearly more worried about anticlericalism and chanted "Viva Cristo Rey," "We want the keys of the Cathedral," and "Down with the Red and Black Banner." Demonstrators demanded that Cárdenas depose Ramos and his Callista "gangsters," permit honest elections, and guarantee freedom of the press, education, and religion. The state authorities forbade pro-Cardenista demonstrations, arrested the participants, infiltrated demonstrators with undercover agents, and supplied miners with beer in return for disturbing opposition meetings. Throughout the state, municipal out groups jockeyed for position and sent petitions to the president calling for the dismissal of Callista city councils. In general, such movements denounced Callismo, "bolshevism," and *agrarismo*, and demanded freedom of speech and religion.[37]

The regional press, generally critical of socialist education and religious persecution, played an important role. *El Heraldo* of Magdalena used the Calles-Cárdenas rift as well as regionalist rhetoric to legitimize the fall of Ramos. "The gross and grotesque imposition . . . perpetrated by that tyrant Rodolfo Elías Calles, so hated by every good Sonoran, in favor of Ramón Ramos, is the most impudent offense and challenge that we have witnessed until now. Down with Callismo! Long live Cárdenas and freedom! Long live Sonora and don't let yourself be dishonored!"[38] In Guaymas, *La Gaceta*, believed to be paid by the Cárdenas faction, published many "absurd" and "obvious falsehoods" about "the pygmy Sun King," Ramos. Israel C. González's *El Pueblo* did the same in Hermosillo.[39] Opposition leaders wrote to influential "patriotic Sonorans" in Mexico City, asking them to convince Cárdenas to repudiate Ramos.[40] A group of prominent businessmen met with Cárdenas to discuss the removal of Ramos. Thus, the civic campaign was waged on many fronts, local, regional, and national, by means of persuasion, agitation, and subversion. But these efforts were in vain: Ramos was elected governor. An armed rebellion now seemed inevitable.

The Callista clique, supported by Cárdenas, decided to proceed with the imposition despite all warnings. From the point of view

of the president, Ramos was the perfect candidate for the governorship. He followed a brilliant career in Sonoran politics, becoming Calles Jr.'s secretary of government. Although both were
Callistas *de hueso colorado*, they could also be considered loyal
Cardenistas and participated in the Cárdenas campaign. Ramos
became secretary general of the national Cardenista campaign organization.[41] After Calles Jr. was rewarded by being appointed secretary of communications, Ramos was a natural choice for the
governorship. But Hermosillo and Mexico City were unable to stem
the rising tide of opposition.

Ramos's inauguration in September 1935, boycotted by leading businessmen, was a tense event. It was postponed for ten hours
while police and federal troops searched automobiles arriving in
the capital for arms. During the function, demonstrators chanted
"Abajo Ramos," occasionally throwing bottles, one of which narrowly missed the garrison commander.[42] However, it would be a
mistake to underestimate Ramos's support from *agraristas*, workers, and teachers. Municipal authorities staged pro-Ramos labor
counterdemonstrations.[43]

Ramos moved rapidly to replace councilmen of dubious loyalty with solid Callistas. But, in doing so, he dug his own grave.
Factional strife and the general discontent with his election were
reproduced at the municipal level. By October the zone commander
spoke of "an almost unanimous discontent with the local authorities." The main problem was that the new authorities were *más
papistas que el papa* and alienated broad sectors of the population.[44]

Municipal Politics, Labor, and Ethnicity

Class and ethnicity dominated municipal politics in Sonora. Callista
labor and agrarian factions struggled for control with economic
elites and, in southern Sonora, with the Mayo Indians. Local conflicts were particularly bitter in the Yaqui and Mayo Valleys, and
in northern ranching areas. The Mayo Valley, where booming haciendas, commercial towns, and Mayo villages formed a unique sociocultural quilt, had become the focus of increasing tension years
before the revolt erupted. It is hardly surprising that Navojoa, a
former bulwark of Maderismo, became the center of Vasconcelista
opposition.[45] In January 1934 rebels under Vasconcelista politician
Pedro Salazar Félix tried to depose the municipal government by
force. Their armed attack was timed to coincide with a visit by the
governor, who claimed that Salazar planned to assassinate him and

declare Vasconcelos president. The government responded by jailing prominent dissidents, many of whom had nothing to do with
the rebels. Salazar was tracked down by rurales and shot in Sinaloa.
The Mayo Valley remained restless, however. Shouting "¡Viva Cristo
Rey!" rebels led by Salazar's brother-in-law, Gilberto Quintero,
attacked the police station and the garrison of Navojoa on December 31, 1934. Although unsuccessful, these precursor movements
demonstrate the factional nature of discontent in the Mayo region.[46]

The combination of factionalism with ethnic and religious resistance would soon spark a serious revolt. The Mayo Indians, with
a population of at least six to seven thousand, formed the rank and
file of a rebel force led by "outs" such as Quintero and Medardo
Tellechea.[47] Ethnicity, religious culture, and labor relations were factors in the Mayo rebellion. Resistance focused on the Callistas responsible for the anticlerical campaign, such as school inspector
José Bernal, teacher Arturo Madrid, Chief of Rural Police Juan P.
Pacheco, and the *agrarista* mayor of Huatabampo, Praxedis Gastélum. Teachers played a crucial role, dedicating themselves "almost
exclusively" to "radical anti-fanatic work."[48] As one teacher recalled:

> The chaotic . . . situation that the Mayo region is socially
> experiencing has undoubtedly been caused by . . . our young
> former governor of Sonora Rodolfo Elías Calles and also
> by the mayors, police commissaries, and lower authorities,
> who were possibly convinced to open spiritually among
> the unredeemed proletarians an era of progress, introduc-
> ing the defanaticizing Socialist School. We teachers were
> entrusted with the task of defanaticization, but were nearly
> unprepared, for it seemed that we only occupied the cathe-
> dra to insult; only a few occupied it to persuade; but if such
> a teacher didn't raise the tone of his speech to insult some
> saint or other, that was enough to consider him as not very
> radical.[49]

The 1934 religious persecution in the Mayo villages had serious
repercussions. Teacher Madrid admitted to having alienated the
Mayos by cracking down on fanaticism and alcohol: "The majority
is displeased with me."[50]

But the man most hated by the Mayos, still remembered today,
was Juan P. Pacheco. The burning of the Little Children had profound consequences. "[The antireligious campaign] is far fresher
in Mayo memory than their participation in the revolution, etched
even more sharply than the loss of their land and their impress-
ment into the haciendas during the nineteenth century."[51] The event

"strikes a deep chord in their sense of Mayo history."[52] The Mayos considered the burnings a major disaster, which interrupted the continuous cycle of religious fiestas necessary to avert supernatural sanctions, possibly the end of the world. Pacheco did not merely destroy a building and some statues but the heart of the Mayo religious symbolic structure, the *Sagrada Familia* (Holy Family), which consisted of the Church (symbolic of Our Mother, *Itom Aye*) and Her Children (*Ili Usim*, representative of both the saints and church members). It formed the symbolic base of the entire Mayo social, political, and ceremonial organization. The burning of the Little Children paralleled a cataclysmic end of the world, which was expected to come in the form of a dreadful flood of the Mayo River.

The Mayos reacted first by withdrawing from mestizo society, and then with violence. The defanaticization campaign strengthened the development of a Mayo opposition culture, in particular millenarian cultural revivalism, which had begun in the late nineteenth century with prophets such as Santa Teresa de Cabora. The disturbances of the 1930s were incorporated into the symbolic world of the Mayos and played a pivotal role in the religious revival movement. This was a response to extreme dislocation by the revolution, land encroachment, and *mestizaje*. The Mayos struggled for more than land; they sought complete political, cultural, and economic autonomy. Even after the rebellion, the Mayos, who, unlike the Yaquis, never received land from the Cárdenas government, continued to resist acculturation through occasional armed outbreaks of millenarianism. Political out groups skillfully manipulated their fears in 1935 and once again in 1939.[53] Although armed Mayo resistance was brief, cultural resistance, in the form of recurring messianic movements and opposition to education, lasted into the 1960s.[54]

The burning of the Little Children is remembered even today. The Mayos celebrate the ceremony of San Juan Bautista every year on June 24, at the very spot where the saint jumped into the river. The church bells of Júpare are considered sacred, having been returned by Governor Yocupicio in response to pleas by a young virgin, who is revered as a saint. Tuesday, the day on which the incident took place, is seen as a day of bad luck. The Mayos express their disappointment at Pacheco's peaceful death, though they are quick to point out that one of his children died in a drowning or shooting accident. They still say that "Iton [Achai] knows that man, he knows [Pacheco]. San Juan knows him too. They know who he is, and what he has done."[55]

Religious persecution sparked a full-blown Mayo uprising in 1935. In August restless, disgruntled Mayos simply left their houses, and police and military units tried to track them down. In a belated effort to pacify the Mayos, Ramos considered reopening Mayo churches and returned a revered statue of San Cayetano.[56] One should not automatically consider the Mayo rebels Cristeros. There is no evidence documenting contacts with the clergy or Cristeros in the Sierra Madre. Actually, the Mayos maintained a largely autonomous religious life, depending on Hispanic priests only for certain sacraments. They generally disliked the priests, who, they believed, sent their money to Rome, and blamed their greed for the burnings.[57] The participation of mestizo agitators explains the timing, which coincided with other revolts. An additional factor may have contributed to Mayo discontent. The Mayos' role in the agricultural economy pitted them against the *yori* (mestizo, white) *agraristas*, who formed part of the Callista coalition. Although many Mayos worked small plots, growing corn, beans, and chickpeas, the mainstay of their economy was seasonal labor in the Mayo and Yaqui Valleys. Some one to three hundred Mayos worked permanently as *peones* on haciendas in the Yaqui Valley alone, while another five to seven hundred traveled there during the harvest. Mayo laborers might earn wages as high as 5.25 pesos per day, while most were paid more than the minimum wage. Thus, Mayo interests were not necessarily antagonistic to those of the landowners. This explains why the rebel Mayos led by "*El Melón*," who stormed the town of Bacobampo in September 1935, chanted, "We don't want unions, we don't want farming associations, we don't want minimum wages, and we want our churches back."[58]

The Mayo Valley conflict centered on municipal politics, especially after Ramos imposed labor governments controlled by *agraristas* and teachers in towns like Navojoa, Etchojoa, Huatabampo, Tesia, and Bacobampo. Relations with the Mayos were strained.[59] Local opposition factions and Mayo Indians seized on the Calles-Cárdenas conflict to try to topple municipal governments. Violence also erupted in largely Hispanic towns (Tesia, Quiriego), usually expressing antagonism between *agraristas* and landowners. In Quiriego, tension increased during the summer of 1935, and the village witnessed attacks against the Casa del Pueblo, established in the former church, while property of the peasant union was burned.[60]

The general situation in the Mayo Valley can easily be summarized. A dominant coalition of Callista politicos, police *comisarios*, *agraristas*, and teachers struggled for power with conservative out factions, while the Mayos continued their battle for autonomy. These cleavages were utilized by regional and national factions. Cárdenas personally admonished the conspirators to avoid bloodshed. But the opposition replied that ten thousand Mayos were ready to rise up in arms.[61]

The conflict was also acute in Ciudad Obregón, the booming center of the Yaqui Valley, where militant urban workers (mill-workers, service employees) and *agraristas* (*jornaleros*) struggled for control of the municipality with conservative agribusiness groups. This led to a rapid turnover of municipal councils and frequent intervention by state governments. Union leaders, *agraristas*, and teachers, such as Matías Méndez, Maximiliano "Machi" López, Jesús P. Retamoza, José D. Oropeza, Jacinto López, and Rafael M. "Buqui" Contreras, were to play a crucial role in state politics. Ramos decided to throw his weight behind labor; and, in 1935, Méndez won clean elections handily, bringing the new labor faction to power.[62]

In northern ranching communities, such as Magdalena, Altar, Santa Ana, and Querobabi, where ranching elites had traditionally been influential, fissures similar to those in the Mayo Valley were visible. Under Ramos the power of the ranchers was openly contested. In Magdalena, for example, rancher Roberto Urias lost elections to a Callista candidate supported by teachers and peasants. Most northern municipalities, including mining and commercial centers such as Cananea and Nogales, witnessed the rise or entrenchment of Ramista labor councils.[63] Throughout Sonora, municipal politics became polarized between Callista labor groups and conservative factions linked to the economic elites.

The Yaqui Indians: From Resistance to Accommodation

> [The Yaquis] may always be regarded as a revolutionary potential.[64]
> —Thomas W. Voetter

The greatest fear of any government was that the Yaqui tribe, with an estimated population of 8,400 to 9,600 in 1937, would join a regional rebellion to defend their ancestral lands and culture, as they had done on many occasions, as recently as 1927. This tenaciously resistant ethnic group manipulated regional and national politics to pursue its own agenda. Mestizos stereotyped the Yaquis as shrewd, lazy, religiously fanatic, rebellious, cruel savages who were not *gente de razón*. However, mestizo contempt was tempered by profound fears, the product of centuries of bloody Yaqui resistance, and a begrudging admiration of the Indians' supposed mysterious powers. For example, the Yaquis were believed to be immune to rabies and to live a hundred years. Likewise, the Yaquis harbored a deep distrust of Mexicans after the recurrent attempts at genocide perpetrated against them. They considered them deceiving, aggressive, uncouth—when the first Mexican was born of dirt and ashes, his first word was *"chingada"*—irreligious *cualquieristas*.[65]

The authorities devised numerous schemes to incorporate and civilize the Yaquis. Their relative success is evidenced by the absence of Yaqui participation in the 1935 revolt, despite considerable agitation. After nearly two centuries, the Yaquis were finally brought under control by a combination of brutal repression and co-optation. A 1927 rebellion generated "the most savage persecution this region has ever witnessed." It took a year-long campaign involving 20,000 troops under the command of General Román Yocupicio, a Mayo, to subdue the Yaquis. The army even used bomber planes to shake the rebels out of their hiding places in the Sierra de Bacatete. Afterward, some 400 were deported—as some remember, by Yocupicio himself—and impressed into the army, while many more fled to Arizona. Many did not return until 1934. An occupation force of 10,000 was deployed to maintain peace.[66]

Repression, however, was deemed insufficient. The military and teachers both sought to "settle them (*arraigarlos*) and change their habits of sloth, rapine, and cattle thieving" as well as their extreme fanaticism, and convert them into productive agriculturalists. "Since time immemorial [the Yaquis] have posed a threat to the development and progress of . . . Sonora." It was time they were "converted into elements useful to their state."[67] Again we see the ideological program of progress clash with traditional, in this case indigenous, culture. A sense of caution (not a real understanding of "the other") is evident in these projects. Reformers stressed the need for tact: "The Indian is suspicious of any sudden innovation." As one teacher noted, "Their fanaticism is tremendous, they spend most of their time preparing their fiestas and religious ceremonies. . . . This vice will have to be corrected bit by bit, because if a formal campaign were to be launched, the teachers involved would die and we might even cause another armed rebellion."[68]

In 1929, Cárdenas ordered General Juventino Espinosa Sánchez to incorporate the Yaquis into a new military structure, which, while

facilitating control, would also leave them with a sense of military
pride and independence. Federal troops occupied the Yaqui camps.
The *broncos*, or rebellious Yaquis, were divided in order to "destroy
their . . . esprit de corps." By 1937 the Yaquis had been organized
into three battalions of three to four hundred men each: the first
group at Bataconsica was headed by Colonel Francisco Pluma
Blanca, the second battalion at Estación Vicam was dedicated to
farming, while the third group at Pótam consisted of troops on active duty. All received a monthly salary (1.50 pesos per day for officers, 1.40 for soldiers). Trustworthy Yaquis were placed in charge
of local *comisarías*. By 1935 the zone commander felt so confident
of their loyalty that a Yaqui battalion was used against Mayo rebels
and Yaqui rustlers in the Sierra de Bacatete. The plan for incorporation seemed to be working.

Yaqui soldiers surrendering to U.S. 10th Cavalry for internment, 1929. *Earl Fallis Collection, Courtesy of the Arizona Historical Society*

Military authorities implemented a program of agricultural
colonization (the *Colonias Yaquis*) and tried to familiarize the Indians with commerce. The Yaqui project reflected the grand scheme
that the developmentalist elite envisaged for the entire nation. The
Yaquis received land, seed, cattle, farming implements, tractors,
and trucks. The authorities established communication links (tele-
phone, roads), an irrigation system, and schools. Yaqui farmers,
exempt from taxes, cultivated 4,200 hectares of irrigated land, sowing wheat, beans, maize, chickpeas, watermelon, and vegetables.
The six to eight hundred Indians not included in the *Colonias* were
organized in five logging cooperatives. All this was done to "cre-

ate established interests," to instill the Yaquis with an individualist, capitalist spirit so foreign to their communitarian mentality. This
expensive program was hardly charity but rather born of decades
of experience with Yaqui resistance. The authorities realized that
coercion had failed, and hoped that new capitalist habits and dependency on salaries would finally break the Yaquis' spirit.[69]

The authorities founded schools in an effort to civilize the Indians, but teachers had difficulty in gaining their confidence. The
Yaquis refused to send their children to school and used this as a
bargaining chip in their negotiations. Teachers tried to buy their
trust with promises of wood, clothing, flour, and beans.[70] The
government's willingness to permit the revival of Yaqui religious
life was important after the Yaqui diaspora and the abandonment
of their lands and churches. Although the Yaquis were not strict
Catholics, they were a profoundly religious people. During the
defanaticization campaign, they were specifically exempted from
the extremist actions of the state authorities ("because they were
afraid of the Yaquis"), and what little was left of their religious
sites remained unmolested.[71]

Faced with the 1935 revolt, the Yaqui chiefs, led by Francisco
Pluma Blanco, reiterated their loyalty to the president and pointed
out that the Yaquis were more peaceful than the *yoris*. Still, they
held deep-felt grievances, expressed in a rambling 1939 petition to
Cárdenas:

> The injustices which the Eight Pueblos, which are our heri-
> tage, as we have suffered much and the pain that we must
> not feel alone because it is ours because we know well of
> our dear land and it is so that we want our eight churches
> and our Holy doctrine and our Holy jurisdiction. . . . This
> has been the cause of the shedding of our blood of inno-
> cent brothers, old people and of our children who are de-
> fenseless and could have served us now. And consequently
> we are letting you know, Mister President, that in those days
> the eight Holy Churches which were not in the poor condi-
> tion that they are today had all their valuable elements com-
> plete, much of them with silver ornaments, and due to all
> this interest they have been lost to the jealous men and revo-
> lutionary politicians who took them away. This revolution
> was made to take our dear owned land away as these were
> the people who took everything and benefited from it all,
> as well as our Valley and the entire bank of the River on
> both sides which were bountiful with cattle and horses as
> well as goats and all kinds of domestic animals, as well as

in our sierra and streams which were all taken by these
politicians and revolutionaries. . . . And as we already said
our Churches are in poor condition . . . and we . . . want the
greatest guarantees from the Nation of the Mexican Republic that our Church[es] will be constructed for the well-
being of our children and everyone in general. . . . President of the Mexican Republic, this is the greatest favor that
we ask you and that you concede to the wishes of our Yaqui
tribe [*sic*].[72]

Land, community, and churches are what the Yaquis demanded.
The church was particularly important, not only as a place of worship but also as a symbol of social cohesion. The term "Eight Pueblos" must be interpreted as a reference from nineteenth-century
mythology to the unity and distinctness of the Yaqui people, their
tradition and historical experience.[73]

In 1935 there was still some danger that the Yaquis would participate in an uprising. Agitators provided Yaquis in Sonora and
Arizona with arms and ammunition.[74] But they refused to join.
Small bands remained in remote mountain areas such as the Sierra
de Bacatete and the district of Sahuaripa, living off cattle rustling
and robbery like social bandits. They occasionally claimed lives in
incidents that evoked widespread terror among mestizos. But during the 1935 revolt a column of troops patrolling the Sierra de
Bacatete, the traditional staging ground for Yaqui rebellion, only
discovered a small band of some thirty Yaqui cattle rustlers. Their
families—twenty-one women, thirty-two children, and an old man,
found hiding in caves—were brought to Vícam with some stolen
horses and cattle.[75] As late as 1949, Yaqui bands were rumored to
roam the Bacatete mountains, though in reality they had largely
abandoned the area by the early 1940s.[76] Military colonization severely weakened their capacity for resistance. The Yaquis would
"soon be negligible as a fighting force."[77]

Conclusion

The national political crisis of 1935 sent shock waves through the
state of Sonora and galvanized slumbering opposition to Callista
rule. Excluded factions, Catholics and Mayos disgruntled by
defanaticization, and economic elites opposed to laborism and
agrarismo now threatened to unite in opposition to Governor Ramos.
These were, in effect, the first "Cardenistas" in Sonora, not the
Callista workers and peasants.

Ramos sought to strengthen his position by courting labor and toppling conservative factions. He turned to the mass arrest of opposition leaders. This action would be insufficient to stem the growing tide of discontent. Aware of the conspiracy, and doubtful of federal support, Ramos purchased rifles and ammunition in San Antonio. Armed supporters, fearful for their lives, slept in the Governor's Palace at night, awaiting attacks. The revolt was in the last stages of preparation. In California and Arizona, rebels purchased rifles, machine guns, and ammunition, which were smuggled across the border on muleback along old trails blazed by Yaqui insurgents. By October a rebellion was imminent.

3

The 1935 Revolt

In October 1935 a hunting party of wealthy Americans made its way through the inhospitable sierra of northeastern Sonora. Much to their dismay, the hunters were held up by armed men and led to the dusty village plaza of Huachinera. Here, about 130 rebels, "largely cowboys who owned their own mounts and rifles," had gathered around a banner inscribed with the words "Viva Cristo Rey." The sportsmen were treated well and spoke at length with the leader, "general" Luis Ibarra, "a man of character and intelligence," and with his confederate, an educated padre who spoke English fluently. While the priest addressed the assembled villagers, calling the state administration godless and Bolshevik, the Americans busied themselves taking photographs and motion pictures of the parading rebel troops. Afterward, the hunters were permitted to continue their quest for trophies before returning to New York, while the rebels went off in pursuit of human quarry.[1]

Ibarra's band was part of a wider, though fragmented, statewide movement against Governor Ramón Ramos. The Sonoran revolt was clearly linked to national political developments. By 1935 national politics was characterized by rising tension between President Cárdenas and the conservative power behind the throne, General Calles. It is against this background that events in Sonora must be analyzed. The 1935 revolt demonstrates how national and regional politics were closely intertwined and interacted in unpredictable ways. Events in Mexico City created a political opening at the regional and local levels, which opposition groups manipulated for their own specific goals. Their actions, in turn, created a new regional political configuration that strongly influenced decision-making in the center and led to the later eclipse of Cardenismo.

Cárdenas lacked a power base in Sonora when he became president. As the conflict deepened, most government and military officials, and many civilians, supported Calles Sr. and applauded his "patriotic" June 12, 1935, declarations criticizing the Cárdenas administration. Cárdenas responded quickly. He forced the cabinet to resign, secured the loyalty of zone commanders and governors, and assured Calles's retirement to Sinaloa. Regional political elites gradually switched allegiance, albeit grudgingly. Sonoran politicians found themselves caught between Cárdenas and the possibility of a Callista countercoup. Cárdenas's July toppling of one of Calles's closest associates, Governor Garrido of Tabasco, was a signal to out factions in Sonora and elsewhere that it was time for action.

In Sonora, opposition forces smouldered beneath the surface until the Calles-Cárdenas conflict erupted. The national crisis of 1935–36 constituted the breaking point that enabled excluded regional factions and other opposition groups to gain the initiative. The anti-Callista movement snowballed and assumed nationwide proportions: "The Senate is being showered with messages of accusation, memorials, open letters, lists of charges, etc. against various state governors who are unlucky enough to have opposition parties. . . . Practically all the governors whose terms expire next year and who seem to have any chance whatever of being reelected are accused by opposing parties."[2] The cleavages that emerged in Sonora prior to the revolt offer rare insights into the influence of variables such as factionalism, culture, class, and ethnicity on the development of the Mexican political system. Diverse, mostly conservative groups, including Catholics, out politicians, landowners, Mayo Indians, and priests, took advantage of the crisis and joined the rebellion in defense of their own particular interests, precipitating Callismo's collapse. To them, Cardenismo meant little more than an opportunity to gain influence and reconstruct the political system.

The grievance that mobilized the largest number of disgruntled Sonorans was undoubtedly the anticlerical campaign, which threatened the cultural practices of broad sectors of the population. Passive resistance gave way to violence, culminating in an armed Cristero rebellion. But the anti-Callista movement in the states was usually spearheaded by excluded factions. In Sonora and elsewhere, factional protest was often successful, despite the small number of persons involved. This was due to superior organization, mobilization capacity, and resources (finances, control of the press). Factional leaders were able to manipulate and harness popular cultural (religious) grievances and national politics for their political aims.

Factional considerations sometimes partially overlapped with class interests. Factions were cross-class alliances, indirectly linked to the economic elites, which in Sonora must be distinguished from political elites. Although merchants or landowners might indirectly support politicians, they mostly avoided holding office. Resistance was at its strongest at the municipal level. Callista *ayuntamientos* became prime targets, and it is here that we find the most violence.

The conservative opposition could not, however, topple Sonoran Callismo without the support of Cárdenas. He finally decided to back the anti-Callistas after some initial hesitation to abandon an ideologically compatible state government. This led not only to the collapse of Sonoran Callismo but also, paradoxically, to the rise to power of forces that would soon oppose Cardenista reform. This was the fundamental meaning of Cardenismo in Sonora during 1935–36. Once in power, these temporary allies, who had evoked the name of Cárdenas during their struggle against Callismo, would turn against him, leading to extreme polarization during 1937–1939.

These tensions finally exploded in a full-blown anti-Callista/Ramista revolt in October 1935. Mayo Indians raided southern towns, while rebel bands spread terror throughout northern Sonora and the sierra. This movement, which lasted until December, reflected diverse grievances which combined to form a broader anti-Callista movement. The outcome ultimately depended on whether Cárdenas would throw his weight behind the rebels against Callismo, or repress them by force.

Revolt in the Mayo Valley

In southern Sonora, the rebellion was complex: *yori* agitators, supported by out factions and landowners, incited Mayos to rebel in defense of their beliefs against repressive Callista municipal governments. While the Mayo rebellion is seen by some as part of the Second Cristiada, its origins must be sought in the Mayo struggle for autonomy.[3] Hostilities commenced on October 26, when Mayo guerrilleros burned railroad bridges and moved toward Etchojoa. On November 2, some fifty Mayos rose in arms, led by Mayo leaders and *yori* agitators such as Antonio Armenta and Gilberto Quintero, who provided arms and ammunition. The inhabitants of the valley lived in fear of Mayo Cristero attacks. In Etchojoa, San Pedro, Bacobampo, Quiriego, and Huatabampo out groups violently expressed their dissatisfaction with the Callista municipal authorities. During a night raid, rebels looted the municipal offices of Etchojoa. Some *regidores* slept in the hills for fear that they would be murdered in their sleep. Troops barely averted the lynching of the mayor of Huatabampo and his council by an angry mob.[4]

Cristero unrest combined with anti-*agrarista* sentiments. On November 11 a group of rioting "reactionaries," led by a local landowner, attacked Quiriego, shouting, "¡Viva Cristo Rey y muera el mal gobierno!" (Long live Christ the King and death to bad government). They stole the town's red and black banner, and, in protest of socialist education, wrote on the school door: "Rascally, hypocritical, cowardly soviet dogs who defile the flagstaff of the symbol of our fatherland with their filthy red and black rag." In the shoot-out that ensued, the mayor and armed campesinos killed two of the perpetrators.[5]

The movement was rapidly suppressed. The zone commander considered the Indians to have been misled by agitators and offered mediation. But when a negotiating team headed by Mayo Román Yocupicio failed to reach an agreement, bomber planes pounded the fleeing Mayos in the thornbush forest near Pozo Dulce. Cavalry pursued the enemy with the goal of exterminating them, occasionally encountering fatal ambushes. Demoralized, the Mayos fled, marching through the night. They remained in hiding until March 1936, long after the *yori* agents had disappeared.[6]

The Cristiada in the Sierra Madre

> La sierra madre es mi gran amiga,
> ella me cuida de la traición.
> —Corrido, "El Prófugo de Sonora"[7]

The closest approximation to a "pure" Cristiada (if one can speak of such a thing) in Sonora would be the uprising of Luis Ibarra Encinas in the Sierra Madre. The interpretation of this movement is problematic. Some believed that it was "actually the result of political agitation, partly manipulated by the clericals"; others considered it "landowner inspired."[8] Was it a pure Cristiada, part of a wider factional struggle, an anti-*agrarista* revolt, or a *serrano* reaction? Factionalism was an important factor. The 1935 revolt demonstrated an uncanny likeness to the Obregonista-Vasconcelista-Cristero pact formed in 1929 against Calles. Ibarra did not operate in a vacuum; his rebellion was premeditated, backed by "powerful individuals," and his men were well armed. He maintained contact not only with Bishop Navarrete but also with other rebels such as Pablo Rebeil and Jesús María Suárez, who denied being Cristeros and represented ranching interests.[9]

Published statements of the Cristeros demonstrate the breadth of their grievances. Ibarra called himself chief of military operations of the National Guard of the Popular Liberation Army (Ejército Popular Libertador). The EPL's six thousand troops operated in various *focos* throughout the nation. He thus considered his struggle to be part of the wider Second Cristiada and adhered to the Cristero Plan de Cerro Gordo signed in Jalapa, Veracruz, on November 20, 1934, which called for the reconquest of "the Fundamental Liberties of Man"—that is, religion, family, and property—and the "annihilation of the ruling regime." The EPL considered itself to be "the foremost opponent of . . . communism in Mexico." It believed that Cárdenas was inspired by Russia, and that Mexico would soon be converted into a "communist nerve center for the invasion of all of Latin America."[10] In his "Manifesto to the People of Sonora," Ibarra claimed that "I am not motivated or inspired by any other ambition than reconquering the essential Freedoms and absolute respect for the three fundamental institutions of Society: RELIGION, FAMILY and PROPERTY. . . . The EPL . . . will not put down its arms until it has conquered. . . : FREEDOM OF CONSCIENCE, FREEDOM OF EDUCATION, OF ASSOCIATION, of the press, of charity, and the civil rights of the vote and proportional representation of all parties in the Chamber of Representatives."[11]

He also mentioned specific grievances such as socialist education, control of the press, electoral fraud, the closed shop, *agrarista* manipulation of the peasantry, and the economic hegemony of revolutionary elites. This revolt was unique within the broader anti-Callista movement due to its clear Cristero linkage and tradition, absent in the other *focos*. But demands went far beyond religion and included the Vasconcelista emphasis on democracy and on private property—the privatization of ejidal lands—that appealed to both rural elites and sectors of the peasantry.

The presence of Bishop Navarrete and his disciples in the vicinity of the *foco* indicates the direct involvement of the clergy. Navarrete and priests Luis Barceló and Luis Valencia traveled from their mountain hideaway to towns such as Granados, Huásabas, and Bacadéhuachi to preach against socialist education. The school director of Bacadéhuachi noted a significant drop in student attendance after these clandestine visits by priests, or *pulpos negros* (black octopuses), as he called them. Some parents, especially mothers, considered founding a clandestine Catholic school on a nearby ranch. Navarrete and Barceló visited the homes of local *beatas*, where they administered the rite of confirmation in private chapels. The village headmaster accused the mayor of tolerating these visitations. The teachers felt "isolated, without any support," and asked for military protection. The entire population was against them: "no one, absolutely nobody, neither young nor old, wants to serve as witnesses" against the priests.[12] The mayor reported Navarrete's passing through town on his way to El Paso but claimed that little could be done as "the opposition is cloaked in an impenetrable silence." Some villagers actually settled in the mountains with Navarrete. Local authorities promised the state government that they would search for the elusive priests, but without result. By October, Barceló was believed to be smuggling arms into the sierra by truck from Hermosillo.[12]

There were several conspicuous leaders in this movement. Ibarra, a Sonoran by birth, had been one of Guizar's generals during the Cristiada in Jalisco and was well connected with prominent members of the Catholic hierarchy. Others were Navarrete's two priests and several ranchers, in particular the Durazo brothers.[14] Rank-and-file participation must be interpreted as a classic *serrano* reaction (to use Knight's concept) against intruders, in particular the teachers who endeavored to change traditional religious culture: "Nearly all of the inhabitants of these villages . . . are staunch Catholics. The communities are agricultural and the residents are small ranchers who are independent and conservative individuals. The means of communication between the various villages mentioned and the outside world are poor, thus making a section that is somewhat isolated and self-supporting. . . . The communities where turmoil existed have been always, because of their isolation and independence, somewhat critical of government interference and intervention in their affairs."[15] In these villages, parents refused to send their children to school "so as not to offend God," thereby giving rise to serious conflicts with municipal authorities, who threatened to arrest the *padres de familia* if they continued to sabotage education. As elsewhere in Sonora, during the summer of 1935 the *serranos* protested religious persecution.[16]

The mini-Cristiada in the Sierra Madre finally erupted in October 1935. On September 22 the bishop had ordained two priests under the ancient pines of his mountain redoubt. The celebration was a grand event, attended by more than four hundred persons from all parts of the state. Several days later one of the new priests, Juan Crisóstomo Barceló, descended to the village of Granados to celebrate Mass. There he was promptly jailed by the local teacher. A furious mob chanting "We Don't Want Socialist Education" freed the young priest and then attacked the teacher, who was knocked unconscious, dragged through the streets by his hair, and beaten with clubs until his skull was fractured.[17]

The die was cast. Ibarra, Cipriano Durazo, and their chaplain, Father Luis Barceló, decided that the moment had come to rise in arms. The Cristeros consulted Navarrete, who reportedly told his seminary students: "If your conscience tells you to defend yourselves with arms, I leave you in liberty."[18] A few days later, some twenty to thirty rebels entered Granados. After brief hostilities, during which several persons were injured and one rebel killed, they beat and shot to death Mayor José María Moreno, making off with one hundred pesos.[19] Ibarra's army grew rapidly as local ranchers and cowboys joined his ranks. Initial reports spoke of some 150 to 200 rebels (the American hunters counted 130 vaqueros). Their base was said to be at Navarrete's camp at Los Ciriales.

The rebels moved rapidly northward past Buenavista, Las Delicias, and La Cueva, taking the villages of Huásabas, Huachinera, and Bacerac on October 8, and continued in the direction of El Tigre. Municipal authorities, federal officials, and teachers fled before they arrived. In each village, Ibarra proclaimed an edict, forbidding drinking and prostitution, and establishing the death penalty for crimes of robbery, assault, and homicide. By midmonth the Cristeros tried to link up with the Mayo rebels, reaching Suaqui de Batuc on October 24. The next day they exchanged fire with the *pelones* for several hours before disappearing into the mountains, leaving behind several dead and wounded.[20]

The zone commander responded rapidly in an effort to encircle Ibarra's men. A company of the Sixteenth Battalion and a cavalry squadron of the Thirty-second Regiment were transported to Moctezuma from whence they entered the sierra on horseback. A squadron of the Seventh Regiment moved from Esperanza toward Sahuaripa to cut off Ibarra from the Mayos. Two hundred cavalrymen advanced from Casas Grandes to Bavispe, aided by scouting planes, thus blocking a possible move to Chihuahua. After surrounding the rebels, soldiers combed the sierra, but to no avail. By October 18 the rebels had vanished, "swallowed up by the earth."[21] Troops did finally discover the secret seminary at Los Ciriales, where classes had just begun. In a letter the army warned the *seminaristas* of the coming attack, promising to spare their lives if they would surrender. Instead, they fled, aided by ranchers and hiding in caves at night. Troops burned the seminary, complete with its milpa, chicken coops, and library, thereby forcing the students into yet another diaspora that would eventually lead them to the United States.[22] The Sonoran Cristiada was followed with great, often exaggerated attention in Catholic newsletters in Mexico City. Exiled Apostolic Delegate Ruiz wrote Archbishop Díaz about erroneous U.S. press accounts that the Yaquis were rebelling and that Nogales was on the verge of falling. Obviously, this was little more than wishful thinking.[23]

After the revolt, military detachments were stationed throughout the region, while airstrips were constructed in such towns as Granados. The situation remained tense. Six months later some of Navarrete's seminarians were still roaming the sierra.[24] In *serrano* villages the unfounded rumor circulated that the conservative opposition leader, Román Yocupicio, would soon arrive, accompanied by armed Mayo and Yaqui warriors, to celebrate the saint's day of San Isidro Labrador and demonstrate his support for the Cristiada.[25] Clandestine religious services continued, and opposition to federal education remained a problem into the 1940s. Officers monitored illegal religious practices. The new mayor of Granados was required to fine or arrest parents for not sending their children to school. When the local officer tried to mediate and called a meeting, the villagers closed their houses and fled to the mountains. At Huásabas, amnestied rebels were holed up in their houses and refused to send their children to school. In Sahuaripa, townsmen rioted against a "cultural mission," fearing that the educators would destroy the church. As late as the mid-1940s, municipal authorities in villages such as Huépac, Ojo de Agua, and Las Delicias opposed education, including adult literacy campaigns.[26] Change would arrive slowly in the Sierra Madre.

Ranchers' Revolt in Northern Sonora

In the north of Sonora, rancher Pablo Rebeil and landowner/teacher/politician Jesús María Suárez led a quite different revolt, which reflected both the statewide factional struggle and fears of rural elites about anticipated agrarian reform. A U.S. vice-consul went so far as to qualify the movement as "Bourgeois versus Proletariat." Even today, ranchers fear "communist" agrarian reform and call the *agraristas* "*bolsheviki*."[27] Religion, on the other hand, was of secondary importance. During a meeting with Navarrete, Suárez declined the bishop's suggestion to join Ibarra's Cristeros.[28]

Since the Ley de Desamortización of 1856, northern and eastern Sonora had experienced a continuous struggle, which persists to this day, between ranchers bent on expanding their pasturage and communities defending traditional communal grazing lands, the ejidos. *Serrano* communities lived mostly from agriculture and petty commerce, possessing only small numbers of cattle of poor quality, while the largest cattle companies commanded land as extensive as the 261,000 hectares of the U.S.-owned Cananea Cattle Company. Although encroachment was never completely successful, figures from the San Miguel and Sonora river valleys suggest that communities lost as much as one-third to one-half of their commons, and agricultural lands as well. These losses became especially painful during the postrevolutionary years, when ranchers started fencing in their lands.[24]

Thus, the question of agrarian reform was at the heart of the cattlemen's fears. In a broadsheet the rebels called for a return of ejidal parcels to family ownership, guarantees for private property, and indemnization of landowners already affected.[30] During the revolt several rebels, including Suárez, met with a mediator sent by Cárdenas to express their concerns about agrarian legislation. After the revolt, cattlemen traveled to Mexico City to confer with the president on the possibility of changing the maximum ranching property size from four thousand to forty thousand hectares.[31] Ultimately, this pressure led Cárdenas to make an exception to his land reform program by issuing *certificados de inafectabilidad* (certificates of immunity) that exempted cattle ranches from agrarian reform.

The leaders of the revolt, such as Rebeil of Altar and the Durazo brothers of Agua Prieta, were all cattlemen or farmers. The Suárez brothers, Jesús María and Alejandro, would later become involved in a long struggle with the ejidatarios of Querobabi, who accused them of resorting to *pistolerismo* to stop land reform.[32] The religious issue was used as a means of attracting a popular following. In an interview with journalists in Tucson, a "saddle worn and weary" Rebeil denied being a "religious fanatic," but, during an opposition meeting in Altar, organizers called for the suppression of socialist education and the reopening of churches.[33]

Factional politics, the settling of old scores, was of particular importance. The out group publicly boasted that "they'll see how we regain what we lost."[34] Suárez was a leading member of the Vasconcelista opposition. The rebels rejected Ramos and called for elections: "As long as Ramos heads the Sonoran government, there

will be no peace in this state." They pledged their loyalty to Cárdenas, stressing the purely regional dimension of the conflict.[35] Who
financed the revolt is unclear, but reports mention Francisco S.
Elías.[36] Despite wild exaggerations, rebel bands were actually small,
consisting of ranchers and their vaqueros. Cowboys generally sided
with the *patrón* due to their dependency on wage labor and the
survival of paternalistic relations on the ranches. Suárez later recalled that the number of rebels ranged from twenty to one hundred at different moments.[37]

The goal of the rebels was to depose the municipal authorities
in the districts of Ures, Magdalena, and Altar. They set about this
task in a systematic fashion. To slow down federal troops they
burned railway bridges on the Hermosillo-Nogales line. On October 14, Rebeil, seconded by Juan E. Caballero and twelve men, entered Santa Ana and executed the police commissary and the
agrarista mayor, Manuel Caudillo, a major collaborator in the
defanaticization campaign. In Altar, the rebels murdered the mayor
and appointed Caballero as his successor. They deposed the councils of Pitiquito, Caborca, and Oquitoa, and forced those of Atil and
Oputo to join the movement. In some cases the authorities, threatened with execution, were forced to send telegrams to the president denouncing Governor Ramos. The rebels also seem to have
been responsible for the murder of the teacher at the Mineral El
Plomo. The uprising soon calmed down and ended completely by
December.[38]

This small, elite-led band without broad backing eliminated
Callista *ayuntamientos* in an almost surgical manner, using
Cardenismo as a legitimizing factor for their bloody deeds. They
played to both regional and national audiences (hence, the telegrams to Cárdenas). There was little popular fervor, no pretense of
democracy, but instead a caudillistic approach characteristic of the
ranching communities, which remained under the sway of cattlemen. The rebels' goal was elite and factional control of local and
regional power structures with the maintenance of the agrarian
status quo.

Cárdenas and the Response to Revolt

Cárdenas's response was decisive in the outcome of the revolt. He
might have decided to back Ramos by suppressing it militarily, an
easy task considering the limited resources of the rebels. But the
rebels were decidedly anti-Callista and invoked his name. Ulti-

mately, political expedience and factional alliances, not radical ideology, were to dictate the reaction of the center. This pragmatism actually led to the destruction of ideologically compatible but factionally opposed power groups, a move that made sense in the short term but dangerously weakened the ability of the Cárdenas regime to implement its reform project and eventually led to its demise. Sonora is an excellent example of the contradictions inherent in Cardenismo. The president faced a dilemma: on the one hand, he felt compelled to consolidate his position by purging all Callistas; on the other hand, Ramos seemed a natural ally, since he supported the tenets of Cardenismo. But realpolitik outweighed personal or ideological affinities. Although the president initially encouraged opposition leaders to cooperate with Ramos, his ambiguous response to rebellion sent a different message to Sonora, thereby undermining the legitimacy of the Callista state government.

The behavior of the military, which did not apply repression uniformly, indicated how the center viewed the conflict. While popular, ethnic, or Cristero resistance was met with a strong show of force, factional revolt, even when violent, was tolerated. Troops never pursued Rebeil's movement, and negotiations were initiated at an early stage. While regional elites willing to cooperate within the national political system were tolerated, savages and fanatics were to be dealt with harshly.

Zone commanders were the most important instrument of the president at the state level. Although their responsibilities were "theoretically . . . wholly military, . . . in actual practice *jefatura* commanders intervene to a considerable extent in civil affairs, chiefly in furthering the policies and plans of the President." Cárdenas replaced the staunch Callista *jefe militar* and continued to rotate commanders regularly.[39] The military's often vacillating reaction to events infuriated the Sonoran authorities and led them to believe that it was collaborating with the enemy, possibly on Cárdenas's orders. The state legislature accused the new zone commander, General Juan C. Zertuche, of conspiring to overthrow the governor. In late October, Zertuche's successor, General Espinosa Sánchez, promised reconciliation and safety to the rebels in an effort to end the bloodshed.[40]

Cárdenas negotiated with the rebels by means of personal emissaries and correspondence, realizing that the revolt was not directed against the federal government. The insurgents wisely declared their loyalty to the president and stated that he must be ignorant of the injustice perpetrated against the people of Sonora.

Cárdenas was expected to address complaints and restore peace by punishing local tyrants and offering amnesty to the insurgents. Resistance was deemed admissible as long as grievances were justified and rebels proclaimed their loyalty. Instead of treating the movement as an uprising against the government to be suppressed by force, the president sent his confidant Colonel Beteta to negotiate.[41]

The Sonoran rebels played their hand shrewdly, claiming to be Cardenista, though they were, of course, opposed to his project. This murky use of political labels left the door open for reconciliation and co-optation. Government leniency paid off: even before Cárdenas removed the Ramos government, rebels started giving up their arms and offering their services to Cárdenas. The northern rebels surrendered first in late October. Cárdenas's representative merely scolded them. After receiving a pledge to cooperate, the authorities released these "honest, hardworking elements." The southern rebels, who never negotiated, did not surrender until late December, when Quintero capitulated in Sinaloa, followed by Mayo leader Luciano Leyva in March 1936. Ibarra remained in hiding until 1941.[42]

The reason for Cárdenas's leniency was the political instability of the moment. Tension mounted when Calles returned to Mexico City on December 13, 1935, after a stay in the United States. The government feared a Callista coup d'état. Even the rank and file of the army could not be trusted. The zone commander of Guerrero described how, when the news of Calles's return was announced, "there was general rejoicing and everybody expected an immediate attempt to overthrow the government. That night in one of his regiments every enlisted man deserted but four. Most of these have not yet returned."[43] As the struggle between Calles and Cárdenas reached its climax, the president finally decided on action in Sonora. On December 16, days after Calles's return, Governor Ramos was relieved of his position. All executive, legislative, and judicial authorities were deposed. The zone commander assumed control, and officers substituted local police chiefs. As troops patrolled the streets, municipal governments either resigned or were ousted. Government committees arrived to investigate the municipalities and nominate new authorities. On December 21, Cárdenas appointed General Jesús Gutiérrez Cázares as interim governor. The Sonoran case was typical: during his presidency Cárdenas deposed fourteen governors.[44] An *arreglo*, including a general amnesty for all rebels, was reached with the government. Even the assassinations in northern Sonora were eventually pardoned. Many of the rebels were to obtain positions in the new state and municipal governments.[45]

Conclusion

The Sonoran revolt of 1935 was not merely a local political conflict. It reflected broader structural and cultural contradictions that emerged throughout Mexico as the result of long-term processes, in particular the increasing influence of the State in regional politics, the deepening of agrarian capitalism and the concomitant exacerbation of class tensions in the countryside, and the implementation of a developmentalist project by modernizing, Jacobin elites.

The revolt was far from uniform but bound by a common antipathy toward Callismo. In the Mayo Valley, ethnic (religious) resistance combined with factionalism to generate a Mayo revolt. In the Sierra Madre a violent Cristiada involved Catholic villagers, ranchers, cowboys, and priests. Cristero attacks reflected a reaction against religious persecution and socialist education. In northern Sonora ranching elites linked to anti-Callista factions took up arms to gain local power and avert land reform. The Yaqui Valley remained surprisingly calm due to the vigilance of the army and the pacification project under way among the Yaquis. The dreaded replay of the 1927 Yaqui rebellion never materialized.

Cárdenas, desirous to avoid an escalation of violence, endeavored to pacify the situation by pledging support to Ramos, while at the same time maintaining a dialogue with the rebels. Total repression of the revolt was deemed unwise, as the president might soon need the anti-Callistas to stay in power. But when the Calles-Cárdenas conflict reached its climax in December, the president moved swiftly against the Callistas, deposing Ramos and granting amnesty to the armed opposition. It was on this diverse and conservative group of anti-Callistas that he would now have to rely for support.

II

"Sonora no es Abisinia": Cardenismo and Regional Politics, 1935–1937

4

The Sonoran Reconstruction

Regional Autonomy and
Failed State Intervention, 1935–36

Interpretors of Cardenismo mark the defeat of Callismo as the triumph of a new progressive coalition of workers and peasants allied to the Cardenista state over the "reactionary" Callista cabal of the old and new bourgeoisie and foreign capital.[1] Although this may reflect Cárdenas's long-term objectives, it does not explain the political realignment in states such as Sonora, Puebla, and Tabasco. In Sonora, it was not a Cardenista worker-peasant alliance that toppled Callismo, but a combination of conservative regional groups and sheer military force. In 1936 the president faced a difficult decision. To gain control of Sonora, he had to reconstruct its political system, purging all vestiges of Callismo, including progressive laborite municipal councils. Cárdenas then allowed the conservative anti-Callista opposition to gain power in the 1936 elections, setting the stage for polarization during 1937–1939.

State Intervention, Religion, and Regionalism

General Gutiérrez Cázares, a revolutionary who had fought at Cárdenas's side, assumed the governorship on December 21, 1935. He installed a conservative bureaucracy headed by an outsider, *secretario de gobierno* Francisco Arellano Belloc. "*El comemierda de Valles*" (as Gonzalo N. Santos nicknamed Belloc with his customary vulgarity) was a confidant of both Cárdenas and his right-hand man Múgica. But more than that, he was an opponent of Cárdenas's conservative rival Saturnino Cedillo and later directed Cárdenas's efforts to undermine Cedillo's *cacicazgo* in San Luis Potosí.[2] Belloc was a troubleshooter, whose task it was to tackle recalcitrant regional strongmen.

Cárdenas set about purging Callistas. Government committees fanned out across the state to investigate, depose, and replace municipal councils, which were parcelled out to anti-Callista job hunters. In many cases, such as Nogales and Cananea, this meant substituting Callista labor councils with conservative, business-oriented ones, sparking workers' demonstrations. In Cananea, Mayor and mineworkers' leader Ramón Meneses was replaced by a trusted employee of the mining company. In Bacobampo the governor imposed Luciano Leyva, a leader of the 1935 revolt. In the Yaqui Valley a radical labor group linked to the Federación Obrera y Campesina del Sur de Sonora (FOCSS) had gained control of the *presidencia* of Ciudad Obregón. Now a government-inspired press campaign reminiscent of A. Mitchell Palmer's Red Scare claimed that Ciudad Obregón was to be the center of a massive labor uprising planned for the first of May. Gutiérrez unsuccessfully tried to depose *obrerista* Mayor Matías Méndez on charges of financial irregularities. In isolated rural areas, peasant unions complained that local caciques and the governor conspired to gain municipal power.[3]

Cárdenas, under pressure from nationwide Catholic civil disobedience and Cristero revolts, mounted a slow retreat on the religious issue. He publicly declared that "it is a lie to say that there is religious persecution in Mexico."[4] But he merely allowed churches closed by gubernatorial decree to be turned over to Catholic neighborhood committees for maintenance, not reopening, while religious celebrations remained outlawed.[5]

The petition campaign accelerated during March and April 1936. There was hardly a village that did not participate. A group of wives of prominent businessmen coordinated the drive, which was supported by María Tapia Viuda de Obregón, the widow of the deceased ex-president. They presented the state government with some nine thousand signatures. The campaign was not always peaceful. In May, hundreds of women stormed the Government Palace, almost knocking down the doors of the secretariat. Violence against teachers continued in the countryside, despite some moderation of socialist education. Schools were burned, and red and black banners were desecrated. Irate parents brutally beat and killed the teacher in Bavispe, a *serrano* town in an area considered "dangerous."[6]

Catholic violence, including riots, the occupation of churches, and the assassination of teachers, also occurred in Veracruz, Puebla, Campeche, Guanajuato, and elsewhere. It coincided with an offensive by the Catholic hierarchy to restore religious freedom and with government efforts to placate Catholics by showing increased tolerance.[7] The government, fearful of losing face, tried to shift responsibility for the enforcement of anticlerical measures to the governors, who responded by referring disgruntled Catholics to Mexico City. In Sonora this sensitive issue would not be resolved until after the gubernatorial elections.

Sonoran regionalist rhetoric was an important element in state-federal relations, a useful weapon against political foes, who, if non-Sonorans, were accused of being pernicious outsiders (known as *guachos*) who did not understand the Sonoran psyche and the idiosyncracies of Sonoran culture.[8] Conservative Sonorans liked to describe themselves as tough, modern, liberal, and individualistic, and their state as a place where labor and capital cooperated harmoniously and religious fanaticism hardly existed. Although such rhetoric often masked vested interests, it should not be discarded as meaningless in itself. Chauvinist perceptions came to color Sonora's political discourse and appealed to a wider audience than just the upper classes. The Sonoran longing for freedom from intervention by the center, which Sonorans had dominated for many years, focused on demands for free state elections. But Cárdenas refused to permit elections in an effort to buy time to line up pro-Cardenista forces.[9]

The regional reaction to outside intervention is exemplified by the scandal that led to the dismissal of Arellano Belloc, Cárdenas's watchdog. In February 1936, Belloc made a forceful public statement that antagonized many Sonorans: "Until recently one could say that the revolution had not entered the State. . . . The hour of liberation of the proletarian class has already arrived in many other parts of the country. In Sonora we barely hear an echo of this desire for freedom."[10] Belloc's declaration invited a vehement reaction from the local press. "This gentleman asserts that we are a people to be conquered, at least for the Revolution. . . . Is Sonora Abyssinia? . . . Civilization hasn't arrived in Abyssinia, says Mussolini. The Revolution hasn't arrived in Sonora, says a bureaucrat . . . who doesn't even know the State or its people." The uproar forced Belloc to resign.[11] Cárdenas's hold on unruly Sonora was so tenuous that he could not even ensure the continued presence of his personal representative.

The Gubernatorial Candidates: Yocupicio, Otero, and Tellechea

Cárdenas hoped to launch the candidacy of a trusted Cardenista. The alternative would be to reach a modus vivendi with a popular regional politician, exchanging a degree of regional autonomy for strict loyalty. General Ignacio Otero Pablos was Cárdenas's semi-official candidate. He commanded substantial campaign funds, which he distributed widely among supporters and the press, and utilized the state PNR. A representative of the governor campaigned on his behalf.[12]

Key support came from the old Callista labor clique of the Mayo Valley, including Praxedis Gastélum and Yaqui Valley campesino leader Jesús P. Retamoza, who ran as candidates for state representative. In larger towns such as Nogales and Cananea, he was backed by major unions, but his overall labor backing was local and incomplete. Statewide, Otero's support was considered spotty.[13] A second, less important candidate was Colonel Leobardo Tellechea, a Sonoran career officer and politician. His following was limited; his only chance of being elected was as a compromise candidate.[14]

The representative of the anti-Callistas was Obregonista General Román Yocupicio Valenzuela. Many viewed Yocupicio, a Mayo with some mestizo blood, as a type of noble savage, "a modern Cincinnatus," "the noble Indian of Masiaca."[15] In the racist view of many Sonoran and U.S. observers, the general's lack of education was made up for by his "native intelligence." "He was not a man of culture, . . . but he certainly was a capable administrator . . . Yocupicio was a simple man . . . but a man of vision."[16] He was "one of those natural talents that suddenly emerged . . . during the Revolution," and "unlike most Yaquis [*sic*], he has a good heart."[17] Although supporters compared him to Alexander the Great, Xerxes, and Napoleon and praised his honest, firm, and valiant character, others considered him morose and tactless, unprepared for the task before him.[18]

Yocupicio, one of twelve children, was born to humble parents in Masiaca in the Mayo Valley on February 12, 1890. After entering the state national guard under Luis Medina Barrón, "who realized the uncommon aptitude and intelligence of this soldier and endeavored to have him taught to read, write and figure," he joined the forces of General Obregón in 1913 with some two hundred men from the Masiaca area, mostly cowboys, becoming part of his escort, *los plateados*. Fighting in forty-two battles, Yocupicio became a fanatical follower of Obregón. After the general's death, he and other staunch Obregonistas paid a yearly visit to his tomb in Huatabampo in a "cult to his memory," a cult that continues to this day. From 1920 to 1923 he served as mayor of Navojoa. A brigadier general by 1923, he commanded an infantry battalion and led the brutal campaign against the Yaquis in 1926–27. In 1929, Yocupicio joined other Obregonista generals in the Escobar rebellion. He was among the last to surrender but was permitted to retire to his ranch, "El Sícome," near Navojoa. Here he eked out an uncertain existence, living off "his small business making nets, bags, and rope out of agave."[19]

Yocupicio's first move was to line up old friends, many of them "rustics," on whom he could count to organize local support, especially in the Mayo Valley, where he addressed supporters in his native tongue, and in Agua Prieta, where he commanded support dating back to the Escobar rebellion.[20] Opposition politicos of all types flocked to the Mayo to court him. Yocupicio's campaign was reportedly funded by the farmers of the Mayo and Yaqui Valleys, who feared future agrarian reform, and by merchants opposed to *obrerista* policies.[21] At the national level, Yocupicio was linked to the remnants of the Obregonista faction. He was financed by María Tapia Viuda de Obregón, but also received support from Cárdenas's enemy, Cedillo, and Emilio Portes Gil.[22] In Sonora, Yocupicio was represented by the Partido Democrático Sonorense, a coalition of Obregonistas and Vasconcelistas, such as Marcos Coronado, Melitón Hernández, Enrique Fuentes Frías, Carlos B. Maldonado, Jesús María Suárez, and self-styled labor leader José Abraham Mendívil; bureaucrats such as Ernesto P. Uruchurtu (whose meteoric career would lead him to become chairman of the PRI and secretary of government); and a variety of army buddies and rustic cronies. The economic elites were well represented, including several influential ranchers.[23] Yocupicio built a broad coalition including most factional, class-based, and religious anti-Callista groups.

His platform addressed the main grievances of conservative Sonorans: religion and labor and agrarian reform. He was forced to play a Janus-faced role in order to avoid antagonizing Cárdenas. Although he pledged to collaborate with the Cardenista Plan Sexenal, his real position was hardly a secret. He told the U.S. military attaché that agrarian action had been taken "hastily, ill-advisedly and with too little consideration for the interests of the commercial and agricultural classes."[24] But Yocupicio was also popular among workers of the valleys. It is not clear whether his attempts to attract the Mayo and Yaqui Indian vote by portraying himself as an indigenous leader were successful, but his friendship with Yaqui chief Francisco Pluma Blanca must have been useful. Women, permitted to vote in the PNR plebiscites for the first time, supported the general en masse due to his promise to reopen the churches; and they played a pivotal role in the elections, albeit not the progressive role the president had hoped for. Their importance was reflected in the foundation of women's political clubs, such as the Club Femenil Pro-Yocupicio.[25]

Yocupicio entered the campaign as an independent, an enemy of the PNR, a party that he described as antidemocratic, anticonstitutional, antirevolutionary, and a "sworn enemy of all liberty, responsible for the corruption of many citizens."[26] But Cárdenas, fearful that an independent candidature would weaken the official party, invited Yocupicio to run for the PNR. The two met on several occasions.[27] Yocupicio's surprise decision to join the hated PNR led to a split with many of his supporters, who felt betrayed by their leader's perceived co-optation.[28] Yocupicio remained suspicious of the federal government, however, and made it clear that he would resort to armed rebellion if deprived of the candidature by electoral fraud. This threat was taken seriously, and it was believed, probably erroneously, that Yocupicio could rely on sectors of the army and on the Mayo and Yaqui tribes. Not everyone agreed. *El Hombre Libre* called him a scarecrow who had frightened Cárdenas into accepting his rise to power.[29]

The embattled Cárdenas had no choice but to take such warnings seriously. His advisers deemed a Callista coup likely. General Joaquín Amaro discussed his plans to topple the president (in a "strictly legal" way) with the U.S. military attaché on several occasions. According to U.S. intelligence, "there is no doubt as to the existence of a well organized and well financed plot to overthrow the present Government," which might involve Amaro, Cedillo, Calles, Abelardo Rodríguez, or Antonio Villarreal, and would be financed by the bankers and industrialists of Monterrey.[30] General Almazán of Monterrey, who was heard to say that "he would like to hang every . . . politician in Mexico," openly stated that he considered Cárdenas "very stupid and a know-nothing. . . . According to his lights, which are dim, Cárdenas thinks he is a patriot. He is an unexperienced young man, a fool and on his road to perdition."[31] Meanwhile, Cedillo threatened that "I do not desire any further bloodshed. However, I have participated in more than one revolution and, should my people ever need me, they will find me completely at their service."[32] Nor could the military be trusted, including the rank and file. Cárdenas tried to shore up his support by offering loyal officers seats in Congress.[33] Under these circumstances it was wise to reach an agreement with the restless Yocupicio.

The Elections

The campaign was chaotic and violent. Most complaints concerned Otero, who was widely reported to "stop at nothing," including violence. He bought supporters and officials with seemingly endless funds, organized barbecues, and handed out tequila and money. His unsavory techniques succeeded in mobilizing people, who "considered [the rallies] as a bit of entertainment."[34] Newspapers and broadsheets served as powerful political instruments. *El Mayo* (Navojoa) and *El Heraldo del Yaqui* (Ciudad Obregón) backed the "Indio of Masiaca." Otero counted on *La Gaceta* and *La Tarantula* (Guaymas) as well as on the radio station, XEW.[35]

Finally, Cárdenas gave the green light for elections. The final election was of no importance: the PNR candidate would automatically win. The real struggle took place during the municipal, district, and state PNR plebiscites and conventions, which would ultimately designate the official candidate. The electoral system was complicated: municipal plebiscites, held on September 20, 1936, designated electors to participate in municipal conventions. These, in turn, chose electors for the PNR district conventions. Here electors for the October 11 state convention were designated, who would finally decide on the official PNR candidates for governor and for the state legislature. State elections on November 22 merely served to legitimize the party decision.[36] The goal of any party was to garner sufficient votes in the municipal plebiscites subsequently to dominate the PNR decision-making process. The delegates would form the pool from which future municipal and party officials were drawn, so that one faction would completely dominate the state party structure, which became little more than a factional instrument.

The process began with municipal elections. PNR plebiscites could be lively events. In Nogales, voters marched down the streets chanting and banging drums, or drove through town in decorated cars, honking their horns. The actual voting process was considered relatively fair, despite reports of the usual cheating: "Most everyone is proud of the fact that the election of September 20, 1936, was the first free and uncontrolled election in the history of

Sonora."[37] There were some complaints, however. Oterista supporters tried to be counted twice at the voting stations (the practice of
ruleteo), while Otero reportedly obtained 1,600 votes from a village
with only twenty-five families.[38] Press reports on the initial returns
were contradictory. Both Yocupicio and Otero claimed landslide
victories.[39]

Official returns released by the National Executive Committee
of the PNR indicate a substantial Yocupicista victory of 16,541 votes
versus Otero's 10,866 and Tellechea's 6,696.[40] Yocupicio's victory
was based on landslides in the Moctezuma, Magdalena, and
Sahuaripa districts. He also carried nearly half of the vote in his
native Mayo Valley. Otero did well in Hermosillo and Guaymas,
gaining nearly half of the urban vote. However, returns from the
Mayo were disappointing, largely reflecting ties to his family's
home town of Alamos. His showing in the northeast was weak.
The vote suggests that Yocupicio received support from miners,
ranchers, *serrano comuneros*, the Mayos, and sectors of urban labor.
Otero failed to portray himself as the labor candidate, even among
agraristas. Tellechea's support was purely local. The importance of
personal ties is clear: Yocupicio gained Agua Prieta and Navojoa,
Tellechea won in Etchojoa, and Otero won in Alamos.[41]

On October 8 the PNR reluctantly declared Yocupicio the win-
ner in the municipal elections, producing "for the first time in the
history of Sonora . . . an honest and untrammeled election."[42] The
rest was simple. Yocupicio carried the district conventions and
Otero retired from the fray, leaving the Yocupicistas in complete
control. Yocupicio did not forget to thank Cárdenas. He reminded
supporters that "General Cárdenas has kept his word and allowed
the people of Sonora the freedom to manifest their will." Only
Yocupicistas attended the state PNR convention, which chose
Yocupicio as their official candidate. It also designated the new PNR
state committee, which closely resembled the leadership of Yocupicio's party.[43] When a worried Gutiérrez Cázares visited Cárdenas
to inform him of the Yocupicio victory, the president reportedly
made no objections. He realized that the imposition of Otero would
probably have led to yet another revolt.[44]

Yocupicio was sworn in on January 4, 1937. During his inaugural address in the Casa del Pueblo in Hermosillo he pledged to cooperate with the president but hinted that labor and agrarian reform
would not have a high priority on his agenda.[45] Yocupicio wined
and dined Cárdenas's rival Cedillo as guest of honor: "He was
seated . . . next to the new governor and the two seemed to make a

point of showing the greatest possible cordiality and friendship to each other."[46] A leading Obregonista, the old bearded Aurelio Manrique, created some unpleasantness by openly criticizing the departing governor: "How do you dare to say that you are stepping down with a feeling of satisfaction for having done your duty, while you actually plunged Sonora into disorder and chaos for a year? You have no shame, for if you did you wouldn't even show your face [here]." Friends were barely able to avert an indecorous fistfight.[47]

Conclusion

Cárdenas's purge of Sonoran Callistas was initially well received. Conservatives applauded the elimination of labor *ayuntamientos*, which often reverted to elite control. Catholics, however, remained restive, disappointed by government inaction on the issue of religion. But by 1936 conservative groups became increasingly critical of Cardenista intervention and clamored for free elections. They rallied around the popular candidate General Yocupicio, who received support from anti-Callistas, Catholics, economic elites, and sectors of the lower classes and the indigenous population. Cárdenas made a half-hearted attempt at establishing a progressive coalition of former Callista workers and peasants around the candidature of Otero. His candidate was not to win, however, for several reasons. Yocupicio, who had a stronger electoral backing than Otero, wisely converted his initial independent candidacy into a PNR candidacy, thus demonstrating his willingness to work within the system. This olive branch was combined with the threat of rebellion. This strategy led Cárdenas to accept free elections and refrain from imposing Otero through "electoral alchemy." Cárdenas managed to keep the peace, but at a high cost. By 1937 the Sonoran labor movement was left on the defensive while the state administration was headed by a governor who would soon turn into one of Cárdenas's most stubborn opponents.

5

The Yocupicista Power Base
and Bureaucratic Patronage

Yocupicio rapidly moved to establish a regional power base. Initially he received substantial popular support, but ultimately his power rested on an informal patronage network with local and national factions and power groups. Informal backing was channeled through existing institutional structures—that is, state and municipal governments and the Sonoran branch of the PNR. New bureaucratic sources of patronage became more important than traditional ones. It would be wrong to consider Yocupicio a classic cacique. Instead, he demonstrated all the characteristics of a "new patron."[1] Some elements of traditional legitimacy remained, such as the affective, personalist bonds of Obregonismo, forged during the revolution. But new sources of patronage, which James C. Scott calls "indirect, office based property," were of greater importance: the control of bureaucratic power, employment, financial resources, business opportunities, and electoral machines. Patron-client relationships survived well in the new bureaucratic ambiance of postrevolutionary Mexico, in which Yocupicio, more comfortable in the ranks of the military, was forced to operate. New, institutionalized, or "profane" clienteles were heterogeneous and unstable. Yocupicio relied on a large fair-weather following and only a small core of Obregonista politicians and veterans. The economic elites, Catholics, and allied factions expected him to provide opportunities for employment and enrichment, and halt agrarian and labor reform and religious persecution. The first months of Yocupicio's administration were characterized by efforts to accommodate his diverse clientele. The governor also started jockeying for position in the national political arena, a hazardous endeavor.

The Camarilla

The power wielded by governors during the 1930s should not be underestimated. These "absolute dictators . . . have very little respect for Federal laws, change their own at will, permit only subservient state legislatures, and are generally occupied in the acquisition of worthwhile properties and all the cash available, for their own particular purposes."[2] Governor Yocupicio was no exception. He "governed with an iron fist covered by a fine glove." One U.S. consul considered him "the power in the State."[3]

Following traditional Mexican pork-barrel politics, Yocupicio staffed his administration with a mix of compadres, Obregonista and Vasconcelista allies, and technocrats. The key position was that of *secretario de gobierno*, the governor's right-hand man and replacement. This job was given to Carlos B. Maldonado, an Obregonista rancher from Baviácora who soon became the most hated figure in government because of his anti-labor stance. He was later replaced, but the position of *secretario* would remain controversial throughout the Yocupicio governorship, resulting in a high turnover.[4]

The cracks in the Yocupicista coalition soon became apparent. "The Yocupicista party was heterogeneous, consisting of individuals and groups with distinct ideologies." By the summer of 1937, Yocupicio had lost his initial overwhelming majority. One of the causes of this rupture was dissatisfaction with his division of the booty, which alienated former supporters.[5] The governor's administration was also marred by recurring power struggles, which exposed his unsophisticated and heavy-handed style and at times seriously weakened his power.

The state committee of the PNR was controlled by the Yocupicista faction and thus was useless as a weapon of the central government. The governor's hegemony was reflected in the PNR leadership, which included Melitón Hernández and José Abraham Mendívil. The party was transformed into an effective instrument of the governor. Yocupicio dominated the Sonoran legislature, which was considered a mere rubber-stamp body.[6] Of all government institutions the judiciary proved the most independent. In May 1937 the entire Supreme Court was forced to resign after clashing with the government secretary and was replaced by new magistrates, among them the bishop's brother.[7]

Several of Yocupicio's associates benefited from the customary graft and shady business transactions. The governor's old friend

Roberto Elzy Torres, once a bartender in Cananea, became one of the wealthiest businessmen in Sonora. He received lucrative highway construction and urban paving contracts. The importance of these works cannot be underestimated: 20 percent of the state budget, some two million pesos, was spent on public works, in particular highways. U.S. Consul Lewis Boyle believed that Yocupicio collected substantial kickbacks and cited sources alleging that the governor was frequently seen in Nogales and Tucson, Arizona, where he "spends . . . lavishly in hotels, saloons and houses of ill repute."[8] By 1938 it was commonly assumed that Yocupicio and his *secretario de gobierno* were misappropriating government funds. The U.S. Customs and Border Patrol also suspected Elzy Torres of being the leader of an opium contraband ring, although they admitted that it was "impossible to apprehend him in the act of smuggling." Opium smuggling was common and poppies were cultivated in northern Sonora, despite occasional army raids.[9]

Electoral Politics: A Return to "Normalcy"

The governor's power soon extended into the remotest municipalities: "Virtually every municipal official and employee . . . has been removed and Yocupicio supporters placed in their stead." Democratic euphoria was replaced by widespread disenchantment. The press bitterly denounced Yocupicio's "blatant intervention."[10] Democracy was a cause which he had proclaimed when expedient but could now dispense with. Yocupicio was particularly anxious to rid himself of the labor-controlled city government of Ciudad Obregón, led by Matías Méndez and Maximiliano R. López. He not only disbanded the council but also jailed the mayor on charges of misappropriating funds. An intense political struggle ensued.[11]

The 1937 municipal elections brought Yocupicista mayors to power throughout the state, often through fraud.[12] Yocupicista candidates were often unpopular with labor. In 1938 a popular uprising forced Agua Prieta Mayor Martín S. Burgueño to flee across the U.S. border. Peasant leagues protested the restoration to power of local caciques. In Bavispe, the opposition denounced the "Porfirian nepotism" of the local "sultan" or *todo poderoso*. *Agraristas* from Casa de Teras claimed that the local cacique and hacendado had imposed the new Yocupicista mayor. Unions demanded that the governor reconsider his dismissal of *agrarista* Mayor Antonio C. Encinas of Huatabampo. Congress nullified the victory in Ures of an *agrarista* and instead declared the "reactionary" candidate victorious, generating protests from peasant and labor leaders already incensed by the election of former rebel Jesús María Suárez, "assassin of *agraristas*," as deputy for the district. Some six hundred *agraristas* occupied the municipal palace in September 1937. The *comisariado ejidal* of Caborca complained of the anti-labor attitudes of the new municipal authorities.[13]

Thus, by mid-1937 any semblance of a democratic *apertura* had vanished: municipal autonomy was flouted by electoral fraud, the nullification of inconvenient results, and direct intervention. Indignation was widespread, especially among labor and peasant groups that had enjoyed increased influence under Calles. Yocupicio's blatant intervention laid the foundations for increasing tension. The honesty of the recent gubernatorial election had raised hopes for democracy, which were now shattered by political reality. However, while able to dominate the state congress and PNR, Yocupicio was unable to control the designation of federal deputies, many of whom tended to be a thorn in his side. In addition, the two federal senators from Sonora, Camilo Gastélum and Andrés H. Peralta, were staunch watchdogs of the central government.[14]

Political Mercenaries: The Press

An important role in the governor's power bloc was reserved for the regional press. Yocupicio's associate, José Abraham Mendívil, became director of one of the state's leading newspapers, *El Imparcial* of Hermosillo. Other Yocupicista papers were *El Mayo* of Navojoa, owned by Yocupicio's friend Raúl Montaño, *El Tiempo* of Agua Prieta, and *El Norte,* run by a state bureaucrat. These publications featured articles by conservative writers such as Nemesio García Naranjo, Jesús Guisa y Azevedo, and Rubén Moreno Padrés.[15]

Opposition publications continued to appear, such as *El Pueblo* of Hermosillo, edited by Israel C. González, *El Noroeste* of Nogales, and *El Intruso* of Cananea. They suffered government harassment, in particular pressure on the advertisers, as happened with the pro-labor *El Heraldo del Yaqui* that soon came under the control of a Yocupicista. *El Pueblo* was subjected to a defamation suit.[16] The press constituted yet another political weapon, disseminating disinformation and lies to discredit opponents.

The national press followed developments in the north closely. Yocupicio became the darling of the right-wing *El Hombre Libre* and the bête noire of left-wing publications such as *El Machete* and *Futuro*. By the 1930s, radio had also become an essential means of mass communication. The government of Sonora controlled a radio station, which, according to its detractors, disseminated fascist propaganda.[17]

The Yocupicista Project

At his inauguration Yocupicio made his conservative position abundantly clear. Although he swore to uphold the tenets of Cardenismo, he also pledged to combat "the disastrous, venal, and political *líderismo*" in the labor movement. One deputy ominously added that "the agrarian problem . . . in Sonora does not have the importance nor the urgency that it has in other states."[18] Yocupicio expounded his ideal of class harmony: "Labor needs Capital and Capital needs Labor, and I plan to protect both."[19] Although he intended to resist government efforts to expropriate lands in the Yaqui, and in particular in his beloved Mayo Valley, little could be done but await Cárdenas's initiatives. Throughout the first months of his administration an uneasy sense of expectation prevailed. In private, Yocupicio strongly criticized Cardenismo: "The President is misguided in his policies, because he wants to resolve problems that can only be solved over many generations." Cárdenas's successor would have to dismantle the reform project completely. He described the president in disparaging terms, calling him a peddler and recalling how he had recently encountered him looking like a tramp (*hecho un mugroso*).

Yocupicio summarized his main goals as "the stimulation of public wealth . . . and absolute respect for smallholdings [*la pequeña propiedad*]," which basically signified the protection of capital against organized labor and the Cardenista government.[20] A key component was the creation of a solid infrastructure for development, especially roads, irrigation canals, and dams. Such projects were to provide employment for thousands of workers hurt by the Depression. By 1938 some fifteen hundred were employed on the La Angostura dam project alone.[21] Although the governor's words must have worried Sonoran workers, he probably retained some labor support during the first months thanks to his tremendously popular decision to repeal the Sonoran Law of Prohibition.[22]

Governor Román Yocupicio surrounded by the symbols of development. *Memoria de la gestión gubernamental del C. Gral. Román Yocupicio, 1939*

Reluctant Tolerance: The Religious Problem

According to a contemporary tale, two Pápagos were walking along a river when they encountered an apparition, which they recognized as San Francisco Xavier. They took this to be a portent that the churches of Sonora would soon reopen.[23] The religious problem remained one of the most pressing issues facing the government. The slow reaction of Yocupicio demonstrates that religious freedom was not one of his priorities, although his election had depended to a considerable extent on the Catholic vote. Now, Catholics became worried about the governor's inaction. Under pressure, he started tolerating religious practices. He told the faithful in Cananea that they could use the Buenavista church, even though it was occupied by the mineworkers' union, and authorized a priest to conduct Mass openly.[24]

Churches had been closed either by presidential or gubernatorial decree. While Yocupicio had considerable leeway in the case of state-controlled churches, he could not reopen federally controlled ones. During the summer of 1937, he made a set of "radical proposals" to the president, pressing for the reopening of all Sonoran churches. He made it appear as if this would help Cárdenas counter "reactionary" opposition and strengthen his regime. Sonora, where "a real religious problem does not exist," would be the perfect place for such a policy. Again, regionalist discourse was used for purely political reasons: "If to a certain degree the reopening of churches and the activities of some priests has been permitted, this has been done in an effort to solve . . . the delicate problem that exists not so much in this state but in other parts of the Republic, but that has undoubtedly also had some repercussions in Sonora, although one must say that the inhabitants of the state do not pose a threat due to their traditional liberalism, as it is well known in the entire Republic that in this part of the country the religious problem does not have the same acute characteristics as in the interior."[25]

Cárdenas reacted in an ambiguous fashion: it remained forbidden to return churches closed by presidential decree, but those under state control could be reopened, even though "this might lead some to consider such an attitude as a victory for the clericals." Obviously, face-saving was a prime consideration. The president passed the problem on to Yocupicio. By the end of 1937 it became clear that the religious conflict would be resolved, though hardly from one day to the next. The state government began to return churches under its control. By October at least one church had reopened in most towns.[26]

It would be a mistake to consider religious tolerance as the work of Yocupicio or, for that matter, of Cárdenas, as some have suggested, portraying him as a shrewd "master politician" who manipulated the church issue to his benefit.[27] Tolerance was the result of a massive, nation-wide popular campaign by Catholics using petitions, takeovers, boycotts, and armed resistance to defend their right of worship. Cárdenas was swamped by a deluge of petitions, usually concerning the reopening of churches, from all parts of Sonora. At times, Catholics asked for the recovery of stolen items. The villagers of San José de Gracia petitioned for the return of their church clock, which had found a place at the school of Topahue. The clergy and their congregations stepped up efforts to hold the still illegal Masses. By May several priests and even Bishop Navarrete were openly officiating in private houses, garages, and hotels without encountering much opposition from the authorities.

Catholics grew increasingly impatient and decided to back up their petitions by taking dozens of churches by force. By July 1937, thirty-four Sonoran churches had been reopened by force and occupied by Catholics. Yocupicio, fearful that the movement might escalate, decided in several instances to call in troops to remove the believers, mostly women and children. Some two hundred women and children occupied the churches of Santa Ana Vieja and Nueva. "Several hundred members of the congregation, particularly women, maintained a vigil in [the church of Nogales] both day and night, and to date the building is still open." In Magdalena, a large group of women, led by Mercedes Durazo de Hopkins and Clementina Angulo de Dávila, broke into the main church. Similar takeovers occurred throughout Sonora. Catholics were elated. Their enthusiasm "was displayed by the unorthodox methods of beating drums and playing orchestras inside the churches."[28]

Catholics were not invariably successful in keeping the churches open. Evictions were common when labor organizations were involved, an issue considered politically sensitive. The mayor of Navojoa ordered Catholics out of the local church, which was used by the San Pedro *agraristas* as a granary. Troops removed praying women from the church of Bavispe. In Caborca Vieja, troops ejected women from the church of Nuestra Señora de la Purísima Concepción, occupied by the *comisariado ejidal*. Catholic schools reopened at their own risk: after a brusque raid in 1938 the Guaymas federal school inspector closed down an illegal school run by nuns.[29]

Yocupicio could do little more than tolerate most of these takeovers, caught as he was between an increasingly militant Catholicism and a reluctant central government. During the spring of 1937 impatient Catholics had criticized his inactivity, staging mass demonstrations in Hermosillo, Huatabampo, and even in front of his home in Navojoa.[30] The threat of armed resistance continued.

By late 1937 the religious situation in Sonora and other states was slowly returning to normal. Cárdenas finally gave in to Catholic pressure. Churches were reopened by federal permit in Hermosillo, Guaymas, and Alamos, while churches taken by force were often permitted to remain open. Thirteen priests were allowed to officiate, while several more, including Bishop Navarrete, returned without official permission. Mass was now held in churches rather than in private homes. Once again, prominent Guaymas families dared to stage lavish church weddings. Religious authorities even discussed reinstating the fiesta of San Francisco Xavier in Magdalena, despite the recent incineration of the saint's image.[31]

From 1938 on the process of re-Christianization, though slow, moved inexorably toward a complete restoration of the status quo. The federal government finally granted permission for the holding of Mass in 1938, and more churches reopened. Thirty-two nuns, previously occupied in schools and hospitals, returned to Sonora.[32] In September 1938, Bishop Navarrete addressed a crowd of Sonoran pilgrims in the Basilica de Guadalupe in Mexico City. With satisfaction he concluded: "Ahora . . . ya no más vida de catacumbas; podemos decir ¡Viva Cristo Rey!" (Now, no more catacomb existence; we can say: Long live Christ the King).[33]

Re-Christianization generated strong opposition from groups that had benefited by receiving church real estate, such as unions, *comisariados ejidales*, schools, and municipal councils. The church of Cumpas, for example, had been turned into a Centro Cultural, where the local union held its meetings, classes were taught, and a printing press had been installed: "If yesterday this was a place of fanaticism, where truth was a myth, today the truth is taught and matters of interest to the community are discussed." Where, workers complained, were they to go now?[34] The *comisariado ejidal* of Ures stated that, "although our religion is Catholic by tradition, we must say that for the moment this Church serves us better as a communal granary."[35] The church of Cócorit served a similar purpose: "[It was] taken by a lot of Red agrarians . . . who have used it for a loafing, propaganda hangout and warehouse for corn, beans, wheat and broken parts of machinery, oil cans etc. It was covered with red flags but they have faded, rotted and blown away."[36] Often unions reacted diplomatically, realizing that many of their members were devout Catholics. The CTM federation of Nogales stressed that it would not try to close down the recently reopened church there, as it respected the spiritual needs of its members. Elsewhere, workers demonstrated against the return of church property. In Cananea, the refusal by the mineworkers' union to give up a church nearly led to a pitched battle with militant Catholics.[37]

It was not until the 1940s that the conflict was entirely resolved. By 1943 the number of priests had risen to twenty-seven, while most of the state's eighty-five churches and chapels had reopened. Still, Sonora remained an area relatively understaffed by the clergy (in this sense Yocupicio was correct in stressing the liberal character of Sonoran spiritual life). While the average for Mexico was one priest per 5,126 inhabitants, Sonora's figure was much lower at one priest per 13,488.[38] By the early 1940s, the elites, so timid and cautious during the period of persecution, had reestablished their close ties with the Catholic hierarchy. A planning committee for the bishop's *bodas de plata episcopales* was staffed by prominent businessmen, ranchers, and farmers. The political elite did not volunteer, maintaining the well-established rule of avoiding direct ties with anything reeking of fanaticism.[39] Thus, by late 1937 the cultural clash had been largely defused by a combination of Catholic militancy, official state tolerance, benevolent ambiguity from the Cárdenas government, and a generally diplomatic stance on the part of organized labor.

Yocupicio Jockeys for Position in National Politics

During 1936 the position of the Cárdenas government remained shaky. The president's skillful manipulation of factions and the military had allowed him to survive the stand-off with Calles. But his intervention against the Callistas, far from resulting in the establishment of a loyal body of Cardenista governors, actually caused the rise to power of a group of conservatives such as Yocupicio and Maximino Avila Camacho of Puebla. Their rising influence and the survival of right-wing caciques and officers such as Generals Cedillo, Almazán, and Rodríguez augured ill for the future.[40] To make matters worse, Cárdenas was forced to allow many former rebels, especially Obregonista exiles, to return to Mexico, where they soon became involved in conspiratorial, right-wing, anti-Cardenista parties.[41]

As early as February 1937, amid this instability, Governor Yocupicio started drawing attention as a possible leader of the disgruntled right. In a radio address, he denied entertaining such plans, but the right-wing national *El Hombre Libre* stated that "Yocupicio could be another Juárez, all we need is a Lerdo de Tejada to repeat those words 'now or never.' "[42] The feasibility of a Yocupicio presidential candidacy must be doubted; and it seems to have been a ploy used by the right to pressure Cárdenas, and by the left to create an anti-Yocupicista scare, rather than a serious bid for power. In reality, the governor's power did not extend far beyond the borders of Sonora. What he lacked was a powerful patron in Mexico City.

Relations with the United States

The governor of Sonora maintained excellent relations with the United States, particularly with the government of neighbor state Arizona, presided over by Governors Robert T. Jones and Rawghlie Clement Stanford. At banquets in Nogales, Arizona, Yocupicio praised the United States and eulogized Franklin D. Roosevelt. "He [Yocupicio] speaks little or no English, but has many friends among the officials . . . of Arizona. The American mining interests in Sonora as well as the cattlemen . . . consider that General Yocupicio has been the ablest Governor in Sonora since the formation of the State." Governor Jones became a welcome guest in Sonora. During one of their famous banquets, offered by the Tucson Chamber of Commerce, the now nearly octogenarian General John J. Pershing stated that "personally, I would like the next Mexican president to be one of my Mexican friends like, for example, General Román Yocupicio." Pershing also jokingly recalled his former exploits in Mexico, in particular his futile search for Pancho Villa, which failed "because he had looked for the Mexican in all the wrong places." His joke was graciously received by the guests with laughter and applause, but to the Mexican Left such chumminess with the gringos, certainly with Pershing, seemed inappropriate.[43] Protests against Yocupicio's visits started to appear in the press.

Close ties with the United States were, however, essential for the Sonoran economy, which had been closely intertwined with that of neighboring states across the border since the nineteenth century. The primarily U.S.-owned Sonoran mining sector was an extension of the Arizona operations. U.S. companies and individuals also owned many ranches, which depended on exports. From 1939 to 1945, Sonora provided 30 percent of Mexican cattle exports to the United States. Sonoran agricultural enterprises, partly U.S.-owned, exported rice, wheat, and winter vegetables to markets across the border.[44] The drawbacks of dependency became evident during the Depression, when the U.S. market collapsed. The Hawley-Smoot Tariff Act of 1930 had a disastrous effect on Sonoran exports. Conversely the U.S.-Mexican agreement concerning the purchase of Mexican silver by the U.S. Treasury from 1934 to 1938 was an important boost to Sonoran mining.[45] Although the 1930s witnessed a temporary decline of these close economic ties due to the Depression, by 1938–39, Sonoran exports expanded once again and boomed during World War II.

The combination of Cardenista economic nationalism with the prominent position of U.S. capital in Sonora resulted in rising anti-Americanism. Xenophobia was expressed by organizations such as the Comité Nacionalista of Nogales, which distributed handbills calling for the expulsion of the "exploiting satraps": "May the white Chinese leave Nogales the way the yellow Chinese did!"[46] Sentiments flared after presidential candidate Hamilton Fish bluntly stated that Mexico City should pay its petroleum debt to Washington by ceding a strip of Sonoran territory to give Arizona access to the sea.[47] However, anti-Americanism never caused serious problems. The Good Neighbor policy of President Roosevelt resulted in a low U.S. diplomatic profile in Sonora, despite the expropriation of U.S. landholdings.

Yocupicio, the "Mexican Mussolini," or Creole Fascism

After lambasting Yocupicio for having toadied to the United States, the Mexican Left, led by CTM leader Vicente Lombardo Toledano, devised a more effective ploy to undermine the credibility of the governor, accusing him of being in league with the fascists and of organizing a Fifth Column. Such accusations, though largely false, did succeed in making Yocupicio suspect in the eyes of foreign observers and undermined his position as the possible future standard-bearer of Mexico's conservatives. The "Mexican Mussolini," as his detractors called him—compare the equally ludicrous comparison between Cedillo and the Führer—was investigated by the U.S. press, anti-fascist organizations, and military intelligence as part of a larger fascist scare. Most of the hype was the result of propaganda, in particular by Lombardo, who passionately warned his compatriots that an extensive espionage network had converted Mexico into a fascist staging ground.[48]

Such hysteria was echoed by U.S. observers such as Betty Kirk, who claimed that "Japan has a skeleton army in Mexico. It is under the direct command of Premier Hideki Tojo. This skeleton army . . . has two plans. One is to direct the invasion . . . of the United States through the Mexican states of Sonora and Sinaloa. The other is to promote, in cooperation with the Spanish falangista allies, the rebellion of Mexican Indians against the whites—in particular, against the 'Yankees.' These race riots will be co-ordinated with the invasion attempts."[49] However, journalist Salvador Novo dismissed the scare as a "Macbethian specter," stating that "nowadays, if Don Vicente [Lombardo] suffers from a colic, it's the fault of Morones; if an earthquake occurs in Mexico, the CTM, through its secretary general, declares that Morones and Calles and the reaction planned and orchestrated the seismic movement; if it does not rain, or if it rains too much, Lombardo Toledano explains dialectically that this is due to the secret scheming of CROM. Plutarco Elías Calles, Adolf Hitler, Luis N. Morones, Benito Mussolini, Julio Ramírez, and the King of England are all personal enemies of Lombardo Toledano and Joseph Stalin."[50]

Rumors suggested clandestine links between Yocupicio and Japanese agents, who were infiltrating Sonora in the guise of fishermen. It was said that Yocupicio had conceded Japan the right to establish a large fishing and espionage fleet in the strategic Bahía de Magdalena.[51] These reports reflect an unhealthy combination of xenophobia and Fifth Column paranoia. In reality, the Japanese colony was small, numbering less than six thousand. They were concentrated in Sonora (786) and Sinaloa (498), where many engaged in shrimping, and in Mexico City.[52] In 1938 visits to the colony in Sonora by the Japanese consul and naval attaché sparked wild speculations. But closer examination led U.S. diplomats to conclude that these rumors "were of so exaggerated and impossible a nature as to tax the credulity of even the uninformed" and "apparently designed to stir up feeling against the Japanese."[53] The anti-Japanese campaign was probably a ploy by business interests to gain control of the lucrative shrimping industry, just as racist rhetoric had been used earlier to take over Chinese merchant houses and shops. In 1940, Abelardo Rodríguez, who had started his economic empire by investing heavily in the Sonoran fishing sector, signed a contract with the fishing cooperatives of Guaymas for the delivery of all shrimp previously caught by Japanese fishermen.[54]

The activity of European fascist regimes in Sonora, denounced by Yocupicio's detractors, seems to have been minimal as well.[55] Spanish fascist organizations such as Falange Española had no branches in Sonora. That U.S. intelligence, usually all too eager to grant credence to ill-founded Fifth Column rumors, could find no proof of Yocupicio's complicity is telling. One example of U.S. intelligence-gathering capability involved the infamous brothel "El Rancho Grande" in Agua Prieta, which was operated by an agent of the Douglas police, who used prostitutes to obtain information on German subversive activities.[56]

The accusations against Yocupicio that emerged in Mexico City were soon echoed by his enemies in Sonora, especially CTM-affiliated unions. The Sonoran government strongly denied the allegations: "The government of General Yocupicio is ANTIFAS-CIST because it emerged from entirely democratic elections."[57] Yocupicio defended himself in an interview: "As far as the charge of being a fascist, . . . everyone . . . knows by now that whichever citizen doesn't support [Lombardo's] goals runs the risk of being qualified that way." However, he only made matters worse by ac-cusing CTM workers of being "unconscious instruments of inter-national Judaism."[58]

Anti-Semitism, though probably strengthened by European fascism, was nothing new in Mexico. It became fashionable during the 1930s, even among intellectuals such as José Vasconcelos. His magazine *Timón* denounced the Judeo-Bolshevik conspiracy, led by such villains as Roosevelt, to dominate the world. *Timón* defended the "liberating totalitarianism" of Hitler, the "broom of God that is sweeping the accumulated evil of centuries from the face of the Earth . . . especially, the Jewish conception of the world of taking advantage of humanity by gathering its legitimate wealth through usury." Meanwhile, well-known painter Dr. Atl diligently collected the addresses of Jewish establishments in downtown Mexico City, possibly in preparation for a Mexican *Kristallnacht*.[59] Mexican anti-Semitism was not, however, part of a broader fascist ideologi-cal project. In Sonora, xenophobia was closely related to economic nationalism, as evidenced by the cases of the Chinese and Japa-nese. In 1938 a Comité Pro-Comercio Nacional called for a boycott of all Jewish establishments in Hermosillo. Protesters bearing anti-Semitic placards used force to stop customers from entering. It was believed that the picketing was sponsored by competing busi-nesses. The actions were stopped by the authorities, and Yocupicio assured a Jewish delegation that they would receive equal rights.

But Jewish shops were expressly taxed, as has happened earlier with the Chinese.[60]

Other accusations concerned the government's links to small ultraright-wing or pseudo-fascist organizations such as Acción Mexicanista, the successor to Nicolás Rodríguez's outlawed *camisas doradas* or Gold Shirts, and the Unión Nacional de Veteranos de la Revolución (UNVR). These representatives of classic fascism—strongly nationalist, anti-liberal, anti-Communist (anti-Bolshevik, pro-Franco), racist (anti-Semitic, anti-Chinese), violently authoritarian movements—never gained a wide following. However, they did have substantial political, though not necessarily ideological, influence.

The Sonoran branch of the UNVR became one of the governor's main pillars of support. This seemingly innocuous veterans' organization was often used for political purposes. It criticized Cárdenas's "communist" policies and advocated the creation of privately owned *colonias agrícolas* worked by veterans. The Sonoran UNVR, founded shortly after Yocupicio's inauguration, was headed by Zenón Jiménez Ponce, the Hermosillo police chief. Various high-ranking state officials played a role, either as consultants or members, including Yocupicio. The UNVR became a Yocupicista instrument financed by the state and municipal governments. Its membership grew rapidly to some one thousand people, with chapters throughout Sonora. It functioned as a pool of support for Yocupicio's countercorporatist schemes to undermine the CTM and *agrarismo*. The veterans formed, as we shall see below, an important constituent of the Yocupicista labor federation, CTS. Spurious unions such as the Sindicato de Trabajadores Veteranos de la Revolución, led by Jímenez, padded the federation's membership. The governor also hoped to use the veterans to initiate land colonization schemes in an effort to undermine official land reform. The federal government, which considered organizations like the UNVR dangerous proto-fascist gangs, was less than pleased. Zone Commander Enríquez unsuccessfully pushed for the UNVR's disbandment, reportedly losing his patience and brandishing a pistol "in the privacy of the Governor's office." But little could be done to outlaw an avowedly patriotic and revolutionary veterans' group.[61]

Conclusion

By the summer of 1937, Yocupicio had established a well-entrenched bureaucratic power base. It relied on informal ties of factional, military, and personal allegiance, which permeated the increasingly bureaucratized state apparatus. The economic elites supported the governor's stance against Cardenista reform and in favor of organicist labor-capital relations.

One essential component of the anti-Callista opposition could not be placated by *amiguismo*. An increasingly impatient and vocal Catholic movement demanded an end to religious persecution and resisted attempts to found a revolutionary civil religion. It responded with petitions, demonstrations, school boycotts, illegal Masses, the violent reopening of churches, and a series of rebellions collectively known as the Second Cristiada. In Sonora, this opposition originated not only with the Church but also with many individual Catholics, especially women, Indians, and *serranos*. Yocupicio reacted by tolerating religious practices and negotiating with the government. Cárdenas reluctantly agreed to moderate intolerance and opted for a slow, face-saving re-Christianization process. By 1937–38 churches were reopened, services tolerated, and priests allowed to return. Teachers were admonished to concentrate on their tasks as educators and relinquish their role as disseminators of the revolutionary creed. Socialist education was phased out and Catholic schools reopened. By 1938 the Catholic movement began to lose its critical influence due to the restoration of religious freedom. The cultural revolution was the product of what François Furet calls the "illusion of politics" and merely sparked a "reassertion of real society."[62] As the revolution entered Thermidor, the State began dismantling the institutions that would have implemented the cultural revolution, a revolution that proved a politically dangerous fiasco.

Yocupicio maneuvered for national position, though without much initial success. He did, however, manage to attract the attention of the Cárdenas government. The development of close ties with the United States was the logical outcome of the increasing importance of the Sonoran export sector and failed to strengthen the governor's position significantly. U.S. diplomats did not play an important role in Sonora due to the Good Neighbor policy. Allegations concerning close links between Yocupicio and the fascist nations were based on propaganda. European fascist ideology did, however, influence the political ambiance, as attested by rising anti-Semitism.

One key sector was still excluded from the Yocupicista power base—namely, the workers and campesinos previously influential during the Callista administrations. Yocupicio would now turn to their incorporation, initially through the mobilization of veterans into the UNVR, which would form a pool for a Yocupicista labor federation. But he would have to compete with Cárdenas for the loyalty of Sonoran labor.

III

Cardenismo, Labor, and
the Polarization of
Sonoran Politics, 1937–38

6

The Cardenista Counteroffensive

Sonoran Labor and the CTM

An unruly crowd awaited Vicente Lombardo Toledano, the leader of the national labor federation, the Confederación de Trabajadores de México (CTM), when his train arrived at the Hermosillo station on the night of September 22, 1937. A mob of hundreds of Yocupicio followers chanting "Death to Lombardo" rushed the train when it came to a halt. What followed is unclear, but Lombardo later claimed that the heroic intercession of railworkers narrowly averted a conspiracy to assassinate him. The CTM prepared nationwide demonstrations. Yocupicio vehemently denied any involvement and laughed off the whole affair, claiming that Lombardo had fled from the scene dressed as a woman, and scoffed that he was "more cowardly than a sterile hen."[1]

This incident reflected the growing power struggle between conservative regional groups and the CTM. Historians working within the populist/corporatist paradigm see the unification of labor by the CTM as a populist *política de masas*, by means of which Cárdenas sought to strengthen his power base, empower the State, and, some add, stimulate capitalist development. The CTM became "the instrument by which the masses of workers would be mobilized in support of the decisions of the State."[2] Unfortunately, this approach denies the Mexican workers any historical agency. Some recent studies advocate a more balanced view of relations between the labor movement and Cardenismo, and stress the capacity of workers to shape policies and the political system.[3]

The Sonoran case demonstrates that this relationship was not one of simple mobilization and manipulation, but rather an alliance, at least during the period from the CTM's foundation in 1936 through 1938, when it was absorbed into the corporatist PRM and lost much of its militancy and political clout. Labor historians stress that the goals of the CTM were, first and foremost, economistic, and they list the following objectives: collective contracts, wage hikes, compliance with the Federal Labor Law, the right to organize and to strike, the closed shop (by means of the *cláusula de exclusión*), and the elimination of company unions. In these areas, organized labor met with great success.[4] But to state that it limited its demands to economistic goals, or that the "Leviathan state" did not allow labor to "mature politically" and participate in politics, is misleading.[5]

The CTM actually stimulated worker participation in municipal and state electoral contests, and also tried to purge the political system of conservatives. Although often unsuccessful, certainly in gubernatorial elections, labor did manage to gain control of influential political positions, not just the sinecures reserved for labor bosses in Congress but also the city councils of important towns such as Ciudad Obregón, Puebla, Veracruz, and Los Mochis.[6] Another example of the "relative autonomy" of labor is the drive for workers' control among key sectors of the proletariat, such as petroleum workers, railwaymen, and millworkers, a project that at times went well beyond the goals of Cardenismo.[7]

In Sonora, the CTM allied itself with a militant, autonomous labor movement, centered in the Yaqui Valley, which sought allies at the national level. It hoped these would help it obtain not only economic benefits and agrarian reform but also political power, such as control of the hotly contested Ciudad Obregón municipal council and the governorship. In return, the CTM and the Cárdenas regime could count on a loyal labor base in Sonora, to be used in support of reform and as a counterbalance to anti-Cardenista forces. The CTM formed alliances of this kind in many states, such as Puebla, Sinaloa, Nuevo León, and Jalisco. In some cases (Oaxaca, Nuevo León, Coahuila), the formation of CTM-affiliated regional federations through so-called labor unification only succeeded after heavy-handed intervention by CTM leaders Lombardo and Fidel Velázquez, an indication of the *charrismo* to come. Elsewhere, in Sonora, fairly independent federations maintained a degree of autonomy. These alliances paid off handsomely: regional federations received national support and in return attacked anti-Cardenista strongmen such as Yocupicio, Cedillo, Alfredo Delgado, and Anacleto Guerrero. Lombardo's shrill campaigns against fascism, which Arturo Anguiano aptly describes as "a terrifying spectre that could only be exorcised by organization, unification and discipline," served to strengthen these attacks and attract broader national, and even international, attention.[8] However, the resulting discipline would lead to the dissipation of the CTM's power and degenerated into classic *charrismo*, which involved a system of government payoffs to a "union oligarchy."[9]

The Sonoran Work Force

The composition of the Sonoran labor force had not changed significantly since the late Porfiriato, despite rapid demographic growth, largely due to migration. In 1930 the population was still overwhelmingly (two-thirds) rural.[10] The economically active population numbered 99,951 (including 4,199 women), of whom the vast majority worked in agriculture.

Economically Active Population of Sonora, 1930[11]		
Agriculture	64,112	64%
Industry	14,768	15%
Communications,		
transportation	2,247	2%
Commerce	4,819	5%
Other	14,005	14%
Total	99,951	100%

Sonoran industry consisted of the previously dominant but now declining foreign-owned mining sector; food processing plants, in particular flour and rice mills; a textile mill (the old Fábrica de los Angeles in San Miguel de Horcasitas); a brewery (the Hoeffers' Cervecería de Sonora in Hermosillo); a cement factory in Villa de Seris; cigar factories (El Toro, La Mexicana); tanneries (La Monarca, Francisco Fourcade y Sucs. in Guaymas); shoe and clothing workshops; electrical plants; and numerous smaller establishments producing candles, matches, soap, foodstuffs, furniture, and bricks.[12]

There were only several thousand factory workers. The mining sector was a key employer. The Cananea Consolidated Copper Company alone employed one thousand miners in 1938, although employment had dropped off dramatically after 1926. Several other companies employed hundreds of workers, such as the Los Angeles mill and the Cervecería de Sonora. Flour and rice mills were located in most towns, especially in the north and in Ciudad Obregón, in the heart of the Yaqui Valley. They varied in size and capacity. Large mills such as the U.S.-owned Cía. Molinera del Río Yaqui and the Cía. Arrocera del Río Yaqui in Ciudad Obregón employed as many as 125 workers, although most averaged some twenty employees.[13] Industrial workers formed only a tiny minority of the total labor force. A traditional sector of small industries and artisanal workshops (*talleres*) predominated, employing on average one to three workers and producing everything from furniture and leather goods to batteries.[14] The commercial sector included large merchant houses, such as the Hoeffers' Abarrotera de Sonora; Tapia Hermanos in Hermosillo; El Puerto de Guaymas, owned by Spaniard Gaspar Zaragoza, with outlets in Guaymas, Navojoa, and Ciudad Obregón; and Agustín Bouvet's La Francesa in Navojoa, which all employed more than one hundred workers. Automobile dealerships and agencies of farming machinery grew rapidly as the agricultural economy expanded. Smaller stores selling hardware, groceries, shoes, clothing, drugs, and liquor were, however, the norm and generally occupied less than ten employees.[15]

The wage gap between skilled and unskilled labor was marked. While skilled miners, millworkers, mechanics, and trainmen might earn anywhere between 7 and 17 pesos per day, common laborers (*jornaleros, obreros*) made as little as 1.60 to 3.20 pesos per day. Wages in the service sector were considerably lower than in industry. Store clerks usually received only the minimum wage (in 1936 the minimum wage was 1.50 to 2.25 pesos).[16] Wage differentiation tended to be greatest in the modern sectors, such as mining and railways, although substantial differences existed between skilled and unskilled labor in all sectors. As real wages declined due to inflation, unskilled labor tended to press for the equalization of wages. Low-paid laborers sought wages and working conditions comparable to those in the "labor aristocratic" sectors, such as mining or the petroleum industry. This led to considerable pressure on capital for higher wages and enhanced collective contracts.

Young women in their teens and twenties constituted a significant part of the industrial labor force, in particular in the tobacco factories, where they worked as cigarette rollers (*envolvedoras*). In urban areas considerable numbers of women worked as seamstresses, laundresses, waitresses, maids, and cooks. In Navojoa alone more than 250 women belonged to the Sindicato Femenil de Costureras (seamstresses). Of this group almost half were single and under thirty.[17]

The vast majority of Sonoran workers were rural laborers, men and women attracted to the fertile Yaqui and Mayo Valleys, where they found employment as vegetable pickers, packers, loaders, and *peones*. In addition, hundreds of unskilled day laborers found employment in state road construction and paving works. Numerous migrant workers from Sinaloa and other states came to the valleys in search of jobs. The Yaqui Valley employed some five thousand *jornaleros* (day laborers), including several thousand migrant workers and some five to seven hundred Mayo Indians. Their wages were low: an unskilled worker earned a mere 1.50 to 2.62 pesos per day. Mayo Valley vegetable packers earned 0.35 pesos per hour, while some tasks were done on a piecework basis. Although low, such wages were considerably higher than in neighboring Sinaloa.[18] Hundreds of women were employed in commercial agriculture. They were overwhelmingly single (80 percent) and very young (35 percent under twenty, 80 percent under thirty). Men found work as *cargadores* (loaders) for the packing companies. They were largely single, and young (64 percent under thirty, more than 90 percent under forty).[19] The number of *peones acasillados* working permanently on haciendas was relatively small. Most Hermosillo area farms employed less than ten *peones*; a large force of more than thirty was exceptional. In the Yaqui Valley, numbers of *peones* on farms ranged from forty-seven to as few as two. The average was about thirteen.[20] Ranches were not a major source of employment. They usually hired a foreman and several cowboys who received the minimum wage. In some cases, wages were still paid in kind, thus perpetuating the old *tienda de raya* system.[21] Most inhabitants of the sierra lived as sharecroppers and renters (growing wheat and maize), prospectors, small ranchers, or muleteers for the mining companies, often combining various activities to survive.[22] Conditions in the sierra were bleak, which resulted in a steady stream of migrants to the coast, a process that still continues today.

Background to the Sonoran Labor Movement

The Porfiriato witnessed the emergence of liberal clubs and urban mutualist organizations (*hermandades, sociedades de artesanos*) such as the Sociedad de Artesanos Hidalgo in Hermosillo and Guaymas. Modern union formation was introduced by the railworkers' Unión de Mecánicos Mexicanos (UMM). The revolutionary years saw the organization of miners' and railworkers' unions affiliated with the UMM and the Unión Minera Mexicana.[23] By the early 1920s labor organization was still characterized by its craft orientation and largely limited to skilled workers in the mining, railroad, and textile sectors, who were close to the artisanal tradition. The Callista national labor federation (CROM) was moderately successful in extending its control over Sonoran labor and stimulating organization during the 1920s, establishing or incorporating unions of urban artisans, textile workers, miners, railwaymen, fishermen, longshoremen, and some peasants in the sierra. It never gained complete control, despite the formation of a CROMista Federación Sonorense del Trabajo in 1928. What is particularly striking is the lack of any significant peasant organization prior to the 1930s.[24]

It was not until the late 1920s and early 1930s that mass unionization took place among previously unorganized groups such as service workers, day laborers, miners in small pits, and, especially, rural proletarians. Federal teachers played an essential role in this Callista, state-sponsored process, actively founding unions, leading workers in their struggle for higher wages and compliance with the Federal Labor Law, and serving on union directorates. Industrial workers, in particular the railwaymen, also played a major role.[25] Only more detailed studies will shed light on the question of whether to consider this movement as a "top-down" (state-sponsored, manipulative mobilization for political purposes) or "bottom-up" (spontaneous grass-roots mobilization) phenomenon.[26] The rise of a strong campesino movement, especially in the Yaqui Valley, was the result of the rapid expansion of commercial agriculture and the formation of a new rural proletariat. But it is clear that the impulse from above, or "outside," served as a major catalyst.

It was during these years that the foundation of the later Cardenista labor movement was laid. Most towns witnessed the formation of unions of artisans (shoemakers, typesetters, carpenters, mechanics), construction workers (brickmakers, masons, plumbers), and serviceworkers (bakers, chauffeurs, *cantineros*, hotel and restaurant personnel, shop employees, musicians), especially in larger towns, such as Nogales, Hermosillo, and Ciudad Obregón. In smaller towns, so-called Sindicatos de Oficios Varios consisting of a hodgepodge of workers were common. But Sonora also saw the massive organization of unskilled labor, as demonstrated by numerous unions of *cargadores*, stevedores, and *jornaleros*, especially in the south.[27] This was the beginning of the unionization of all types of labor, including the "campesinos," a vague and misleading term applied to both the peasantry and the rural proletariat, two diverse groups with divergent interests. By the early 1930s campesino groups petitioning for land, *uniones obrero-campesinas*, constituted the core of the new labor movement.[28] Agrarian reform during the 1920s and early 1930s was, however, still a top-down paternalistic enterprise in which teachers played an essential role. Governor Calles spent considerable time personally supervising the new ejidos. In the sierra, the process was different, characterized by struggles between *comuneros* and ranchers for control of village commons.

An important milestone in the history of the Yaqui Valley campesino movement was the founding in 1934 of the Federación Obrera y Campesina del Sur de Sonora (FOCSS), which unified the militant rural proletariat of Campos 80, 60, and 74 under the leadership of men such as Jacinto López, Maximiliano López, Matías Méndez, and Rafael Contreras. Some key FOCSS leaders, including Jacinto López, a shoemaker born in the *serrano* town of Banámichi, and Maximiliano López, a *peón*, were schooled in union tactics by the miners of Cananea and the Empalme railroadworkers and transferred their "mature" union experience to the campesino movement. Most were, however, landless *peones*, while teachers also figured prominently among the leadership. It was this organized rural proletariat in states such as Sonora, Coahuila, and Sinaloa that was to play a key role in Cardenista politics and agrarian reform.[29]

By the late 1930s women's unions of seamstresses, laundresses, *planchadoras*, cooks, maids, midwives, waitresses, and vegetable packers, as well as all-female unions of *oficios varios*, became a significant factor.[30] The general trend to incorporate new groups into the union system undoubtedly stimulated the formation of new unions, as well as women's leagues in the ejidos.

In Sonora, the trend toward labor unification—the conglomeration of unions in regional federations—so marked during the Cárdenas presidency, began during the early 1930s. Regional *federaciones obrero-campesinas* were formed in Hermosillo, Huatabampo, Navojoa, Guaymas, Ures, Ciudad Obregón (FOCSS), Nogales, and Alamos. These were not uniformly militant: the FOC de Hermosillo, led by the flamboyant José Abraham Mendívil, later formed the core of the conservative CTS, while the FOCSS became the nucleus of the radical CTM-affiliated Federación de Trabajadores de Sonora (FTS). Efforts to create an overall Confederación General de Trabajadores de Sonora failed due to the unstable situation in 1935.[31] Thus, by 1935 the Sonoran labor movement was not only well organized but also quite militant, playing an increasing role in municipal politics. However, it was closely controlled by Governors Calles and Ramos. Also, unification had not been achieved, while the struggle for higher wages and collective contracts was just beginning.

Creating a Cardenista Power Base in Sonora

Yocupicio was solidly in control of Sonora by early 1937. This was an unpleasant prospect for the shaky Cárdenas administration, which desperately sought to consolidate its power base beyond the old-style alliances with ideologically opposed regional power groups forged in 1935–36. The price paid for toppling Callismo was high indeed: conservative factions dominated the state and could be expected to do their utmost to obstruct the implementation of reform. It was now a high priority to form loyal, radical state power groups on which Cárdenas could count for political and, if necessary, armed support. During 1937–38, Cárdenas distanced himself from his conservative allies and embraced campesino and workers' unions. This transition from a factional to a class-based alliance would never be complete and generated intense conflict. Conservative columnist Diego Arenas Guzmán believed that the president consciously used the CTM and the PNR (the latter was of only limited use in Sonora) to destroy conservative strongholds and avert the presidential candidacy of Cedillo or Yocupicio: "Both [the PNR and the CTM] have aimed their batteries against . . . San Luis Potosí and Sonora. . . . Neither Cedillo nor Yocupicio has taken to the mania of greeting with shaking hands, of reverently uncovering their heads before the banner of the hammer and sickle, or of standing at attention on hearing the 'Internationale.' And this is more than sufficient proof to brand them abominable reactionaries, lackeys of the clergy and lieutenants of the Fuehrer or the Duce."[32] The CTM targetted a number of "reactionary" governors in Sonora, San Luis Potosí, Sinaloa, Querétaro, Puebla, and Coahuila, and their conduct was debated in Congress.[33]

The CTM launched a fierce anti-Yocupicio campaign calling for his resignation. CTM leader Lombardo accused Yocupicio of being an "enemy of [the government], closely allied to the hacendados and the clergy of the state, as well as to the fascists of the United States Southwest and the heads of the Catholic Church in the neighboring states of the United States." He wrote the president that in Sonora a fascist government repressed labor, suppressed constitutional liberties, and ignored the Federal Labor Law. Lombardo's magazine *Futuro* accused him of kowtowing to foreign mining companies, tolerating feudalism in the sierra, betraying his own Indian race, and of having invited the reactionary par excellence, José Vasconcelos, to reside in his state. In the wake of the failed Cedillo rebellion of 1938 the governor was depicted as the leader of *la Reac-*

ción: "Once Saturnino Cedillo was eliminated . . . the reaction took it upon itself to find a substitute as captain and standard-bearer of their program. They easily found him in Román Yocupicio."[34]

Cardenistas used a rather broad definition of *la Reacción*, that mythical coalition reviled by nineteenth-century liberals and still evoked by paranoid *priistas* today, which reminds us of the eternal "aristocratic conspiracy" of the French Revolution. "In its ranks one finds the national bourgeoisie, the clergy, the political debris of all our social movements, the great mercenary journalists, the reactionary leaders of the CROM and the CGT, the governors of Sonora, Chiapas, and San Luis Potosí, a few Callista senators, Saturnino Cedillo, and, in short, all the enemies of the betterment of the popular masses."[35] Charges accusing Yocupicio of planning an anti-Cardenista rebellion sparked calls for his dismissal. The Senate sent a special fact-finding mission to Sonora, which privately advised him to remove the more objectionable members of his *camarilla* and stop harassing union leaders. However, in public these issues were not mentioned, and the committee's official conclusions seemed to vindicate the governor's position. Obviously, Mexico City was willing to offer Yocupicio an honorable, face-saving opportunity to mend his evil ways.[36]

For Cárdenas the task at hand was to construct an alternative Sonoran power bloc along the lines of the corporatist project being implemented at the national level. He would later claim, with some exaggeration, that "when we retired . . . the working class was perfectly organized. . . . The peasant class was also organized and had land and a rifle in its hand as army reserve and defender of the people. The teachers were organized as well, and their union deserved the respect of all. The same with the government employees, who already enjoyed the legal statutes that recognized their rights. The military was in an identical situation."[37]

The government attempted to re-create this national project at the regional level with some, though not complete, success. The president's attention was directed toward workers, peasants, and teachers, potential allies who could serve as a counterbalance to Yocupicio's "reactionary" coalition. First, these groups were to be organized or, more accurately, allied with national Cardenista organizations. Then Cárdenas would press for agrarian and labor reforms to satisfy their demands. Lombardo would later boast that he personally organized the workers of the Yaqui and Mayo Valleys.[38] His claim is rather exaggerated; this was not a process of mobilization from above. Concentrating on Cárdenas's and

Lombardo's efforts gives us a misleading picture. Mobilization would have been impossible without the existence, since the early 1930s, of a militant labor movement, which now actively sought allies at the national level, just as national factions sought a clientele at the regional one. In Sonora, Cárdenas would have to do without a loyal PNR apparatus, which remained solidly in the hands of the Yocupicistas. It was the CTM that was to play a key role in Cárdenas's campaign against the governor, together with the federal bureaucracy, teachers, and sectors of the army.

This new power bloc, backed by the central government, was to make Yocupicio's life unpleasant for the next few years. The Sonoran labor movement hoped to receive payoffs in the form of land, higher wages, better working conditions, workers' control of sectors of the economy, and political power, including direct or indirect control of city councils, the governorship, and seats in Congress. By the 1930s, the Mexican labor movement had developed a mature political agenda with clear objectives: "The determination of the CTM to gain control of the worker and peasant organizations of Sonora is essentially political. Its immediate goal is to win the elections for governor. But at the same time the election of a CTM governor . . . prepares for a mediate aim: the presidential elections in 1940."[39] Far from being an immature, manipulated cipher, organized labor strongly influenced the course of Cardenismo.

The Failure of Campesino Unification in Sonora: The Liga de Comunidades Agrarias

Among the rural workers and peasants of Sonora, expectations had risen since Cárdenas's presidential campaign tour in 1934, "when we were lucky enough to hear from his own lips and in this very town [Ciudad Obregón] the promise that as soon as he would be inaugurated as President he would grant us the land."[40] In an effort to tap their power, the PNR convened a Convention of Campesino Unification in Hermosillo for February 20–21, 1937, with the purpose of founding a Liga de Comunidades Agrarias y Sindicatos Campesinos del Estado de Sonora (LCASC), a state federation that would unify all unions of peasants and rural laborers and integrate these into the future national peasant league, the Confederación Nacional Campesina (CNC). Much to the dismay of Yocupicio, who attended the meeting, PNR president Silvano Barba González promised the *agraristas* a rapid redistribution of the Yaqui Valley lands. Congress degenerated into a rowdy and, for the governor, unpleasant affair. *Agraristas* criticized his stance on land reform and labor. The U.S. vice-consul at Guaymas was not amused by the numerous allusions to Yankee imperialism and denounced those "outsiders who come to Sonora expressly for the purpose of stirring up trouble for [Yocupicio]." The event was a major embarrassment for the governor and undoubtedly sharpened his already profound dislike of the Cárdenas regime and labor.[41]

The new Liga never became a pillar of Cardenismo. Instead, "the CNC entered to divide us even more," recalls one campesino leader.[42] When founded, it counted only 387 members in the Yaqui Valley.[43] In their search for national patronage, most Sonoran peasants, rural laborers, *agraristas*, and ejidatarios joined the CTM instead. This outcome belies the conventional wisdom of a clear demarcation between peasant and workers' unions organized in the CNC and CTM, supposedly masterminded by Cárdenas in an effort to divide and rule. The Liga denounced the intromission of the CTM into its field of operations. Ultimately it became part of the national peasant federation CNC, founded in 1938, and absorbed many of the conservative, anti-collectivist ejidatarios backed first by the Sonoran government and, subsequently, by the anti-Cardenista national governments of Avila Camacho and Alemán. A major battle between the two organizations commenced, the Liga/CNC championing the interests of *individualistas*, the CTM of *colectivistas*.

The CTM in Sonora

It was the CTM that became the prime weapon in the struggle against Yocupicio. It soon attracted a mass following among urban and, especially, rural workers. In Sonora, San Luis Potosí, Sinaloa, Nuevo León, and other states, the CTM became an instrument of intervention for the central government. Aggressively seeking to control fragmented regional labor movements, the CTM now sent its delegates, or "agents provocateurs" as their detractors called them, to the provinces (Sonora, Coahuila, Sinaloa, Baja California, México, Oaxaca, Nuevo León).[44]

In March 1937, CTM delegate Enrique Torres Calderón arrived in Sonora to organize a labor congress that would establish a CTM-affiliated Sonoran labor federation. He publicly denounced the governor's labor policy. Yocupicio soon protested that Calderón was busy fomenting strikes and dividing the workers. Calderón retorted that he had visited the governor twice, only to be received with insults and threats to expel or jail him.[45] The Yocupicio-CTM conflict turned ugly when Calderón mysteriously disappeared. Lombardo accused the Yaqui Valley police of having kidnapped and possibly assassinated the CTM delegate on orders of Yocupicio, and threatened a general strike in Mexico City if he were not found immediately. Yocupicio responded that the case was a sham, an *autosecuestro*. What actually happened is unclear, but the delegate reappeared a week later, "safe and sound." In response to this "agitation" the authorities jailed fourteen CTM leaders.[46]

The CTM-sponsored Congress of Unification was finally held in Ciudad Obregón, the heart of Sonoran radicalism, from June 10–12, 1937. This conference established the Federación de Trabajadores de Sonora (FTS/CTM) as an umbrella organization for the regional federations of Nogales, Ciudad Obregón, Huatabampo and Etchojoa, Alamos, Navojoa, and Santa Ana. The most important labor leaders, including Jacinto López, Hermenegildo Peña, Vicente Padilla, Manuel Bobadilla, Matías Méndez, Rafael Contreras, Saturnino Saldívar, Ramón H. Olivarría, Antonio Encinas, Praxedis Gastélum, Francisco Trejo, Pablo Hernández, and Jesús P. Retamoza, attended the conference. The participants elected FOCSS leader Jacinto López as their first secretary general. The delegates, headed by CTM leaders Fidel Velázquez and Rodolfo Piña Soria, lambasted the governor, while workers marched through the streets chanting anti-Yocupicio obscenities. He responded by arresting them and eight other delegates, an act that sparked mass protests, a one-hour strike in Mexico City, and a scolding by the secretary of the interior. Lombardo suggested to the president that the Sonoran government was unconstitutional and exhorted all CTM delegates to agitate against Yocupicio. The left-wing national press echoed these virulent attacks.[47]

The struggle assumed the aspect of a personal vendetta when the CTM leader's train was mobbed by angry Yocupicio supporters on arrival in the Sonoran capital on September 22. Lombardo claimed that the governor had ordered his assassination. Officers present during the incident later discounted Lombardo's version, while others even insinuated that he had conceived the whole incident himself, "making him seem like a martyr elsewhere in the country."[48] The right-wing *El Hombre Libre* opined that the real purpose of this *autoatentado* was to "blow on the embers of a fire that had already begun to die down."[49] Yocupicio vehemently denied the charges and merely made jokes at Lombardo's expense. His jokes masked a great unease with the entrance of the CTM into

Sonora. It now controlled a major sector of the Sonoran federations. This promised increased labor unrest and constituted a direct threat to the economic elites. Some speculated that the escalating attacks against the governor would soon lead to his fall. But Yocupicio continued his blatant repression of the CTM.

The Federación de Trabajadores de Sonora

The CTM was able to absorb an already existant and militant Sonoran labor movement, the core of which consisted of the rural proletariat (not a peasantry) of southern Sonora, sectors of urban labor, and teachers. Unification was swift, profound, but not entirely conclusive. It did, however, provide the president with a weapon with which to undermine Yocupicio's position, as well as a mass constituency with which to support Cardenista candidates for office. The CTM never did gain complete control over the Sonoran labor force, however, and the alliance would later show serious rifts. The independent miners' union SITMMSRM, for example, left the CTM in 1936 and followed an autonomous political line, based more on the miners' specific economistic demands and outlook than on any sense of ideological affinity with Cárdenas.

The strength of the FTS/CTM varied; while it dominated the valleys and some towns, it was relatively weak in Hermosillo and in Agua Prieta.[50] By 1939 the FTS claimed to represent some 19,000 workers. The Yaqui Valley FOCSS provided much of the leadership, which included FTS president Jacinto López, Rafael Contreras, Ramón H. Olivarría, Matías Méndez, Maximiliano López, Manuel S. Corbalá, and Jesús P. Retamoza.[51] The most combative unions belonged to the FOCSS, such as the Sindicato Industrial Progresista Sonorense, the Sindicato Industrial del Valle, and the Sindicato Oriental del Valle del Yaqui Campo 80, all consisting of rural proletarians. After the agrarian reform of 1937–38, the numerous *comisariados ejidales*, *sindicatos obrero-campesinos*, and *ligas femeniles* of the Yaqui and Mayo Valleys formed the prime strength of the CTM. The Nogales federation, the Federación de Uniones y Sindicatos Obreros, had a different makeup, consisting of diverse urban workers: painters, drivers, masons, *abasto* workers, *cantineros*, waiters, restaurant workers, shop assistants, bakers, and day laborers, and, by 1939, federal health-care workers, office personnel and teachers, railworkers, and movie operators. The State contributed to this expansion by adding the federal bureaucrats, a loyal and pliant clientele.[52]

The Unification of the Sonoran Teachers: Federal versus State Teachers

The influential teachers, former allies of Callismo, needed to be converted to Cardenismo through "unification"—the creation of a united Sonoran teachers' federation subservient to the government. Two issues dominated the struggle: the teachers' standard of living, which was repeatedly threatened by the Sonoran government's inability to pay their meager salaries, and political allegiance. Ultimately, federal teachers fell under the control of the Cárdenas government, and state teachers were placed under Yocupicio's state government.

State and federal teachers tried to unify in an effort to strengthen their position vis-à-vis the state government. For many leaders the solution was adherence to the increasingly important Cardenista Confederación Nacional de Trabajadores de la Enseñanza (CNTE). To this purpose the first Congreso de Unificación Magisterial y de Orientación Social was held in Hermosillo in 1936, organized by union leader Hermenegildo Peña. Teachers decided to push for a 6 peso minimum salary (as in Mexico City), distribution of arms to rural teachers (a reaction to the slaying of the teacher of Bavispe), the federalization of Sonoran education, the rehiring of dismissed teachers, continuation of the anticlerical campaign and socialist education, agrarian reform, prohibition, unionization, the expulsion of all Chinese from Sonora, and the defense of the state against Yankee imperialism.[53]

Peña reportedly tried to reach an agreement with the unpopular director general of education, Fernando Ximello: in return for the exclusive recognition of and aid to the union, noninterference in its affairs, and the removal of uncooperative teachers, the union pledged to consult the director on important issues and defend him against political attacks. This agreement, characteristic of the contracts signed throughout the nation between unions and government officials, was never ratified. Instead, teachers supported by the CNTE threatened to strike, finally forcing Ximello's resignation.[54] This episode is of interest as it exemplifies the impact of the national political realignment on regional union politics. Local unions allied with national unions to strengthen their power. Most federal teachers jumped on the bandwagon of the Cardenista CNTE.

The teachers were soon split between a CTM-affiliated group consisting of federal teachers and a faction of state teachers controlled by the state government. At the national level the federal government stimulated efforts to unify the teachers. During the 1937 Unification Congress in Querétaro the Federación Mexicana de Trabajadores de la Enseñanza (FMTE) was established, which would later form the base of the CTM-affiliated Sindicato de Trabajadores de la Enseñanza de la República Mexicana (STERM), founded in 1938. In Sonora the battered remnants of the federal teachers' movement, led by Hermenegildo Peña and Gabriel Rivera, united in 1937 in the Sindicato Unico de Trabajadores de la Enseñanza de Sonora (SUTES), which adhered to the FMTE, and later to STERM, and thus belonged to the CTM and the anti-Yocupicista power bloc.[55]

By now the state government had become quite adept at playing the Cardenista corporatist game, and in June 1937 it convened its own Unification Congress, which founded the Federación Estatal de Maestros Socialistas Sonorenses (FEMSS). Because of its links with the governor and the state labor federation (the CTS), it was reviled as a *sindicato blanco*. This was not entirely inaccurate: the FEMSS received subsidies from the state government, which purged many (reports speak of as many as sixty) of the undesirable "socialist" teachers, replacing them with older, more conservative personnel.[56]

During 1938 the federal teachers fought back. They played a central role in the campaign against reactionaries, as was the case in San Luis Potosí, Puebla, Sinaloa, and Nuevo León.[57] Their main goal was to gain control of the key position of director general of education. The trouble began when Yocupicio decided to remove the progressive director general, Elpidio López, and replace him with a conservative, Leobardo Parra y Marquina, sparking protests by SUTES and the FTS. From then on, relations between federal teachers and the Yocupicista directors remained conflictive.[58]

The governor did his best to purge Sonora of radical socialist teachers—in particular, union leaders and federal school inspectors. In May 1938, Yocupicio presented the Education Ministry (SEP) with a list of twelve "undesirables," mostly militant inspectors and union leaders, including Peña. Some were forced to leave the region, others were harassed, arrested, or shot. Individual village teachers were also targeted. State teachers suddenly replaced federal teachers throughout the state.[59] The Sonoran government hoped to end their "pernicious and systematic opposition" and role as *orientador de la comunidad*. Such repression generated strong opposition at secondary schools in Ciudad Obregón and Hermosillo, where students staged strikes. Yocupicio responded by temporarily closing both schools.[60] The clash assumed wider significance when the teachers' unions contacted Cárdenas and accused Yocupicio of persecution and the promotion of fascist education. Cárdenas personally intervened in the conflict, but in an ambiguous fashion. He admonished SEP to "hold those elements that are not doing their duty accountable," and ordered an inquiry. In October 1938 he finally decided on an act of Solomonic justice: the Yocupicista director general was to be replaced, but at the same time the teachers on the governor's blacklist were to leave the state. However, whether they actually left is doubtful.[61]

The Sonoran teachers' struggle was a perfect training ground for labor leaders. Hermenegildo Peña became one of the first leaders of the national teachers' union, STERM.[62] The Sonoran struggle was replayed throughout Mexico. Divisions between pro- and anti-CTM teachers' unions plagued Durango, Coahuila, and Puebla. Teachers, especially STERM leaders, were purged in Yucatán, Zacatecas, Durango, Chiapas, Tabasco, and Michoacán.[63] The political importance of teachers was soon to decline, however. The Yocupicista press launched a campaign to depict them as irresponsible communists who abandoned their pupils to agitate for utopian goals or personal benefit.[64]

By 1938–39 the heroic days of rural education were over.[65] Rural teachers, playing the role of social catalysts, had helped found unions and ejidos and enforced compliance with labor laws. Their influence had undoubtedly been crucial during the early 1930s. Now the struggle shifted away from individual teachers in isolated villages and mining camps to union leaders, politicos, and bureaucrats from Mexico City. By 1939 a balance of power had emerged in Sonora between the federal teachers of SUTES, with their national allies, and the Yocupicista educational bloc, which controlled state teachers and the directorship general.

Labor Militancy

As elsewhere in Mexico, Sonora witnessed an explosion of labor militancy during the Cárdenas *sexenio*, as evidenced by intense strike activity, in particular among the Yaqui Valley millworkers, railworkers, and miners. Labor unrest in the Yaqui Valley began in 1936 with the workers of the wheat and rice mills of Ciudad Obregón. This was the territory of the Sindicato Industrial Progresista Sonorense (SIPS), one of the most militant unions of the FOCSS. The semi-industrial mode of production of the mills favored the militancy that would spread to the city's proletariat and the rural laborers of the valley. Some 750 workers, including power plant employees and packers, participated in a general strike. They controlled the agricultural and industrial infrastructure, depriving farmers of storage and processing facilities during the harvest.[66] SIPS was not simply interested in higher wages and better working conditions; it admonished Cárdenas to expropriate the mills if no settlement could be reached.[67] Sporadic strikes continued into 1939.

Labor conflicts affected other sectors of the economy as well. Major strikes occurred at the Cananea mines in 1935–36, 1938, and 1940. In January 1937 a strike broke out at the moribund Fábrica de Hilados de Los Angeles, a textile factory notorious for its low wages and poor working conditions. Although an agreement was reached, the mill ceased to operate in 1938, leaving four hundred textile workers in such dire straits that their leaders claimed to be breaking up tables to construct coffins for those likely to die of hunger. The venerable mill was never to reopen its gates. Labor agitation also characterized the operations of the rundown U.S.-owned Southern Pacific of Mexico Railway, where a strike threat by the Sindicato de Trabajadores Ferrocarrileros de la República Mexicana (STFRM) hung over the company. When a negotiated settlement was reached in February 1936, railworkers threw their hats and tools in the air, shouted, rang bells, and blew whistles to celebrate the event. STFRM national secretary Juan Gutiérrez signed a *convenio* with the company, agreeing on a 16.6 percent wage hike, a fifteen-day paid vacation, readjustment of rents, medical aid, schools, a closed shop, and the exclusion of foreign workers from most positions. This agreement, though significant, did not address the most radical desire: workers' administration. "Certain employees were circulating lists containing the names of those employees who were to be the officials of the railway company and boasting that the railway would be turned over to them soon." However, when it became clear that many of their brethren in the nationalized Mexican Railways were actually losing their privileges, the Southern Pacific employees became more conciliatory. By the summer of 1938 their militancy was on the wane.[68]

During 1938–39, conflicts took on a less aggressive style. This decline of militancy may have been due to the abysmal situation of the Sonoran economy, which experienced a severe slowdown during the summer and fall of 1938. Companies teetered on the brink of bankruptcy. The Cía. Industrial del Pacífico, S.A., terminated its operations and fired four hundred workers. Large mines such as the Moctezuma Copper Company and El Tigre were paralyzed.[69] Unemployment remained at peak levels until 1939, and beggars started appearing in the streets. The recession was accompanied by high inflation. During the third quarter of 1938 food prices rose by 20 percent. The state government responded by pegging the prices of prime necessities such as rice, beans, and sugar. The dire situation was reflected in the state's finances, which were "now at such a low ebb that the breaking point is about to be reached." Guaymas municipal employees received no salary for months and the city's credit channels were closed off. Observers spoke of "increasing hunger and dissatisfaction in the lower classes." By December a slow recovery seemed to be setting in.[70] The Sonoran economy remained unstable, but unemployment rates dropped significantly during 1939–40.

Unemployed in Sonora, 1931–1940[71]
(Economically Active Population in 1930: 99,951)

Year	Number
1931	5,787
1932	8,069
1933	7,305
1934	7,243
1935	6,498
1936	8,879
1937	8,218
1938	8,113
1939	6,979
1940	5,752

Strikes took on a new, desperate, defensive character. Office employees and clerks now fought to stop the erosion of real wages. At the Guaymas power plant, workers backed down from previous demands that would have resulted in a contract modeled on that of the petroleum workers. The workers of the Southern Pacific of Mexico Railway line staged "a retreat of labor."[72] The defensive stance is evident from data on conflicts. During 1939 only three officially recognized strikes subject to federal jurisdiction were staged. Of the total of 350 labor conflicts, half were related to the dismissal of personnel.[73] The heady days of Cardenista mobilization had come to an end.

Conclusion

By 1937 the CTM had become the prime component of the Cardenista power bloc in Sonora and controlled important sectors of urban labor, the federal teachers and bureaucrats, and the bulk of the *agraristas*, thousands of whom had been armed. Once organized, the CTM became an essential Cardenista weapon against the conservative government of Yocupicio.

Was the massive incorporation of Sonoran labor into the Cardenista machine the result of populist, top-down manipulation of the Machiavellian *política de masas* criticized by revisionist historians? Actually, little real mobilization was needed. The CTM merely allied with a well-organized Sonoran labor movement, especially the militant rural workers of the valleys. The Yaqui Valley campesinos provided the bulk of the leadership of the FTS/CTM. There was undoubtedly an important external element involved: teachers, school inspectors, railwaymen, and Callista politicians all played a role in shaping agrarismo. But the movement maintained a high degree of autonomy and was generally led by home-grown leaders, in particular in the Yaqui Valley. More than a product of secondary mobilization, the movement of rural proletarians was largely the result of spontaneous mobilization in a rapidly expanding capitalist agricultural sector.

The alliance between labor and Cardenismo led to increased militancy until 1938. The CTM's objectives were not merely economistic. Spurred on by Cardenista rhetoric, labor went further, and called for workers' control of railroads and flour mills. Political goals, such as the control of municipalities and the governorship, were crucial as well. Workers' agency molded the course of Cardenista politics to a substantial extent. Yocupicio could not turn a blind eye to the increasing power of the CTM. One of his prime aims was its exclusion from power, if possible by corporatist schemes similar to those employed by Cárdenas, and, if necessary, by repression.

7

Yocupicio's Response

From Repression to Countercorporatism

Yocupicio proved adept at countering the CTM, not only by repression but also by the incorporation of labor into his conservative machine. This was achieved by the formation of a corporatist regional federation, the Confederación de Trabajadores de Sonora (CTS). By 1938, Sonoran labor politics was characterized by a pitched battle between Cardenista labor and the CTS.

Repression

The Yocupicio years were marred by the harassment of union leaders. The governor responded to growing opposition by jailing union leaders such as Jacinto López, Matías Méndez, Aurelio García, Praxedis Gastélum, and Antonio Encinas as well as school inspectors and presidents of *comisariados ejidales*. Their lives were constantly threatened, and many were killed in shoot-outs. The state government invariably dismissed such incidents as vendettas or bar brawls, while the victims' supporters usually described them as assassinations at the hands of hacendados, caciques, *pistoleros*, or policemen. The truth probably lies somewhere in the middle. Sonora was a dangerous place; men carried firearms, which were often used during commonplace cantina brawls or street fights. But many of these incidents were undoubtedly politically motivated.

Yocupicio's *pistoleros* were identified as the perpetrators of assaults on school inspector Juan Oropeza and Teodoro Villegas Ayala, a Masiaca peasant leader shot to death in 1938. The police were also blamed for numerous attacks. Even FTS leader Jacinto López became the target of an assault.[1] Yocupicio had few qualms about the repression. He boasted to the U.S. military attaché that he "promptly imprisoned every emissary sent by the labor syndicates to agitate and organize in Sonora. Thus far (he stated in a perfectly simple and matter-of-fact manner) he had thrown into jail more than 50 agents of the CTM and other labor organizations and meant to keep them there indefinitely."[2]

White Corporatism: The CTS

Repression alone was insufficient to stem the rise of Cardenismo. In addition, the state government sought to undermine individual CTM unions by divisive tactics, such as the creation of so-called white unions. The terms *sindicato blanco* (white union) or *sindicato de paja* (straw union) were used to describe government-controlled or company unions. The Yocupicista Federación Obrero-Campesina de Hermosillo became, according to its detractors, an "apocryphal" federation. The Sindicato de Empresa at the Cía. Molinera del Río Yaqui in Ciudad Obregón was founded with the purpose of undermining the militant Sindicato Industrial Progresista Sonorense.[3]

The state authorities went a step further and created what its enemies branded a white labor federation, the Confederación de Trabajadores de Sonora (CTS). The only way to fight a powerful federation with corporatist ties to the government was for the state government to duplicate this system at the regional level. Some conservative governors counted on pre-existing national labor federations (CROM, CGT) to battle CTM infiltration. *Cetemista* federations met fierce resistance from repressive state governments in Hidalgo, Tabasco, San Luis Potosí, and elsewhere.[4]

Divisionismo and repression did not in themselves generate broad labor support for *anti-cetemista* state federations. Conservative governments had to "deliver the goods." Initially, white unions were placated by negotiating deals with state and municipal authorities granting them lucrative contracts for public works, especially roadbuilding, drainage, pavement, and construction projects. The authorities also had to demonstrate a willingness to protect their unions from exploitation by capital; hence, a marked increase in the number of rulings in favor of white unions. By playing the Cardenista corporatist game and operating within the framework of the Federal Labor Law, conservative governors were ultimately forced to accept, albeit reluctantly, the necessity of reformist labor policies. In return, the economic elites received a docile labor force, and the political elites developed an essential power base.

Corporatism characterized the relationship between the CTS and the Yocupicio administration.[5] The Cárdenas years are often considered the formative period of modern Mexican corporatism, which developed with the creation of the CTM and the CNC and their incorporation into the PRM, together with the military and popular sectors. Cardenista corporatism was mimicked and even perfected by governors like Yocupicio, who realized that it might also serve regional political interests. In terms of dependency on the State, the CTS was a more successful corporatist construction than the CTM. The repression of CTM delegates in the spring of 1937 enabled Yocupicio to beat the CTM at its own game. By May, a month before the CTM convention, he had already formed a state federation. The CTS became one of the pillars of his regime. "The *plan de campagne* against the CTM" was carefully orchestrated. There were still sufficient independent groups with which to establish the new federation: urban artisans, day laborers (many of whom found work in Yocupicio's construction projects), members of conservative ejidos, hacienda *peones*, teamsters, veterans, and the multifarious workers of *oficios varios*. The state labor authorities found a bona fide union base in the moderate Federación Obrero-Campesina de Hermosillo. The first step was to sow dissension among its leaders. Labor Department head Montaño and Inspector General of Labor José D. Oropeza met with union leaders José Abraham Mendívil and Fernando A. Galaz. It was decided to start with a labor congress, along the lines of the postponed CTM convention. The FOC of Hermosillo launched a propaganda campaign, using the state radio station, while state labor inspectors proselytized among workers.[6]

On May 23–25, 1937, a well-orchestrated Unification Congress was held in the Teatro Noriega in Hermosillo, which founded the CTS. Yocupicio was advised to retire after the opening, so as not to give the impression of dominating the meeting. However, Montaño and Oropeza kept tight control over the proceedings, drawing up statutes and removing troublesome workers, several of whom were jailed.[7]

The CTS Leadership

Enemies of the CTS claimed that its leadership hardly represented the working class and depended completely on the Yocupicio administration. Indeed, there is some truth to this. The leadership included numerous police officers and politicians but relatively few authentic labor leaders, many of whom were actually independent contractors. The first secretaries-general were Colonel Zenon Jiménez Ponce, onetime Hermosillo police chief and leader of the right-wing UNVR; José Abraham Mendívil and Tiburcio Saucedo, Yocupicista politicos and union leaders from Hermosillo; Porfirio Valencia, former mayor of Casa de Teras and UNVR member; and Alberto F. Maldonado, a machinist from the Sonora Brewery. Policemen and UNVR members dominated the Nogales CTS federation. Simón Mercado, CTS leader in Ciudad Obregón, was secretary general of the white Sindicato de Empresa del Yaqui.[8] Key positions were occupied by men with dubious claims to a proletarian background. All were closely linked to Yocupicio and the state government.

Official Subsidies and Support

The CTM depended on subsidies from the Cárdenas government.[9] This was equally true of the CTS. There are clear indications that the CTS was financially dependent on the State Treasury rather than on union contributions. Yocupicio was rumored to have spent

CTS May Day celebration in Hermosillo. *Memoria de la gestión gubernamental del C. Gral. Román Yocupicio, 1939*

30,000 pesos on its formation alone. The CTS received a monthly subsidy of 1,500 pesos from the Treasury. The government paid for the formation of a CTS-affiliated Federación Obrera de Ciudad

Obregón. Payments were also made to the teachers' union, FEMSS, and to other Yocupicista organizations.[10]

The CTS also received political backing. The state government urged mayors to offer their full support. The CTS was recognized within the *sector obrero* of the official party in 1938. The state-controlled Junta Central de Conciliación y Arbitraje, the municipal Juntas, and the Labor Department usually favored CTS over CTM demands. The state labor authorities and the CTS leadership cooperated closely in revising and signing collective contracts. This was hardly surprising, as the labor representatives on the Junta Central were leading CTS members.[11]

CTS strikes were kept to a minimum, only five during 1938–39. "The truth is that our [CTS-affiliated] workers, who distance themselves from the intransigent and extremely radical conduct that the unions of other workers' sectors have adopted . . . , study their problems and carefully take prudent measures which will avert failures, striving for prior agreements or at least explanations from the companies . . . before deciding to go on strike."[12] These few strikes were generally resolved in favor of the workers. But the CTS was ultimately less interested in better working conditions or higher wages than in control of the labor market. Its final goal was the total exclusion of the CTM.

CTS unions benefited from their close ties to state and municipal government by reaping important contracts to the exclusion of their CTM rivals. In Nogales, the mayor and the state labor authorities were instrumental in the formation of the CTS-affiliated Unión de Troqueros, Estibadores y Similares. It was agreed upon "to exclusively hire members of the union in the municipal public services."[13] Such *arreglos* could be terminated if the unions involved strayed from the official line. Labor pacts were ultimately based on political expediency.

Politicians were tempted to seek support from the strongest unions in town. The CTM-affiliated Federación de Uniones y Sindicatos Obreros de Nogales signed a pact (a written document, not an informal verbal agreement) with mayoral candidate Manuel Mascareñas, pledging its vote in return for specific concessions, including exclusive control of municipal drainage and cleaning works, specific positions in the city council, support for agrarian reform, and enforcement of collective contracts.[14] The CTS had to pay a price for its cozy, corporatist relationship with government. During the 1939 elections it loyally supported Yocupicio's candidate for governor.

National Linkage: CGT or CROM?

"Independent" state federations required national allies to counterbalance the CTM. There were two options: the CROM and the Confederación General de Trabajadores (CGT). Usually, well-entrenched remnants of the CROM were chosen. Rifts between the CROM or CGT and the CTM occurred in Baja California Norte, Yucatán, and Nuevo León.[15] The CTS finally opted for the CGT. On June 29, 1939, Governor Yocupicio inaugurated the second Gran Convención of the CTS with a speech lauding its "essentially *obrerista* position, untainted by politics." Both CGT Secretary General Julio Ramírez and a representative of the CROM were present. After some debate the CTS decided to adhere to the CGT. The decision was a risky one that might have had negative electoral repercussions for the Yocupicista faction. Only union organizations recognized by the new official party, the PRM (1938), were permitted to vote in state primaries, and there was some danger that CTS adherence to the CGT would disqualify it from inclusion in the CTM-dominated party labor sector. However, this problem was eventually solved, and both the CGT- and CROM-affiliated unions were allowed to participate.[16] By adhering to the CGT, the CTS was obliged to aid CGT affiliates in other states.

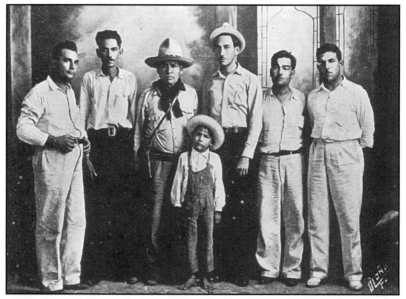

Julio Ramírez (center), secretary general of the CGT, visits Yaqui chief Francisco Pluma Blanca (center, with pistol) and members of the CTS leadership, including Porfirio Valencia (left). *Memoria de la gestión gubernamental del C. Gral. Román Yocupicio, 1939*

The CROM also supported Yocupicio, as it struggled against the CTM to maintain its hold on packing plants, tanneries, and docks in the Guaymas and Mayo regions. The small CROM hardly posed a threat but actually served as a useful ally. In 1938 the Sonoran CROM and the CTS signed a mutual-aid agreement against the CTM.[17] They cooperated in the 1939 elections, voting against the CTM candidate.

CTS-Affiliated Unions

By 1939 the CTS claimed the affiliation of 202 unions and five regional federations: the Federación Obrero-Campesina de Hermosillo, the Federación de Trabajadores del Distrito de Alamos, the Federación de Guaymas, the Federación Obrero y Campesina de Ciudad Obregón, and the Federación de Trabajadores del Distrito de Magdalena. Official CTS estimates claimed 10,000–19,000 members, as compared with the CTM's 19,000. A more accurate figure is 6,500. The CTS had considerable strength in northern Sonora, while the CTM dominated the rural proletariat and ejidatarios of the valleys.[18]

Within a matter of months, Yocupicio had managed to gain control over an important sector of the working class, creating a powerful rival to the CTM. Despite its less than spontaneous birth, the CTS managed to retain its position as one of the leading federations in Sonora. During the mid-1980s, 80 unions representing 8,800 workers were still affiliated with the CTS, while the CTM's 182 unions had a membership of 15,400.[19] The table below offers a breakdown of CTS unions:

Estimated CTS Union Membership in 1938[20]

Sector	Membership	Number of Unions
Factory workers	601	8
Miners	540	2
Artisans, skilled urban labor	297	8
Service workers, teamsters	1,634	27
Construction, road workers	373	3
Office workers	82	2
Teachers	110	2
Rural laborers, loaders, packers	1,060	9
Oficios varios, veterans	1,803	5
Total	6,500	66

Industrial workers, for example tannery and tobacco workers, formed a significant part of the CTS. The CROM, a CTS ally, retained the adherence of the textile workers. What these industries have in common is their antiquity. Most were nineteenth-century factories located in Hermosillo and Guaymas. Newer industries, in particular the flour and rice mills of the valleys, fell under the control of militant CTM unions. The CTS controlled the miners of Pilares, a recently reopened mine, without the continuity and tradition found in Cananea, and the new cooperative of Churunibabi. However, most miners belonged to the independent national mineworkers' union, the SITMMSRM. Urban artisans and service workers constituted another important group within the CTS, but the majority was drawn from the mass of semi-rural proletarians that had not been absorbed into the agrarian movement and found work in road construction projects and as day laborers in the valleys. Such groups lacked organization and were frequently absorbed into the CTS for electoral purposes and in schemes to undermine CTM unions.

CTS-affiliated Painters' Union, Hermosillo. *Memoria de la gestión gubernamental del C. Gral. Román Yocupicio, 1939*

Almost one-third of CTS members belonged to unions not easily categorized, called Sindicatos de Trabajadores Veteranos de la Revolución or Sindicatos de Oficios Varios, which were formed under Yocupicio.[21] They had certain characteristics indicative of white unionism. The bulk (60–80 percent) of the members were day laborers, and the rest served as artisans and service workers (20–35 percent). Some were even landowners, merchants, industrialists, state employees, policemen, and politicians. These individuals were probably the agents of Yocupicismo, responsible for manipulating the unions for political purposes. Their mobilization during elections was appealing, as individual membership in more than one CTS union was not uncommon.

How to Undermine the CTM: Divisionism and Sonoran Labor

Having established the CTS, Yocupicio went beyond "containment" and endeavored to "roll back" the CTM. Unions could only operate if they were registered by the state Junta de Conciliación y Arbitraje. The Junta was controlled by representatives of labor and capital friendly to Yocupicio. Most labor members belonged to the CTS, while the board was presided over by the governor's trusted crony, Enrique Fuentes Frías. The CTM lodged numerous complaints against the board's decisions.

This leads us to the issue of *divisionismo*—that is, the encouragement of splits within opposing unions, the creation of parallel CTS organizations, and, ultimately, the destruction of the non-CTS union. The CTM and the SITMMSRM claimed that the state used coercion and chicanery to divide the working classes and incorporate workers into CTS-affiliated white unions. Yocupicio and the CTS were relatively successful in this endeavor. For example, although most miners' unions adhered to the SITMMSRM, workers of the Moctezuma Copper Company in Pilares de Nacozari, organized in the Sindicato "Héroe Jesús García," joined the CTS. The CTS majority pressed the company, with which the union had signed a collective contract, to use the *cláusula de exclusión* against pro-SITMMSRM dissidents. The issue at stake was control of the mine's work force by one union, and the methods employed by the CTS differed little from those used elsewhere by the CTM.[22] However, the largest mining center, Cananea, remained solidly in the hands of the SITMMSRM. Thus, a miners' elite, consisting of those continuously employed during the recession, supported the SITMMSRM, while the CTS was backed by unemployed miners and members of cooperatives (Churunibabi) as well as by the "new" miners of Pilares de Nacozari, who were more easily co-opted than those of Cananea.[23]

The numerous day laborers employed in public works projects formed another pliable clientele. Some six hundred road construction workers alternated between the CTM-affiliated Sindicato Nacional de Carreteras y Obras Públicas (SNCOP), organized by a federal labor inspector and a teacher, and two CTS-affiliated unions controlled by the state Labor Department. Their case demonstrates how complex the political game had become. Through skillful manipulation of labor legislation concerning preference in hiring, Yocupicio and the CTS were ultimately able to authorize the construction company to fire the SNCOP members and hire the CTS-affiliated workers.[24] These new CTS unions would play an important role as tools of the Yocupicista machine.

Examples of inter-union struggles abound. In Ciudad Obregón, a CTM and a CTS-affiliated Sindicato de Albañiles fought for control, the first backed by the state government, the latter by the federal labor inspector. During harvesttime in the Mayo Valley, the CTS and CROM battled the CTM for control of packers' and loaders' unions. In 1936–37 an all-female vegetable packers' union in Huatabampo became the object of a tug of war between Yocupicio and the CROM, on the one hand, and Mayo Valley radicals, on the other. The CTS also moved into the Yaqui Valley flour and rice mills. At the Compañía Molinera del Río Yaqui a state labor inspector aided in the formation of a CTS-affiliated *sindicato blanco* consisting of renegade CTM members.[25] In some cases it proved possible to reach a collective contract with two unions of different affiliation, as happened with the vegetable packers of Etchojoa and the tannery and construction workers of Guaymas. Tasks were split between unions.[26] Both federations were quick to spot opportunities to undercut their opponent. When the Teatro Obregón in Nogales fired employees belonging to the *cetemista* Sindicato de Trabajadores de la Industria Cinematográfica del Pacífico, the CTS offered workers at a discount.[27]

Divisionismo was a game that all parties could play, including employers who preferred the more docile CTS unions. The Irish owner of the Hermosillo bakery "El Modelo" cooperated with CTS leaders in undermining the old *cetemista* bakers' union and formed a new company union with dissident workers. Landowner Ramón Salido was said to support the "white" Sindicato de Trabajadores de Bácamen against the "red" Sindicato de Yoremes Unidos de Bacobampo.[28] Such accusations are not always easy to evaluate.

Divisionismo could also reflect power struggles between antagonistic workers' factions bent on controlling jobs and contracts, struggles that lacked class significance. In 1936 the truckers of Nogales and Santa Ana, who accused each other of white unionism, fought a violent battle for control of the lucrative route to Mexicali.[29]

The most easily manipulated sector of labor consisted of the federal and state employees. While Cárdenas organized federal employees in the FSTSE, which would join the new PRM as the backbone of the popular sector, Yocupicio managed to do the same with state employees. In 1938, CTS leader Fernando A. Galaz presided over the founding of the Sindicato Unico de Trabajadores al Servicio del Estado y de los Municipios de Sonora (SUTSEMS). Yocupicista bureaucrats like Lorenzo Garibaldi (a stray scion of the Italian revolutionary) dominated the meeting.[30] SUTSEMS would provide Yocupicio with a captive labor sector which could be mobilized for elections and demonstrations.

Divisionismo was also reflected in the realm of ritual. Both the CTM and CTS were eager to appropriate the symbols and festivals of the international labor movement, such as Labor Day. In Nogales, Labor Day 1938 was celebrated by two parades, one of workers and federal employees affiliated with the CTM, the other of CTS unions, state bureaucrats, and teachers.[31]

Regionalist Discourse

The CTS defended its strategy in the regionalist discourse so typical of the period:

> Because of its geographic position, and . . . its historical position or antecedents, Sonora needs to be better understood in terms of its mentality, its customs, its sentiments and aspirations. The federal officials who come here from outside of the state . . . abound in moral, social, and political prejudice. . . . Most of them expect . . . to find the Sonoran in a state of primitive culture or in constant rebellion. . . . And this erroneous judgement . . . leads them to mistakes and excesses, always to the detriment of the people of Sonora. . . . Our reluctance or failure to join the CTM is not caused by ideological inferiority or retardation. We have always resisted the strategy of violence and conquest employed by its leaders, a procedure that the dignified Sonoran resists and rebels against as any conscientious and honorable man would. This conduct is humiliating to Sonora. . . . The current activity of the CTM consists of little more than

snatching away unions from us. That is why we reject their branding our unions "white" and theirs "Red" or "leftist," as if the declaration of affiliation when a union switches from one confederation to another would modify the judgement or the mentality of the masses.[32]

Yocupicio used similar discourse when he stated:

> The Sonoran worker is well fed and well clothed, his union organization is perfect, and only those complain about it who cannot tolerate the fact that the worker and peasant organizations of the state remain independent. . . . No, you third-rate politicians, agents provocateurs, bad Mexicans, unwitting instruments of international Judaism, Sonora will not be a problem for the Fatherland, but . . . be aware that if . . . one of those travelling mystificators [*mixticadores, sic*] has the nerve to look for trouble in the state, they can be sure that the government and all the good sons of Sonora will know how to face any situation in defense of the decorum and sovereignty of the PATRIA CHICA.[33]

He denounced the intrusion of "outside agitators" who did not understand the idiosyncracies of the Sonoran people and decried "destructive ideas coming from the center." In his "Answer to Lombardo," he stressed the special nature of Sonoran culture:

> Each . . . state . . . has its own needs and faces specific and distinct problems, to which no solution should be offered that does not concretely correspond to its idiosyncrasies. That is why we do not want nor accept commonly used formulas that are not compatible with the political and social organization of the country and with our mode of being. . . . My state has closed its gates to the invasion of doctrines that fundamentally clash with our institutions, and energetically opposes the destructive and corrupting work of the emissaries of agitation, those who sow disorganization and confusion. . . . The government of the state cannot permit the incursions of leaders who with personal aims and under the pretext of union propaganda only manage to cause unrest and conflicts . . . and thus distract the attention of governors and governed toward sterile campaigns. . . . Possibly Mr. Lombardo Toledano feels restless because he has not been able to extend his influence to the working masses of Sonora . . . because there the worker doesn't need the tutelage of men who do not understand the regional environment and problems.[34]

Revolutionary discourse was now mixed with anti-communist rhetoric, used effectively against Cárdenas, and becoming predominant during the 1940s. Bizarre *indigenista* overtones were also adopted. Yocupicio was depicted as "an Indian Governor who gave an example of patriotism to the europeanizing whites . . . he is a natural product of the north, of the state of Sonora."[35] Ironically, this populist discourse was also evident in Cardenismo. Like Cárdenas, Yocupicio was portrayed as a man of the people, easily accessible to humble peasants and Indians. The *comisariado ejidal* of Etchojoa was cited as saying, "I enter his house in Navojoa as if it were my own." An element of sentimental fondness for the governor was introduced: "Nacha la Pascola, the widow of a Yaqui tribal chief, who refers to President Cárdenas as 'my little son Lázaro,' was telling me that she was going to Hermosillo to visit her other son, and explained to me: 'That's Román, the Governor.' Yocupicio became a caring father figure: 'El vaquero,' Chief of the Seri tribe . . . assured me that 'when you talk to our Governor, everything is taken care of.' "[36] Regionalist discourse could even be used to undermine class solidarity. Many southern CTM workers were outsiders, migrant workers from Sinaloa and elsewhere. The state government used chauvinism to attack these workers as aliens who competed for jobs with "authentic" Sonorans.[37]

Conclusion

During 1937, Sonora witnessed the creation of a "Cardenista machine" consisting of former Callista radicals (teachers, campesino leaders, politicians), the rural laborers and *agraristas* of the south, and urban labor organized in the CTM. This alliance was bolstered by federal agents, such as school and labor inspectors, the zone commander, and the federal bureaucracy. In response, Yocupicio managed to forge an effective coalition of urban and rural day laborers, state teachers and bureaucrats, and other sectors of labor. Two increasingly well-demarcated power blocs emerged: one under state, the other under federal control.

What is striking is the ease with which a blatantly antireformist state government could incorporate labor into its bloc. To dismiss the Sonoran case as one of mere "white" unionism is to miss the point. Workers were willing to support whichever faction promised to deliver benefits and political power, whether progressive or otherwise. It is undeniable that the CTS maintained close relations of a corporatist nature with the Yocupicio government. It was purely a government creation, unlike the FTS/CTM. The CTS leadership consisted to a large extent of Yocupicio's cronies, many of

Opposing Machines

State Government	Federal Government
State/municipal PRM committees	National PRM committee
State legislature/Supreme Court	Federal Congress/Senate
	Political emissaries
Municipalities	
State police	Military zone commander
	Armed reserves
UNVR	
State labor authorities	DAT/labor inspectors
CTS	FTS/CTM
FEMSS	STERM/school inspectors
LCASC (CNC)	*Comisariados ejidales*
	Yaqui colonies

them former police chiefs. Union finances were subsidized and its demand-making process controlled by the government, which resulted in low levels of labor conflict. CTS unions were at times fictitious or at least of a dubious nature (veterans' unions, *sindicatos de oficios varios* controlled by non-workers, double membership, etc.). The CTS fulfilled several functions: it was an arm in the struggle against the CTM and the Cárdenas government; it helped limit labor demands; and it served as an electoral tool of the Yocupicista faction.

However, despite its unabashedly white character, the CTS could not have existed without genuine labor support. CTS unions may not have been as combative as those belonging to the CTM, but they did receive certain benefits from their close ties to the government, in particular generous contracts, to the exclusion of CTM workers. For such unions, patronage was at least as important as the application of the Labor Law or higher wages, certainly at a time of high unemployment. Many workers, threatened by the Depression, may also have been attracted by the macho regionalist rhetoric of Yocupicio and the CTS directed against hated outsiders, such as Lombardo or non-Sonoran migrant workers. The Yocupicio government was able to deliver the goods thanks to Yocupicista and CTS control of the labor boards. These factors led to the establishment of a powerful labor federation which survived the Yocupicio years.

8

Agrarian Reform in Sonora

We campesinos all hold the name of Lazaro Cárdenas in honor.
... When we were kids, we heard our parents say that it would
be better if he would be president for another 20 years.
—Campesino, Hermosillo, to Cuauhtémoc Cárdenas, May 15,
1988[1]

El ejido fue una alcahuetería.
—Reyes Anaya Zamorano[2]

"I have been waiting, waiting and waiting! ... This is going to
lead to something serious."[3] By the summer of 1938, Edward R.
Jesson, a U.S. landowner in the Yaqui Valley, was "so desperate
over losing his life's savings with the loss of his property that he
seems to be on the verge of losing his mind."[4] Ever since Cárdenas
had announced the land reform project during the previous fall,
Jesson had watched as his life's work, a farm of some eight hundred hectares, disintegrated. He was besieged by squatters who
built shacks on his property, stole his farming implements, and cut
and sold his timber. Tenants now refused to pay rents, claiming
that he did not own the land. *Agraristas* armed with machetes and
rifles threatened to "run or shoot me and my friends." They "cut
my fences, running horses, mules, burros and cattle in my fields."
And when he sent a worker to fix the fences, one agrarian "told
[him] to send his gringo boss down to fix [the fence] and he would
show him something." The local authorities were impotent. Yocupicio advised him to write to the president. The U.S. Consulate
could do nothing but try to calm the nervous Jesson and complain
that "the situation here ... is one of illegality, uncertainty, destruction of the means of production, [and] anarchy." For some the tension became unbearable. The wife of one of Jesson's British
employees went mad worrying over the expropriation, and one
night jumped into a forty-foot-deep well.[5]

The *agraristas* were confident that Jesson's land would soon be theirs. Little did they realize that Cárdenas had already granted those same lands to the Yaqui Indians. In March, two truckloads of Yaquis drove onto the Jesson farm and told the campesinos that they would have to leave. The deadline for the evacuation was set for June 20. The exodus nearly turned into a chaotic flight. Jesson desperately tried to move out his valuable equipment, but could find no trucks. Government lorries finally evacuated the tenants and squatters, and "dumped [them] in the bush without shelter and with what little food they had." Jesson remained after the deadline to salvage part of his property: "If I were a Mexican I would not be here, but as the Indians told my brother that the Americans always paid the Indians well and never cheated them, I know they will give me a little, the best in a pinch." His final departure was somewhat tragic. His old car broke down in the pouring rain, and he was forced to sell horses and burros at discount prices, "barely enough for a trip to San Francisco." He finally made his way back to the Golden Gate city, where he immediately fell ill, spending his days in bed writing letters to the U.S. consul in Guaymas.[6] Jesson was but one of thousands of Sonoran residents whose lives were dramatically affected by the Cardenista land reform of 1937–38.

The most loyal followers of Cárdenas, those who even today have not forgotten the memory of "tata Lázaro," were the Mexican campesinos. Sonora, like other agricultural regions such as Yucatán and the Laguna, was subjected to Cardenista agrarian reform, which destroyed the Porfirian hacienda and profoundly altered the structure of rural society. Besides being a vehicle of social justice and economic restructuration, agrarian reform was a political weapon, used to create a campesino power base and to undercut conservative strongmen like Yocupicio. Land redistribution also pacified the Yaqui people, who were always a potential threat. The Yaquis finally received title to tribal lands from Cárdenas after centuries of ethnic warfare.

Although revisionists maintain that Cardenista agrarianism was an alien imposition on the peasantry—this is certainly true of the collective ejido—land reform in Sonora was relatively successful, at least during the initial phase. It addressed the grievances of rural workers, created a viable, market-oriented ejidal sector in the valleys, and ensured Cárdenas the support of a well-organized and armed campesino sector. However, its long-term impact was less profound. The ejidal sector survived the onslaught of the counter-reform of the 1940s, but in a seriously weakened form. The old landed elites, strengthened by new groups of urban entrepreneurs, continued to develop a strong capitalist agricultural sector which came to dominate the ejidos.

Sonoran Rural Society
Prior to the Cardenista Reforms

When speaking of agrarian reform, we must define distinct zones, which received varying treatment from the Agrarian Department. The best lands of Sonora are located on the Pacific coastal plains, in particular in the Yaqui and Mayo Valleys. Before the 1890s the Yaqui Valley was a largely uninhabited wasteland which, as the result of an important Porfirian surveying contract, was opened to settlement and production around the turn of the century by the U.S.-owned Richardson Construction Company. The company built an irrigation system and sold blocks of land, or *campos agrícolas*, to U.S., Mexican, and European investors and settlers, who cultivated wheat, rice, maize, vegetables, and chickpeas for markets in Mexico, the United States, and Spain. A dynamic agrarian bourgeoisie developed, a mélange of old and new economic elites.

Yaqui Valley farms were far removed from the stereotypical feudal hacienda. Wage labor predominated. Speculation, risk-taking, and the search for new markets were the prime concern of these entrepreneurs, many of whom fared poorly in this perilous pioneering adventure.[7] The Yaqui Valley haciendas were relatively small, highly capitalized operations, employing a considerable work force of resident *peones* and seasonal migrant workers. Not all farmers worked the land themselves; there existed a considerable group of tenants.[8] By the 1930s the Yaqui Valley had become a northern cornucopia, yielding 11 percent of Mexico's wheat production during 1935–36, turning Sonora into the nation's leading wheat producer. The valley's acreage continued to expand due to new irrigation works, from 10,000 hectares in 1911 to 41,000 in 1928. This phenomenon created favorable conditions for the consolidation of an agricultural bourgeoisie, and mitigated the severity of rural conflict by continuously expanding the field of opportunities. Expansion levelled off during the Depression but accelerated once again during the late 1930s, reaching 55,000 hectares in 1937 and 70,000 by 1943.[9]

The Mayo Valley was a bustling mosaic of Mayo Indian villages, booming towns such as Navojoa, Etchojoa, and Huatabampo, and large, modern haciendas producing cash crops, such as winter

vegetables and the lucrative but risky chickpea. The most important estates were El Bácame, Las Parras, Bachantahui, Citavaros, El
Sahuaral, and Basconcobe. The Mayo Valley landowners often belonged to pre-revolutionary elites. Some, such as the Salido and
Otero families, dated back to the late colonial period.[10]

The oldest haciendas were located in the Hermosillo Valley.
Some were founded before independence and remained in the
hands of elite families, such as the Camous, Gándaras, and Astiazaráns. The largest were El Zacatón, El Carmen, El Molino de
Camou, La Labor, Santa Teresa, Codórachi, El Alamito, El Cerro
Pelón, Topahue, El Saúz, La Victoria, and San José de Gracia. They
combined cattle grazing on vast expanses of arid pasture lands with
the cultivation of wheat and other crops on smaller irrigated plots.
Their primacy was contested by a new group of farmers, mostly
Italians, as well as merchants like the Mazóns, who established
small, flourishing estates indicative of future development.[11]

The northern Sierra was a different world, a landscape of mountains and deserts covered by sprawling ranches and dotted with
mines and commercial towns. The size of cattle estates was dictated by ecological necessity: in Sonora at least 1,000 hectares are
required to run a viable ranch.[12] Here the revolution had little impact on land tenure. Huge estates, such as La Arizona and Santa
Barbara, not to mention the U.S.-owned Cananea Cattle Company,
dominated the rural economy. The Nogales area was controlled by
a pre-revolutionary elite of *ganaderos* such as Guillermo Mascareñas, Arturo Morales, Jesús Elías, and other members of the Elías
clan.[13] Raising cattle for U.S. and domestic markets was a risky
but lucrative business, which, after collapsing during the revolution, recovered during the late 1920s. Despite a sharp drop during
the Depression, exports boomed after 1935. In that year, Sonora
exported 80,000 head of cattle, nearly one-third of the national
total.[14]

The Cananea Cattle Company dominated the cattle sector, grazing about 40,000 head on 170,000 hectares. The company consisted
of seventeen subsidiaries (a ploy necessary to avert expropriation)
combined in a parent company, the Cía. Mexicana de Inversiones,
S.A., the real value of which was estimated at 3,100,000 pesos. J. E.
Wise of Nogales, Arizona, owned La Arizona, one of the larger
operations with its 22,234 hectares and 2,500 head of cattle. A typical medium-sized ranch was the Hacienda Guiracoba in the Alamos
district, owned by W. C. Lucas and C. E. McCarty. It consisted of
4,108 hectares, of which 300 had been cleared for agriculture, a

house with six rooms, corrals, and eight pastures. Total investments were estimated at U.S.$30,000.[15]

Serrano life still maintained vestiges of the feudal past, such as the paternalism of ranchers towards their *labriegos* and cowboys, payment in kind, the *tienda de raya*, verbal contracts, and sharecropping. Cohesive peasant communities engaged in the defense of ancient ejidos (commons), which usually consisted of grazing lands without water and *mesetas* covered with mesquite and brush, useless for cultivation. Ranches, which had been expanding for decades, started fencing in these lands during the 1930s, and clashed with *serrano* villagers. The *comuneros* of Arizpe sought to mark the boundaries of their old ejido on which ranchers Jesús and Domingo Elías had encroached. In Terrenate, *comuneros* struggled against the Dávila family to protect rights to their *antiguo ejido*. The confirmation of titles to communal lands owned by the communities *desde tiempo inmemorial*, usually dating back to the 1880s, was also an issue in Opodepe, Arivechi, Soyopa, and Suaqui.[16] Ranchers also clashed with sharecroppers, renters, smallholders, and *jornaleros*. All dabbled in small ranching, woodcutting, muledriving, petty commerce, or prospecting to supplement their meager income. In the narrow strips of fertile land along the Magdalena, Sonora, San Miguel, Moctezuma, and Bavispe rivers, a few small haciendas coexisted with *minifundias* of several hectares, barely sufficient for subsistence, while the majority of the population was landless. The rate of land concentration in areas like the Ures Valley accelerated during the late Porfiriato.[17]

Conflicts between *serrano* landlords and sharecroppers frequently centered on the stipulations of the often verbal contracts. In Sonora, sharecropping was hardly a benign institution, and certainly no avenue for social mobility. A typical agreement involved the landlord providing the sharecropper with land, seed, water, animals, and plows in return for one-third of the crop (*al tercio*). Some contracts were even worse, as at Mazatán: the landowner "gives the person a piece of land; he gives him seeds, usually maize, one or two pairs of mules, farming implements . . . that's all, the person who receives this is obligated to cover the expenses of preparing dams, irrigation ditches, sowing the land, cultivating the plants, irrigating, weeding, and finally harvesting, and when that is done to cart half of the crop to Mr. [Rafael] Córdova who gets that as well as the stubble."[18] By 1936, teachers and sharecroppers were fighting for better contracts *al cuarto*, even *al quinto*. Life in the Sierra was rough and uncertain. The population often lacked food and clothing, and frequently left for the coast in search of a better life.[19]

Prior to Cardenista reform, Sonoran rural society had not changed substantially since Porfirian times. Most economic elites maintained their land and economic power, despite the revolution. The contention is exaggerated that in Sonora, after the 1916 expropriation of properties belonging to *enemigos de la causa* by Governor Plutarco Elías Calles, "the take-over of Porfirian property, and the rise of a new, revolutionary elite was more complete than in any other state." Actually, many affected individuals managed to continue their business activities without interruption. Most Porfirian landowners survived right up to the Cárdenas reform.[20]

It was not until the late 1910s that limited *agrarista* pressure was felt. Agrarismo originated not with the rural proletariat of the valleys but with villages and towns seeking boundary settlements and the redistribution of communal grazing lands lost to ranchers or during the nineteenth-century liberal Reforma.[21] Most petitions would not be solved until the early 1930s. During the Obregón presidency (1921–1924) agrarian reform made a modest beginning: some 74,300 hectares were ceded as *dotación* (land grant) or *restitución* (land restitution). Most was grazing land; only 2,503 hectares were irrigated. Two-thirds of the grants consisted of national lands. This process slowed down during the Calles presidency (1924–1928), but modestly accelerated during 1928–1935.[22]

Dotaciones (Land Grants) in Sonora, 1916–1940[23]

President	Total Area	Irrigated Area	Beneficiaries
Carranza (1916–1920)	1,208 has.	1,208	1,192
De la Huerta (1920)	37,106	550	818
Obregón (1920–1924)	44,259	0	1,859
Calles (1924–1928)	26,961	777	1,801
Portes Gil (1928–1930)	52,706	1,868	1,313
Ortiz Rubio (1930–1932)	4,755	1,998	787
Rodríguez (1932–1934)	122,007	6,021	3,941
Cárdenas (1934–1940)	528,507	26,317	11,547
Avila Camacho (1940–1946)	243,486	2,016	3,430
Alemán (1946–1952)	90,782	910	513

Note: These figures do not include *restituciones*.

Governor Rodolfo Elías Calles took a lively interest in agrarian reform and initiated many of the later "Cardenista" land grant procedures in the Sierra and in the Hermosillo Valley.[24] However, the valleys remained largely untouched. There had been Callista plans to change land tenure in the Yaqui Valley, but these differed substantially from later Cardenista reform. Plutarco Elías Calles hoped that the Yaqui Valley would be redistributed, not to ejidatarios but to colonists—that is, private landowners—with support from the State. This would create the class of yeoman farmers so popular in Callista agrarian ideology. Reform would have a trickle-down effect, raising wages and living standards of rural workers, whose increased purchasing power would stimulate the development of a national market. This was the basic capitalist development model for rural Mexico espoused by the Sonoran revolutionaries.[25]

In Sonora, teachers played a leading role in the agrarian movement of the early 1930s, during which there was a degree of "secondary mobilization," or top-down mobilization by the State.[26] Teachers were expected to organize *uniones campesinas*, petition for land, and "strengthen the class spirit in the Peasant Unions by intervening in all their inter-union difficulties, and taking care to eliminate those perverse people who block the revolutionary conquests; . . . [and] to identify the Peasant Unions with the Schools, to create sympathy among the proletarians for the redeeming work of the Teacher."[27] Teachers participated in the activities of *comités agrarios*, negotiated contracts for *peones*, and petitioned for land. "There is not a single rural village where the inhabitants are covered by agrarian legislation that has not been counseled to petition for its ejidos, not one community where workers' organizations exist where the teachers have not participated in the unions . . . as advisors."[28] A school inspector explained his responsibilities: "Because agrarian problems are common and the villagers invariably turn to me to solve their problems with irrigation, grants of farming implements, the condition in which they are to receive the fences, etc., I have already taken the necessary steps toward the formation of a resistance league which will meet every week to explain to them the rights and obligations of the landowners and sharecroppers."[29]

The rural population realized the utility of teachers and often petitioned to have one sent: "We believe it is urgently necessary to send us a MALE TEACHER who identifies himself with . . . the Ejido so that he can guide us along a good path, as the majority of us compañeros are ILLITERATES."[30] Teachers were welcome in the Yaqui Valley *campos*: "Hardly had we arrived when the campesinos surrounded us, and then the teachers sang songs, recited appropriate poems, and one of the teachers or myself would give a talk about the problems of that place."[31] This poetic appeal by the teacher of Remedios is typical: "You who continually struggle in the solitude of the fields to feed your family; you who know nothing of the sweetness of rest; you who know nothing of the sung beauties of the sunsets, because the fatigue of arduous labor doesn't leave you any time for poetic contemplation. . . . In the solitude of your hamlet the Revolution has placed the beacon that guides your liberation, that illuminates the darkness of your taciturn life . . . THE SCHOOL. . . . Come to it; there you will learn to know your rights, to defend yourself with honor."[32] This pivotal role of the Mexican teacher was soon to end, however, as agrarian reform became increasingly the terrain of campesino unions and bureaucrats of the Agrarian Department.

External agents would have little impact without pressure from the rural population. The struggle of the *comuneros* of the Sierra was the type of traditional primary mobilization in defense of village lands that sparked the revolution in Villista Chihuahua. The groups mobilized during the early 1930s were quite different, largely consisting of rural laborers in the Yaqui and Mayo Valleys. By the time of the Cárdenas reforms, such groups had developed considerable autonomy. To consider them mere pawns in a process of secondary mobilization would not do justice to the strength and sophistication of the *agrarista* movement, which survived Cardenismo and continues its struggle today.

Pre-Cardenista reform failed to change the pattern of land tenure in Sonora substantially. By 1930 thirty-eight ejidos, covering an area of 188,000 hectares, mostly grazing lands of poor quality, had been granted to 4,071 ejidatarios. This was an inconsequential figure. Land ownership was still highly concentrated. In 1927, 721 holdings maintained control of 96 percent of the total area of rural properties. The ejido, including the old commons, controlled 13 percent of Sonoran lands, 25 percent of grazing lands, and only 7 percent of irrigated lands. In 1934, 90 percent of the population was still landless. Foreigners played an important role in agriculture and ranching. Of the principal Sonoran landowners in 1927, 658 were Mexican nationals who controlled 474,000 hectares, and 124 were U.S. citizens who owned 415,000 hectares. The value of the average U.S.-owned plot was nearly four times that of Mexican properties.[33]

A close look at specific subregions gives us a more balanced view of Sonoran land tenure. Prior to the Cárdenas reforms, of a total of 44,000 hectares of irrigated land in the Yaqui Valley, some 28,000 were owned by eighty-five landowners. Large tracts were held either by individual farmers, such as the Stocker, Astiazarán, and Richardson families, who owned more than 500 hectares, or by companies owning between 1,000 and 2,000 hectares, such as Los Miles, S.A., the Cía. Agrícola del Naínari, and the Cía. Agrícola Occidental. Most plots ranged from 150 to 500 hectares.[34] Land was quite concentrated in the Mayo Valley as well. The leading haciendas belonged to the Salido, Campoy, Terminel, Urbina, Zaragoza, and Ruiz families, who possessed thousands of hectares.[35] We have some figures on concentration in the cultivable strip along the Río Sonora, characteristic of most Sierra valleys. In Baviácora, eight owners held 64 percent of lands, but in plots of an average size of only 49 hectares, while 13 percent of owners possessed the remainder, mostly *minifundias*. Eighty-six percent of the population was landless. Other *serrano* municipalities, such as Aconchi, Banámichi, and Huépac, showed a similar pattern. Land concentration in the ranching areas was more extreme than in the Sierra valleys. Here ejidos controlled a minority of lands.[36] The general picture that emerges is one of considerable land concentration and high levels of landlessness throughout Sonora. More than fifteen years of revolutionary agrarian reform had not altered the structure of rural society significantly. Most *dotaciones* involved poor grazing lands, often *baldíos* (public lands). Few large landholdings were affected. This pattern was to change dramatically during the Cárdenas years.

Counter-agrarismo

By 1935 agrarian reform dangled like a sword of Damocles above the heads of landowners. Unrest, reflected in the 1935 rebellion, at times assumed religious overtones. The countryside of Alamos was visited by a roving preacher, who posed as a "messenger of God" and railed against Cárdenas and agrarian reform.[37] In the Sierra, *agraristas* confronted cattlemen and their ranch hands. In Querobabi a conflict emerged between the Suárez brothers, both members of the Yocupicio *camarilla*, and ejidatarios: "They have spared no effort to pit the *agraristas* against their salaried rural workers and cowboys, fomenting the hatred of the worker with a patron against those who have no patron, that is, the Ejidatarios." The two groups constantly exchanged insults and gunfire.[38] At Casa de Teras, "the omnipotent cacique Francisco Fragoso" clashed with his tenants.[39] In the isolated mountains along the Chihuahuan border at El Gavilán, a feud festered between *agraristas* and the unscrupulous Villa and Mendoza families, who, officials admitted, "are capable of anything." The conflict resulted in the burning of the *agraristas'* fences and houses and culminated in a day-long shootout in which three ranchers were killed.[40] Other ranchers, such as J. E. Wise of La Arizona, or the Monroy brothers at San Lorenzo, used surreptitious methods, often leaving gates open to allow cattle onto ejido lands to destroy the crops. *Agraristas* and tenants often struck back using the "weapons of the weak" at their disposal. A favorite method was the slaughter or mutilation of the landlords' animals.[41]

Some landowners went further, and in 1938 spoke once again of staging an uprising. One prominent landowner hinted to a U.S. consular official that "the 'day was coming,' but that he and men like him would not move until they believed that 'Washington would be neutral.' " Most, however, were painfully aware that they lacked the power to stop reform by force and would "lose an armed revolt together with all hope of salvaging anything."[42]

Their caution can be explained by the fact that *agraristas* constituted a significant armed force in Sonora, especially in the Yaqui Valley. Cárdenas created a solid *agrarista* power base by forming paramilitary campesino reserves trained by the army. By 1936 more than 3,000 Sonoran *agraristas* had been provided with rifles and ammunition. The *defensas* kept order in the ejidos, protected the fields, and became active in municipal politics, especially in Ciudad Obregón, where they toppled an unpopular mayor. They played a role in suppressing Mayo unrest in 1939 and were involved in the bloody internal struggles among agrarian factions of the Mayo Valley. Overall, Cárdenas claimed to have armed some 200,000 *agraristas* nationwide.[43] By 1938 the reserves constituted a significant military, or at least political, factor in the state. As one landowner succinctly put it, "As the agrarians are armed, they can pretty much do as they please."[44]

The days of armed rebellion had passed. Now, landowners took to lobbying the government, at times with success. When in 1935 Cárdenas threatened to limit the size of ranches to 4,000 hectares, a delegation of Sonoran cattlemen, including representatives of the Cananea Cattle Company, made a hurried visit to Mexico City, and received promises that the limit would be set at 40,000 hectares.[45] Landowners in Sonora and elsewhere (the Laguna, Sinaloa, Puebla, Veracruz, Chiapas, Michoacán) tried to appropriate agrarian reform in an often vain effort to stop the inevitable. In 1931 the national Confederación de Cámaras Agrícolas proposed to cede portions of its members' land to solve the agrarian problem once and for all.[46]

This type of counter-agrarismo, as I shall call it, was well developed in the Mayo Valley. Here landowners formed a Committee for the Resolution of the Agrarian Problem, which consisted of representatives of the Chamber of Commerce, landowners, real estate agents, and state officials. They sought a "solution" that would leave landowners largely unaffected. In 1932 the Mayo landowners agreed to assess a tax of 3 percent on the value of all harvests in order to finance the construction of the La Unión canal and the formation of four ejidos—La Unión, San Pedro, Navojoa, and San Ignacio—to be populated by day laborers and smallholders. In 1932, 112,880 pesos were spent on the project. Landowners contributed 76,710 pesos and the state government lent the rest. Despite initial opposition from many campesinos, the project was politically successful in that these ejidos later formed a clientele for conservative governors. But it was a mere drop in the bucket.[47] Desperate to save the Mayo Valley, where he reportedly owned some 4,000 hectares, Yocupicio revived this policy in 1937. Local hacendados decided to develop another irrigation canal, Las Pilas, of which half of the cost would be paid for by a tax of 10 pesos on every metric ton of wheat harvested, in addition to the existing 3 percent tax. The state pledged to provide the other half (600,000 pesos). At least 119 landowners participated in this last-ditch attempt to avert expropriation.[48]

This plan appealed to the Yaqui Valley farmers, organized in the Confederación de Asociaciones Agrícolas del Estado de Sonora (CAAES). They sought a similar rapid solution and considered assessing a 3 percent tax on the 1937 bumper wheat crop. The Yaqui Valley was still largely untouched by reform; only four ejidos had been formed in 1935 in Cócorit, Bácum, San José, and Esperanza. Landowners sought to maintain the status quo and proposed a plan by which land, water, and the clearing of land (*desmonte*) would be paid for by the farmers. Seventy-three landowners, organized in the Junta de Agricultores de la Región del Yaqui, met in 1936 to locate acreage for the project far from the best agricultural lands. Meanwhile, campesino leaders such as Pascual Ayón complained of CAAES pressure, including an assassination plot against him.[49]

Colonization schemes were also seen as a means to undermine agrarismo. Saturnino Cedillo, the conservative secretary of agriculture, travelled to Sonora in early 1937 and spoke with the CAAES and *agraristas*. He claimed that they preferred to purchase ten hectares each as colonists instead of receiving four in ejidal form. Yocupicio had policemen offer potential colonists fifteen hectares with water rights in an effort to stop the formation of ejidos. These efforts failed due to lack of time.[50] He was more successful in the case of the Colorado River Land Company near San Luis Río

Colorado, where he stimulated colonization by smallholders, especially veterans, according to the Colonization Law. A significant
part, 60,000 hectares (of a total of 160,000), was finally settled by
colonists who received the land on a fifteen-year rent basis.[51]

As reform loomed large, landowners hoped to avert disaster
by subdividing their latifundios among family members. In 1935
the Obregón family subdivided its Yaqui Valley holdings among
eight members in plots of 134 to 136 hectares in a futile effort to
limit the damage. Such tactics were seldom successful unless separate farming administrations were established. U.S. owners at times
used *prestanombres* (that is, they transferred title to Mexican nationals in order to mask ownership).[52]

The *Reparto*

The landowners failed to stave off the inevitable. In 1935 the Agrarian Department made an extensive study of the Yaqui Valley, where
tension mounted as more than 3,000 *agraristas* demanded land.
Finally, on October 28, 1937, the president announced the long-
awaited redistribution in the Yaqui Valley, but the final *reparto* was
postponed pending negotiations between Yocupicio and Cárdenas.

It was in the realm of agrarian reform that the weakness of the
Sonoran government vis-à-vis the federal government was most
obvious. Yocupicio and the landed elites had no means of taking
on the armed *agraristas* backed by Cárdenas, the CTM, and, if push
came to shove, by the military, without provoking full-scale class
warfare and a regional rebellion: "The State administration is impotent as regards agrarianism, except to . . . try to claim to be an
advanced advocate of agrarianism for the consumption of the agrarians and the central government or a conservative for the consumption of capital."[53] The governor left for Mexico City to discuss issues
such as indemnization, respect for *la pequeña propiedad* (the 100 hectares each landowner was permitted to retain), and the fate of the
harvest standing in the fields. Cárdenas pledged to respect
smallholdings and granted the landowners time to harvest.
Yocupicio, in turn, promised that he and the landowners would
peacefully cooperate. Steven Sanderson suggests that there was
more to this *arreglo*, namely, a pledge by Cárdenas to permit
Yocupicio to remain in power in return for acceptance of agrarian
reform.[54] Such a deal sounds plausible given the general ambiance
of *pactos* that pervaded this period. The governor may have secured
his tenure by promising to cooperate. He also profited in terms of

his image. The press described how "Yocupicio is in the Yaqui making the real Revolution, the Cardenista Revolution of granting ejidos to the pueblos and converting the pariahs of the countryside into honorable and strong citizens."[55]

The Yaqui Valley remained tense until the October 31 deadline. Farmers feverishly gathered their last harvest, often facing bands of armed, impatient *agraristas*. This tense, rumor-laden atmosphere gave way to wild celebration with fireworks, Sinaloan bands, and dancing in the streets when Cárdenas and Yocupicio officially announced the *reparto* to a vast crowd of thousands in Pueblo Yaqui. A "new sense of equality," but also of revenge, especially against the hated foreign landowners, permeated the festivities. Details about the indemnization were ironed out in November: landowners were to receive bonds with an annual interest of 9 percent. More importantly, they were promised future farming land to be irrigated by the La Angostura dam, then under construction. The rapid expansion of agricultural lands in Sonora not only allowed for the survival of the pre-Cardenista agrarian bourgeoisie, but it also left space for the emergence of a new group of *agricultores nailon*, such as merchants (the Mazóns and Hoeffers), officials (Maldonado, Horacio Sobarzo, the Uruchurtu family), and landowners (the Pavlovich family), in the Costa de Hermosillo during the 1940s. Though called *pequeñas propiedades*, some plots well exceeded the legal limit of 100 hectares.[56]

In the Yaqui Valley, 17,400 hectares of irrigated land (of a total of 43,700) and 36,000 hectares of *agostadero* (grazing lands) were distributed to 2,160 campesinos organized in thirteen new collective ejidos, with an average of eight hectares per ejidatario. The remaining properties were limited in size to 100 hectares. By 1940 the amount of land controlled by ejidos in the valley had increased to 25,500 hectares of irrigated lands (of a total of 62,500), due to the expansion of arable land by clearing.[57] The impact of Cardenista reform on land tenure in the Yaqui was significant. Some sixty-eight landowners and companies such as the Cía. Los Miles and the Cía. Agrícola del Naínari of the Obregón family lost thousands of hectares. On average, owners lost 50 to 300 hectares.

Land reform dramatically altered the pattern of ownership. By 1937, of a total of 3,604 landowners, 2,765 were ejidatarios, while 158 farmers owned medium-sized holdings of 90 to 100 hectares or more (32.5 percent of the total). Sixty-seven plots remained of between 50 and 90 hectares, 367 of 10 to 50 hectares, and 247 *minifundias* of less than 10 hectares. Land concentration thus decreased considerably. The Yaqui Valley now became a mix of ejidos and small- to medium-sized farms.[58]

The Yaqui Valley reform was particularly sensitive because of the large number of U.S. landowners involved. Cardenista reform actually targeted their properties in accordance with economic nationalism. U.S. citizens controlled almost half of the Yaqui Valley, or possibly more, if one considers that some Mexican land corporations were mere holding companies for U.S. investors, and individual Mexican citizens held lands for U.S. owners. Several of the largest operations were controlled by the holding company of one man, C. V. Whitney. These included the Yaqui Valley Land Company and the Cía. Agrícola Occidental. Some 21,179 hectares of U.S.-owned land were affected by the expropriation, including large companies such as Los Miles, S.A., the Cía. Agrícola Larrimore, French and Reed, and individuals such as Wirt Bowman and Z. O. Stocker.[59]

U.S.-Owned Lands in the Yaqui Valley, 1936[60]

Number of Properties	Area, Each	Total Area (has.)
64	1–50	1,349.67
19	51–100	1,383.10
2	101–150	260.00
12	151–250	2,392.84
11	251–400	4,274.00
7	401–1,000	4,184.10
2	>1,000	2,932.60
Total 117		16,776.31

There was a sense among U.S. landowners that they were targeted for expropriation. Many decided to give up farming, deeming their remaining 100 hectares insufficient. Absentee owners often lost even the 100 hectares, unless they had influential contacts, as did William Frankie, who was married to the sister of the governor of Puebla. Others used their ties with Mexico to argue their case. Z. O. Stocker's Mexican wife pleaded with Yocupicio to stop the expropriation of their hacienda, reminding him of her husband's pioneering work in the Yaqui, his acquaintance as a revolutionary soldier with men such as Maytorena, de la Huerta, and Obregón, and the Mexican nationality of their child. Her husband, she wrote, now "ill, silent, sad, and demoralized," had always idealized Mexico, once paying thirty-five dollars to an orchestra in the Astor

Hotel in New York just to hear the national anthem.[61] Outside the Yaqui Valley, U.S. landownership was less pervasive, consisting primarily of ranches in the north and in the Alamos district.

Yocupicio's hopes of sparing the Mayo were in vain. During July 1938, 73,949 hectares, of which 12,676 were irrigated, were granted to 4,489 ejidatarios in individual plots. Vast haciendas, such as Basconcobe and Las Parras, were whittled down to 100 hectares. José Tiburcio Otero lost 5,623 hectares to the ejido Basconcobe. The practice of subdivision among family members was usually futile, although the Salidos succeeded by establishing independent administrations for each plot, a move necessary to avoid accusations of *neolatifundismo*. As it was, the family lost large tracts of land, including Ildefonso Salido's Hacienda Bacobampo, Epifanio Salido's El Comparto, and Ramón Salido's El Bácame.[62]

In the Sierra the *reparto* was limited. Of a total of 15,224,050 hectares of grazing land, only 319,717 were affected. The most important ranches, including those of the Cananea Cattle Company, were declared *inafectable* for twenty-five years by the Cárdenas administration in an effort to revive the lucrative cattle export business. Nationwide, 745 ranchers (especially from Chihuahua and Coahuila) received these *certificados de inafectabilidad* for more than nine million hectares of grazing lands. In 1937, after intense lobbying from the Cananea Cattle Company, Cárdenas declared the expropriation of Sonoran ranch lands terminated. The government granted forty-one *certificados* for nearly 600,000 hectares to Sonoran landowners between 1938 and 1950. These protected J. E. Wise's La Arizona, Guillermo Mascareñas's 39,314-hectare spread Santa Barbara, Gilberto Ramos's Hacienda Aribabi in Imuris (16,093 hectares), Arturo Morales's San Rafael near Nogales (35,000 hectares), and the Hacienda Cuchuta near Esqueda. The Cananea Cattle Company was also exempted for the moment. In some cases, lands occupied by *agraristas* were returned to the original owners. Not surprisingly, today some ranchers speak fondly of Cárdenas.[63] The impact of Cardenista reform on the ranching sector was negligible.

In the Sierra valleys, where small-scale farming predominated, change was greater, though not profound. In the Río Sonora Valley, several ejidos were formed during 1934–35, which received primarily grazing lands. A small part of the population, about 12 percent, received land grants. Agrarian reform was hampered by the fact that most holdings were smaller than 100 hectares and thus immune to expropriation. In the Bavispe area, for example, only one landowner was affected. The federal and state governments provided the rest. Figures for the middle Río Sonora Valley indicate a 9 percent decrease in landlessness due to reform.[64]

Overall, Cardenista land reform in Sonora involved the granting of 528,000 hectares to 11,500 campesinos—a substantial increase in the percentage of irrigated land possessed by ejidos, from 7 percent in 1930 to 40 percent in 1940, and of *temporal* (semi-arid lands) as well, from 25 percent to 40 percent.[65] The total of land owned by ejidos grew from 13 percent in 1930 to 40 percent in 1940. This process would, however, be reversed during the 1940s *contrareforma*, as the ejido stagnated and private holdings were established in rapidly growing areas such as the Costa de Hermosillo and Caborca-Altar. By 1950 the figure had declined to 17 percent.[66] In the short run, reform was a severe setback for the Yocupicista coalition, while Cárdenas gained the support of many ejidatarios, armed and in possession of the richest lands in the state. The ejidos remain an important part of Sonoran rural society. But, seen from a long-term perspective, land reform had less impact.

Agrarian Reform and the Rural Bourgeoisie

How did Cardenista reform affect the rural bourgeoisie of Sonora? This question is at the heart of the debate on continuity and change before and after the Mexican Revolution. To what extent did the class structure of Mexico change due to the revolutionary process, which reached its peak during the Cárdenas years? Some historians correctly interpret the revolution as bourgeois, in the sense of greatly stimulating capitalist development.[67] However, this does not necessarily mean that the old Porfirian economic elite was displaced by a new revolutionary bourgeoisie, consisting of Artemio Cruz-like figures who used their political and military influence to accumulate wealth. The so-called Sonoran group, petty bourgeois revolutionary entrepreneurs such as Alvaro Obregón, Benjamín Hill, and Plutarco Elías Calles, are invariably mentioned to illustrate this point.[68] That a group of "millionaires of the revolution" emerged is undeniable. But it was never powerful enough to completely destroy the old economic elites.

If, then, the Porfirian elite was not displaced by a new revolutionary bourgeoisie, what did happen? Most historians speak of a fusion or syncretization of the old and new bourgeoisie through business connections and intermarriage.[69] As novelist Abelardo

Casanova aptly put it, "He who goes up needs to hold onto he who goes down, because the rich man who is becoming impoverished has more than the poor man who is becoming wealthy."[70] Even these fusion theories may be overstated, however. As Meyer writes, "The new men, the politicos, get involved in . . . business enterprises which . . . often turn out to be paltry compared with those of the real impresarios. The Sonorans who became involved in modern agriculture, and all the millionaires of the revolution . . . remain tiny in comparison with the real financial, commercial, and industrial fortunes."[71] Revolutionary entrepreneurs often had little success establishing themselves. According to Hernández Chávez, "the new rulers did not consolidate as a dynamic and vital sector" of the bourgeoisie.[72] On the other hand, the Porfirian economic elites demonstrated a great capacity for survival. The Terrazas Creel group of Chihuahua, the Redos of Sinaloa, and the industrialists of Monterrey all managed to recoup. In Chiapas, writes Thomas Benjamin, "the distribution of power and wealth . . . has changed very little . . . since the 1890s. . . . Continuity reigns."[73]

The Sonoran case sheds light on the process of class formation in postrevolutionary Mexico and the role of the State in this process. The contention that "practically the entire Porfirian oligarchy" of Sonora, "the most powerful businessmen, merchants and politicians," were affected by revolutionary confiscations in 1916 is overstated. The majority survived such travails.[74] The real challenge was the Cardenista land reform of 1937–38. But even here the impact was spotty at best. The lack of change was most evident in the Sierra, in particular in the ranching areas, where agrarian reform made little headway. Even today cattlemen control much of the grazing land in areas like Cucurpe. Clashes between ranchers and *comuneros* for control of communal lands continue.[75]

In the Yaqui, Mayo, and Hermosillo valleys, however, a serious blow was dealt to the landowning class. Here most of the old haciendas and many modern farms were affected. This does not mean, however, that new revolutionary groups displaced the old elites. They retained small, highly capitalized enterprises, capital, human capital (education, technical know-how), and political influence. *Neolatifundismo*, the reconstitution of large family-controlled farming operations through subdivision among family members and friends, the use of *prestanombres*, the renting of ejidal lands, the repurchase of lost plots, and other tricks were rife. A special characteristic of Sonora was the rapid growth of acreage from the 1940s on. Lost lands could be replaced by lands opened by the La Angostura dam, in the Costa de Hermosillo, or in the Caborca-Altar area.[76]

The "new" economic elite was hardly a revolutionary bourgeoisie. It consisted of various components: old nineteenth-century elites, often of foreign merchant extraction, such as the Astiazarán, Camou, Zaragoza, Escalante, Salido, Gándara, and Parada families; a new elite of merchant origins, which diversified into agriculture from the 1920s on, but especially after 1940, such as the Mazón, Robinson Bours, and Tapia families; and a small group of revolutionary origin, basically the Obregón and Elías Calles families. These groups today control diversified investments in agriculture, industry, ranching, commerce, and banking. The concentration of land in Sonora is considerable, certainly when the holdings of entire families are analyzed, and when the widespread practice of renting is taken into account. The Parada, Ciscomani, Camou, Mazón, Tapia, and Valenzuela families control estates of thousands of hectares, often of a size even the Porfirian elites would not have dreamt of.[77]

After the Reparto: The Struggle between Collectivists and Individualists

The Sonoran *agraristas* formed an integral part of the Cardenista coalition. Did the new ejidos formed in 1937–38, in particular the collective ejidos, function as bastions of Cardenismo? Actually, the serious rifts that developed in many ejidos immediately after their foundation weakened their unity as a *political* institution. The formation of collective ejidos in the Yaqui and Mayo Valleys may be considered one of the prime feats of Cardenista land reform. According to classic accounts, the collective ejido (that is, an ejido exploited in collective form) functioned well until the so-called agrarian counter-reform of the 1940s, when the government began to stimulate the development of private properties and individually exploited ejidos. The Banco Nacional de Crédito Ejidal and the CNC started exerting strong pressure on the collective ejido. This new policy resulted in factional divisions, corruption, and the final disintegration of many collectives. External factors are seen as having caused the collapse of this last vestige of Cardenismo.[78]

This interpretation is inaccurate for two reasons. First, it ignores the deep conflicts that developed within the ejidal sector, in Sonora and elsewhere, immediately after the redistribution. These rifts were not invariably the result of external pressure. Some interpretations also overstress the counter-reformist nature of the Avila Camacho government, which actually continued protecting the exclusive position of the collective ejido in areas such as the Yaqui Valley.

In Sonora we find the typical problems of many Mexican ejidos, such as the misappropriation of funds, the illegal use of ejidal farming equipment and trucks, the control of large tracts of land by ejido leaders, and the inevitable *amiguismo*. At the ejido 1° de Mayo in Bácum, for example, an ex-manager was arrested in relation with the misappropriation of 30,000 pesos. The cooperative shop was robbed, 18 tons of rice and 2,000 liters of gasoline disappeared, while the accountant sold equipment to local farmers.[79] The renting of ejidal lands to neighboring farmers or enterprising *ejidatarios ricos* became an endemic problem. This process, which began during the late 1930s, reached enormous proportions by the 1960s. In 1962, 11,480 hectares of Yaqui Valley ejidal lands were rented, while three Mayo Valley ejidos alone leased 3,314 hectares. In 1940 the Mayo Valley ejidos El Bácame and La Cuchilla leased hundreds of hectares in return for 25 percent of the crop. This often seemed lucrative from the ejidatario's perspective. In 1942 landowners offered the ejido La Victoria the option to rent 150 hectares of unused land for three years at a price of 10,000 pesos. They would clear the land and install a pump, which could be repurchased by the ejido.[80]

Conflicts within the ejidos arose for a variety of reasons. The agrarian reform process in Sonora was chaotic. One of the most serious problems was the fact that thousands of *agraristas* with legal rights remained without land after the redistribution, while many non-Sonoran migrant field-workers (*braceros*) did receive land. In Pueblo Yaqui, for example, numerous *vecinos* felt tricked after only 189 of a total of 470 *agraristas* received titles. In Ures, 463 campesinos remained landless, as did nearly 300 *agraristas* of Campo 60 in the Yaqui Valley. At Quechehueca, many distrustful campesinos refused to accept land, calling the *agraristas carne de cañón* (cannon fodder) and *soldados del gobierno:* "Se van a ir a la guerra por pendejos" (You are going to go to war because you're idiots).[81]

Thus, the *agraristas* were immediately divided between haves and have-nots. Groups excluded sought allies in an effort to vindicate their rights. Even those who received land were not assured of the automatic continuation of their rights. In many ejidos the original *censos agrarios* were reviewed after several years, and thousands purged, including not only ineligible ejidatarios but also the victims of power struggles. The purges had a major impact on the composition of ejido membership. The 1941 Yaqui Valley purge led to 2,122 names being dropped and 1,357 added to the list of title-holders. This obviously led to serious conflicts. Many of those added were non-Sonoran field-workers. During the 1940s, one-third of the Yaqui Valley ejidatarios were from outside Sonora.

Origin of 2,251 Yaqui Valley Ejidatarios with Ejidal Rights, 1941[82]

Sonora	1,462
Sinaloa	402
Chihuahua	151
Jalisco	56
Durango	54
Nayarit	38
Other states	66
Mexicans born in the U.S.	20
Foreigners	2

Many ejidatarios left to work on private farms, where they received salaries of 6 to 8 pesos per day, considerably more than the 2.5 offered by the Sociedad de Crédito Ejidal. Work on the ejidos was often performed by young men in their teens and twenties, who constituted a third of the Yaqui Valley work force.[83]

Such problems pale, however, when compared with the crucial division within most ejidos between so-called collectivists and individualists. Clashes erupted immediately following the expropriation in 1937–38, not, as some suggest, during the later counter-reform. The agrarian Thermidor started under Cárdenas and was partly the result of internal divisions among the ejidatarios. Many demanded parcelization, the subdivision of ejidos for individual exploitation.

Various arguments reminiscent of Samuel Popkin's "freerider" problem were heard in favor of individual exploitation. "In the collective system there exists no equity because while some of us ejidatarios work 190 days during each agricultural cycle, others only work 30 days, and these persons don't contribute to the work in the fields because they want to work in easy businesses, for example as drivers."[84] In 1940 ejidatarios of El Sahuaral complained that "the collective system . . . is simply an ideal—there is excessive bureaucracy in the Banco Nacional de Crédito Ejidal, it is an insurmountable obstacle that undermines the hope of the campesino, while the agent of the bank enriches himself at the expense of the suffering ejidatario and his family."[85] Vicente Lombardo Toledano, speaking in Ciudad Obregón during his unsuccessful presidential campaign in 1952, rejected critics of the collective ejido as campesinos "misled, pressured, hallucinated by promises, pacts, and lies," victims of "peasant leaders . . . who betrayed their class brethren for a couple of pesos and set about to destroy collective work to become individualists."[86]

While the division between individualists and collectivists resulted from internal conflicts, it was stimulated by external actors. At a confused meeting of the ejidatarios of Bácum, three orators, including FTS leaders Rafael Contreras and Maximiliano López, publicly defended collectivism, while three opponents spoke in favor of individualism.[87] Governors Yocupicio and Macías supported the individualist cause. More importantly, the split was exploited by the two rival sectors of the PRM: the CTM, which supported collectivism; and the CNC, in Sonora represented by the Liga de Comunidades Agrarias, which backed the individualists.[88]

The individualist-collectivist division was the rule in most Yaqui and Mayo Valley ejidos, many of which split into distinct groups working the land separately. During the late 1930s individualist groups started petitioning for the parcelization of ejidal plots. Later, during the 1950s, many ejidos were legally divided into two distinct sub-ejidos with different forms of exploitation.[89] Conflicts within the ejidos, often "divided like mortal enemies," became violent, especially because ejidatarios had been armed by Cárdenas. Divisions within the ejido of Bacobampo, combined with Yocupicista manipulation, resulted in bloodshed. On January 11, 1939, a force of some eighty *individualistas*, supported by the mayor of Etchojoa and his police force, clashed with two hundred *colectivistas* supported by the *defensas* of Basconcobe and El Sahuaral and Yaqui Valley reserves, leaving one policeman and four *agraristas* dead.[90]

The collectivist-individualist conflict started in the late 1930s and continued through the 1940s and beyond. The so-called counter-reform of the 1940s took some time to develop. In 1941, President Avila Camacho, faced with the problems in the Yaqui and Mayo Valleys, decreed that the Yaqui Valley would remain the exclusive domain of the collective ejido. The Mayo Valley, where individualist ejidos had a longer history, was designated a zone of mixed exploitation. It was not until 1948 that an *acuerdo presidencial* permitted both collective and individual ejidal exploitation in the Yaqui Valley, thus enabling individualist groups legally to demand the division of collective ejidos.[91]

Thus, from the very onset the ejidos of Sonora were the scene of intense strife between factions allied to rival labor organizations.

Far from constituting a unified pillar of Cardenista support, the *agrarista* movement splintered into antagonistic groups (ejidatarios versus landless *agraristas*, collectivists versus individualists, CTM versus CNC), weakening the political influence of the Cardenista agrarian movement.

The Successful "Solution" of the "Yaqui Problem"

> We, all the Yaqui Tribe of the eight pueblos, . . . want all our territory and all property . . . to be respected. The eight pueblos in general would like all those who receive the Presidency to attend us the way Señor Lazaro Cárdenas did.
> —Yaqui Tribe to Cuauhtémoc Cárdenas, November 5, 1988[92]

Land tenure in Sonora was also changed by another important measure of the Cárdenas administration: the granting of tribal lands to the Yaqui Indians. The age-old resistance of the Yaquis and their willingness to ally with any political force promising greater autonomy and the return of ancestral lands made them a political wild card. By granting the tribe half a million hectares and providing them with generous material support, Cárdenas managed to put a definite end to centuries of violent Yaqui resistance to *yori* encroachment.

The cornerstone of Cárdenas's plan was the restitution in October 1937 of 485,000 hectares of tribal lands on the north bank of the Yaqui River. Water rights to the Yaqui River and the future La Angostura dam were included, as well as the Bacatete Mountains. This unique agreement would be the basis of a long-lasting peace. One observer correctly assessed its profound historic importance: "This decision . . . could mean . . . the end of the old Yaqui wars, the continuous insurrection of the Yaqui and his struggle against the white man."[93]

Peace was not the only major consequence of this momentous decision. It also served to bind the Yaqui Indians to Cárdenas in a patron-client relationship. They were henceforth expected to remain loyal in moments of crisis. Yaqui soldiers were later sent to Nogales to guard against rebellious Almazanistas.[94] It was the Mayos, who received no land, not the Yaquis, who would stage millenarian revolts during the late 1930s and early 1940s. The Yaquis demonstrated their respect for Cárdenas during his June 1939 visit to the village of Torin. Chief Luis Matus told the president that "we have always been exploited and repressed by ambitious elements, [but] I have felt your good and healthy intentions toward our race."[95]

Even today, Cárdenas remains popular: "If there is any Mestizo whom the Yaqui regard as a tribal hero, it is Lázaro Cárdenas."[96] But the Yaquis' enduring independence and tenacity were demonstrated by the following incident during a meeting with Cárdenas:

> To the explanations of the President . . . the [Yaqui] Governor . . . answered, . . . "When the government was defeated. . . ." General Cárdenas made the observation that the government had not been defeated, and invited the Governor to continue: "You know, that when the government was defeated. . . ." General Cárdenas repeated his explanation that the government had not been defeated; that it had thousands and thousands of troops, arms and airplanes with which to fight, but that it preferred to come to a peaceful agreement and that that was exactly the reason why he was there; and that if he understood this, he should continue: "Look, President, when the government was defeated and came to ask us for peace. . . ." General Cárdenas responded: "Very well, when the government was defeated . . . please, go on."[97]

To consider Cárdenas's interest in the Yaquis as purely Machiavellian—one observer stated that the redistribution was "not really altruistic" but a "strategic necessity"—would not do justice to his keen personal interest in and empathy for the indigenous peoples. In Sonora his attention was not limited only to the powerful Yaquis but also included the politically insignificant remnants of the Pápago tribe. Cárdenas paid considerable attention to the "Yaqui problem," which he considered a delicate issue. He personally drew up plans and corresponded extensively with everyone involved, from the Yaqui governors to the engineers in the field, keeping up with the most minute details. He visited the Yaqui villages on several occasions, conducting long meetings with the chiefs. This marked a dramatic change in his attitude. During the 1926–27 Yaqui uprising, Cárdenas had volunteered his services to put down what he then considered the rebellious, ignorant, fanatic Yaquis. His proposed solution for the Yaqui problem had been drastic: after a "vigorous" campaign, "it will be necessary to expel from Sonora every indio [*sic*] who gives himself up."[98]

Now the president's goal was to integrate the Yaquis into Mexican society as modern, virtuous, hard-working farmers while still maintaining elements of Yaqui culture. In June 1939 he initiated a comprehensive development plan to be carried out by the Yaqui governors, the military heads of the *Colonias Yaquis*, and virtually every branch of the federal government. The Ministry of Agriculture would construct an extensive irrigation system and road network, establish sanitary services and cooperatives, and promote the development of small-scale agricultural, ranching, and salt-mining enterprises. The plan included schools, notably a boarding school, the Internado Indígena in Vícam, run by the Department of Indian Affairs to educate a future generation of "collaborators." The linguist Dr. Morris Swadesh would train teachers to speak fluent Yaqui. The Ministry of the National Economy would establish a granary in Vícam and consumers' co-ops. The government would aid in reconstructing the traditional Yaqui towns of Belem, Huiviris, Ráhum, new Bácum, and Cócorit. In 1940 the tribe received 150 mules, forty plows, trucks, carts, pumps, and other items ordered by the president. Sums involved were substantial: in 1938 the tribe had a budget of 204,600 pesos, of which 52,000 were spent on farm implements, 75,000 on loans for repairs, and 30,000 on livestock.[99]

This missionary activity was not limited to material issues but contained an element of social engineering that sought the complete restructuration of Yaqui society. Cárdenas's thirteen-point plan dealt with every aspect of Yaqui life, from government to sports. Living conditions would be improved by new housing, water supplies, baths, and medical facilities. The Yaqui communities would be uplifted by meetings, conferences, and sports events. Technical skills would be developed by the establishment of a carpentry workshop, a smithy, a saddlery, and orange groves. Strong liquor, which plagued the tribe, was banned. Such reforms, it was hoped, would bring about a change of mentality. Cárdenas entreated the Yaquis that only unity and collective effort would lead to success: "The . . . Yaqui Tribe should join in the Nation's effort."[100] "You should organize yourselves to take better advantage of your lands, to improve your houses, and to sanitize your villages." Rebel Yaquis, would be persuaded to abandon their lairs in the Sierra del Bacatete and join the *mansos* settled in the *Colonias*.[101]

Obviously, there was a huge gap between the president's earnest wishes and daily reality. Numerous problems arose. Farming implements and livestock often disappeared, and outsiders abused tribal resources. The Yaquis accused the head of the Yaqui Colonies, Teófilo Alvarez, of forcing them to sell land. Cárdenas reacted by inviting Alvarez to Mexico City for a little tête-à-tête, during which he granted him a pay raise of 1,000 pesos, undoubtedly in return for a pledge to end his illicit practices. The Yaqui governors also complained about the illegal construction of houses on their lands. Chief Francisco Pluma Blanca, considered a traitor by his Yaqui detractors, reportedly grazed cattle on the reservation. General Gutiérrez Cázares and others made considerable sums exploiting tribal forests for railroad ties. Efforts to establish a salt-mining cooperative soon collapsed and the business was taken over by outsiders.[102]

Some Mexicans remained in the area. The 1,500 to 2,000 *yori* inhabitants of Vícam were appalled by developments, and cited two Yaqui attacks during 1937–38 as the result of renewed Indian recalcitrance. They complained of the Yaquis' "hatred and fear toward the white man, whom they consider foreigners and harmful beings," a hatred that supposedly contrasted with the white man's willingness to cooperate with the Indians. (Note the terminology applied, the Indian-white dichotomy, more reminiscent of the United States than of, say, central Mexico, where a more nuanced racial vocabulary was used.) Demonstrating their sense of racial superiority, they complained that the Yaquis believed "that the whites, or 'Yoris,' as they call us, exploit them, that they don't pay their contractual obligations, that the 'yori' shouldn't live near us; but we believe that you haven't understood the fact that we are the ones to incorporate them and that we have lived in harmony with them."[103]

The president, disturbed by such reports, ordered General Gutiérrez Cázares, who had extensive experience with the Yaquis, to draw up a personal report. His 1939 conclusions were hardly encouraging. Agricultural production remained low, despite the arrival of modern farming equipment. The Yaqui governors severely restricted the development of woodcutting. Roads had fallen in disrepair, workshops were abandoned, canals neglected. The town of Vícam no longer had a fresh water supply. No schools functioned, except the Vícam boarding school, but many of the institution's thirty pupils were actually non-Indians. Thanks to the laxness of the authorities, alcohol sales remained high, especially on payday. Assaults and cattle rustling were commonplace. Local government was a shambles: "Complete anarchy reigns in the administration of the Yaqui Colonies." The cause of this bleak situation, states the report, was the "criminal conduct of the present [state] government," its "policy of isolation" and "complete tolerance." The Yaquis considered this approach as "a sign of weakness" and took advantage of it. While earlier heads of the Yaqui Colonies had tried to limit the power of their governors to purely ritual affairs, their successors had, since 1936, allowed the governors' prestige and influence to rise once again, to the point that *yoris* were actually expelled from Yaqui lands and the old policy of integration and acculturation abandoned. The Yaqui government administered its own justice system, which, according to an officer in Pótam, included burning convicted criminals to death.[104] Cázares, echoing the musty debate on civilization versus barbarism, argued that the only solution to the Indian problem would be the colonization of the region by white people: "The Yaqui problem differs entirely from that of other tribes . . . due to the indomitable character of the aborigines, who have practically never considered themselves subject to the Government." If no solution were found, a new rebellion might haunt Sonora once again.[105]

This report may have painted too negative a portrait, however. In 1938 the Yaquis were enthusiastically sowing and harvesting wheat on 1,000 hectares of tribal lands. Neither Cárdenas nor Cázares was able to understand the Yaquis on their own terms but still dreamt of civilizing and integrating them—one by the love, patience, and dedication of a missionary, the other by force and cultural erosion. Cárdenas's policies at least slowed down the process of deculturation that occurred elsewhere. The Mayos, for example, lacked an enclave, and responded to cultural encroachment with a series of desperate millenarian rebellions. Half a century later the Yaquis are still in possession of tribal lands and have maintained a degree of autonomy. But the process of integration that Cárdenas hoped for did, to some extent, take place. Today the Yaquis operate much as other ejidatarios, having become the economic subjects of the Banco Rural and the Agriculture Ministry. They produce cash crops with the aid of modern technology as yet another sector of the Sonoran agribusiness establishment.[106] Whether they will be able to maintain their autonomy within this changed setting is an open question.

Conclusion

What were the consequences of Cardenista land reform in Sonora? From a short-term perspective, the *reparto* was a great success. A total of 528,000 hectares were redistributed to some 11,500 ejidatarios. A sizeable and economically viable ejidal sector was established in one of the most important agricultural zones of the nation. Most Porfirian haciendas and farms were dealt a serious blow. Cárdenas seemed to have gained the loyalty of thousands of *agraristas* and of the Yaqui Indians, who ceased to be a serious threat to his regime. It was the rural folk of Sonora, not the industrial proletariat, that would form the backbone of Cardenista power. By 1939 almost half of the population economically active in agriculture was involved in agrarian reform, either as members of ejidos or as *agraristas* petitioning for land.

Members of Comisariados Ejidales and Comités Ejecutivos Agrarios in Sonora, by District, 1939[107]

Altar	1,914	Moctezuma	3,762
Arizpe	2,863	Ures	2,860
Magdalena	1,495	Sahuaripa	1,369
Hermosillo	1,482	Alamos	10,303 (incl. Yaqui Valley)
Guaymas	4,846 (incl. Mayo Valley)		
Total			30,894

However, agrarian reform was not as complete nor as successful as Cárdenas might have hoped for. The ranchers were exempted. The ejidal sector in the valleys was undermined by *neolatifundismo* and internal strife, which would neutralize it as a political factor. Conditions in the Yaqui tribal lands remained poor, due in part to Yaqui resistance and abuse by *yori* officials and entrepreneurs. The Mayo tribe never received land and remained restless. The 1940s and 1950s witnessed increasing attacks on the Cardenista collective ejido. The ejidal sector maintained its hold on some of the state's most fertile lands but lost its relative importance due to the expansion of private holdings elsewhere in Sonora. The campesinos did not, however, entirely lose their militancy. Large-scale mobilization occurred repeatedly in the wake of Cardenista reform, as recently as 1976.

9

Industrial Workers and Cardenismo

The Sonoran Mineworkers

Estos hombres del trabajo
son dignos de admiración
que se exponen diariamente
dando vida y corazón.
—*Corrido*, "La desgracia del 69"[1]

In Sonora, mineworkers constituted the most numerous representatives of the industrial work force, which, on theoretical grounds, might be expected to possess a mature, class-conscious world vision and play a vanguard role in the labor movement. Although this period displayed a high level of mineworkers' militancy, Cárdenas failed to create a close alliance between the State and the mineworkers. At the national level, miners abandoned the fledgling CTM and maintained the independence of the mineworkers' union, the SITMMSRM.

The Sonoran miners tended to play an isolated political role, seldom allying with other sectors of the working class. The miners' movement that emerged in Sonora during the 1930s was not the result of top-down mobilization but rather a defensive reaction to the world economic crisis. However, it was greatly stimulated by the intervention of representatives of the Cardenista State, without which it would have been unable to secure, during a recession, the wage hikes, union recognition, and improvement of working conditions that made miners even more of a "labor aristocracy"—that is, a privileged upper stratum of the working class—than they had been before.[2] This period witnessed the transformation of a weak, fragmented, and defensive movement into a combative, successful, and relatively autonomous labor sector. The State not only failed to harness the political power of the miners, but it also remained dependent on foreign mining companies for a substantial part of its revenues. Cárdenas was unable to forge a progressive alliance with the industrial proletariat of Sonora. Miners generally favored independent or conservative political candidates. The labor-aristocratic skilled mineworkers followed their own autonomous, economist, often conservative interests and displayed a semi-artisanal mentality instead of that of a radical archetypal proletariat. Miners were often quite militant, as is clear from the numerous strikes and takeovers of mines in Sonora during the 1930s, but at the same time they had a narrow, parochial political vision that precluded a radical role within the Cardenista coalition.

The Mexican Miner: Archetypal Proletarian or "Independent Collier"?[3]

Theorists have allotted miners a special role in the development of the working class, elevating them to the venerable position of "archetypal proletarian," the embodiment of working-class solidarity and militancy. To this day, much of the discussion on miners continues to take place within the framework of the antiquated "isolated mass" hypothesis postulated by Clark Kerr and Abraham Siegel in 1954. Kerr and Siegel explained the miners' "empirically demonstrated" propensity to strike in terms of their industrial environment, which dictates their existence as a homogenous isolated mass. They form "a race apart," which develops a high level of solidarity and union organization. These "tough, inconstant, combative and virile workers" will, by nature, be inclined to strike.[4]

Recent historiography criticizes the structuralist notion of a universal miners' experience. Royden Harrison, for example, demonstrates for the British case how miners' traditions actually stunted the growth of a genuine working-class consciousness and militancy, resulting in the labor-aristocratic mentality of the "independent collier." British colliers were no archetypal proletarians but formed a hereditary caste of craftsmen who maintained close ties to the land. The collier considered himself not a wage laborer but an independent tradesman who contracted with the mine owner for a specific task. The mines, in a sense, existed for the miners. The independent collier strongly resisted industrial discipline, rationalization, and proletarianization. Like any group of craftsmen, miners defended their status through an exclusionary attitude toward newcomers in the industry.[5]

These theoretical reflections bring new insight to the story of the Latin American miners, on whom historians, correctly or incor-

rectly, have conferred an important revolutionary role, especially
in the cases of Bolivia, Chile, Peru, and Mexico. According to conventional wisdom, the miners of industrial centers such as Cananea
spearheaded the revolutionary movement.[6] Charles Bergquist
boldly proposes a reinterpretation of the Mexican Revolution, stressing the importance of export workers in the foreign mining and
plantation enclaves where, supposedly, a combative working-class
consciousness should be expected to emerge.[7] Ramón Eduardo Ruiz
argues that in Sonora the penetration of foreign capital and the formation of production enclaves led to the development of a radical
"classic proletariat," predestined to revolt.[8] Such ideas are also reflected in the Guerra-Knight debate on Mexico's *révolution minière*.
François-Xavier Guerra argues that the initial phase of the revolution must be interpreted as a mining revolution, while Knight, on
the other hand, argues that miners played a minor role and did not
display a consistently revolutionary or anti-imperialist consciousness. They were neither radicals nor revolutionaries but, rather, liberal pragmatists who founded reformist associations and pursued
economist goals, readily entering into alliances with the State.[9]

If the Mexican miners of the 1930s can be considered archetypal proletarians, then they would have formed an important element, perhaps even the vanguard, of the progressive Cardenista
alliance. They also would have experienced a high level of labor
militancy. Indeed, the 1930s did witness the rise of a militant, well-
organized national miners' union as well as major unrest in Sonora
and elsewhere. However, there are many difficulties with this approach. Mobilization and militancy did not translate into a broader,
radical political movement. The miners comprised a heterogenous
group in terms of geographic origin, cultural background, position
in the labor process, and wage levels. Thus, the notion of a homogenous unified proletariat must be qualified. The miners' political
affiliation is also quite revealing. Instead of forming a progressive
alliance with Cardenismo, many actually supported independents
or even conservative anti-Cardenista politicos.

Mining Labor

Sonoran miners of the 1930s were characterized by a heterogeneity, which belies the notion of a homogenous isolated mass. The
term "miner" actually included everyone from highly paid mechanics and drillers to independent placer miners, ore thieves, and
scavengers. "Mines" might be foreign-owned, highly capitalized

operations, or primitive shafts worked by peasants and Indians in the remote Sierra. Even in the most modern mines it was hard to find a fully proletarianized, homogenous, and radical work force during the 1930s. Labor was divided in terms of geographical origin, culture, class background, skills, and wage levels. In Cananea an elite existed of skilled miners and proletarianized artisans, including *contratistas* (team heads), mechanics, electricians, carpenters, solderers, and smiths. They bore a superficial resemblance to a classic proletariat but actually demonstrated many features of an artisanate, including an exclusionist, labor-aristocratic mentality.[10] One must distinguish between the miners who worked in teams, or *cuadrilla,* according to semi-artisanal labor systems, and the more fully proletarianized surface workers found in the concentrating plants, foundries, and workshops. The miners' elite contrasted markedly with the mass of common laborers (*peones, jornaleros*) who comprised about 75 to 80 percent of the work force. This stratum consisted of dispossessed *serrano* campesinos and *peones* who formed an unstable element which retained ties to the land and thus never became completely proletarianized. During mining crises an easy "repeasantization" process would take place. The Sierra constantly expelled its surplus population to the large mines or agricultural centers.[11] These workers formed the core of the floating population of the Depression years, who roamed the state in search of work.

These differences were reflected in widely diverging wage levels. Although the large majority of workers earned the lowest wage on the pay scale (2.50 to 3 pesos per day), some skilled laborers could make as much as 15 pesos.[12] Within the mine there existed a clearly defined hierarchy or *escalafón* that workers had to ascend before reaching the position of *contratista: cochero, ayudante perforista, perforista, encargado de obras a destajo, ayudante destajero, contratista.*[13] Not only the great diversity in types of labor but also the nature of the work itself makes it difficult to speak of complete proletarianization. Work practices retained significant artisanal elements, such as team or *cuadrilla* work and piecework (*destajo*). Work in the interior of the mine was executed by *cuadrillas* of six to twenty men headed by the *contratista,* a skilled worker who acted as a broker between his men and the foremen and engineers. Teams worked independently on assigned tasks arranged by a team head who received the tools and pay and was responsible for his men's performance. This production system, which one might describe as semi-artisanal, lasted well into the 1930s.[14] Skilled miners preferred team work, as it involved "the intelligent use of workers' faculties."[15] Payment was also indicative of incomplete proletarianization. The miners received a relatively low basic minimum wage (credited to their account at the company store), supplemented by earnings for piecework. In 1929, 79 percent of underground workers at Pilares and 50 to 60 percent at Cananea were on this contract system, which strongly stimulated production. It was generally favored by miners, as it allowed for a degree of independence and resulted in higher wages.[16]

The *cuadrilla* and *destajo* or *tarea* (task) systems have been interpreted as a successful attempt by miners to resist industrial discipline and maintain control over the work process. A pure wage-labor system, as used above ground in processing, was considered unworkable below. Managers' constant complaints about the miners' inefficiency and drinking are also indicative of workers' resistance. Miners preferred working only several days per week if that would provide them with sufficient income. One observer estimated that at any given moment one-fifth of all mineworkers at Nacozari were absent due to drinking.[17] Another interpretation stresses the fact that companies actually preferred this semi-artisanal system, as it forced miners to discipline themselves while requiring little supervision. During the crisis of the 1930s, managers deliberately lowered minimum wages in the *cuadrillas* to force miners to boost production.[18] However, as late as the 1930s, the process of proletarianization in the mines remained incomplete, and a semi-artisanal production mode continued to exist even in technologically advanced enterprises.

At least as important as the *gran minería*, in terms of the number of workers involved, were the small and medium-sized mines. Here we find even less evidence of advanced proletarianization: most miners were common laborers, peasants who worked in the mines on a seasonal basis or during subsistence crises.[19] In addition, there were large groups of independent, unorganized, and lawless *gambusinos* or *buscones*, employed in placer mining or in legally or illegally exploited abandoned shafts. Some were dependent on the companies, such as those *buscones* who were "free workers . . . permitted to work in the [usually abandoned] mines on a basis of paying the owner of the property a certain agreed-upon percentage of the ore mined as royalty." Others worked independently in small teams, aided by women who ground the ore. Their numbers increased due to the Depression. Such independent miners were unpopular with the unions because of their resistance to organization.[20] At the bottom of the hierarchy, we find those people (often women or children) who scavenged in the refuse waters and along the transport lines and resold copper waste to the companies (for example, Cananea's *cobreras*).[21]

Thus, we find a highly diverse labor force in the Sonoran mines: well-paid, semi-proletarianized, and proletarianized skilled laborers, some working for basic wages, others still working according to artisanal traditions; peasant miners and new proletarians working as common laborers on a temporary or seasonal basis; independent and semi-independent *gambusinos*; and scavengers. This obviously did not constitute a homogenous, isolated mass. It might be expected that the type and intensity of political action would differ from group to group. Differences in wage levels, types of labor, and culture weakened group solidarity and inhibited the rise of full class consciousness.

The Moral Economy of the Mexican Miner

Instead of searching for the classic proletarian, it may be more useful to indicate certain general traits of the "moral economy" of the Mexican miner.[22] Many mineworkers, especially skilled miners and independent *gambusinos*, considered mining not merely a job but also a family tradition and way of life to which they had a moral right: "In many Mexican mines, *buscones* or their fathers have worked for many years. They believe they have a right to work there and therefore cannot be prevented from working except by force. . . . Companies cannot prevent them working, and it is of course inadvisable for a foreign company to act so contrary to *established customs* as to try to remove them."[23]

Their semi-artisanal work habits reflected the independent mentality and relative freedom of the miner. Mining skills were passed down from father to son. Because mine work was frequently a supplementary activity, many *gambusinos* tended to work in a casual and irregular way, at loggerheads with modern industrial discipline. If placed in an industrial environment, miners toiled in *caudrillas* under relatively little supervision and preferred piecework to base wages. This gave them greater freedom to work as they chose, and when they chose, while at the same time offering higher wages based on individual effort. Many Sonoran miners remained semi-agrarian workers, supplementing their incomes from agricultural or ranching activities with seasonal or irregular mine work, thus avoiding a risky dependency on either the unstable mining cycles or the vagaries of nature. Their relationship with the mines might be characterized as symbiotic.

According to their moral economy, miners viewed themselves as entering a reciprocal agreement with the owners, not as wage laborers but as skilled workers contracted for a specific task. They were willing to accept the management's authority if it took the risk of exploitation, paid them fair wages, and treated them with respect (disrespectful *mayordomos* were common targets of frustrated miners). However, if a company halted its operations, thus breaching the reciprocal agreement, miners would eventually resume working the mine illegally, considering it their right. From their perspective, mines existed for the miner. Private ownership rights were not automatically acknowledged. A temporarily abandoned mine was likely to be invaded and exploited by independent *gambusinos* or former miners.

Thus, the miners' worldview led them to radical collective action and the denial of government-sanctioned property rights. Such collective action does not automatically reflect a well-developed class consciousness or a revolutionary political agenda. Professional miners were more vulnerable to mining cycles and unable to fall back on subsistence farming. This factor, combined with their position in the miners' hierarchy, made them more susceptible to organization, in particular in defense of their labor-aristocratic status. Such groups joined the first *fraternidades* and unions and later formed the core of union leadership. In this case, the elite were more radical in times of economic downturn, as they had no other livelihood to fall back on.

Companies learned to adapt to the moral economy of the miner, accepting artisanal production systems (*cuadrilla*, piecework), which often led to a happy symbiosis of modern industrial production with semi-artisanal work methods. They even contracted with independent *gambusinos* on a leasing basis, thus neatly avoiding legal responsibilities toward their employees. Companies often preferred semi-artisanal production because of its higher productivity and lower overhead costs. Here the moral economy of the miner was consistent with the capitalist mode of production.

Company and miners' interests clashed, however, when mineworkers thought that the company did not fulfill its moral obligations and seized abandoned company property. The moral economy of the miner was not accepted by the State (that is, the Labor Department), or by the unskilled, proletarianized workers (especially surface workers) within the industrial unions, who pushed for the homogenization of the work force and fixed wages, measures that would undermine the relative freedom of both the skilled miners' elite and the independent *gambusinos*. The prime enemies of the unions were the *gambusinos*, who resisted labor legislation, base wages, and unionization, preferring the independence and freedom of their pre-proletarian working conditions.[24] Thus, the process of proletarianization was in a way promoted by the State and the national union, partly in an effort to offer all workers better and more stable working conditions and partly to control them in State and union patronage systems. It was this process, combined with the introduction of new technology, that would ultimately destroy traditional artisanal mining practices.

The Economic Conjuncture: The Crisis of the Mexican Mining Industry

The world economic crisis of 1929 led to a collapse of metals prices, which, coupled with high U.S. import taxes, nearly destroyed the Mexican mining industry.[25] The mines were hardest hit during 1930–1932, when production dropped by an average of 16.6 percent, and, once again, after 1938. Hundreds of mines went bankrupt or suspended operations. By 1932 half of Mexico's 90,000 miners were unemployed. Of 879 companies, 559 closed down between 1934 and 1940. Cardenista labor and mining legislation, especially that which limited the duration of concessions to thirty years, contributed to an atmosphere of pessimism among mineowners.[26] Sonora felt the repercussions of the Depression strongly. It has even been suggested that the mining crisis led to a reorientation of the Sonoran economy away from the foreign mining enclaves to the new commercial farms of the south.[27] The crisis affected the largest companies, such as the Cananea Consolidated Copper Company (4C) in Cananea, the Moctezuma Copper Company in Nacozari, and El Tigre Mining Company in Oputo. These giant U.S.-owned firms exploited numerous mines and ran smelters, railroad lines, cattle ranches, stores, and complete company towns. The livelihood of thousands of miners, mechanics, *peones*, merchants, clerks, and their families depended directly on the erratic international metals market.

U.S. companies were responsible for 99 percent of Sonoran mining production.[28] The largest operation was the Cananea Consolidated Copper Company, controlled by Anaconda. It owned more than 150,000 hectares, a modern smelter, concentrating and precipitating plants, a power station, railroad lines, and the company town. In 1929 the company employed 2,276 Mexican and 146 foreign workers, the latter mostly mechanics, office workers, smelterers, supplymen, geologists, engineers, and managers. In 1927 total investments in Cananea were estimated at U.S.$50,000,000. A town of nearly 17,000 inhabitants in 1930, Cananea boasted numerous shops and even exclusive clubs, such as the sixty-member Cananea Country Club, which owned a clubhouse, swimming pool, and tennis courts. Obviously, life in Cananea was not quite as glamorous for the large majority of the population. Mining camps were rough places, known for their rowdiness, massive *bacanora* consumption, nightly shootings, and vice. In Cananea, miners frequented cabarets such as Monte Carlo and Bohemia. Alcoholism, seen by some as a reaction to the extremely insecure life-style of the miner, and prostitution, organized in *zonas de tolerancia* such as Cananea's Moscú, were rife. Many smaller *minerales* lacked schools.

The second largest complex was the property of the Moctezuma Copper Company, a subsidiary of the Phelps Dodge Corporation, valued at U.S.$15,000,000. It exploited mines at Pilares de Nacozari, operated a 3,000-ton concentrator and a power plant at Nacozari, and possessed 86,000 hectares of grazing lands. The squalid poverty of company housing in the segregated "Mexican town" contrasted with modern amenities such as a recreation center with library, billiards, a dance hall, and a bowling alley for the U.S. employees, who also enjoyed a golf course and a portable tennis court. During the company's heyday in the 1920s, it employed up to 3,500 workers. By 1930 this figure had declined to 2,500, and it continued to drop to a low of 800 due to the Depression. Nacozari and Pilares were both company towns.[29] The largest silver mine, valued at U.S.$1,500,000, was operated by El Tigre Mining Company. By 1930 its rich silver veins were depleted and the company's labor force had dropped from 1,000 to 800.[30] The crisis also affected numerous smaller, usually U.S.-owned mines. Many had not been worked for years, while others employed small numbers of miners. Medium-sized companies had roughly between fifty and several hundred workers, while the smallest mines employed between fifty and a dozen workers.[31]

The Mexican Revolution seemed to have changed the attitudes of the Sonoran miners significantly. Cananea in 1930 was "a hot spot of changed and changing conditions," where "respect and welcome toward foreigners and foreign capital" and "the cringing attitude of people toward government authority" were all things of the past. The U.S. employees at the Moctezuma Copper

Company noted a new "independence of mind" among workers.[32] But the negative impact of the Depression was arguably of greater importance. By 1932 virtually all mining operations in Sonora, with the exception of the 4C, were paralyzed.[33] The owners of dozens of long-inoperative mines ceased to pay taxes and abandoned their properties. In 1931 the Moctezuma Copper Company closed down, leaving 1-2,000 workers unemployed. During late 1931 some 7,000 persons streamed out of Pilares and Nacozari in search of a new livelihood: "By train, truck or trail, families were going out every day. . . . The young people who boarded the train for distant points carried guitars and other musical instruments, babies and bundles, lunch baskets and bottles, as if they were going on a picnic. But the old folks hugged framed pictures of dead children and saints to their bosoms and had not trusted even their little trinkets and heirlooms to be packed in trunks or boxes. So when it came leaving time, they and their feebleness could hardly be lifted on the train for their burdens."[34]

Large numbers of Mexican repatriates, expelled from the United States, joined the jobless miners, making the situation in the northern Sierra intolerable. Observers reported widespread suffering. After a temporary recovery, a second spate of bankruptcies occurred in 1938 as silver prices fell once again due to the cancellation of the U.S.-Mexican silver-purchasing agreement. A rise in export taxes also devastated the smaller silver mines. El Tigre Mining Company requested permission from the federal government to suspend operations. Other companies, such as the Cía. Minera El Porvenir, abandoned operations without notice, leaving their miners in dire straits.[35]

The mining crisis was not only the result of the economic conjuncture. Before the Cárdenas presidency, foreign companies maintained a comfortable modus vivendi with regional elites and state and federal governments, which aided them with tax breaks, permission for layoffs, and wage reductions. Revenues from mining taxes were a key source of income for the State. It would not be an exaggeration to speak of an alliance between foreign capital and the State, even in the years following the economic nationalism of the Constitution of 1917. In 1931, for example, Governor Calles tried to use his father's influence to exempt the Moctezuma Copper Company from taxes.[36] Governor Yocupicio renounced state mining taxes and pleaded fruitlessly with the Cárdenas government in an effort to keep the company open. Successive governors overlooked the tax arrears of the La Colorada mine and even protected abandoned shafts from invaders. The Moctezuma Copper Company insisted on "some assurance of stable operating" from state and federal officials, by which it meant the pacification of labor.[37]

This cooperation came under pressure during the Cárdenas *sexenio* due to the implementation of the Federal Labor Law, rising taxes, and government-sponsored labor agitation. From the onset, the president made it clear that it was time that mining wealth actually benefited the Mexican people instead of foreign capital. Mineowners were reluctant to invest and generally failed to renew expired leases, while prospective U.S. investors shied away from the industry. What kept companies from closing down completely was the strict labor indemnity legislation: "The [Moctezuma Copper] Company had no intention of closing down its Sonora properties because it was cheaper to operate at a small loss rather than pay the bonuses provided by the Mexican Labor Law for indefinite cessation of operations. . . . If the . . . companies . . . found it unprofitable to operate, they would nevertheless be forced to produce at a loss in order to retain ownership because if they shut down, under Mexican law, the unemployed miners might then be declared to have the right to take over the mines." But Cárdenas never expropriated the foreign mining companies, largely because they constituted the principal source of income of the State, providing as much as 28 percent of government revenues. In 1940 mining still accounted for 48 percent of total foreign direct investment in Mexico.[38]

Unemployment, Survival, and *Gambuseo*

The onset of the Depression raised the question of what was to happen to the thousands of unemployed mineworkers and their families, who were now eking out an uncertain living in barren mining camps. Besides human suffering, the State had to worry about the social and political repercussions of mass unemployment. The state government and the mining companies reached an agreement providing for the repatriation of non-Sonoran workers to their home states and the sending of Sonorans to the agricultural valleys in search of work as farm laborers. Travel expenses were covered by the companies. Public works projects were implemented to absorb hundreds of ex-miners and repatriates. Many were able to fall back on subsistence farming, either returning to the land or working garden plots. Some ex-miners later benefited from land distribution and colonization.[39] Most preferred to work as *gambusinos*, independently or under contract to a company, in the exploitation of placers and abandoned shafts, or to form cooperative mining associations and continue to work unproductive mines collectively.

Placer mining was crucial. "At the onset of the world wide depression, the extensive placer fields . . . offered practically the only means of earning a livelihood to the unemployed, and many of the poorer classes of people took advantage of this opportunity to avoid starvation."[40] Placer mining employed not only ex-miners and repatriates (some 540 ex-miners from Cananea worked 4C silver fields in 1937) but also many peasant-miners. In remote villages such as Soyopa the entire population relied on the returns of placer mining, which was considered a traditional family enterprise. Techniques involving gold pans and crude dry-washing machines were handed down from father to son. Entire families would leave their homes in search of gold. A gold rush occurred in 1939–40, when as many as five thousand men, women, and children feverishly made their way in cars, carts, and on foot toward El Mezquite, southeast of Magdalena, where up to ten kilos of gold were produced per day by washing sand and gravel. Within no time, a rowdy, lawless shantytown had sprung up. Few *gambusinos* actually became wealthy: "Their efforts are usually crowned with very little success. Each individual earns only enough to supply the bare necessities of life, but efforts are continued on account of the lack of employment elsewhere."[41]

Gambusinos often took to working closed mines illegally, breaking their way into the shafts and exploiting the ores with stolen tools and machinery. This behavior was completely in accordance with the miners' moral perception of property rights. When agreements with mineowners broke down, they believed that they had a right to work the abandoned mines. At the La Colorada mine, 150 *gambusinos*, only one-third of whom were former employees, earned sufficient wages (reportedly five pesos per day) to support two cantinas and a band of musicians. Their work methods were undisciplined: "It was a common occurrence for the miners to take from one to five cases of beer into the mines when they entered to steal ore."[42] At times independent *gambusinos* and company management reached ad hoc agreements for the exploitation of shafts. This occurred at the Cía. Minera "La Libertad" at La Campana, which stopped operations in February 1938, leaving some eighty-six workers unemployed. The company lent funds to the miners so that they could take over exploitation on a lease basis.

Independent *gambusinos* clashed with miners engaged in cooperative mining. These disputes clearly demonstrate the difference between organized miners and the independent, unorganized, and drifting *gambusinos*. In 1938, after the closedown of the Pedrazzini Gold and Silver Mining Company at Las Chispas, the Sindicato de Obreros Unidos agreed to work the mine cooperatively, while the company promised to purchase the ores at previously established prices. Unfortunately, some fifty armed *gambusinos* broke into the mine shaft and began to exploit the veins illegally. These men had been previously employed by the mine as independent *buscones*. Armed company guards and federal troops finally secured the mine for the cooperative.[43] Both miners' unions and the Labor Department consistently opposed *gambusino* work, whether independent or under contract to a company on a royalty basis. Not only were *gambusinos* difficult to organize, but they also fell outside existing legal labor categories.[44] Many ex-miners preferred the freedom of *gambuseo* in terms of the lack of industrial discipline, the liberty to sell ores to any buyer, and flexible working hours.[45]

Unionization in the Mines

By the mid-1920s miners' unions were still plagued by "a great dispersion and organizational heterogeneity" and an "organizational vacuum."[46] The final impulse for unification came from regional caudillos and ultimately resulted in the formation of the Sindicato Industrial de Trabajadores Mineros, Metalúrgicos y Similares de la República Mexicana (SITMMSRM) in 1934. The CTM had little direct influence over the miners' unions, since the SITMMSRM left the federation almost immediately after its foundation in 1936 in protest of CTM meddling in its internal affairs.[47] In Sonora, miners' unions remained weak until the early 1930s.[48] As the repercussions of the Great Depression were felt, a handful of miners retained a precarious hold on their jobs. The government allowed companies to undermine the standard of living of the remaining miners dramatically. Production levels were reduced, wages cut, and jobs eliminated. The Moctezuma Copper Company and El Tigre Mining Company cut minimum wages in an effort to boost productivity.[49] By the time Cárdenas became president, Sonoran miners were in a particularly weak position.

At the large mines in Sonora, Coahuila, Hidalgo, and elsewhere, unionization was usually a futile reaction to cutbacks. During two massive layoffs at the Cananea Consolidated Copper Company in 1930 and 1932, 900 of a total of 1,700 workers lost their jobs.[50] As one miners' leader recalled, "When they heard about the reduction of the workday and the dismissals, the compañeros started to get organized . . . in unions, which didn't have much power and were thus destined to fail." In Cananea the Sindicato de Oficios Varios "Nueva Orientación" was founded in 1930 as the fusion of two weak unions of skilled mechanics, railwaymen, and miners. The background of this union can be found in the weekly meetings of miners at cultural centers such as Fraternidad Buenavista and especially Luz y Fuerza, as labor leader Agustín M. Pérez later explained:

> In those days [around 1930] we had an anarchist center in Cananea called "Luz y Fuerza" [Light and Power], where we got together every week; and it was here that, between discussions, we got interested in making possible a union. . . . The meetings we had in the Club "Luz y Fuerza" were of an anarchist tendency, but we didn't really know anything about that. . . . All the compañeros got together to discuss social and other topics, right?, but mostly things related to the organization of the workers. During the meetings . . . we read a lot of anarchist books like those of Zola, of this author I really enjoyed one book that dealt with miners; we also read books by Russian authors; the newspapers that we read were from New York and Tampico, the magazines were *Cultura Obrera*, *Cultura Proletaria*, *Verbo Rojo* and *Sagitario*. But our favorite books were those that Lázaro Gutiérrez de Lara wrote in Cananea: *Los Bribones*, in which he criticized the North American company. . . . After reading, we always had a discussion, one of our favorite topics was free love, another that we really liked was the strategy that we had to follow to create a new world: without government, without capital, and without God. It was during these discussions of the Club "Luz y Fuerza" that the Sindicato Nueva Orientación was born.[51]

Management at Cananea did not accept unionization without a struggle. Union members were prime victims of the layoffs. A company union which consisted of surface workers, called *blancos*, signed a collective contract with the 4C, and fused with the Sindicato "Nueva Orientación" in 1932 to form the Gran Sindicato Obrero "Mártires de 1906," led by Ramón C. Meneses. The merger was an unsuccessful effort by the arbitrating state government to defuse radical tendencies among the miners. The result was a movement split between collaborationist *blancos* (surface workers) and militant *rojos* (interior mineworkers).[52]

In the small *minerales*, rural teachers were instrumental in organizing unions and defending the legal rights of workers during the 1930s. They frequently headed miners' unions or served as advisers. The main purpose of such unions was to extract a maximum of benefits from the dying companies before their closure or to guide the transition to cooperative status. Increasing opposition to teachers' radicalism led the Cárdenas regime to limit their role as ideological and political emissaries of the State. In 1937 a federal labor inspector forbade the teachers to attend union meetings at El Tigre, and the Sonoran director of education warned teachers not to get involved in "personalist politics." They were increasingly supplanted by representatives of the Labor Department or of the mineworkers' union.[53]

The Mining Cooperatives

During the 1930s the mining zones experienced the seizure by workers of numerous foreign-owned mines, including some of the largest operations, which were converted into worker-administrated cooperatives. At first glance, this would seem to be a reflection of the economic nationalism espoused by the Cárdenas administration, thus indicating a marked correlation between State and working-class ideology. However, in this case a moral economy approach offers a better tool with which to analyze the mineworkers' behavior.

Cárdenas regularly spoke out against the predominance of foreign capital in Mexican mining: "The mineral production of our country has been fantastic. . . . And these enormous riches—have they perchance served to help our lower classes? Have they even created Mexican millionaires? Have they helped better the living conditions of those who . . . produce this untold wealth for the foreign companies?"[54] The Cárdenas government introduced measures to control foreign capital and strengthen the participation of Mexican nationals. It regarded cooperativism as a means to break dependence on foreign capital. Popular pressure frequently resulted in mines being turned over to the workers. By 1937 unions could blackmail companies: if they refused to give in to their demands, lengthy strikes could result in the mine being turned over to the miners according to the labor laws. For many smaller operations this was the only alternative, as they could not afford severance payments. They usually agreed on exploitation by workers in return for royalties, or illegally abandoned operations altogether. For larger companies with substantial investments, this was not an option, and they continued operations at a loss, usually giving in to workers' demands.

When companies did stop operations, the miners frequently formed cooperatives. As late as 1946, seventy-five mining cooperatives existed in Mexico, employing 19,000 associates. Foreign capital considered them masked expropriation. They were generally not a success due to insufficient capital, the bad condition of the mines, and the poor technical skills of many miners. The trend was toward short-term exploitation in an effort to guarantee at least a meager livelihood to miners who otherwise would have lost their jobs.[55] Sonoran examples show that the formation of cooperatives had little to do with popular economic nationalism. Miners invaded foreign mines because they believed that they had a moral right to work them, preferably without government interference. Their "radical" denial of private property rights was a reflection of their traditional worldview. The State superimposed its own cooperativist ideology on the miners' moral economy.

The formation of cooperatives was hardly a spontaneous development. Miners were frequently abandoned by their U.S. bosses, leaving them with few alternatives but to attempt exploitation on their own, either legally, as a government-sanctioned cooperative, or, preferably, illegally, as independent *gambusinos*, selling ores to brokers of dubious reputation. At the Churunibabi mine, workers established the Sociedad Cooperativa Productora de Mineros Unidos de Churunibabi, which signed a contract with the Moctezuma Copper Company.[56] Negotiations between El Tigre and Section 87 were so lengthy that some 125 miners started working the mines illegally as *gambusinos*, preferring irregular, independent work to cooperative exploitation. To the great dismay of the federal labor inspector, many miners refused to join the cooperative, as they were fetching excellent prices for their ores and expected to receive lower wages from the cooperative. They immensely enjoyed their newfound freedom, a clear indication of how deeply ingrained certain elements of the miners' moral economy still were: "This way they work on the days they want, enter whenever they like, and, above all, they have no foreman and no responsibility to anyone." Their enthusiastic scavenging seriously endangered the stability of supporting arches in the mine shafts. Finally they were convinced, in part by the presence of troops, that a cooperative would be a better long-term solution. In 1938 an experimental agreement was signed with the company, including an 11 percent production royalty. However, the cooperative ultimately declined and the miners reverted to unregulated *gambusinaje*.[57]

Labor Conflicts

During the Cárdenas years the original lack of organization of Sonoran miners was transformed into a surprising combativeness that resulted in wage hikes and new collective contracts and strengthened miners' unions. The strike was the favored weapon. Often, threatening with a work stoppage was sufficient to obtain concessions from the mining companies. The nature of the miners' demands underwent an evolution during the 1930s. While strikes before 1935 still involved many traditional demands and reflected a defensive reaction against layoffs, those of the Cárdenas years focused on new issues such as union recognition, collective contracts, the closed shop, and union control of hiring, and had a markedly aggressive nature. Union action was responsible for dramatic wage increases which protected real wages of miners and positioned them among the best paid workers in the nation.[58]

Labor conflicts at the huge 4C complex at Cananea obviously had the greatest economic and political impact. During the early 1930s, the Gran Sindicato Obrero "Mártires de 1906," led by Ramón C. Meneses, fought for the establishment of a collective contract that would resolve traditional grievances related to working conditions and benefits. In 1932 a collective contract was signed, which addressed many of these issues but also strengthened the union considerably through a series of novel concessions: recognition of the union and hiring and promotion preference for union members.[59] A wildcat strike in 1935 resulted in a substantial wage hike of forty to fifty-five centavos and additional pay raises depending on the price of copper of up to sixty-five centavos.

The Sonoran miners' movement was galvanized by its adherence to the new national mineworkers' federation, the SITMMSRM, founded in 1934. In November 1935 the SITMMSRM's leaders, Agustín Guzmán and Carlos Samaniego, presided over a meeting that transformed the Gran Sindicato into Section 65 of the SITMMSRM, dissolved the old collective contract, and presented a whole new series of demands. The company initially refused to recognize the new union. The SITMMSRM followed a radical new national strategy, aimed at wage hikes to offset inflationary trends, union control of hiring through the closed shop, a limit on the number of foreigners to 10 percent of the work force, the reduction of hours, and general benefits to raise the miners' standard of living. The ultimate goal, frustrated by presidential pressure to limit demands, was a nationwide miners' contract and, possibly, the nationalization of the entire industry. The means to reach these goals was the strike. In 1935 alone, eighteen thousand miners of the SITMMSRM were involved in thirty-six strikes.[60]

Backed by the national miners' union, the demands of the miners of Cananea became considerably bolder. One important change was a greater emphasis on the closed shop (the *cláusula de exclusión*) and union control of hiring. Demands also included a 30 to 50 percent wage hike and pay for seven days as well as a series of points related to working and living conditions. The 4C refused to accede to the demands, especially the closed shop, which would include foremen and thus make the union, in the words of 4C Vice President Charles L. Montague, an "autocratic political power."[61] Cárdenas played an important role in the Cananea conflict. His watchdog, *secretario de gobierno* Arellano Belloc, advised Montague to give in completely to the union.[62] A three-month strike finally broke out in January 1936. Miners suffered considerably due to a lack of strike funds. The conflict soon spilled into the arena of municipal politics. The governor, who supported the 4C, deposed the municipal government presided over by mineworkers' leader Meneses and tried to place a yes-man in the *presidencia*. Troops broke up miners' demonstrations.[63] Meanwhile, Montague was summoned to Mexico City by the head of the Labor Department. When he refused to come, Secretary General Cantú Estrada threatened to send soldiers to bring him. Talks in Mexico City proved fruitless. Cantú claimed that Cárdenas wanted to place control of the 4C in the hands of the SITMMSRM. Montague concluded that "the actual conflict lies primarily between the Copper Company and the Government rather than between the Company and the laborers."[64]

In the final settlement the 4C made important concessions. It recognized the union and accepted the closed shop. The flexible wage scale was allowed to increase by as much as twenty-five centavos. In return, the company received from the federal authorities a (somewhat dubious) guarantee of labor peace for two years. However, "the point which was most distasteful to the company, namely, that the hiring and firing of foremen should be subject to the approval of the union, had been completely withdrawn."[65] In general, the result of this collective contract was to strengthen the union's position and improve living conditions of 4C employees. Real wages rose dramatically, the lowest wages by some 70 to 100 percent.[66]

The year 1938 witnessed another major strike at the 4C. Workers demanded union control over hiring and firing, the reduction of the workday to six or seven hours, more rest days, and an across-the-board wage hike. The strike only lasted two weeks. The final agreement included a minimum wage hike of 1.25 pesos and a series of points related to living conditions. A total of 209 new clauses were added to the collective contract.[67] A third serious strike broke out in April 1940 and lasted more than five months. By then the union was particularly strong, while the size of the work force was back up to about 1,200. The miners demanded a revision of the collective contract to include a wage hike and the dismissal of several employees, including Vice President Montague and the head of personnel, Saturnino Campoy. Work was resumed after the contending parties reached an agreement that included wage increases for piecework and several other concessions.[68] Strikes occurred at many other companies. At the Moctezuma Copper Company, miners struck in 1930, but the company closed its gates less than a year later, leaving 1,600 miners without income.[69] Even at the smaller mines, strike threats became common.

Despite the new character of many demands, which were strongly influenced by Cardenista labor legislation, traditional grievances, such as abuse by foremen, continued to play a major role. One of these cases involved Henry Forest, a generally hated foreman of the 4C. Miners accused Forest of tyrannical and violent behavior. He was said to threaten workers with dismissal, insult them, refuse to allow them to go to the toilet during work periods, deny them pay, work them too hard, and prevent injured miners from leaving the shafts. His language was less than edifying. As one observer said, "[Forest] treats the Mexican workers in an immoral and hostile way and . . . I believe it is unreasonable that a foreigner behaves like that on our native soil." A brawl between Forest and a drunken miner who was fired led to work stoppages, the refusal by miners to allow the *mayordomo* into the La Colorada mine, and sabotage. Forest was finally shot and wounded by a disgruntled Mexican mineworker in the main street of Cananea. He recovered, only to be shot and killed a year later, this time by an American.[70]

The Forest incident was not an isolated case. There was a general anti-American (and anti-Chinese), xenophobic trend among miners, which was often stimulated by labor leaders: "Soap box speakers have been quite eloquent in their recommendations of taking things away from the American owners and dispatching owners and employees out of the country."[71] Popular pressure led to a gradual decline in the number of foreign employees in the large mining companies. Foreign companies learned their lesson. When the Moctezuma Copper Company reopened in 1937, the management wisely limited the number of foreign employees to a handful of supervisors. In 1940 only twenty foreigners worked at the mine, of which just ten were U.S. citizens.[72]

Miners' militancy in Sonora and elsewhere resulted in major victories: by the late 1930s unions, the closed shop, and collective contracts were generally accepted, while health provisions, working conditions, and wages (which rose by 40 percent in 1934–35 and another 25 percent in 1936) all improved dramatically.[73] Workers were less successful, however, in controlling the hiring process, which remained a bone of contention.

The Inter-Union Conflict at Pilares de Nacozari

Some miners stubbornly opposed incorporation into the national union. Should the resistance be interpreted as a manifestation of working-class autonomy, or should it be dismissed as the result of devious efforts by conservatives to maintain a docile work force through the manipulation of *sindicatos blancos*? At Pilares de Nacozari, the 600-man-strong Sindicato Minero "Héroe Jesús García" (HJG) refused to join the SITMMSRM and instead adhered to the state-sponsored Confederación de Trabajadores de Sonora (CTS). Its relations with Governor Yocupicio were excellent. Federal labor inspectors tried to influence the union to join the SITMMSRM, but the Sindicato Minero was able to maintain control of the workers, possibly aided by threats from management. Adherents of Section 114 complained of intimidation by armed company guards.[74]

A major difference between Cananea and Nacozari was the fact that the Moctezuma Copper Company had closed for several years. The new work force lacked cohesion and a sense of identification with the company's history and with the miners' struggle. Many workers were new to the industry and unsure which course to follow. One labor inspector evaluated the union as a *sindicato blanco* because it never issued demands or complaints, while many of its leaders were *mayordomos* or *empleados de confianza*; the secretary was, he claimed, a local judge who also owned a shop and mules. He asserted that the collective contract signed by the *sindicato* was a flimsy affair of one page.[75]

The supremacy of the Sindicato HJG was consolidated in the 1940 contract, which acknowledged the union as the sole representative of the workers. All hiring would take place from a pool of workers designated by the union.[76] The Sindicato HJG also controlled the mining cooperative of Churunibabi, which belonged to the CTS and was rewarded with financial support from the Yocupicio government.[77] The CTS came to control some 540 miners at Churunibabi, Pilares, and Nacozari. The miners of the Sindicato HJG constituted an important clientele of Yocupicio and invariably voted for Yocupicista candidates.

Conclusion

Classic explanations of mineworkers' behavior within the framework of the isolated mass theory are of little use. The Sonoran miners constituted a highly heterogenous group. Many demonstrated an artisanal, labor-aristocratic mentality and tradition. The moral economy of the miner, which stressed his moral right to exploit the mines, made for a lasting tradition of independence and resistance to proletarianization. Organization was strongest among the skilled workers, who were organized along craft lines, initially together with mechanics and railwaymen, until the 1930s. During the Depression, what was left of the mineworkers' movement was strengthened in a defensive effort to maintain real wages and jobs. In smaller mines top-down mobilization, especially by teachers, played an important role. However, independent *gambusinos* and many of the unemployed remained unorganized.

This defensive posture changed once the SITMMSRM made its entry into Sonora in 1935. Under the influence of Cardenista labor policy, the mineworkers' movement became increasingly aggressive. Surprisingly, this development took place during a period of decline within the mining sector. It was Cardenista mining legislation that made it difficult for large companies to discontinue operations, while smaller ones often abandoned their mines to the workers so as not to make severance payments. Under these circumstances many companies had no alternative but to accept most labor demands. The mineworkers of Cananea, who struggled against the 4C in a series of major strikes, were successful in defending real wages and extending union control through the closed shop. The majority of miners were now *gambusinos*. They reverted to pre-proletarian modes of exploitation that were, in some aspects, quite radical, in particular the invasion and illegal exploitation of foreign-owned mines. These were traditional reactions to the violation of their moral economy, most likely to occur when the miners' perceived "right" to work the mines was threatened. These invasions did not, however, reflect agreement with Cardenista economic nationalism. Actually, the State grafted its economic nationalist, cooperativist vision onto the *gambusinos*, who merely sought to continue their traditional way of life independently. In many cases they agreed to the formation of cooperatives only after pressure from the State.

The Sonoran mineworkers were not incorporated into the Cardenista political alliance. The SITMMSRM left the CTM and maintained an independent position. During the 1939 gubernatorial elections, many of the Cananea miners voted for the independent candidate. Other groups even joined the Yocupicista machine by adhering to the CTS. During the 1940 presidential elections many supported the conservative candidate, Juan Andreu Almazán, via the Partido Minero Almazanista. Technological developments and state actions would ultimately destroy the last vestiges of artisanal behavior among mineworkers. But in many ways it was the State, and not capitalism per se, that speeded up the process of proletarianization through the levelling of wages, de-skilling, and mass unionization.

IV

The Politics of Cardenista Reform and the Reform of Politics, or the Demise of Cardenismo, 1938–1940

10

Cardenista Politics and the Mexican Right

A Mexican "Thermidor" began in 1938.[1] Cardenista reform stagnated and in many cases was reversed due to strong opposition, especially among conservative governors. In states such as
Sonora, rising discontent was channeled away from overt resistance
toward a more subtle opposition within the system. This change
was related to two major political crises in 1938: the Cedillo rebellion and the expropriation of the foreign petroleum companies,
combined with a serious financial and economic situation, in the
wake of which Cárdenas and his conservative opponents accepted
the necessity of negotiating a modus vivendi on reform. Although
this dialogue prevented further armed revolts, it also forced
Cárdenas to moderate his policies, and ultimately led to the demise of Cardenista reformism during the 1940s.

Hermosillo Blues

The first anniversary of the Yocupicio administration was celebrated
with a *gran baile popular* in the handball court, with free beer provided by the Sonora Brewery and a more exclusive ball at the Club
Trece. The governor had little reason to celebrate, however. Ugly
rumors about his imminent demise began to surface in October 1937,
during the *reparto*. U.S. military intelligence predicted that "there
will be a major rift within the next 30 days. Yocupicio has sent most
of his family from the state and has been reported to have threatened the Federal Government with open warfare if he is not permitted to conduct the affairs of his state in his own manner."[2] The
U.S. vice-consul in Guaymas expected a rebellion at any moment,
which might actually benefit U.S. interests. "Such an outbreak might

be temporarily detrimental to . . . the Americans who are being deprived of their properties, . . . even endangering their lives if no precautions were taken, but in the end the result might conceivably mean the salvation of their life's work."[3]

Yocupicio was, indeed, despondent: he "bitterly denounced the agrarian policies of the . . . Administration [and] said that he hoped . . . that he would be able to prevent the expropriation of the land that was given . . . to the Yaqui Indians but that he was unable to do so when he visted Mexico City." The authorities had treated him poorly, making him wait in the anteroom of the Agrarian Department for three days: "General Yocupicio said that it was his opinion, an opinion that was shared by many patriotic Mexican landholders, . . . that if the Government of the United States had indicated to the Mexican Government it viewed with concern the expropriation of the Yaqui River lands that the lands would not have been expropriated. . . . He said that the agrarian policies of the Government will, if continued, in all probability create a condition of affairs similar to the situation that has existed in Spain for more than a year."[4] In another private conversation he stated that "the Administration disliked him intensely because they believed he was too conservative in his attitudes toward agrarianism and that all his acts were closely observed by government agents in Hermosillo. The General stated . . . that in view of the Government's suspicion of him, it is necessary for him in all of his acts to create the impression that he was a sincere friend of the Administration and that any other policy at this time would be dangerous not only politically but in other ways also."[5] By early 1938, Yocupicio "sometimes even thinks that it is impossible for him to cope with the situation."[6]

Yocupicio was a survivor, however. He "has certainly not allowed this attitude to bring him into open conflict with the Federal administration. Probably in this he has shown himself a good politician since open opposition to the Federal administration would undoubtedly have cost him his position."[7] His survival can also be attributed to hard work lobbying the president. He spent much of January in Mexico City, where he made a point of praising Cárdenas's record. He also worked through his trusted ambassador in Mexico City, Adolfo Ibarra Seldner, who did an excellent public relations job and claimed that Cárdenas had assured him that Yocupicio was "in good standing" and that his "future [was] assured."[8] Cárdenas reciprocated by inviting the governor to accompany him on several presidential tours. He actually praised

Yocupicio's work: "The government of Sonora . . . is a revolutionary government because it has demonstrated its interest in aiding
the campesinos, while in addition it has always granted the necessary guarantees to organized labor, . . . I have information that there
is complete tranquility in Sonora and that . . . reports [concerning
repression] have been stirred up by some person who doesn't know
the personality of the governor of Sonora." This was quite a change.
Some believed that Cárdenas considered Yocupicio harmless now
that agrarian reform had succeeded; the governor had been "obliged
to fall in line."[9] However, this conclusion may have been somewhat premature.

Yocupicio and the Cedillo Rebellion

In 1938, Cárdenas faced major trials: the petroleum expropriation
in March and the Cedillo rebellion two months later, both of which
were set against the background of a severe economic slump. In
either case, Yocupicio decided to back the president, despite their
differences. By the summer a new situation had arisen: intense polarization subsided as conservative factions decided to work within
the system, while Cárdenas moderated his policies dramatically in
an effort to accommodate these groups. His regime was still far
from stable. A powerful conservative group controlled many state
capitals and the army remained distrustful. "President Cárdenas
has attempted to guard against the material opposition of high
military officers by placing all inactive generals on the active list,
by frequent changes in Commanders of units, . . . and by the
shifting or substitution . . . of 18 of the 35 Military Zone Commanders."[10] He took measures to placate privates and lower-
ranking officers by raising their payments in the Army and Navy
Savings Bank, an effective measure against desertion. He also increased salaries by 10 percent for most ranks, and promoted some
1,000 officers.[11]

Some of the more politically inept opposition groups finally
joined an anti-government uprising led by the disgruntled cacique
of San Luis Potosí, Saturnino Cedillo, in 1938. The Cedillo rebellion was more than a pathetic last gasp of primordial caciquismo.
It threatened to unify the right and reflected widespread discontent with Cardenista reform among business groups, the urban
middle classes, rural elites, and even sectors of the lower classes.
Opposition centered on the military; a smattering of small right-
wing, semi-fascist organizations such as the Unión Nacional de

Veteranos de la Revolución (UNVR), Acción Revolucionaria Mexicanista (the *camisas doradas* or Gold Shirts), and the Confederación de la Clase Media; and out groups, such as the Callistas. Their influence should not be underestimated. That the Cedillo rebellion ultimately failed was due to the fact that important sectors of the Right decided to operate within the system, backing the presidential candidacy of General Manuel Avila Camacho instead of gambling on the uncertain and violent solution of Cedillo.[12] The secular right sought to lead the country back to the Sonoran path of development of the 1920s, though stripped of Jacobinism. Conservatives espoused a simple, strongly anticommunist ideology: they opposed Cárdenas's socialist rhetoric, educational policies, the CTM, and collectivist agrarian reform, and stressed the importance of agrarian capitalism based on *la pequeña propiedad*.[13]

Conspiracies had been brewing ever since Cárdenas came to power in 1934, especially among disgruntled officers and politicians linked to the Calles faction or to Emilio Portes Gil, the *éminence grise* of Mexican politics.[14] Cedillo's appeal as an alternative to Cárdenas started to decline in 1937, when he was ousted as secretary of agriculture and retired to his home state, San Luis Potosí. The sense prevailed that, to quote Santos, "Cedillo is an ignoramus who doesn't know what he's doing."[15] He counted on a small group of conspirators, including Yocupicio, Gildardo Magaña, governor of Michoacán, Félix Bañuelos, governor of Zacatecas, and General Francisco Carrera Torres, zone commander of San Luis Potosí. He set out to recruit followers among the military and solicited funds from foreign companies. "The oil companies have received three different letters from General Cedillo inquiring how much backing he could expect from them in case he chose to lead an armed movement against the present régime. General Cedillo assured the companies that he could count on the support of Governor Yocupicio of Sonora."[16]

Yocupicio was a logical ally. Besides maintaining close ties with Cedillo, he came from the same rural revolutionary background, was a strong opponent of Cardenismo, and was considered a *socio* of Portes Gil.[17] By the summer of 1937, reports surfaced concerning arms smuggling in preparation for a pro-Cedillo revolt. Yocupicio was also said to be preparing landing strips on isolated beaches for the *corsario* airplanes he had purchased for the Hermosillo Aviation School. Three former aviation teachers from Sonora were arrested while carrying a subversive letter from Cedillo. At this time,

Cedillo also started building a personal air force, which was used during the rebellion.[18] Such accounts were taken seriously by both Mexican and U.S. military intelligence: "Yocupicio is the only one . . . who might join forces with Cedillo."[19] However, secret agents discovered little evidence of arms contraband. Many rumors were undoubtedly exaggerated by Yocupicio's enemies. His moves seem to have been more defensive than offensive. But by September 1937, "General Yocupicio was very well organized and would not have tolerated a violation of the sovereignty of Sonora." His agents contacted Cedillo and various anti-Cardenistas in Mexico City.[20] All seemed poised for a rebellion.

These political problems came at a time of serious economic and financial crisis, caused in part by massive government spending on agrarian reform and infrastructure projects. By early 1938, Mexico's economy was plagued by rising inflation, declining real wages, capital flight, supply shortages, and a government budget crisis. This crisis threatened to spark anti-Cardenista opposition and destabilize the government.[21] However, the political situation changed dramatically for two reasons: the March 1938 petroleum expropriation created a surge of pro-Cardenista patriotism; and the underground presidential campaign of Manuel Avila Camacho, the secretary of defense, had begun to attract many conservatives such as Yocupicio, who were still not entirely convinced of the feasibility of a rebellion. Magaña, Yocupicio, and Bañuelos now tried to persuade Cedillo of the futility of his desperate plan.[22] Cedillo was unable to enlist Yocupicio's support "because he was very Cardenista despite everything that Lombardo Toledano had done to him. . . . [H]e said that he and his Yaquis were behind General Cárdenas and wouldn't back a Cedillo or a Lombardo Toledano, but that they shouldn't stir up things in Sonora, and that he was governor and a general; then Cedillo told Córdova that they were stroking Román Yocupicio's self-esteem to make him switch sides to Cárdenas, and he said that that was a very malicious and very caddish answer."[23]

Yocupicio pledged his loyalty to the president in April, then conveniently left for surgery in Los Angeles. "He asked me to tell you [Cárdenas] that he had absolutely no agreement with General Cedillo, because before being inaugurated as governor . . . he had clearly indicated to the Señor President that in questions related to the politics of the state . . . he would only be guided by the instructions of the President, and that the Señor President knows very well that he keeps his word." He promised that, once recuperated, he would travel to Mexico City to speak personally with Cárdenas.[24]

The Cedillo rebellion finally erupted in May 1938. By then, Cedillo had been abandoned by his erstwhile supporters. Yocupicio reiterated his pledge of loyalty to Cárdenas in a sentimental telegram: "All of us old soldiers of the state are at your orders."[25] Cedillo was distressed by what he considered the betrayal of Yocupicio, Magaña, and Bañuelos. He reportedly sent an envoy to Hermosillo, "severely upbraiding [Yocupicio] for not joining [him]."[26] In July 1938 federal agents arrested a brother of *camisas doradas* leader Nicolás Rodríguez in the Government Palace in Hermosillo and found a letter from Cedillo sewn in the leg of his trousers. In the letter, Cedillo complained that he could not understand why Yocupicio had not come to his aid as promised. In his last "Manifesto to the Nation," issued in June–July 1938, Cedillo bitterly denounced "the treachery of the Governments . . . of Sonora, Michoacán, and Zacatecas, which had a Pact of Honor with the Government of San Luis Potosí, so that if General Lázaro Cárdenas, the Dictator modelled after Stalin, should carry out his threat to declare the Power of any of the before-mentioned States dissolved, they would support it in order to defend its sovereignty."[27]

Why Yocupicio did not join Cedillo is unclear. In a recent interview, Sonoran campesino leader Bernabé Arana offered an intriguing and plausible hypothesis that might explain the ambivalent relationship between Yocupicio and Cárdenas. He suggested that the president never removed Yocupicio because "he was the fifth column, he was the one who sent all the reports to General Cárdenas."[28] Unfortunately, the evidence does not corroborate this hypothesis, and we will probably never know what Cárdenas and Yocupicio discussed during their private meetings. Cedillo was on his own. Yocupicio had been quite wise not to follow the old cacique on his desperate adventure. Cedillo was tracked down by federal troops and executed on January 10, 1939.[29] The time for rebellion had definitely passed.

The Petroleum Expropriation and the Politics of Loyalty

On March 18, 1938, President Cárdenas declared all foreign petroleum holdings in Mexico the property of the State. This momentous decision, the culmination of Mexican economic nationalism, created a completely new political scene. The expropriation was followed by a massive outpouring of declarations of support and loyalty, campaigns to collect funds to liquidate the petroleum debt, and demonstrations in support of nationalization. It also sparked an economic crisis involving a drop in government tax revenues, a slowdown in trade, and a bout of panic-driven inflation.[30] These circumstances forced the opposition to assume a patriotic stance and pledge loyalty to the president. Right-wing opponents, in particular Cedillo, who had begged the foreign oil companies for support, faced the prospect of being branded traitors to the *patria*.

For Yocupicio and other conservative governors, and for the economic elites, the expropriation created a new set of problems. However, they were able to overcome these at the price of operating within the system. They appropriated Cardenista economic nationalism for their own purposes, in return expecting the president to reward them by addressing their grievances. Even the Catholic Church seized the moment to search for a détente with the state. The new archbishop of Mexico, Luis María Martínez, an acquaintance of Cárdenas, called on Catholics to support the expropriation.[31]

These events are usually interpreted as a genuine, spontaneous outpouring of nationalist support. Actually, the Right and economic elites generally opposed nationalization in a muted way but used events to ingratiate themselves with the president. Popular support was exaggerated by the press; many of the "spontaneous" demonstrations were staged, and participation was obligatory for government employees.[32] Yocupicio reacted slowly, waiting until the 20th to declare his solidarity and traveling to Mexico City on the 23rd. That same day, massive demonstrations were held in Hermosillo and other towns. The authorities ordered business establishments closed. The atmosphere was panicky, and Sonorans hoarded silver and staples.[33]

The U.S. consulate worried about rising anti-Americanism: "The attitude of the predominating lower classes against aliens is reaching dangerous proportions." But no serious threat to U.S. interests materialized. The director of the Moctezuma Copper Company stated that "employees have become a little more bumptious," but he was not overly concerned.[34]

While the lower classes may have favored the expropriation, this could not be said of the economic elites. "Merchants, cattlemen, mine-owners and executives, even though they make public avowals of support, . . . are not in reality in sympathy with the program. They fear the power of the Administration and express their opinions reluctantly and only to persons in whom they have complete confidence."[35] But they soon realized that loyal cooperation with government efforts to pay off the debt would be politically more rewarding than passivity or outspoken hostility. The Chambers of Commerce urged members to collaborate with union demonstrations. The ranchers of Sonora collected 100,000 pesos for the cause and received warm thanks from the president. Ejidos and farmers pledged 3 to 5 percent of the value of their harvests. Businessmen founded the Comité Pro-Rendición Nacional. As elsewhere, women were mobilized to collect money. Patrocina A. de Yocupicio, the governor's wife, emulated the example of Amalia Solórzano de Cárdenas and headed the fund drive, collecting large sums from the *damas* of Hermosillo society.[36]

The elites would, of course, expect a payoff. Yocupicio's secretary, Ibarra Seldner, traveled to Mexico City to discuss sensitive issues such as the protection of *la pequeña propiedad*. He expected these to be resolved favorably, as the cooperation of ranchers and landowners had made a favorable impression on the president.[37] Thus, the impact of the expropriation was twofold: it undercut the position of the extreme Right, making the success of the Cedillo rebellion almost inconceivable; but, conversely, it also resulted in the "loyal Right" being able to push its conservative agenda with more success, now that Cárdenas needed broad support.

The Governors' Lobby

Many of the governors who rushed to Cárdenas's side after the expropriation hardly qualified as staunch Cardenistas. The conflictive relationship between the Cárdenas administration and the government of Sonora was by no means an exception. The role played by Yocupicio was mirrored by that of numerous other conservative governors and caciques. These could easily be dealt with when isolated, as happened with the unhappy Cedillo. Once combined, however, they formed a formidable opponent. They soon forced the president to moderate his radical policies and ultimately placed their candidate, General Manuel Avila Camacho, in the presidency, defeating Cárdenas's preferred successor, the radical Francisco J. Múgica.

Many governors had come to power for reasons of political expediency during the Calles-Cárdenas confrontation. Emilio Portes Gil had been influential in their appointment during his presidency of the PNR. The governors of Sonora, Michoacán, Zacatecas, Coahuila, Durango, Hidalgo, México, Nuevo León, Oaxaca, Querétaro, Sinaloa, Tabasco, and Tamaulipas were all considered Portesgilistas.[38] They constituted the remains of the Portesgilista-Cedillista faction, which fragmented in the wake of Portes Gil's removal as president of the PNR and Cedillo's ill-fated rebellion. As a group, they lacked cohesion. But in their home states they followed policies similar to Yocupicio's, combating the CTM, backpeddling on agrarian reform, and building conservative power bases.

Governor Maximino Avila Camacho, the "Mad Czar of Puebla," formed the center of another bloc of conservatives. A brother of Manuel, this egregious character, a former bullfighter, rose to power during the Calles-Cárdenas conflict when Cárdenas relied on him as zone commander to establish Cardenista hegemony. In return, Cárdenas allowed him to use electoral fraud and violence in his successful bid for the governorship in 1937. He proceeded to construct a solid *cacicazgo* which would dominate Puebla until the 1960s. Avila was considered "a menace to the existence of a free labor movement." He supported the CROM and the Federación de Trabajadores de Puebla (FTP) against the Federación Regional de Obreros y Campesinos (FROC)/CTM, and controlled the *poblano* peasant league LCA/CNC. He repressed socialist teachers by founding a state teachers' union, Sindicato Unico de Trabajadores de la Educación de Puebla (SUTEP), curbed anticlerical measures, built close relations with the regional bourgeoisie, and espoused an anticommunist regionalist rhetoric. He was considered so dangerous that when Cárdenas fell ill in 1940, it was rumored that Maximino had ordered him poisoned.[39]

Likewise, in Veracruz, Governor Miguel Alemán (1937–1939) presided over the demise of a vigorous peasant movement and battled the CTM. In Michoacán, Gildardo Magaña, a "precursor of the Revolution" and old Zapatista, and a friend of Cárdenas, clashed with the local Liga de Comunidades Agrarias and the CTM and exerted pressure on the collective ejido. He ran for the presidency as an independent in 1940 on a platform defending small property ownership and states' rights. We see a similar scenario in Nuevo León, Tlaxcala, Zacatecas, and Tamaulipas.[40] There were, of course, regional Cardenista power blocs that remained loyal, for example in Chiapas and Jalisco.[41] But these governors never had the strength of the anti-Cardenista clique and depended heavily on the center. They were easily outflanked by conservatives during the presidential campaign.

By 1938 three conservative governors' factions became visible: that of Portes Gil, who made a discreet comeback in 1938, and the Veracruz and Puebla groups led by Alemán and Maximino Avila Camacho, respectively. Combined in support of Manuel Avila Camacho, they formed a formidable anti-Cardenista bloc. The group's ideological stance was expressed in simple, anticommunist rhetoric. As Santos, who described them as *anticomunistas francos* (as opposed to the pro-Múgica *comunistoides*), put it, "there was chaos in the streets with so many marches by workers carrying red and black flags proclaiming communism, beating on drums and scaring people, all of this provoked by Múgica and Lombardo Toledano. . . . Múgica is going to lead Mexico to communism and that will be the ruin of the country."[42]

A major rallying point was the so-called *defensa de la pequeña propiedad*. The conservatives, echoing Cedillo, favored colonization schemes—that is, the sale of private plots to individual smallholders (*colonos*), and the parcelization of existing ejidos instead of collective exploitation. They also addressed the grievances of smallholders hurt by illegal expropriation. Yocupicio's slogan was "Land for those who have a right to it and respect for smallholdings." This position should not be discounted as mere elite manipulation. It reflected, as in the case of the Sonoran collective ejidos, the demands of sectors of the rural population that preferred private ownership over collective exploitation. Cedillo, Yocupicio, Avila Camacho, Magaña, and Bañuelos all became champions of *la pequeña propiedad*. Bañuelos and Magaña formed state defense leagues for smallholders.[43] In addition, the governors of Sonora, Veracruz, Michoacán, Tamaulipas, México, Puebla, Sinaloa, Nuevo León, and Tlaxcala all endeavored to keep the CTM out of their states, using violence if necessary, and sought state control of federal education. Many resented the constant attacks in the left-wing press and in Congress. A new solidarity could be noticed among governors. When the governor of Tabasco came into conflict with radical teachers, Governors Alemán and Yocupicio made a public show of support.[44]

Such informal links soon solidified into an official governors' lobby, which met with the president regularly, presented demands, and received important concessions which seriously weakened the Cardenista program. The first meeting occurred a week after the petroleum expropriation, a critical moment for the president. The governors, demonstrating their solidarity, presented him with checks worth 100,000 pesos to cover part of the national petroleum debt. In return, they desired more influence on agrarian reform, the arming of *agraristas*, and respect for *la pequeña propiedad*.

Yocupicio was pleased with the results: Cárdenas pledged to allow the governors more say in these issues, respect smallholdings, and return lands illegally expropriated to the lawful owners. He even founded the Oficina de la Pequeña Propiedad in May 1938. The governors were permitted to "closely watch" the federal teachers and to propose candidates for the state directorships of federal education. Yocupicio's announcement of the agreement led to protests by Sonoran teachers.[45] The governors renewed their demands during a second meeting held in July in the Centro Sinaloense in Mexico City. Cárdenas promised to speed the solution of agrarian cases, and he reiterated that "there will be absolute respect for '*la pequeña propiedad*.' " Committees were established to investigate the ejidos, federal education, and labor. Cárdenas went out of his way to criticize the "unfounded" complaints against the governors, specifically mentioning the case of Sonora. Many congressmen were appalled: "The ejido has been abandoned by the governors."[46] The meetings continued in 1939 and assumed increasingly political overtones.

The governors organized informally to support a conservative presidential candidate from within the system. According to Santos, a clique of politicians, including Yocupicio, discussed the candidacy of "unknown soldier" Manuel Avila Camacho, largely out of desperation. On learning of their plan, Manuel's brother Maximino threw a fit:

> Maximino jumped up from his chair and said, with a red face: "That's impossible! My brother Manuel candidate for the presidency of the Republic? He was never even council member of our village, Teziutlán. . . . I should be president. . . . I am the eldest of the family, I raised all of them when they were children. When Manuel was small, I made him ride on a wild burro and gave him a centavo." Maximino became excited with his own words, and said: "Manuel is a 'steak with eyes' and I am the governor of a very important state, Puebla, which used to be a scorpion's nest and which I now control entirely (and that was true). . . . I will contact the governors so that they listen to you, but in the sense of [promoting] my candidature.[47]

By late 1938 the pro-Manuel Avila Camacho movement gained momentum, supported by Alemanista, Avila Camachista, and Portesgilista governors, including Yocupicio and his successor

Macías. Masonic lodges also played a role: Yocupicio and Maximino Avila Camacho were honorary presidents of the Gran Comité Nacional Masónico Pro-Avila Camacho. On November 16, 1938, the governors signed a pact in Agua Azul, Puebla, in support of Avila Camacho. This solidified the governors' movement, which was to emerge victorious from the electoral fray. They would spend the next years doing at the national level what they had tried to do in their home states: dismantle Cardenista reform.[48]

Conclusion

The two crises of 1938, the Cedillo rebellion and the petroleum expropriation, set the scene for a renegotiation of the balance of power between Cárdenas and his conservative opponents, including governors such as Yocupicio. The failure of the Cedillo rebellion clearly demonstrated the futility of armed revolt and convinced Yocupicio and others that resistance within the system would be more productive. They soon presented Cárdenas with the bill for their loyalty. The governor's lobby demanded concessions in the key fields of agrarian reform and socialist education. The president responded by moderating his stance and indicated that further reform was not to be expected. The emerging détente can also be explained by the success of the conservative Avila Camacho candidacy, which led the opposition to believe, correctly, that in the near future it would gain control of the political machine constructed by Cárdenas.

11

From Polarization to *Continuismo*, 1938–39

Al final tiene que pactarse, porque de no pactarse, no sé donde
hubiera parado.
—Campesino leader Bernabé Arana on electoral politics in the
1940s[1]

Opposing Power Blocs

During 1938 the tense national situation was magnified through
the prism of Sonoran politics. This resulted in violent clashes
between two well-defined regional power groups: the Yocupicista
bloc (the state government, bureaucracy, and PNR organization,
municipal governments, the police, the CTS, the FEMSS, and the
UNVR); and the Cardenista bloc (the federal bureaucracy, the zone
command, the CTM, the *defensas sociales*, the ejidos, and SUTES).

The FTS/CTM had become a force in the state and clamored
for power. Its anti-Yocupicista campaign continued unabated and
gained momentum during the months prior to the Cedillo rebellion. At the 1938 national meeting of the CTM, both Lombardo and
FTS leader Jacinto López reiterated their attacks, while the Cardenista *bloque revolucionario* in the Senate called for Yocupicio's dismissal. The governor responded by jailing more labor leaders.[2]
During the fall, CTM labor groups launched a nationwide anti-
Yocupicista telegram campaign, orchestrated by the national CTM.
The *comisariado ejidal* of Palos Chinos wrote the president a typical
complaint: "The revolution accuses [Román Yocupicio]: of being a
servile instrument of the reaction, an enemy of the Socialist School,
an enemy of all progressive movements and of . . . the Mexican
Social Revolution; because he delays and obstructs the unification
of workers; . . . because he shelters fascist-style groups and gives

. . . the best jobs to representatives of these groups; because he seeks to disband the Defensas Sociales; . . . and because he seeks to . . . expel from the state the honorable Director General of Education."[3] The campaigns seemed to be paving the way for federal intervention.

Municipal Politics, 1938–39

Municipal politics reflected the growing power and confidence of workers and campesinos, and the increasing polarization between popular forces and the Yocupicio administration. As one campesino recalls, "Nos sentíamos jodones, que eramos muy fregones. . . . Nos metimos a gatos bravos, queríamos poner todo."[4] In many municipalities, a labor faction, often ousted from power after the fall of Callismo, battled a conservative Yocupicista faction. The state government controlled municipal politics through the regional committee of the PRM, which designated the heads of municipal PRM committees.

In the Mayo Valley, the Yocupicista authorities harassed a radical faction of school inspectors, teachers, campesino leaders, and Callista politicos, and sacked union offices and schools. The Hermosillo council was controlled by a Yocupicista faction including CTS leader Tiburcio Saucedo, the police by UNVR/CTS leader Colonel Jiménez Ponce. Only in rare cases did labor dominate the councils: Cananea, controlled by the powerful miners, was an exception.[5] The case of Agua Prieta exemplifies the tension between Yocupicista mayors and the working classes. On March 24, 1938, a full-blown uprising against Mayor Martín S. Burgueño erupted when armed ejidatarios stormed the municipal palace at 2 A.M. and disarmed the police force. Burgueño escaped through a window and fled to Douglas, Arizona. Agua Prieta remained the scene of an occasional violent outburst.[6]

The most conflictive and politically significant case was Ciudad Obregón, that "hotbed of radicals," where labor fought a fierce and prolonged battle for power. After discovering "evidence" of fraud and bootlegging, Yocupicio jailed the entire city council, including Matías Méndez and Maximiliano López. This sparked protests and violence, including the shooting death in the mayor's office of mayoral candidate José Moreno Almada, a compadre of Yocupicio's, and an assassination attempt against Maximiliano López, who was wounded. Yocupicio tried to convince the federal authorities that the latter incident was merely "a common brawl, probably caused by a personal grudge or some other banal reason."[7]

The fiercest clash came on March 21, 1938, in response to the arrest of FTS leader Jacinto López. Some two hundred armed *agraristas* invaded the town, stormed the police headquarters and jail, freed López, and disarmed the police. They then occupied the municipal palace and laid siege to the council members, who were holed up in a private home. The FTS declared a general strike and disconnected utilities. *Agraristas* held the town until troops arrived to reestablish order. Several more unstable councils, one of which lasted only two weeks, came and went during 1938–39. Workers raided the municipal palace once again in 1939. The new Governor Macías placed an FTS government in power to placate labor, possibly the result of a rumored Macías-CTM pact. But in the 1940 elections an independent with ties to the business community, Faustino Félix, surprisingly beat popular campesino leader Maximiliano López and established a council with CTS leader Simón Mercado. Businessman Abelardo Sobarzo replaced him for the 1941–1943 period. The struggle continued well into the 1960s.[8] These chaotic events demonstrate how polarized municipal politics had become by the late 1930s, especially in areas with a working-class power base.

The Watchdogs of Cárdenas: Military Zone Commanders and Politics

The president's power ultimately rested in his control of the military. Troops were concentrated in the north, with the Sixteenth Battalion stationed in Hermosillo, part of which was moved to the rebellious south of Sonora for temporary duty in 1938, and the Forty-third Cavalry Regiment spread out in small garrisons. These contingents were insufficient to cope with a full-scale rebellion but sufficed to suppress urban demonstrations. An additional 420 armed civilian reserves, with headquarters in Santa Ana, were scattered across the north. Troops based in Esperanza and reserves watched over the Yaqui and Mayo Valleys.

The military tended to be conservative. The U.S. consul in Nogales was thoroughly impressed by the officers, who were "extremely friendly" and "willing to dispatch troops to scenes of trouble where American interests were involved."[9] By the 1930s the military had reached a degree of professionalism, possibly due to the high turnover in command. It loyally followed orders from Mexico City and refrained from building close ties with regional elites.

The zone commander, designated by the president as a personal watchdog, was the key military actor. This was obvious during the restless days of 1937–38, when Cárdenas sent several generals to throw their weight behind the anti-Yocupicista opposition. In April 1937, Cárdenas appointed General Miguel Henríquez Guzmán, a trusted associate who had served in his home state of Michoacán and had commanded five different military zones, including the violence-ridden post-Garridista Tabasco, before being sent to Sonora. He was later transferred to San Luis Potosí, where he replaced the rebellious Cedillista Carrera Torres. In Sonora he assumed an openly anti-Yocupicista position: "Since his arrival [Henríquez] has taken advantage of every opportunity to attack the Governor."[10]

General José Tafolla Caballero succeeded him in August 1938, and immediately became the center of a national scandal. The general, who had served as cavalry commander in Michoacán, publicly pledged to support the collective ejido, unionization, socialist education, and the emancipation of the Indians. His strong comments were applauded by the left-wing press and the Cardenista establishment. The national *El Popular* cited Tafolla in a front-page article under the headline: "Sonora will be reincorporated into the Revolution. . . . General Tafolla is going to do it."[11] Cardenista senators warmly congratulated him for his courageous remarks: "Sonora was the only hope of the antirevolutionaries, and when the reactionaries saw the attitude of General Tafoya [*sic*], they saw their ambitions collapse."[12] The Right, however, was appalled and called for a reprimand: "A chief of operations . . . has nothing to do with the land question . . . neither is it his business to organize the proletariat or guide labor struggles; . . . much less is he affected by the problem of education." *El Hombre Libre* called him an "arrogant proconsul."[13] Defense Minister Manuel Avila Camacho finally censored him, calling his speech an "erroneous expression." As a sign of his disgust, Tafolla returned an automobile that Yocupicio had given him and implicated Yocupicio's treasurer in a tobacco-smuggling scheme.[14]

He created a commotion by intervening in several labor conflicts in the Mayo Valley. Yocupicio blew these conflicts out of proportion, raising a nationwide outcry which led to Tafolla's recall. The first incident involved an intra-union conflict among the seamstresses of Navojoa. Tafolla made the mistake of openly backing dissident seamstresses who sought to leave the CTS and join the FTS/CTM. Yocupicio denounced his statements as an attack against the sovereignty of Sonora.[15] The situation in the Mayo rapidly deteriorated. The election for *comisariado ejidal* of Bacobampo in October 1938 caused another serious conflict. For several months the mayor of Etchojoa and the state authorities had tried to oust the anti-Yocupicista *comisariado*. They made numerous arrests and disarmed the ejido's *defensa social*. The Bacobampo incident reflected the struggle between collectivist ejidatarios supported by the CTM and individualists backed by the Yocupicistas. The FTS/CTM tried to influence the election, as did Tafolla. The authorities responded by arresting dozens of *agrarista* leaders.[16] The Yaqui Valley *agraristas* dispatched 150 armed *reservas sociales* to the Huatabampo area. Yocupicio publicly accused the reserves of staging a rebellion and Tafolla of having instigated the events: "I have reached the conclusion that the agitation has been purposefully provoked, using the *defensas sociales* of the Yaqui Valley as an instrument, and invading this region with army units in open rebellion." The Sonoran Legislature passed a resolution censuring Tafolla and granted Yocupicio special powers to defend state sovereignty. This constituted a clear and dangerous act of defiance against the center.[17]

It was at this tense moment that the governor's close ties to Defense Secretary Manuel Avila Camacho became evident. Avila Camacho deemed it time to calm the inflamed spirits and bolster the position of Yocupicio. He arrived by plane in Navojoa the next day and traveled throughout the state with Yocupicio, visiting the Mayo. In Santa Ana the two, who were "extremely friendly to each other," were received with music, *bellas señoritas*, and an impressive *barbacoa*. Both the CTS and the CTM were on their best behavior and staged street demonstrations in favor of Avila Camacho. But the CTM soon grew openly critical of his conciliatory press declarations. "There have never been any troubles in Sonora, nor do I believe that there are any now. . . . You can convince yourself that all is quiet, and that everyone is happy and is tending to business. Whatever rumors about unrest that may be circulating in the capital and other places are baseless and are spread by persons interested in misleading the general public. . . . I am convinced that General Yocupicio will have justice done for all, following the wishes of President Cárdenas, who seeks the well-being of the people."[18] Avila's message to the CTM was to remain calm and support the governor. But in an effort to placate labor, he ordered that jailed CTM leaders be released. Consequently, CTM plans for a general strike were shelved. He left behind a somewhat pacified Sonora. Several days earlier, General Tafolla had departed for Mexico City, never to return.[19]

Yocupicio had weathered yet another challenge from the center, but only by allying with the increasingly influential faction of Avila Camacho. By making this move, and not joining the ill-fated Cedillo rebellion, Yocupicio secured his position as governor and was able to hand over his post to a hand-picked successor without major interference from Mexico City. By 1939, with Cardenismo on the wane and the Avila Camacho candidacy gaining steam, Yocupicio's future seemed more secure than ever.

Political Reform: The Formation of the PRM

Cárdenas had failed to control the Yocupicio government by means of the zone command. Now the reorganization of the official party along corporatist lines seemed a more subtle and promising method to strengthen the role of organized labor in unruly states such as Sonora. He tried to use the new PRM party structure to channel the popular vote in support of a Cardenista candidate for the governorship in the 1939 elections. Once Cárdenas had managed to implement crucial reforms, these had to be guarded for the future by a stable political system purged of reactionary elements which, in states such as Sonora, had infiltrated and gained control of the old Partido Nacional Revolucionario (PNR).

In 1938, Cárdenas boldly reconstructed the party into a semi-corporatist structure, the Partido de la Revolución Mexicana (PRM), which consisted of four sectors: labor, unified in the CTM; the peasantry, organized in the CNC; the "popular" or middle-class sector; and the military. One of the short-term results of this reform was to enhance the political clout of *agraristas* and organized labor. PRM primaries opened channels of representation to previously excluded groups. The sectoral nature of party elections converted organized labor into a crucial element. Women, too, participated in elections, though only in PRM primaries.[20] The PRM also allowed for a degree of upward mobility for labor leaders.

In Sonora this trend forced conservatives to include labor groups, in particular from the Yaqui Valley, in the political equation. From 1940 onward, we see labor and campesino leaders, such as Jacinto López, Saturnino Saldívar, Rafael Contreras, Aurelio García, Manuel R. Bobadilla, and Matías Méndez, serving as federal congressmen and senators alongside old Yocupicistas, such as Jesús María Suárez and Carlos B. Maldonado. The PRM gave these leaders national visibility and respectability and incorporated them into the political establishment. This process did not immediately convert Sonoran union leaders into dependent *socios en el poder*.[21] The rise of *charrismo* (the control of labor by union bosses) was an uneven process, and Sonora would still witness large-scale popular mobilization during the 1950s and 1970s. But union democracy perished quickly, due to the rising power of labor leaders, who functioned as intermediaries between the government and the masses. Ironically, in the long run the PRM's corporatist system of interest representation would afford the State with yet another means to control the popular sectors.

The increasing influence of labor was hotly contested by the Yocupicistas, who tried to take over the new party in the same way they had controlled the PNR earlier. The first step was to gain control of its leadership. The first president of the PRM regional committee was Yocupicio's trusted secretary, Adolfo Ibarra Seldner, a suave lawyer who had "earned a high reputation as a specialist defending capital against labor in Mexico City."[22] The important Secretariat of Peasant Affairs fell to the leader of the increasingly conservative Liga de Comunidades Agrarias/CNC. Although FTS/CTM leader Jacinto López was initially appointed head of the Secretariat of Labor Affairs, he was soon replaced by CTS leader Porfirio Valencia. The state PRM presidency changed hands rapidly but finally fell to Yocupicista state representative Francisco Ceballos.[23]

The Gubernatorial Elections: The Candidates

The 1939 gubernatorial elections were a test of Cardenista control of the new PRM. The contest would either result in the continuation of a conservative Yocupicista regime or in the rise to power of a pro-labor Cardenista administration. By the spring of 1938 it was clear that the race would be between Cardenista General Ignacio Otero Pablos and General Anselmo Macías Valenzuela, the Yocupicista *tapado*, with General Francisco Bórquez as a dark horse.

With Yocupicio substantially weakened, Otero, a career officer born in the Mayo, was in a better position than during the last elections, but much depended on the creation of a solid electoral base. It was here that he ultimately failed. It was essential to gain the backing of the FTS/CTM. For this purpose, Otero turned to

Lombardo, with whom he signed a pact in Mexico City. FTS leader Jacinto López was supposed to sell this agreement to his Sonoran constituency. This was yet another example of the phenomenon of *pactar*, the bargaining between politicians and labor so common during the 1930s. According to this pact, the state government was not to intervene in municipal politics, thus enabling labor to control towns such as Ciudad Obregón. It would recognize the FTS/ CTM as the state's most important labor federation and cancel the registration of *sindicatos blancos*—that is, dismantle the CTS. The FTS would gain representation in the state and national legislatures. The state bureaucracy would be purged of specific "enemies of the workers and peasants." Otero pledged to support agrarian reform, disarm *guardias blancas*, and stop "outside influences" from gaining control of CTM peasant organizations—that is, suppress the *individualista* ejidos.[24]

There was some disagreement in the ranks of the FTS on whether to chose Otero or Bórquez. An FTS convention was held in June, with serious repercussions for the Sonoran labor movement and for Otero. Afterward, Jacinto López proudly wrote to Cárdenas that the FTS had unanimously endorsed Otero. In reality this was not the case. A bitter feud erupted between López and other delegates who, distrustful of the FTS leader, accused him and Lombardo of having violated the federation's democratic decision-making process. The dissidents decided to back Bórquez. Many delegates, including Maximiliano R. López, Manuel R. Bobadilla, Matías Méndez, and Aurelio V. García, influential leaders of the Yaqui Valley ejidatarios, left the meeting, stating that they would not permit "a group of compañeros [to] try to commit an imposition without the authorization of their unions, designating the candidate from the capital of the Republic, without even letting their constituency know."[25] Echoing Yocupicio's regionalist rhetoric, they denounced Otero as "one of those professional politicians who don't know our environment, and who can't know the real needs of our State after an absence of twenty years or more, who only receive their information by means of correspondence from a distance of two thousand kilometers and gain support through bribes and promises."[26]

The split was backed by some two hundred of the four hundred CTM delegates, representing unions belonging to the Unión Agrícola del Valle del Yaqui, led by Maximiliano López, Méndez, and García; the Unión Agrícola Ejidal del Mayo; delegations of the SITMMSRM, Sections 6 (Cananea) and 76 (Cucurpe); delegations of the Federación del Distrito de Altar; and some delegations of the FOCSS and the STFRM of Empalme. Whether they formed a majority is less important than the fact that the FTS/CTM was thoroughly divided, with some of the most militant sectors backing Bórquez and repudiating the imposition.[27] *Charrismo*, closely linked to the government, had reared its ugly head, but it was hardly a success. López's decision to back Otero made political sense but seriously undermined union democracy. The dissidents could find no better alternative than to support the out candidate. Labor played according to the system's rules of pacts and alliances but was not ready to make a direct bid for the governorship. The results were catastrophic: with labor divided, Otero's candidacy was bound to fail. His campaign organization, the Partido Liberal del Obrero, Trabajador y Campesino de Sonora, consisted of a weak hodgepodge of politicos (Jesús G. Lizárraga, once again in the opposition, and Senator Andrés H. Peralta, a Cardenista watchdog); part of organized labor and the agrarian movement (Jacinto López, Saturnino Saldívar, and teachers' leader Hermenegildo Peña); and elites who joined to gain access to the political system. It was hardly a match for the Yocupicista machine.[28]

Yocupicio's candidate was General Anselmo Macías Valenzuela, born in 1896 in Agiabampo, Sinaloa, to an Alamos family. His enemies disparagingly nicknamed him *el sinaloense*, once again introducing the *patria chica* theme. He served in the Constitutionalist forces and became zone commander in various states. U.S officers described him as "young, intelligent, affable and ambitious . . . particularly partial to America . . . very friendly indeed with Almazán . . . and a good horseman and fair polo player."[29] Macías could boast excellent connections with the influential Portes Gil, having served as *jefe militar* in Tamaulipas, and as commander of the Presidential Guards during the Portes Gil interregnum, becoming his business partner and compadre. Equally important were his links to the campaign of Avila Camacho.[30]

Macías maintained close ties with Governor Yocupicio and was officially endorsed by the Sonoran Chamber of Deputies, the UNVR, the Liga de Comunidades Agrarias/CNC, and the CTS. This machine worked effectively at the local level, often through coercion. Yocupicio reportedly spent 20,000 pesos on the campaign, which also received support from merchants and landowners. Perhaps he backed Macías because he believed "that he would do as he was told," as "he appears to be much less forceful and to have much less character than . . . Yocupicio."[31] Macías's candidacy attracted support from Catholic women due to his moderate stance on the religious question. The Maciista party had a broad base, including Obregonista politicos such as former Governor Alejo Bay, pliant labor leaders such as José Abraham Mendívil and Porfirio Valencia, and members of the farming and ranching elites. Support was strong among the pre-Cardenista "official" Mayo Valley ejidos. He even courted the STERM teachers, indicating that he sought to abandon the more confrontational style of Yocupicio.[32] This pragmatism and tendency toward conciliation became evident when Macías reportedly dined with Lombardo in Mexico City and pledged to aid the FTS/CTM after his election. This move led to a distancing, if not a break, between Yocupicio and Macías.[33]

The third candidate was General Bórquez, a proponent of "real democracy" and *sufragio efectivo*. Most of his labor support came from dissident CTM groups of Yaqui and Mayo Valley ejidatarios opposed to the imposition of Otero. He was also popular with many Cananea miners.[34] What some considered a last-ditch attempt by Cárdenas and Lombardo to unify the CTM around a labor candidate occurred when a little-known former federal deputy and bureaucrat, Gustavo Padrés, arrived in Sonora in November 1938. His style was aggressive: he proposed to punish Yocupicio and attacked Otero as a corrupt antirevolutionary and criminal: "He assassinated people and buried them alive to get their money." Padrés was, however, unable to garner a significant following in such a short time.[35]

The central government desperately tried to impose a Cardenista candidate by using CTM control over key sectors of the working class, in particular the campesinos of the valleys. Jacinto López, a man closely linked to Lombardo, sought to harness his following in support of Otero. The center was not interested in an actual labor candidate but instead resorted to unpopular or unknown generals with factional ties. Such imposition from outside was a slap in the face to many workers and campesinos. This emerging *charrismo* led to a split within the ranks of the FTS and weakened Otero's chances. The Oteristas proved no match for Macías's well-oiled campaign machine.

The Campaign

The intensity of the campaign was reflected in mudslinging speeches and broadsheets. Otero told the press that "the situation in my state is terrible. Yocupicio is an absolute dictator." He accused Macías of being the candidate of landowners and reactionaries, of mobilizing followers by paying 10 pesos per horseman and 50 centavos per pedestrian, and of arresting and assassinating Oteristas. Broadsheets portrayed Macías as a corrupt, anti-Cardenista, fascist outsider. Padrés wrote to Cárdenas, complaining that during a speech Macías had said that "here in Sonora there is only one law: the BALLS [*HUEVOS*] of Yocupicio."[36] The Maciista press published statements by Otero's creditors complaining about debts related to the purchase of large quantities of beer.[37] The political culture of the era was characterized by personal insults, vendettas, street fights, cantina brawls, shootouts, assassinations, and occasional full-scale agrarian uprisings. Politicos regularly resorted to beatings, pistol-whipping, and chair throwing in the streets and in cantinas such as La Bohemia or the Club Social. The press reported several near duels, one involving Otero's brother.[38]

The candidates, adopting the classic Mexican campaign style institutionalized by Cárdenas, traveled throughout the state. Rallies were lively, at times rowdy, events, often characterized by drunkenness and violence, as the candidates frequently provided free beer.[39] Otero's tour was marred by disturbances that often reflected the split between CTM- and CTS-affiliated workers. On entering Nogales, his motorcade ran into sharp tacks and nails, which nearly caused several cars to overturn. When he tried to give a speech at the Customs House, he was received by a Maciista mob, "stomping, whistling, and howling like animals," who displayed a coffin with a sign stating: "Otero, May He Rest in Peace." Fistfights broke out between inebriated Oteristas and Maciistas.[40] Padrés was pelted with tomatoes and rocks, and during one of his speeches, the electricity was cut off. Followers were armed to the teeth. Padrés accused Macías of being supported by truckloads of drunken supporters armed with machine guns. It is hardly surprising that violent clashes led to fatalities: in Baviácora an altercation resulted in four dead and nine wounded. The unrelated assassination of Horacio Clark, a leading Agua Prieta Oterista, heightened tensions considerably.[41]

The PRM Primaries

Between December 1 and January 22, the PRM held primaries to designate candidates for governor and for state representatives. As a result of Cárdenas's reorganization, the election was not a plebiscite but organized, like the party, along corporatist lines. Individual sectors of the party, such as labor, the peasantry, and the popular sector, voted in separate assemblies. Votes were cast by members of unions, *comisariados ejidales*, women's leagues, and other organizations, which tended to cast bloc votes. Although women were not to receive the vote until 1953, they did participate in PRM primaries, constituting at least 10 to 20 percent of the vote. Women cast their ballots in so-called *ligas femeniles*, instead of through unions. Some observers considered these *ligas* populist machines, useful for expanding and manipulating the vote.[42]

The electoral machine was controlled by Yocupicio, who used it to impose conservative candidates. State officials spread Maciista propaganda and exerted pressure on the electorate. Government employees and CTS-affiliated workers were threatened with dismissal if they did not vote for the correct candidate. PRM committees and electoral delegations were all in the hands of Yocupicistas.[43] This did not leave the central government entirely powerless, however. The PRM representative sent from Mexico City to oversee the elections was rumored to be a relative of Otero and was bitterly denounced by Maciistas.[44]

The primaries were marred by massive, though unquantifiable, fraud. Maciistas and Oteristas spent the night prior to the elections handing out free beers, so that by election day many voters were drunk. They also mobilized large groups of workers, for example the CTS roadworkers, and trucked them into "enemy territory." Yocupicio tried to stop truckloads of Oteristas being transported from Ciudad Obregón to participate in the Etchojoa elections. The vote at the ejido San José de Bácum was cast by men driven in from elsewhere. Borquistas claimed that delegates failed to set up ballot boxes in heavily Borquista areas, while police officers stopped Padristas from voting in Hermosillo. Many of the Maciista unions voting in Ciudad Obregón were heavily padded with non-members, usually ejidatarios from Esperanza, Bácum, and El Júvani, who had already voted elsewhere and were now paid two pesos for their services. The assembly of the Sindicato de Veteranos de la Revolución in Ciudad Obregón was presided over by a PRM delegate who also happened to be the town's police chief. He appeared dressed in uniform with a pistol at his hip, accompanied by three uniformed policemen and four plainclothesmen. Violence and intimidation by politicians and police officers armed with Mausers and rifles was reported. Non-existent unions cast their vote. The usual "electoral alchemy"—tampering with voting lists, the robbery of ballot boxes, the cancellation of votes, and other tricks—occurred on a massive scale. Jacinto López reportedly suppressed

results from several Borquista mining camps.[45] The blatant character of the fraud, which strongly contrasted with the previous gubernatorial election, was well reflected by a comment, whether
apocryphal or not, of one PRM delegate: "Mr. Padrés, we want you
to be happy, so why don't you fabricate the votes that you still need
on the blank forms that we are willing to give you so that you can
fill them out the way you want, and I will sign them accordingly.
What else do you want?"[46]

The final result was close, despite massive fraud: Macías received 35,530 votes, Otero 33,449, Bórquez 1,413, and Padrés next
to none. These figures, which reflected the strength of the machines
more than popular choice, are obviously of limited significance.
Bórquez correctly pointed out that it was odd that while during
previous elections a total of 37,000 votes had been cast, now both
the individual Maciista and Oterista tallies nearly equalled that figure. He identified massive fraud in the so-called popular sector,
where Macías received more than 18,000 votes, more than his combined vote from the agrarian and labor sectors, with Otero not far
behind with almost 15,000.[47] It was here that large-scale manipulation probably occurred.

The contest in the agrarian and labor sectors was more interesting. Although fraud was rampant, one can glean some conclusions from an analysis of the results. The Hermosillo district results
showed a major victory for Macías thanks to support from the CTS,
including dubious unions such as the Sindicato de Veteranos
Trabajadores, some ejidos, and many newly formed women's unions
of domestics, seamstresses, and cooks. Otero carried local CTM
unions (bricklayers, movie projectionists, tobacco workers), and federal employees such as the health-care workers and federal teachers.[48] These results reflected a balance between the CTM and the
CTS, tipped in favor of Macías by the machine. Northern Sonora
was largely in control of the Maciistas, especially in towns such as
Nogales, where Macías was supported by veterans' organizations,
CTS unions, and state teachers, while Otero received votes from
federal employees and the CTM. Bórquez carried the independent-
minded Cananea miners of the SITMMSRM, while Macías controlled the Yocupicista miners of Pilares. In Guaymas, Otero fared
poorly, faced with the opposition of strong CTS unions, including
the dubious roadworkers' union, certain ejidos, railworkers, veterans, and CROM unions.[49]

Electoral control of the Mayo Valley, with more than ten thousand ejidatarios and *agraristas*, was essential. Here Macías won

handily with support from old prosperous town ejidos and the large, conservative ejidos formed from above during the Calles governorship, including La Unión, San Pedro, Moroncarit, San Ignacio, Tesia, and Navojoa. Otero won in radical strongholds such as Etchojoa and Basconcobe, both new Cardenista ejidos, and in numerous smaller ejidos with meager resources and a membership ranging in the dozens instead of the hundreds. This pattern reflected a split between the haves (large ejidos with access to water, land, and credit, and with political ties to Hermosillo) and have-nots (the smaller ejidos). Obviously, the fact that Yocupicio hailed from Masiaca and that one of his relatives, Miguel Yocupicio, was running for representative also helped Macías. In the Mayo ejidos, women formed 20 percent of the electorate and tended to follow the general vote.[50]

The Yaqui Valley, with 3,750 ejidatarios and *agraristas*, thousands of rural proletarians, and the population of the booming town of Ciudad Obregón, was another key area. Here results were clear: the Maciista machine was too weak to defeat Otero, who garnered 2,705 votes, Macías 1,385, and Bórquez 714. But this tally does not reflect the vote of a unified *agrarista* movement against a manipulative machine. The issue is more complex. The vote (and high abstention rates) reflected severe divisions between a pro-Otero, Lombardista faction led by FTS leader Jacinto López, who exerted strong pressure on ejidos to follow the official line, and a "democratic" sector led by Maximiliano López, consisting of the ejidos of Cócorit, Providencia, El Yaqui, and Campos 47, 77, and 60. There existed an additional split within many ejidos between collectivists and individualists, the latter favoring Macías, who, like Yocupicio, advocated the parcelization of collective ejidos. Thus, the ejido vote, 35 percent of the total, was split three ways: 537 votes for Otero, 660 for Bórquez, and 500 for Macías. The natural clientele of Cárdenas, those who might be expected to have been easily incorporated into the populist corporatist machine, failed to support the official candidate unanimously. It was not the ejidatarios but the rural proletarians (30 percent of the vote), the field and irrigation workers (*jornaleros*) organized in CTM-affiliated Sindicatos de Obreros y Campesinos, which overwhelmingly backed the Cardenista candidate: from them Otero received 1,255 votes, as opposed to 159 for Macías and 53 for Bórquez. It seems that the Cardenista-Oterista populist campaign appealed most to the have-nots. Urban labor (construction workers, bakers, carpenters) constituted 18 percent of the vote and were split between Oterista CTM unions and Maciista CTS unions. It was here that the Maciista machine was most capable of manipulation, especially with the large, rapidly formed CTS union of Jornaleros de Caminos, the Sindicato de Empresa del Yaqui, and in particular the Sindicato de Veteranos de la Revolución, whose members were ejidatarios from pro-Macías ejidos who could be counted on to vote twice. Such manipulation was, however, unsuccessful in giving Macías the needed edge. A mere 10 percent of the vote consisted of women's leagues, who overwhelmingly favored Otero. Finally, a small but loyal group of followers were the federal teachers, who voted for Otero, and the state teachers, who voted for Macías. We thus find a pattern of divided ejidos, not easily manipulated by the Cardenista machine, a largely Oterista-Cardenista rural proletariat, and a divided urban work force, of which the recently organized sector of *jornaleros* was easily manipulated by the CTS and Yocupicio. The divided agrarian movement was incapable of defeating the Macías-Yocupicio machine outside of the Yaqui Valley.

Electoral Results in the Yaqui Valley[51]

Percent of Total Vote	Otero	Bórquez	Macías	Total
Ejidatarios (35%)	537	660	500	1,697
Rural proletariat (30%)	1,255	53	159	1,467
Urban labor (18%)	301	0	556	857
Teachers, office workers (3%)	77 (43)*	1	62*	140
Women's leagues, unions (10%)	399	0	108	507
Others	136	0	0	136
Total	2,705	714	1,385	4,804

Note: An asterisk indicates votes by teachers.

The Hermosillo convention of the PRM reviewed the results on February 5. It was then that the Sonoran and national machines had to reach agreement. After a last-ditch effort by the PRM National Executive Committee to avert his victory, Macías was finally declared the candidate anyway, reportedly after pressure by Yocupicio and Avila Camacho. Rumors, denied by Macías, spoke of a Macías-Lombardo pact, in which Lombardo would choose the candidates for *secretario de gobierno*, three state representatives, the president of the state Conciliation and Arbitration Board, the head of the Labor Department, and several municipalities. Relations between Yocupicio and Macías rapidly deteriorated due to the latter's willingness to talk with the CTM. The FTS/CTM and the Oteristas initially claimed treason by the PRM and Lombardo but ultimately abided by the decision, later endorsing Macías.[52] Bórquez, who called the election a blatant imposition, decided to run against Macías in the final elections as an independent. The primaries also involved the election of state representatives, mayors, and police chiefs and thus permitted the Maciista machine to gain a firm hold on the entire state apparatus.

In the final election, Bórquez's Partido Democrático did not have a chance against the well-oiled machine of Macías, who was, of course, declared victorious. His candidates for representatives, a group of Maciista-Yocupicista politicians and CTS leaders, formed the 1939–1941 legislature as the reward for their services. They included campaign managers, the governor's relative Miguel Yocupicio, CTS leaders, and a former Yocupicista representative.[53] Municipal politics reflected the domino effect as well, but not as neatly, since local politics was much harder to control. In restless Ciudad Obregón, Maciista Faustino Félix defeated the popular campesino leader Maximiliano López. In Bácum, the ejidatarios' candidate Vicente Padilla claimed victory, but the regional PRM committee decided in favor of his opponent instead. Ranchers came to power in many northern towns: Roberto Urias in Magdalena, Manuel Mascareñas Jr. in Nogales, and Juan Caballero, a 1935 rebel, in Altar. Captain Armando E. Carrillo won in Arizpe, despite accusations that he was a crony of the region's largest rancher, Jesús Elías. Intervention by the state Congress also settled the elections in labor strongholds such as the railroad town of Empalme, where it overturned the victory of the railworkers' candidate. It declared Maciista Abelardo B. Sobarzo mayor of Hermosillo. The municipal elections were extremely messy. Results were nullified in most Sonoran towns, but opposition to blatant imposition led Governor Macías to adopt a conciliatory stance in certain municipalities. The most striking case was in Ciudad Obregón, where the new governor designated a provisional CTM *ayuntamiento* after Mayor Félix resigned due to growing CTM opposition. He realized that political space had to be given to labor to calm down tensions that had mounted under Yocupicio.[54]

Conclusion

In 1938, Sonora was polarized more than ever between a popular Cardenista coalition and a conservative government. The conflict, which focused on labor representation, was particularly fierce at the municipal level, where Yocupicista mayors faced a strong, at times armed, labor-*agrarista* challenge. The Yocupicista power bloc, which controlled the municipalities, excluded workers and peasants and tried to exert its influence in the ejidos. By 1938 many of these groups had been armed by the Cárdenas government and reacted to exclusion by openly rebelling in Agua Prieta, Ciudad Obregón, and Bacobampo. Cárdenas endeavored to strengthen popular forces by sending an outspoken, loyal zone commander to intervene. This plan was foiled by Yocupicio, who relied on his clientelist ties with Defense Secretary Avila Camacho to undermine the position of Cárdenas's emissary. After the Tafolla fiasco, Cárdenas turned to Sonoran electoral politics in an effort to oust the conservative faction, once again with little result.

The 1939 elections demonstrated how Cárdenas tried to use the new corporatist PRM structure to mobilize support for Cardenista candidates. His effort failed for several reasons. In the first place, Yocupicio managed to assert his control over the Sonoran PRM, adding it to his already formidable machine, which also included the CTS, an essential vehicle for the mobilization of rural laborers, veterans, and members of older, individualist ejidos. Cárdenas failed to impose unity on the Sonoran workers because of his use of *charrismo*—that is, the Lombardo-López-Otero pact, which only managed to create divisions. Important sectors of labor, such as the Yaqui Valley campesinos and the miners, refused to accept this violation of union democracy. Thus, Otero's main support did not come from the ejidatarios, whose vote was split, but from the landless rural workers of the valleys. The ejidatarios, with their organization, arms, and land, did not constitute an easily manipulated clientele.

The result of this disunity was conservative *continuismo* and the defeat of labor. The Yocupicista-Maciista machine won the elections without serious problems. Yocupicio had managed to outwit Cárdenas once again. But the new governor had learned an important lesson: the state's political system would remain unstable without some type of modus vivendi with the CTM. Macías discarded Yocupicio's stubborn approach and soon demonstrated a new willingness to negotiate with Cardenista labor.

Epilogue

The New Accommodation

2 Muertos hay junto al quicio
vigilando eternamente,
pues temen que Yocupicio
resucite de repente.
—*El Imparcial*, November 2, 1939

The Cárdenas Visit

Once the situation in Sonora had calmed down, Cárdenas deemed it time to visit the recalcitrant state. His stay symbolized the moderate, conciliatory approach that prevailed in the wake of the 1938 petroleum expropriation. The president assured Sonoran elites that further reform was not to be expected. He arrived on May 22, 1939, entering through the desolate Cañón del Púlpito on the Chihuahua border. His motorcade was awaited by Governor Yocupicio, Governor-elect Macías, and an honor guard of mounted ranchers and cowboys. The next day he visited Agua Prieta, where he promised cattlemen that further land expropriation would not occur: "The pleasing personality of the President has had the effect of winning to him many of the individuals who disliked his so-called radical policies."[1] He traveled by train to Nacozari, where, in the *casa grande* of the Moctezuma Copper Company, he received miners' unions and a delegation of *damas católicas*. In Pilares, Cárdenas drank coffee with members of the miners' cooperative, seated on the ground under the welcome shade of an old mesquite tree. In Ures, campesinos entertained him with a grand fiesta during which forty calves were served, washed down with eighty kegs of beer.

He made his entry into Hermosillo on foot, flanked by Yocupicio and Macías. Here he remained for several days, receiving hundreds of visitors in Yocupicio's office in the Governor's Palace, attending a banquet in the Casino, a sports festival, a *gran baile*, and the 4th

Industrial, Agricultural, and Ranching Exposition. The cattlemen offered him a *comida ranchera* with "grilled beef, *barbacoa*, green chile salsa, beans, beer, music, camaraderie, simplicity, an absence of formality, and affection for President Cárdenas and Governor Yocupicio." The president was soon joined by his wife Amalia and the young Cuauhtémoc. From Hermosillo he made trips to the north, where he was given "a rousing welcome by the laboring classes."[2]

President Lázaro Cárdenas (center) and Governor Yocupicio (right) at the opening of the IV Exposición Industrial, Agrícola y Ganadero del Estado de Sonora, 1939. *Memoria de la gestión gubernamental del C. Gral. Román Yocupicio, 1939*

Cárdenas spent more than a week in the Yaqui Valley, not, it must be stressed, in Ciudad Obregón, which he only visited for a day, but in Pueblo Vícam, in the heart of the Yaqui tribal lands. There he received delegations from all the Yaqui pueblos, granted them water rights, and forbade the sale of liquor. He also met with some thirty *comisariados ejidales*. In Ciudad Obregón, the CTM staged a mass demonstration of two thousand workers and campesinos. Cárdenas pleased Obregonistas by paying a visit to María Tapia, the wife of former President Obregón, at the Hacienda El Naínari. From there he traveled to the Mayo Valley and Guaymas.[3]

All in all, the visit by Cárdenas left many Sonorans impressed with his conciliatory demeanor and largesse. He made an effort to listen to all groups and to travel to all corners of the state. Although such factors are intangible, his stay undoubtedly contributed to the increasing accommodation between Sonora's political actors.

The Macías Government and the Politics of Accommodation

The Macías government reflected the new, more subtle, co-optive political system that emerged in Sonora after the period of polarization of 1934–1938. This involved a political pact with the opposing coalition led by Lombardo Toledano and Jacinto López. The less-polarized atmosphere also opened the door for increasing political participation by the economic elites. This pattern was quite distinct from that described by Peter Smith for the national level. Smith identifies two distinct elites in postrevolutionary Mexican society, one political and one economic.[4] In Sonora, however, both elites cooperated closely and even overlapped. The new postrevolutionary political elite was a mixture of diverse origin. It consisted

President Lázaro Cárdenas (right) during his visit to Sonora, flanked by Governor Yocupicio (center) and General Macías (right). *Memoria de la gestión gubernamental del C. Gral. Román Yocupicio, 1939*

of revolutionary politicians, such as Macías and Abelardo Rodríguez, and their offspring, such as Alvaro Obregón Tapia; members of the economic elites (merchants, landowners), including Ignacio Soto and Roberto Urias; middle-class politicos, especially lawyers;

and labor leaders emerging both from the CTM (Jacinto López, Maximiliano López, Matías Méndez) and the CTS.

Macías took the oath of office on September 1, 1939. In his inaugural speech he adopted a conciliatory tone. As Avila Camacho later did during his presidential campaign, Macías called for unity, and pledged to aid both labor and capital and to defend political freedom. He promised to support unions without preference, thus holding out an olive branch to the CTM. More than five thousand workers and campesinos attended the inauguration together with the interior minister, representatives of the governors of Puebla and Arizona, and the presidents of the Chambers of Commerce of Hermosillo and Tucson. The festivities were organized by the Comité de Festejos, the membership of which included not only the Yocupicista-Maciista faction but also prominent landowners and merchants, indicating an increasing intermixture of political and economic elites.[5]

Macías's cabinet, though not a mere recycling of the old Yocupicista clique, featured many familiar faces. The Obregonista faction was represented by Alejo Bay, who received the Treasury. The CTS leadership played a prominent role: José Abraham Mendívil headed the Labor Department. The legislature was staffed with prominent Maciistas and Yocupicistas. The municipalities presented more problems, leading Macías in rare cases (Ciudad Obregón) to abrogate local power in return for political peace. Macías irritated Yocupicio by moving toward a settlement with the CTM. Several of Yocupicio's former supporters, now disgruntled, even drifted into the ranks of right-wing opposition movements, such as the Partido Acción Nacional and the Almazán campaign.[6]

The CTM was quite amenable to a closer relationship. In September 1939 the president received a surprising letter eulogizing Macías, signed by Vicente Lombardo Toledano, Fidel Velázquez, Jacinto López, Rafael Contreras, and Roberto Espinosa Pérez: "With the new government of the state of Sonora, presided over by General Anselmo Macías, a new era of Hope has opened for all Sonoran workers."[7] Both parties realized that the polarization of the Yocupicio era had been counterproductive and were under pressure from the federal government to make peace. The debacle with Otero had been a traumatic experience for the workers, many of whom felt betrayed by the manipulation of the PRM and the CTM. During 1940–41, labor conflicts and strike activity declined. The intense power struggle between the CTM and the CTS subsided after CTM leaders Lombardo and Alejandro Carrillo visited Sonora to patch up relations with the CTS and officially endorse Governor Macías.[8] The press scaled down its attacks against the CTM and actually praised the federation's moderation. The days of CTM militancy in Sonora were over. Ex-Governor Yocupicio continued to lambaste the CTM, but his aggressive style now seemed outmoded.

The New Settlement and the Presidential Elections of 1940

With the aid of national leaders, Macías had reached a modus vivendi with the CTM and succeeded in overcoming extreme polarization. His political machine, now supported by the CTM, would be used to ensure the presidency for Macías's ally Manuel Avila Camacho. The Sonoran right still owed Avila Camacho a favor for having protected Yocupicio in times of crisis. And he desperately needed a favor. The "unknown soldier" was not popular among Sonorans. His victory in Sonora would be the result of machine politics.[9]

The conservative opposition candidate was Juan Andreu Almazán, a wealthy businessman and former zone commander of Nuevo León who maintained close ties to the Monterrey bourgeoisie. In Sonora, Almazán drew widespread support from merchants, ranchers, mineowners, and the Catholic Church. Even sectors of the lower classes, such as conservative mineworkers, favored him. Besides this broad following, Almazanismo was represented by such political outs as defeated gubernatorial candidate Bórquez and by such eternal opposition members as Israel González, Jesús Lizárraga, and "El Mocho" Coronado.[10]

In January 1939, Macías himself launched the Avila Camacho campaign in Sonora with the blessing of Yocupicio. This secured the automatic though half-hearted support, generally obtained through "veiled threats of duress by their superiors," of federal and state employees. Organized labor was a crucial element. The CTS, the CTM, and veterans' organizations endorsed Avila Camacho and reportedly provided 150,000 pesos for the campaign. While labor could be manipulated, it was considerably more difficult to gain widespread support from the economic elites. Macías exerted considerable pressure, reportedly forcing the cattlemen to provide 60,000 pesos for the campaign fund, the merchants of Nacozari another 6,000. The elites of Agua Prieta, where Almazanismo was strongly entrenched, failed to cooperate and were punished by tax increases and the closure of several saloons and clubs owned by Almazanistas.[11]

The campaign was run by Maciista and Yocupicista politicos. The machine in itself was not deemed sufficient to ensure an Avila Camacho victory. The authorities and their paid gangs of thugs harassed the Almazanistas. In Navojoa, hundreds of rock-throwing and knife-wielding Avilacamachistas attacked an orderly march of Almazanistas in March 1940. They broke down the door of the Almazán campaign headquarters, destroyed propaganda material, smashed furniture, and stoned trucks carrying Almazanistas. Several persons died in the riots.[12] Much of the violence was the work of the club-wielding goons of El Guarache, a political gang captained by José A. Mendívil and Jesús López. One member later fondly recalled how the group had disturbed Almazanista rallies by sprinkling ammonia among supporters and storming their opponents' platform during speeches. They burned down the Almazanista campaign headquarters in Santa Ana. El Guarache leaders even considered the use of *delincuentes bien enmariguanados* (delinquents high on drugs) as "shock troops."

Violence exploded when Almazán visited Hermosillo on June 26, 1940. According to one account, fireworks went off among the crowd as his train entered the station. These were answered by shots from the train. Chaos ensued: "The tumult was converted into an inferno of gunshots, kicks, yells, moans, laughter, cudgel blows, stone throwing, and bottle throwing." In the commotion one person was shot dead, another wounded. Galaz recalls how the dead man's body was paraded down the streets the next day by a funeral procession carrying large placards denouncing Almazán as an assassin. "I can't avoid a mocking smile when I think about the quick-wittedness and lack of scruples of the politicians, because my dear bemoaned friend Chicho [the victim] WAS AN ALMAZANISTA."[13] Avila Camacho won the elections in Sonora handily. The machine was in place and worked well. Too well, one might say—the PRM primaries were a farce. By September 23, Avila Camacho was leading by 50,566 votes to Almazán's 84.[14]

General Yocupicio

In his farewell speech, Yocupicio announced his retirement from politics "without hate or rancor," stating that he planned to settle in the countryside. He left for Tucson to tend to his wife, who was recuperating from an operation. Rumors about possible appointments or a bid for the presidency never materialized. After his retirement, Yocupicio repeatedly wrote to Cárdenas and visited him in Mexico City and Pátzcuaro, always appealing to the *respetable Jefe*, as he addressed him, for favors for his cronies or the Indians. In 1940 he founded a logging company and asked Cárdenas to grant him a concession in the Mesa del Campanero. Here he received guests such as Abelardo Rodríguez, whom he would proudly drive around the mountain in a pickup truck. Yocupicio died quietly on September 4, 1950.[15]

His retirement was not quite as innocent as it may seem at first glance. He resented Macías's rapprochement with the CTM intensely. Possibly as a warning to Macías, he conspired in one last uprising, once again using the Mayo Indians' profound religiosity as a means of mobilizing popular discontent. The 1939 Mayo revolt was a complete fiasco but undoubtedly served its political purpose.

The Struggle Continues

The modus vivendi between conservative factions and labor lasted until the late 1940s. During this period the CTS gained strength thanks to its close ties with the governments of Macías and his successor, the "millionaire of the Revolution," General Abelardo Rodríguez. Meanwhile, the CTM languished, a reflection of its declining militancy.[16]

The period of accommodation ended in 1948, when Lombardo left the increasingly dependent CTM and founded a new, militant national labor federation, the Unión General de Obreros y Campesinos de México (UGOCM), and an independent party, the Partido Popular (PP). His close associate, the prominent Sonoran labor leader Jacinto López, immediately abandoned the CTM and joined the UGOCM, becoming the federation's first secretary of labor and bringing a large part of the Sonoran ejidatarios with him.[17]

The year 1949 was crucial for Sonoran politics. Popular forces that had lain dormant for nearly a decade now reemerged to support the Partido Popular candidacy of López for governor. Labor finally made a direct bid for power. However, a non-Priista labor governor was unthinkable. Conservative political groups in Sonora and Mexico City imposed an apolitical industrialist, Ignacio Soto, with the aid of troops. This intervention, followed by a purge of UGOCM unions, dealt a demoralizing blow to Sonoran labor. Many leaders were persuaded to rejoin the CTM.[18] The governorship remained solidly in the hands of conservative factions linked to business interests. What could be more telling than the election of Alvaro Obregón Tapia, the son of former president Obregón, in 1955?

Labor continued its efforts to gain control of the fiercely contested municipal government of Ciudad Obregón, but, as before, with mixed success. From 1943 to 1946 the CTM was in power once again, with Heriberto Salazar as mayor. But the pro-labor municipal council of Vicente Padilla was removed from power in 1949, while campesino leader Rafael Contreras failed to win the elections of 1958, despite overwhelming popular support. Even the now rehabilitated Rodolfo Elías Calles had a go at the mayorship, from 1952 to 1954. The repression of labor reached new levels of violence in 1953 with the assassination of Maximiliano López, a much-respected *agrarista* veteran.

The old *agrarista* struggle, characterized by campesino mobilizations and the invasion of latifundios, continued. A massive UGOCM-sponsored invasion of the lands of the Cananea Cattle Company in 1958 forced the Mexican government to expropriate. The latest great wave of agrarismo swept Sonora in 1975–76. Thus, Sonora remained highly polarized during the postrevolutionary years, and witnessed recurrent attempts by the successors of the Cardenista popular coalition to gain political power and access to land. However, the political and economic system remained largely in control of conservative factions, closely allied to the agro-industrial bourgeoisie, as had been the case during the years of Lázaro Cárdenas.

Conclusion

Today in Sonora little remains to remind one of the heady days of Cardenismo, and Sonora certainly cannot be considered a neo-Cardenista bulwark. But as one digs beneath the surface, it soon becomes clear that the Cárdenas period has not been forgotten and is still considered controversial by many Sonorans, who discuss it with some reserve. As Steven Sanderson points out, "Unfortunately, Sonoran historians tend to gloss over the Yocupicio period, and much more work remains to be done to complete this fascinating story."[1] This study does not pretend to complete the story, but my findings can be used to re-examine existing interpretations of Cardenismo and of the Mexican Revolution, and to trace the contours of an important episode in Sonoran history. Avoiding black legend and hagiography, I have tried to flesh out the diverse meanings of Cardenismo to a heterogeneous population and reach a balanced understanding of the way in which the postrevolutionary political culture of Sonora and Mexico developed during the days of Lázaro Cárdenas.

To what extent did Cardenista goals and policies constitute a novel, radical attempt to restructure Mexican society? Was Cardenismo a democratic, popular, bottom-up movement or an authoritarian top-down imposition? How powerful was the State under Cárdenas, and to what extent did sectors of society successfully oppose Cardenista reform? And finally, how radical were Cardenismo's long-term effects?[2] These queries, suggested in the work of Alan Knight, provide an analytical framework with which to approach this complex historical problem.

Cardenismo: A Radical Project?

Sonora did witness a radical attempt to transform society during the 1930s, although it was as much the product of worker and peasant agency as of top-down Cardenista reform. In the new Sonora, workers would play an important political role and enjoy the fruits of their labor. Land reform would create a balanced system of land tenure, while educational and cultural campaigns would foster the development of a secular, modern citizen. This vision of the future had little to do with socialism, despite the frequent use of socialist rhetoric. The Cárdenas administration was acutely aware of the "limits of state autonomy" and operated in a relatively pragmatic, cautious fashion. Cardenismo was not an isolated phenomenon, but an integral part of the revolutionary process, and manifested many similarities with earlier state- and national-level experiences. During the early years, Cardenismo was hardly characterized by progressive politics, but rather by the persistence of traditional, Machiavellian factionalism and by the continuation and radicalization of the revolution's cultural project. It was not until 1936–1938 that Cárdenas attempted to create a new society, and this short-lived, hesitant, and ill-fated effort was largely abandoned by 1940.

One of the most radical aspects of Cardenismo was undoubtedly the cultural project. Mexico's revolutionary elites, the carriers of a liberal, Jacobin ideology, sought to implement a transfer of sacrality away from religion by destroying its symbols and replacing it with a civil religion. Their ultimate goal was the creation of a revolutionary "new man." During the 1930s, leaders such as Cárdenas and Rodolfo Elías Calles intensified the cultural policies of their predecessors, utilizing civic festivals, education, popular theater, and iconoclasm in an effort to suppress "fanaticism" and "backwardness."

Cardenista labor politics were less radical and demonstrated a clear continuity with the past. During 1936–37 the national labor confederation, CTM, sponsored the unification of labor in state federations and tried to suppress its rival, the Callista CROM. This effort was carried out in an often heavy-handed, top-down fashion sure to polarize regional politics. After failing to impose a loyal Cardenista governor in Sonora in 1936, Cárdenas decided to forge a new alliance with the Sonoran workers and peasants, especially the *agraristas*. However, the new Federación de Trabajadores de Sonora was based on a pre-existing labor movement dating back to the early 1930s. Previously organized sectors, such as the mineworkers, railwaymen, and urban artisans, were joined on a massive scale by *jornaleros*, in particular the rural proletarians of the Yaqui and Mayo Valleys. It was this dynamic rural proletariat, organized in militant unions such as the FOCSS, which constituted the backbone of Cardenista labor in Sonora and other agricultural regions of the north such as Sinaloa and the Laguna. Without this support the regime might not have survived. In many states, such as Sonora, Sinaloa, Querétaro, Nuevo León, Puebla, Coahuila, and San Luis Potosí, the CTM and regional labor federations such as the FTS served as weapons against conservative power blocs, provoking mass repression, but seldom succeeding in gaining control of the state government.

Labor benefited substantially from the alliance with the Cárdenas government, which enforced federal labor legislation, defended the right to strike and unionize, boosted real wages, and sanctioned the closed shop. Benefits that had once only reached a limited sector of the working class were now extended to previously neglected groups, such as *jornaleros*, *peones*, and sharecroppers. However, by 1938 labor's militant campaigns in favor of radical collective contracts and workers' control went well beyond what the Cárdenas administration deemed prudent.

Mass land redistribution, a novelty in Sonora, was the linchpin of Cardenismo. The goals of agrarian reform were fourfold: to further the revolutionary cause of social justice, to revitalize the rural economy, to create a body of loyal armed ejidatarios, and to mobilize a new electorate for the revolutionary party. During the Cárdenas presidency, some 11,500 Sonoran campesinos received 528,000 hectares of ejidal lands. The old pattern of land concentration was radically changed. By 1940 the ejidos held a substantial 40 percent of irrigated lands, thus constituting a major component of Sonora's agricultural sector. In 1939, 31,000 Sonoran campesinos, nearly half of the population economically active in agriculture, were members of either ejidos or *comités agrarios*.

The Yaqui Indians were among the principal beneficiaries of Cardenista reform. In an unprecedented move, Cárdenas granted them half a million hectares of tribal lands. In doing so, he sought to end a struggle spanning two centuries, which posed a continuous threat to any administration, and to "uplift" and "assimilate" the Yaquis into the national mestizo culture. This process was, from the perspective of the government, a success. The Yaquis ceased to pose a military threat and even became staunch supporters of Cárdenas. Economically, they were slowly absorbed into the ejidal sector. Other ethnic groups were less fortunate. The Mayos, who lacked an enclave, fell prey to acculturation and loss of autonomy, which they resisted by means of futile millenarian revolts.

Thus, Cardenismo in Sonora was radical in the sense that it endeavored to reshape traditional culture, mobilize workers and peasants in support of the regime, and restructure labor relations and land tenure. But it showed a high degree of continuity with earlier revolutionary experiments and was only unprecedented in terms of scale. Cardenista reform was often a far cry from what workers and peasants actually hoped for and expected, and political motivations were always an important factor. The origins of much of Cardenista radicalism must thus be sought among the popular classes.

Cardenismo: A Popular Project?

If any political actor was radical, it was organized labor and its allies, including federal teachers and labor inspectors. It was among these groups that the outlines of a popular utopia emerged, albeit vaguely. They sought workers' control of railroads, mines, estates, and factories, as well as political power in the workplace and in municipal and state government. Their ultimate goal was to secure the presidency for the working class. Federal teachers also envisioned the emergence of a new Mexican culture.

Such radical ideals were ultimately too much for the Cárdenas administration, and it often felt compelled to rein in popular militancy. Cárdenas stimulated agrarian reform for both political and economic reasons. Workers' control of industry, on the other hand, though reluctantly accepted under special circumstances elsewhere in Mexico, received little support in Sonora. Entire sectors of the economy, in particular cattle ranching and mining, remained off limits. The cultural revolution was soon abandoned as counterproductive. Cárdenas, as much as anything, responded to grass-roots regional pressure. Much of the Cardenista project actually originated with the CTM and regional labor groups. Of course, State backing was essential for the implementation of reform. It is doubtful whether Sonoran land tenure would have undergone such a dramatic transformation without support from the center. But only the cultural project demonstrated all the characteristics of a top-down imposition. Not surprisingly, this project was the first to falter and, ultimately, fail.

Cardenista reform and social conflict in Sonora reflected the deepening of Mexican capitalism, as evidenced by the increasing proletarianization of the rural population, the rise of urban labor, and a fierce struggle for land and political power. Workers and peasants were hardly the puppets of a cynical Cárdenas government, but major political players who shaped the future of their nation. CTM mobilization was not the product of manipulative "populism," of a *política de masas* aimed at establishing an authoritarian Leviathan state. Until the late 1930s, regional CTM federations actually maintained a high degree of autonomy. The CTM's goals were not merely economistic. CTM federations actively sought political control at both the municipal and state levels. But though labor participated enthusiastically in electoral politics, it met with stiff resistance, and the danger of *charrismo* soon became evident. Labor leaders signed pacts with members of the political elite, such as gubernatorial candidate Ignacio Otero Pablos. Labor pacts involved pledges of political support in return for attractive points such as the exclusive right to represent labor, specific government positions, and lucrative contracts. Patron-client relations, though benefiting labor in the short term, caused leaders to lose sight of the interests of the rank and file, undermined union democracy, and opened the door to co-optation.

Likewise, Cardenista land reform was not necessarily an arbitrary, alien imposition on Mexico's peasantry, doomed to failure from the very beginning. It was driven by strong demand from below, especially from the landless rural workers of the valleys. The Sonoran ejido's main problem was political, not economic. Not all *agraristas* could be satisfied: the majority remained landless and soon felt betrayed by the government. Others resented *liderismo* and collective exploitation. Splits emerged between landless *agraristas* and ejidatarios, collectivists and individualists, CTM- and CNC-affiliated groups, old and new, rich and poor ejidos. Paradoxically, the creation of a Cardenista rural clientele undermined the unity of the agrarian movement.

Federal teachers were crucial disseminators of the Cardenista project, acting as cultural brokers between peasants and workers and the government. They served as *mentores socio-políticos* in villages and mining camps, later as union leaders and politicians, and battled conservative governors and caciques in states such as Sonora, San Luis Potosí, Nuevo León, and Tabasco. But by 1938 their days of glory were over. They suffered at the hands of repressive state governments and lost support from the president. Cárdenas responded to conservative pressure by admonishing teachers to tone down their radicalism and distance themselves from political struggles. Their social role was taken over by federal bureaucrats, and they ultimately became a pliant clientele of the central government.

Some labor groups maintained their distance from politics altogether, and concentrated on their own parochial goals. This was the case with the skilled mineworkers, who constituted a labor aristocracy with an independent, semi-artisanal mentality. Those miners who retained their jobs during the Depression benefited from labor legislation and successfully defended their privileges, but failed to form a close alliance with Cárdenas. Instead, many maintained an independent position or joined the state-controlled CTS. The invasion and occupation of foreign-owned mines by militant *gambusinos* was not a reflection of Cardenista economic nationalism and cooperativism, but the logical consequence of the violation of their moral economy.

Thus, the Sonoran case demonstrates that worker and peasant agency was an essential factor in Cardenismo. A cautious and reluctant Cárdenas was often pushed to implement sweeping reform. These findings contradict the extreme revisionist interpretation that views the Mexican Revolution as a process whereby a self-serving, middle-class revolutionary elite mobilized and manipulated the popular classes in an effort to gain control of the State.

Cardenista State Formation

The Cardenista State proved to be weak and incapable of implementing a long-term national reform project. From 1934 through 1936 it teetered on the brink of collapse, dependent on alliances with regional, often conservative, power groups. Cárdenas desperately sought to manipulate regional conflicts in an effort to consolidate his power in the face of the Callista challenge—not, it must be stressed, by mobilizing the "Cardenista masses," but through factional intrigue, military coercion, and the creation of unholy alliances with the enemies of his enemies. It would therefore be deceptive to overemphasize the difference between "reactionary" Callismo and "revolutionary" Cardenismo.

In the short run, Cardenista politics involved trading federal control of the states for a degree of regime stability. In Sonora, Cárdenas tolerated the victory of the popular conservative candidate, General Román Yocupicio, relegating ideological considerations to a secondary position. Radical reform would have to wait. In the long run this policy led to an anomalous situation: it strengthened conservative factions with an ideology diametrically opposed to Cardenismo that would subsequently attack the president's policies. The very process that enabled Cárdenas to consolidate a power base and implement reforms also undermined the future viability of his reform program. Although it guaranteed his temporary survival, it actually sealed the fate of revolutionary reform and set the stage for the counter-revolution of the 1940s.

Later, after surviving the Callista challenge, the government relied on organized, and often armed, workers and *agraristas*, as well as on zone commanders and an expanding federal bureaucracy, to maintain control in the provinces. Organized labor gave Cárdenas the strength to push through reform during a brief interlude from 1936 through 1938. This window of opportunity closed rapidly from 1938 onward, as the Cardenista State once again faced a series of economic, social, and political crises. The corporatist reorganization of the official party in 1938, which was meant to institutionalize working-class political participation and strengthen the revolutionary regime, was a failure in Sonora. Regional conservative groups handily turned the restructuring to their advantage, and forced Cárdenas to roll back his own reform project. Power was wrested from the followers of Cárdenas even before he left office. The president was unable to hand over a strong, centralized State to his successor.

Thus, Sonora can be used as a case study to critique a stubborn misconception concerning Mexican politics and state formation: the idea that Cárdenas established a *"presidencialismo feroz,"* "the Leviathan that ultimately devoured all of society."[3] Actually, as the Sonoran case demonstrates, far from constituting the omnipotent Leviathan state, the Cárdenas regime was vulnerable, relying as much on a multitude of risky regional alliances with often conservative political actors as on popular support. This study thus tends to discount those analyses of federal-regional relations during the 1930s that stress the destruction of regional power blocs by the scheming and coercion of an increasingly autocratic central government.[4] Instead, it emphasizes the manipulation of developments in the center by regional and local actors with their own agendas. One should use labels such as "Cardenismo" with great care. Carlos Martínez Assad depicts the Cardenista movement in Tabasco as "a whole series of disperse forces . . . usually motivated by completely contradictory objectives, united against Garrido."[5] Describing the Cardenistas in Michoacán, Paul Friedrich stresses driving forces such as factionalism, vendettas, and greed for land: "The triumph of Cardenismo also meant the satisfaction of individual avarice coupled with Machiavellian egoism."[6] A personalist and statist interpretation of Cardenismo has overestimated the power of the State and underestimated that of local societies.

The Sonoran case represents an intermediate phase in the state-building process between the predominance of regional autonomy characteristic of post-Independence, Porfirian, and revolutionary Mexico, and the more centralized polity of the postrevolutionary period. Conflicts in Sonora reflected the interplay of local, regional, and national politics. One cannot consider developments in Sonora in a vacuum. Although the postrevolutionary State was a key actor in the regional arena, it was a far cry from the authoritarian entity described by revisionists. Regional power groups could pressure and manipulate the center as well, especially during times of political breakdown, and were as instrumental as the "Leviathan on the Zócalo" in shaping contemporary Mexican society.

Anti-Cardenista Opposition and Its Impact

Opposition to Cardenismo was strong, diverse, and widespread throughout the presidential period. The culture wars of the 1930s clearly demonstrated the limits of revolutionary reform, and in Sonora this project largely failed. It was carried out for a limited period by a small cadre of politicians and teachers with some proletarian support. De-Christianization was vehemently opposed by the Church, Catholics (especially women), indigenous groups, and serrano communities, and became entangled with broader factional and class-based resistance. Opposition in Sonora coincided with widespread passive and armed resistance elsewhere in Mexico, including the Second Cristiada. Catholic pressure was a strong incentive for Cárdenas to moderate his policy of religious intolerance. Adverse to plunging the country into yet another civil war, he staged a slow retreat on religion. By 1938 religious practices were generally tolerated, and it was clear that the status quo would be restored. Mass opposition put a permanent end to State efforts to effect a Jacobin cultural revolution.

Cardenista land reform also met stiff opposition. The Sonoran landed elite actively resisted the threat of mass expropriations. Although the 1935 revolt reflected landowners' concerns, elite resistance was largely limited to lobbying, the harassment of agraristas, and pre-emptive reform, also a common last resort in the Laguna, Sinaloa, Puebla, Veracruz, Michoacán, and Chiapas. But neither the landed elite nor the Yocupicistas had an answer to the swift and profound process of land reform. During the *reparto*, landowners desisted from rebellion because of the threat of armed *agrarista* units. Land reform dealt the rural bourgeoisie, especially foreigners and those unable to fall back on diversified investments, a serious, though not mortal, blow. However, their resistance was not entirely in vain. It led to the wider drive for the protection of smallholdings (*la pequeña propiedad*), championed by many governors. By 1939 their pressure would force the president to moderate agrarian reform, and eventually contributed to the counter-reform of the 1940s. Ranchers were particularly successful. Cárdenas granted them *certificados de inafectabilidad*, and their economic power has since grown continuously.

Economic elites also considered *obrerismo*, especially unionization, as a threat to the status quo. Cárdenas stimulated the development of a strong and politically influential popular alliance with the revolutionary State. Elite resistance was only partly successful; they would manage to minimize, but not destroy, the political and economic power of organized labor. The Cardenista progressive labor coalition, in particular the CTM, also met fierce resistance from many state governments (in Sonora, Hidalgo, Tabasco, Veracruz, Tamaulipas, Michoacán, Puebla, México, Sinaloa, Nuevo León, and Tlaxcala). Eventually, most governors came to realize that repression was less effective than corporatist patronage. They used rival national labor federations (CROM, CGT) and regional federations such as the Confederación de Trabajadores de Sonora to attack and weaken the CTM and divide the working class. The formation of the CTS was a top-down type of mobilization, but surprisingly successful and enduring.

Anti-Cardenista resistance was often complex, and interacted with local and regional conflicts. For example, out factions used the Calles-Cárdenas split in a successful bid to oust dominant political elites and gain control of state, municipal, party, ejidal, and other political structures. The Mexican case coincides with Charles Tilly's theories on collective action: the opportunity arose at a moment of political crisis. The power vacuum was seized upon by regional groups pursuing their own agendas.[7] In Sonora, Obregonistas and Vasconcelistas wrested power from the Callistas, in the process gaining control of the PNR structure. Similar struggles occurred in states such as Jalisco, Oaxaca, Querétaro, and Tabasco. A general political realignment took place throughout Mexico (in Sonora, Puebla, Tabasco) after the fall of the Callistas, resulting in greater regional independence, not Cardenista hegemony.

The Opposition in Power

After coming to power in 1937, Yocupicio, like other governors, rapidly consolidated his power base, which consisted of state and municipal governments, the local PNR, the legislature, and the judiciary. He then set about to avert the implementation of Cardenista reform in Sonora. Informal factional ties permeated state institutions, where *compadrazgo* and revolutionary loyalty mixed nicely with technocracy and bureaucracy. The Yocupicio administration received endorsement from the economic elites, which, however, remained aloof from direct involvement in politics. Yocupicio organized a new, "white" labor federation, the CTS, which incorporated urban workers, veterans, state employees, miners, *gambusinos*, sectors of the industrial proletariat, and, above all, many previously unorganized day laborers. What characterized these groups was their recent organization. CTS members benefited by gaining subsidies, key positions on arbitration boards, lucrative and exclusive contracts for public works, and sinecures in local and state government. The CTS was more interested in establishing a monopoly than in labor rights. In return, it formed a counterbalance to the CTM, an electoral pool, a docile labor force, and a source of loyal Yocupicista politicians.

By 1938, Sonoran society was polarized between two opposing power blocs. The Cardenista coalition consisted of workers, *agraristas*, federal employees and teachers (all unified under the umbrella of the FTS/CTM), and the zone command. The Yocupicista bloc controlled the state apparatus and maintained close links with the bourgeoisie, but it also included popular sectors organized in the CTS and the UNVR, and state teachers and bureaucrats. The two were locked in a fierce and often violent power struggle, especially at the municipal level. Clashes between workers and Yocupicistas were common, as attested by uprisings in Ciudad Obregón and Agua Prieta.

Cárdenas tried one last time to gain control of Sonora during the strongly contested elections of 1939. His reorganization of the official party into the corporatist PRM seemed to offer labor a chance of attaining hegemony in Sonora. The PRM allowed popular organizations, including women's groups, a substantial say in the electoral process. This effort failed, however, when the state PRM fell into the hands of Yocupicio. Prior to the election, CTM leader Vicente Lombardo Toledano, FTS leader Jacinto López, and Cardenista candidate Otero had signed a political pact. However, rifts within the popular coalition soon became glaringly obvious. The ejidos were split between collectivists and individualists, and labor was divided between the CTM, CTS, and CNC. In an effort to unify these sectors, Lombardo and López resorted to *charrismo*, a move that only served to exacerbate the fragmentation of labor. Thus, the last opportunity of establishing a pro-labor, Cardenista government in Sonora was lost.

The Yocupicista machine worked smoothly and assured the victory of the conservative candidate, General Anselmo Macías Valenzuela. Conservative elites maintained their hold on the regional power structure. Labor lost much of its militancy. In response to a slowing economy and declining support from Mexico City, the combativeness of earlier days gave way to a defensive, pragmatic stance in labor conflicts.

Developments in Sonora were reflected at the national level. By 1938 rising regional opposition to Cardenismo in states such as Michoacán, Puebla, Veracruz, Nuevo León, Tlaxcala, and Tamaulipas converged, first in a conservative governors' lobby, which successfully pressured Cárdenas to moderate reform, and later in the conservative presidential candidacy of General Manuel Avila Camacho. In addition, sectors of the military, opposition factions, and the radical right exerted strong pressure on the government. Cárdenas was forced to renegotiate the balance of power with conservative regional groups after their qualified demonstration of patriotism and loyalty in 1938 during the Cedillo rebellion and the petroleum expropriation, which showed their willingness to operate within the bounds of the "revolutionary family."

The governors expressed their grievances during a series of meetings with the president. Their complaints, phrased in anticommunist discourse, included most of the Cardenista reforms, in particular agrarian reform (collectivism and the arming of *agraristas*), which they sought to replace with colonization schemes and support for small- and medium-sized holdings. They also opposed the growing power of the CTM, resented the radicalism of federal teachers, and called for an end to socialist education.

Cárdenas, beset by growing national and international opposition, was forced to tolerate conservative politicos such as Yocupicio and give in to their demands. He curtailed the activity of rural teachers, established the Oficina de la Pequeña Propiedad, discouraged further CTM attacks on governors, and slowed the pace of agrarian reform. Thermidor had begun. The conservative anti-Cardenista opposition soon sidetracked Cárdenas's radical candidate for the presidency, Francisco J. Múgica, in favor of conservative Avila Camacho. He won the 1940 elections thanks to the support of conservative regional machines, including that of Yocupicio. The counter-reform, which had begun as a regional rebellion against Cardenista reform, now controlled the presidency. The anti-Cardenistas would spend the next decade undoing much of the legacy of Cardenismo. The golden age of Cardenista reform, which had barely lasted two years, was over.

Cardenismo: The Long-term Effect

Cardenismo's changes were limited and their significance was ambiguous. Most profound were Cardenista attempts to boost the influence of labor and transform rural society. The Cárdenas years witnessed the entry of organized labor into the realm of politics. Labor demonstrated a keen interest in going beyond economist goals and sought direct political power. In towns with a strong labor presence, such as Ciudad Obregón and Cananea, workers were able to establish tenacious but unstable *obrerista* city councils. Labor was less successful in gubernatorial contests. In the elections of 1936 and 1939 it did not rely on an authentic working-class representative but on an outside politician designated by Cárdenas. The struggle of the Sonoran workers and ejidatarios for representation culminated in the failed 1949 gubernatorial campaign of home-grown labor leader Jacinto López. Power remained in the hands of conservative factions and economic elites, although labor representatives did play a junior role from the 1940s onward.

Cardenismo did not give rise to a new, popular, democratic political culture. Sonoran politics was still dominated by informal networks (factionalism, *compadrazgo*, revolutionary ties), political manipulation (electoral fraud, the purchase of votes, control of the press), and violence (verbal confrontations, assassinations, uprisings). However, there were novel elements that polarized politics: a new self-confidence, if not hubris, of labor, exemplified by mass participation in politics, sometimes via elections, sometimes via popular rebellions. But labor, unable to break the hold of the old system, soon settled for pacts, co-optation, *charrismo*, and economism. In return, labor leaders were incorporated into the political elite, while lip service was paid to their demands. Despite sporadic outbreaks of labor militancy, conflicts were now generally solved within the bosom of the "revolutionary family." Local or national bosses balanced interests and dictated solutions in an effort to maintain patriotic unity and class harmony. Although the Cárdenas years offered workers and peasants a political opening with which to establish a more democratic system, the outcome was authoritarianism.

Official discourse took on a populist note, regionalist, even indigenist and xenophobic. But regionalist discourse was often less a defense of state autonomy against the center than veiled manipulation of chauvinism in defense of class interests. It portrayed Sonora as a special entity where class harmony prevailed over hotheaded conflict. The world context also provided new elements of discourse drawn from fascist and socialist ideology, especially the Bolshevik Revolution. Franco, Hitler, Stalin, Roosevelt, and Mussolini were all added to Mexico's political imagery. Although fascism never congealed in a major movement, it was reflected in a dangerous rise in populist xenophobia. More importantly, regional political discourse assumed a marked anti-communist stance that would become the national norm by the 1940s and 1950s.

The socioeconomic structure of Sonora showed more evidence of change. But many of the gains of Cardenismo in the realm of labor and agrarian reform were ephemeral. Land reform was never complete and was insufficient to solve the problem of landlessness. *Neolatifundismo* soon reared its ugly head. The collective ejidos were plagued by internal strife and subject to official pressure. The relative economic importance of the ejidal sector declined during the 1940s as the dynamic private sector expanded with state support. The official federations, the CTM and CNC, lost much of their combativeness, while the militant UGOCM suffered official repression. The Sonoran bourgeoisie flourished, benefiting from the post-Depression boom of commercial agriculture, trade, ranching, and industry. Businessmen even began to participate directly in politics once again. The continuity of the Sonoran economic elites is marked: neither the revolution nor Cardenista reform replaced this group with a new revolutionary bourgeoisie.

In practical terms, Cardenismo was largely a failure. Its most enduring legacy was undoubtedly the Cardenista myth, an amorphous utopian dream which still retains much of its appeal. As Mexico continues to lurch from crisis to crisis, and as neo-liberalism erases the last vestiges of revolutionary reform, the echoes of Cardenista idealism can still be heard. Mexican historian Lorenzo Meyer, in a recent lament of the "second death of the Mexican Revolution," once again conjures up the hallowed specter of Cardenismo, "the last great utopia that we Mexicans as a nation have had." And he calls on his compatriots "to give new life to the essence of Cardenismo: to make of Mexico a just, democratic, and free nation."[8] But Cardenismo will only be of value as a model for the nation's future if we go beyond the myth and the utopian dream, and try to understand the day-to-day reality of the years of Lázaro Cárdenas.

Abbreviations Used in Notes

AAGES	Archivo Administrativo del Gobierno del Estado de Sonora
AELY	Archivo de Ernesto López Yeacas
AFJM	Archivo Francisco J. Múgica
AFT	Archivo de Fernando Torreblanca
AGN	Archivo General de la Nación
AHGES	Archivo Histórico del Gobierno del Estado de Sonora
APEC	Archivo de Plutarco Elías Calles
ARM/PHS	Archivo de la Revolución Mexicana/Patronato de Historia de Sonora
ASM	Arizona State Museum
CACAC	Correspondence, American Consular Agency, Cananea
CACG	Correspondence, American Consulate, Guaymas
CC	Confidential Correspondence
CPR	Consular Post Records
CR	Confidential Records
DA	Departamento Agrario
DAAC	Departamento de Asuntos Agrarios y de Colonización
DAT	Departamento Autónomo del Trabajo
DEF	Director de Educación Federal
DGEF	Director General de Educación Federal
GC	Guaymas Consulate
GR	General Records
GS	Gobernador de Sonora
HCS	*Historia contemporánea de Sonora*
HGS	*Historia general de Sonora*
MI	Military Intelligence
NAW	National Archives, Washington
NC	Nogales Consulate
OIPS	Oficina de Información Política y Social

PM	Presidente Municipal
RG	Record Group
RG, DGG	Ramo Gobernación, Dirección General de Gobierno
RP, FLC	Ramo Presidentes, Fondo Lázaro Cárdenas
SD	State Department
SEP/AH	Secretaría de Educación Pública/Archivo Histórico
SEP/ARPF	SEP/Archivo de Rurales y Primarias Foráneas
SG	Secretaría de Gobernación
SRA/AG	Secretaría de la Reforma Agraria/Archivo General
SS	Secretary of State
WTD	World Trade Directory

Notes

Introduction, xi–xix

1. Adolfo Gilly, ed., *Cartas a Cuauhtémoc Cárdenas* (México: Era, 1989), 238–39.
2. Frank Brandenburg, *The Making of Modern Mexico* (Englewood Cliffs: Prentice Hall, 1964), 10, 131.
3. John Gledhill, *Casi Nada: A Study of Agrarian Reform in the Homeland of Cardenismo* (Albany: Institute for Mesoamerican Studies, University at Albany, State University of New York, 1991), 28–30.
4. Partido Nacional Revolucionario, *La gira del General Lázaro Cárdenas* (México: PRI, 1986), 11; *Acción y pensamiento vivos de Lázaro Cárdenas* (México: Federación Editorial Mexicana, 1973), 10, 15, 191, 305; Frank E. Tannenbaum, foreword, to *Lazaro Cardenas: Mexican Democrat* by William Cameron Townsend (Ann Arbor: George Wahr Publishing Company, 1952), vi; Roberto Blanco Moheno, *Tata Lázaro: Vida, obra y muerte de Cárdenas, Múgica y Carrillo Puerto* (México: Editorial Diana, 1972), 432.
5. Nathaniel and Sylvia Weyl, *The Reconquest of Mexico: The Years of Lázaro Cárdenas* (London: Oxford University Press, 1939), 10–11, 381–84; Townsend, *Lazaro Cardenas*, 213, 365, 370, 372.
6. Anatol Shulgovski, *México en la encrucijada de su historia* (México: Ediciones de Cultura Popular, 1968); Olivia Gall, *Trotsky en México y la vida política en el periodo de Cárdenas 1937–1940* (México: Era, 1991), 344; Blanco, *Tata Lázaro*, 381–82; Adolfo Gilly, *El cardenismo, una utopía mexicana* (México: Cal y Arena, 1994), 396–404.
7. Nora Hamilton, *The Limits of State Autonomy: Post-Revolutionary Mexico* (Princeton: Princeton University Press, 1982), 281.
8. Ibid., 240–41; Alan Knight, "Cardenismo: Juggernaut or Jalopy?" *Journal of Latin American Studies* 26, no. 1 (February 1994): 79.
9. Gall, *Trotsky*, 225, 344.
10. José C. Valadés, *Historia general de la Revolución Mexicana: Un presidente substituto* (México: SEP, 1985), 189–93; Salvador Abascal, *Lázaro Cárdenas: Presidente Comunista*, 2 vols. (México: Editorial Tradición, 1988–89).
11. Alicia Hernández Chávez, *La mecánica cardenista* (México: El Colegio de México, 1979), 4; Luis Javier Garrido, *El partido de la Revolución institucionalizada: Medio siglo de poder político en México: La formación del nuevo Estado en México (1928–1945)* (México: SEP, 1986), 382–87; Octavio Ianni, *El Estado capitalista en la época de Cárdenas* (México: Era, 1977), chap. 9; Arturo Anguiano, *El Estado y la política obrera del cardenismo* (México: Era, 1975), 138–39, 92–93; Jorge Basurto, *Cárdenas y el poder sindical* (México: Era, 1983), 98.

12. Arnaldo Córdova, La política de masas del cardenismo (México: Era, 1974), 180.

13. Marjorie Becker, "Lázaro Cárdenas and the Mexican Counter-Revolution: The Struggle over Culture in Michoacán, 1934–1940" (Ph.D. diss., Yale University, 1988), 2–6, 23–24, 111, 129, 134. Also see idem, "Black and White and Color: Cardenismo and the Search for a Campesino Ideology," Comparative Studies in Society and History 29 (1987): 453–65; Gledhill, Casi Nada, 28–30, 65–66, 90, 106–7.

14. Marjorie Becker, Setting the Virgin on Fire: Lázaro Cárdenas, Michoacán Peasants, and the Redemption of the Mexican Revolution (Berkeley: University of California Press, 1995).

15. Hilda Muñoz, Lázaro Cárdenas: Síntesis ideológica de su campaña presidencial (México: Fondo de Cultura Económica, 1976), 13; Gall, Trotsky, 267; Ruth Berins Collier and David Collier, Shaping the Political Arena: Critical Junctures, the Labor Movement, and Regime Dynamics in Latin America (Princeton: Princeton University Press, 1991), 232–36; Robert Kaufman, "Industrial Change and Authoritarian Rule in Latin America: A Concrete Review of the Bureaucratic-Authoritarian Model," in The New Authoritarianism in Latin America, ed. David Collier (Princeton: Princeton University Press, 1979), 202. For a critique of presidentialism see Friedrich E. Schuler, Mexican Foreign Policy in the Age of Lázaro Cárdenas (Albuquerque: University of New Mexico Press, 1998).

16. Córdova, La política, 176.

17. Gilbert M. Joseph, Revolution from Without: Yucatán, Mexico, and the United States, 1880–1924 (Durham: Duke University Press, 1988), xxiii.

18. The historiography on the Mexican Revolution is vast. For a historiographical introduction see, for example, Alan Knight, "The Mexican Revolution: Bourgeois? Nationalist? Or Just a 'Great Rebellion'?" Bulletin of Latin American Research 4, no. 2 (1985): 1–37; Paul Vanderwood, "Building Blocks but Not yet Building: Regional History and the Mexican Revolution," in Mexican Studies/Estudios Mexicanos 3, no. 2 (1987): 421–32; Thomas Benjamin and Mark Wasserman, eds., Provinces of the Revolution: Essays on Regional Mexican History, 1910–1929 (Albuquerque: University of New Mexico Press, 1990).

19. Exceptions include Mark Wasserman, Persistent Oligarchs: Elites and Politics in Chihuahua, Mexico, 1910–1940 (Durham: Duke University Press, 1993); Becker, Setting the Virgin on Fire; Wil G. Pansters, Politics and Power in Puebla: The Political History of a Mexican State, 1937–1987 (Amsterdam: CEDLA, 1990); Daniel Nugent, Spent Cartridges of Revolution: An Anthropological History of Namiquipa, Chihuahua (Chicago: University of Chicago Press, 1993).

20. Bryan Roberts, "The Place of Regions in Mexico," in Mexico's Regions: Comparative History and Development, ed. Eric Van Young (San Diego: Center for U.S.-Mexican Studies, 1992), 227–45. Van Young defines regionalism as "the self-conscious identification—cultural, political, and sentimental—that large groups of people develop overtime with certain geographical spaces." See in the same collection idem, "Introduction: Are Regions Good to Think?" 2.

21. On Sonoran and norteño culture see, for example, Barry Carr, The Peculiarities of the Mexican North, 1880–1928: An Essay in Interpretation, Occasional Papers, No. 4 (Glasgow: Institute of Latin American Studies, University of Glasgow, 1971); Héctor Aguilar Camín, La frontera nómada:

Sonora y la Revolución Mexicana (México: SEP, 1985); Miguel Tinker Salas, "Under the Shadow of the Eagle: Sonora, the Making of a Norteño Culture, 1850–1910" (Ph.D. diss., University of California, San Diego, 1989); Friedrich Katz, *The Secret War in Mexico, Europe, the United States, and the Mexican Revolution* (Chicago: Chicago University Press, 1981), 18–21. For an interesting discourse-oriented analysis of *norteño* culture see Ana María Alonso, *Thread of Blood: Colonialism, Revolution, and Gender on Mexico's Northern Frontier* (Tucson: University of Arizona Press, 1995).

22. *Estadísticas históricas de México* (México: INEGI, 1985), 1:19.

23. Juan José Gracida Romo, "Génesis y consolidación del Porfiriato en Sonora (1883–1895)," and "El Sonora moderno (1892–1910)," in *Historia general de Sonora*, Vol. 4, *Sonora moderno: 1880–1929* (henceforth *HGS*), ed. Cynthia Radding de Murrieta (Hermosillo: Gobierno del Estado de Sonora, 1985), 4:54, 102; Evelyn Hu-DeHart, *Yaqui Resistance and Survival: The Struggle for Land and Autonomy, 1821–1910* (Madison: University of Wisconsin Press, 1984).

Chapter 1, "The Revolution Comes to Sonora," 3–21

1. Obviously, radical legislation had been implemented during the armed phase of the revolution and during the 1920s. However, Sonora's socioeconomic and political structure remained largely unchanged.

2. The term "Jacobinism," used by Mexicanists such as Jean Meyer, Alan Knight, and Carlos Martínez Assad, refers here to radical anticlerical and antireligious movements that sought to replace religion with a revolutionary civil religion. See, for example, Jean Meyer, *La Cristiada: El conflicto entre la iglesia y el estado 1926–1929* (México: Siglo XXI, 1973), 2:84–89.

3. François-Xavier Guerra, *Le Mexique: De l'ancien régime à la révolution* (Paris: L'Harmattan, 1985), 1:115; James C. Scott, "Patron-Client Politics and Political Change in Southeast Asia," *American Political Science Review* 66 (March 1972): 91–113.

4. Carlos Moncada O., *La sucesión política en Sonora (1917–1985)* (Hermosillo: Editorial Latinoamericana, 1988), 23–37; Rocío Guadarrama, "Las alianzas políticas," in *Historia general de Sonora: Historia contemporánea de Sonora 1929–1984* (henceforth *HCS*) (Hermosillo: El Colegio de Sonora, 1988), 77; Serie Sonora, 1a serie, reel 9; Fernando A. Galaz, *Desde el Cerro de la Campana: Relatos* (Hermosillo: Editorial Urias, 1964), 2:225.

5. Rocío Guadarrama, "La reorganización social," *HCS*, 151; Maurice W. Altaffer, U.S. Consul, Nogales, to State Department (henceforth SD), 27 August 1930, 30 April 1931; Lewis V. Boyle, U.S. Consul, Agua Prieta, to Secretary of State (henceforth SS), 22 April 1931, Records relating to the Internal Affairs of Mexico, U.S. State Department, 1929–1940, 812.00, reel 18 (microfilm), (henceforth SD/18); U.S. Military Intelligence Reports, Mexico, 1919–1940 (microfilm), reel 9 (henceforth MI-9), G-2 5737, 7 December 1934.

6. A. F. Yepis, U.S. Vice-Consul, Guaymas, to SD, 11 March 1935, SD/19; Guy W. Ray, U.S. Vice-Consul, Guaymas, to SD, 1 October 1934; Altaffer to SS, 24 April 1930, 10 March 1931; Report, Thomas W. Voetter, U.S. Consul, Guaymas, 3 March 1933; Reports, 2 June 1934, 31 August 1934 by Ray, and April 1935 by Yepis, SD/18.

7. José Abraham Mendívil, *Medio siglo de lucha (social y política)* (Hermosillo: Publicaciones Mendívil, n.d.), 2:7; Yost, Nogales, to SD, 30 April 1932, SD/18.

8. Rodolfo Elías Calles to Plutarco Elías Calles, 6 September 1931, Archivo de Plutarco Elías Calles (henceforth APEC), gav. 27, ELIAS CALLES CHACON, rodolfo, inv. 1733, exp. 4, leg. 13/24, ff. 630–3, Archivos Plutarco Elías Calles y Fernando Torreblanca; Josiah McC. Heyman, *Life and Labor on the Border: Working People of Northeastern Sonora, Mexico, 1886–1986* (Tucson: University of Arizona Press, 1991), 9, 34.

9. Report, Voetter, 30 September 1932; Review, Boyle, 31 October 1932; Report, Ray, 1 December 1934, SD/18; Juan Manuel Romero Gil and José Carlos López Romero, "Crisis y resistencia comunitaria (1929–1934): Tercer acto," in *XIV Simposio de historia y antropología de Sonora: Memoria* (Hermosillo: Instituto de Investigaciones Históricas, Universidad de Sonora, 1990), 2:14–25; Manuel S. Corbalá, *Rodolfo Elías Calles: Perfiles de un sonorense* (Hermosillo: n.p., 1970), 154–55, 158; José Carlos Ramírez, "La estrategia económica de los Callistas," and Guadarrama, "La reorganización," *HCS*.

10. R. E. Calles to P. E. Calles, 6 September 1931, APEC, gav. 27, ELIAS CALLES CHACON, Rodolfo, inv. 1733, exp. 4, leg. 13/24, ff. 630–33; Evelyn Hu-DeHart, "Racism and Anti-Chinese Persecution in Sonora, Mexico, 1876–1932," *Amerasia* 9, no. 2 (1982): 1–28. A recent popular publication entitled "cazador de guachos" attests to the endurance of xenophobia.

11. Graham Greene, *The Power and the Glory* (New York: Viking Press, 1968), 11.

12. N. Ross Crumrine, *The Mayo Indians of Sonora: A People Who Refuse to Die* (Tucson: University of Arizona Press, 1977), 21, changed the details. Idem, "Mechanisms of Enclavement Maintenance and Sociocultural Blocking of Modernization among the Mayo of Southern Sonora," in *Ejidos and Regions of Refuge in Northwestern Mexico*, Anthropological Papers 46, ed. N. Ross Crumrine and Phil C. Weigand (Tucson: University of Arizona Press, 1987), 24; Charles J. Erasmus, *Man Takes Control: Cultural Development and American Aid* (Minneapolis: University of Minnesota Press, 1961), 276–77; idem, "Cultural Change in Northwest Mexico," in Charles J. Erasmus, Solomon Miller, and Louis C. Faron, *Contemporary Change in Traditional Communities of Mexico and Peru* (Urbana: University of Illinois Press, 1978), 97.

13. See Alan Knight, "Revolutionary Project, Recalcitrant People," in *The Revolutionary Process in Mexico. Essays on Political and Social Change, 1880–1940*, ed. Jaime E. Rodríguez O. (Los Angeles and Irvine: UCLA Latin American Center and the Mexico/Chicano Project, University of California, Irvine, 1990), 227–64; Carlos Martínez Assad, *El laboratorio de la revolución: El Tabasco garridista* (México: Siglo XXI, 1979); Gilbert M. Joseph and Daniel Nugent, eds., *Everyday Forms of State Formation: Revolution and the Negotiation of Rule in Modern Mexico* (Durham: Duke University Press, 1994); Becker, "Black and White and Color," 453–65; idem, *Setting the Virgin on Fire*; Mary Kay Vaughan, *Estado, clases sociales y educación en México*, 2 vols. (México: SEP, 1982); David L. Raby, *Educación y revolución social en México (1921–1940)* (México: SEP, 1974).

14. Alan Knight, *The Mexican Revolution* (Cambridge: Cambridge University Press, 1986), 1:69–70, 2:501.

15. Aguilar, *La frontera*; Carr, *Peculiarities*, 6–7, 9–13; Jean Meyer, "Mexico: Revolution and Reconstruction in the 1920s," in *Cambridge History of*

Latin America, vol. 5 *(1870–1930)*, ed. Leslie Bethell (Cambridge: Cambridge University Press, 1986), 155.

16. Martínez, *El laboratorio*, 39.

17. Knight, *Mexican Revolution*, 2:238–39, 500; Jean Meyer, Enrique Krauze, and Cayetano Reyes, *Estado y sociedad con Calles* (México: El Colegio de México, 1977), 321, 328–29; Enrique Krauze, *Reformar desde el origen: Plutarco Elías Calles* (México: Fondo de Cultura Económica, 1987), 33, 58.

18. Lynn Hunt, *Politics, Culture, and Class in the French Revolution* (Berkeley: University of California Press, 1984), 24.

19. Meyer, *La Cristiada*, 2:208.

20. Alan Knight, "El liberalismo mexicano desde la Reforma hasta la Revolución (una interpretación)," *Historia Mexicana* 137, no. 1 (1985): 85.

21. See Adrian Bantjes, "Religión y Revolución en México, 1929–1940," *Boletín* 15 (1994) (México: Fideicomiso Archivos Plutarco Elías Calles y Fernando Torreblanca), 4; idem, "Idolatry and Iconoclasm in Revolutionary Mexico: The Dechristianization Campaigns, 1929–1940," *Mexican Studies/Estudios Mexicanos* 13, no. 1 (Winter 1997); Martaelena Negrete, *Relaciones entre la Iglesia y el Estado en México 1930–1940* (México: Universidad Iberoamericana, 1988).

22. Also see Adrian Bantjes, "Burning Saints, Molding Minds: Iconoclasm, Civic Ritual, and the Failed Cultural Revolution," in *Rituals of Rule, Rituals of Resistance: Public Celebrations and Popular Culture in Mexico*, ed. William H. Beezley, Cheryl English Martin, and William E. French (Wilmington, DE: SR Books, 1994).

23. Fray Juan de Torquemada, *Monarquía indiana* (México: Porrúa, 1969), 3:506.

24. *Memoria General: Informe rendido por el C. Rodolfo Elías Calles, Gobernador Constitucional del Estado, ante la H. XXXII Legislatura local, el 16 de septiembre de 1934* (Hermosillo: Cruz Gálvez, 1934), 4, 15, 35.

25. R. E. Calles to P. E. Calles, 12 September 1931, APEC, gav. 27, ELIAS CALLES CHACON, Rodolfo, inv. 1733, exp. 4, leg. 13/24, ff. 630–35.

26. Cárdenas to P. E. Calles, 14 May 1932, APEC, gav. 12, CARDENAS, Lázaro, inv. 820, exp. 206, leg. 5/9, f. 270; Becker, "Cárdenas"; Martínez, *El laboratorio*, 54–55; Negrete, *Relaciones*, 76–77; Instructivo, 1 November 1934, Archivo Administrativo del Gobierno del Estado de Sonora (henceforth AAGES) 235"35"/21.

27. The limit was one priest per 20,000 inhabitants (16); see, for example, Rocío Guadarrama, "Los cambios en la política," *HCS*, 179–80; Voetter to SD, 29 February 1932, SD/18; Relación, 8 November 1932, Dirección General de Gobierno, Ramo de Gobernación, 2.340(22), Archivo General de la Nación, Mexico City (henceforth RG, DGG, AGN); R. E. Calles to P. E. Calles, 12 September 1931, APEC, gav. 27, ELIAS CALLES CHACON, Rodolfo, inv. 1733, exp. 4, leg. 13/24, ff. 630–33; P. E. Calles to Rodríguez, 17 May 1934, APEC, RODRIGUEZ, Abelardo L., gav. 59, exp. 189, leg. 11/11, ff. 541–42; Edward S. Maney, Guaymas, to SD, 4 September 1931; Gibbs to Robinson, 25 March 1934, Record Group 84, Consular Post Records (henceforth RG 84), Correspondence, American Consular Agency, Cananea (henceforth CACAC), 1934–35, vol. XXVII, National Archives, Washington, DC (NAW); Boyle to SD, 31 May 1934, SD/18.

28. Joseph B. Carbajal to Representative John P. Higgins, Affidavit, priest, 8 June 1935, Religious Persecution in Mexico Papers, May–July 1935, Latin American Library, Tulane University.

29. Bantjes, "Iconoclasm"; Negrete, *Relaciones*, chap. 3.

30. Arturo Madrid to Gobernador de Sonora (henceforth GS), 7 June 1935, AAGES 231.5"35"/38; Erasmus, *Man Takes Control*, 276–77; idem, "Cultural Change," 97; Crumrine, *The Mayo*, 25.

31. Guadarrama, "Los cambios," *HCS*, 181–82, 197–99; RG, DGG 2.340(22)29, AGN; *El Día*, 4 March 1967; Gilberto Suárez Arvizu, "Fundación de la Universidad de Sonora," *VII Simposio de historia de Sonora: Memoria* (Hermosillo: Instituto de Investigaciones Históricas, Universidad de Sonora, 1982), 426.

32. Meyer, *La Cristiada*, 2:200–206.

33. R. N. Bellah, *Beyond Belief* (New York: Harper and Row, 1970), 21.

34. David Freedberg, *Iconoclasts and Their Motives* (Maarsen: Gary Schwartz, 1985), 25–37; Martin Warnke, "Bilderstürme," in *Bildersturm: Die Zerstörung des Kunstwerks*, ed. Martin Warnke (Munich: Carl Hanser Verlag, 1973), 10.

35. Director de Educación Federal (henceforth DEF) Fernando Ximello to Celso Flores Zamora, Jefe Departamento de Enseñanza Rural, Informe, October–November 1935, Secretaría de Educación Pública/Archivo Histórico (henceforth SEP/AH) 249.

36. Rosalío Moisés, Jane Holden Kelley, and William Curry Holden, *A Yaqui Life: The Personal Chronicle of a Yaqui Indian* (Lincoln: University of Nebraska Press, 1971), 6, 14, 82, 126; Muriel Thayer Painter, *With Good Heart: Yaqui Beliefs and Ceremonies in Pascua Village* (Tucson: University of Arizona Press, 1986), 83, 130–31, 154; Personal communication, Cynthia Radding, Hermosillo, 1988; Muriel Thayer Painter Papers, MS 18, SG, Series 4, Folder 1, Field Notes, Magdalena, 1947, and Celia A. Duarte, "Mexican-Yaqui Relations during the Revolution," MS, Spicer Papers, Archives A-0384, Arizona State Museum, Tucson (henceforth ASM).

37. José Abraham Mendívil, *Don Juan Navarrete y Guerrero: Como pastor y como hombre* (Hermosillo: Publicaciones Mendívil, 1975); Painter Papers, MS 18, SG, Series 4, Folder 1, Field Notes, Magdalena, 1947, ASM. James S. Griffith, *Beliefs and Holy Places: A Spiritual Geography of the Pimería Alta* (Tucson: University of Arizona Press, 1992), chap. 3, esp. 50–55, concluded that the images are not the same.

38. Painter Papers, MS 18, SG, Series 4, Folder 1, Field Notes, Magdalena, 1947, ASM.

39. Hector Rubén Bartolini Verdugo, *Monografía de Aconchi (Acontzi)* (Hermosillo: n.p., 1983).

40. GS to Comisario Yécora, 26 December 1934, AAGES 235"35"/4; Ray to Yepis, 19 January 1935, RG 84, Correspondence, American Consulate, Guaymas (henceforth CACG) 1935, 5:800, NAW; Report, Ramón R. Reyes, 1935, SEP/AH 211.4.

41. Martín Mercado to maestros, 10 October 1934, SEP/AH 366.6.

42. Moreno to Flores, 20 April 1935, SEP/AH 249.

43. Presidente Municipal (henceforth PM), Navojoa, to Manuel Soto, 1935, AAGES, 235"35"/31.

44. GS to Comisario Yécora, 26 December 1934, AAGES 235"35"/4; GS to PM, Divisaderos, n.d.; Director General de Educación Federal (henceforth DGEF) Fernando W. Dworak to GS, 24 April 1935; Vicente Contreras to PM, Magdalena, 14 June 1935, AAGES 235"35"/29; Madrid to GS, 7 June 1935, AAGES 231.5"35"/38; Francisco Alfredo Larrañaga Robles, *Monografía*

del Municipio de Navojoa. 1982 [Navojoa: n.p., 1985?], 92–93; Interview, Ernesto López Yescas, Bácum, 24 May 1992.

45. Dworak to GS, 24 April 1935, AAGES 235"35"/29.

46. Corbalá, *Calles*, 154–55, 158.

47. Enrique Krauze, *General misionero: Lázaro Cárdenas* (México: FCE, 1987), 59.

48. R. E. Calles to P. E. Calles, 25 July 1934, APEC, gav. 27, ELIAS CALLES CHACON, Rodolfo, inv. 1733, exp., leg. 13/24, f. 1040.

49. Mona Ozouf, *La fête révolutionnaire, 1789–1799* (Paris: Gallimard, 1976), 18, 243–44, 268.

50. PM, Navojoa, to Soto, 1935, AAGES 235"35"/31; R. E. Calles to P. E. Calles, 25 July 1934, APEC, gav. 27, ELIAS CALLES CHACON, Rodolfo, inv. 1733, exp., leg. 19/24, f. 956.

51. Teacher to Secretaría de Defensa Nacional, 1 November 1935, Archivo de la Revolución Mexicana/Patronato de Historia de Sonora (henceforth ARM/PHS), reel 75.

52. Domingo Cultural, 29 July 1934, SEP/AH 366.6; Programa, SEP/AH 249.

53. Leonardo Ramírez to DGEF, 3 May 1935, SEP/AH 211.3; Sabino Linares to GS, 14 March 1935, AAGES 235"35"/27; Daniel Domínguez to DEF, 1 March 1936, SEP/AH 319.12; Ray to SD, 1 April 1935, SD/19.

54. *Alma sonorense: Organo mensual de la Federación de Maestros del Estado de Sonora* (Ures) 3 (June 1934); Interview, Gilberto Escobosa Gámez, Hermosillo, 22 May 1992; SEP/AH 366.7.

55. Speech, Pascual E. Jiménez, 20 October 1934, AAGES 235"35"/6; Arturo García Fomenti, *Desde la tribuna revolucionaria de Sonora (Escuela socialista y otros temas)* (México, 1935), 55–58.

56. Krauze, *General misionero*, 27, 36; Meyer, *La Cristiada*, 2:210.

57. Michel Vovelle, *Religion et Révolution. La déchristianisation de l'an II* (Paris: Hachette, 1976), 232–35, 228, 278.

58. Cited in Mayo Murrieta and Ma. Eugenia Graf, *Por el milagro de aferrarse: Tierra y vecindad en el Valle del Yaqui* (Hermosillo: El Colegio de Sonora, Instituto Tecnológico de Sonora, Instituto Sonorense de Cultura, 1991), 176.

59. Vaughan, *Estado*, 1:9, 28–29; 2:286–87; Knight, *Mexican Revolution*, 1:23; 2:423, 463; Eduardo Ibarra and Ernesto Camou Healy, "Las instituciones educativas," HCS, 579.

60. Manuel Diego Hernández and Alejo Maldonado Gallardo, "En torno a la historia de la Confederación Revolucionaria Michoacana del Trabajo," in *Jornadas de historia de occidente: Movimientos populares en el occidente de México, siglos XIX y XX* (Jiquilpan: Centro de Estudios de la Revolución Mexicana "Lázaro Cárdenas," A.C., 1980), 128–29; Krauze, *General misionero*, 46, 49, 54–55; Victoria Lerner, *La educación socialista* (México: El Colegio de México, 1979), 14–15, 73, 75, 82, 98–99.

61. Martínez, *El laboratorio*, 86.

62. Flores to DEF, 16 April 1935, SEP/AH 249.

63. García, *Desde la tribuna*, 55–58.

64. Ibid., 70–71; Corbalá, *Calles*, 154–55, 158; *El Imparcial* (Hermosillo), 14 August 1966.

65. Lyle Brown, "Mexican Church-State Relations, 1933–1940," *A Journal of Church and State* 7 (1964): 211, n.36; Bantjes, "Religión," 4;

Document, 25 August 1935 by teacher, Cananea, Archivo de Ernesto López Yescas (henceforth AELY), Bácum, Sonora.

66. Circular, 23 April 1934, RG 84, Consular Post Records (henceforth CPR), Nogales, Confidential Correspondence (henceforth CC) 1936, vol. II, NAW.

67. Abelardo Casanova, *Pasos perdidos* (Hermosillo: Imágen, 1986); Robinson to Josephus Daniels, U.S. Ambassador, 1 March 1935; Robinson to SS, 1 June 1934, SD/18; Circular, 23 April 1934, RG 84; CPR Nogales, CC 1936, vol. II; Document, 25 August 1935 by teacher, Cananea, AELY; R. E. Calles to P. E. Calles, 3 May 1934; Dwork to R. E. Calles, 10, 12, 13 June 1934, APEC, gav. 27, ELIAS CALLES CHACON, Rodolfo, inv. 1733, exp. 4, leg. 9/24, ff. 957–58, 983–85; Gibbs to Robinson, 25 May 1934, RG 84, CACAC, 1934–35, vol. XXVII, NAW; Circular, 25 February 1935, SEP/AH 249; Ozouf, *La fête,* 20; Interview, López Yescas, 24 May 1992.

68. Instituto, 17 June 1935, 14 July 1935, SEP/AH 249; R. E. Calles to P. E. Calles, 3 May 1934, APEC, gav. 27, ELIAS CALLES CHACON, Rodolfo, inv. 1733, exp. 4, leg. 9/24, ff. 957–58; Ignacio Almada Bay, "La conexión Yocupicio: Soberanía estatal, tradición cívico-liberal y resistencia al reemplazo de las lealtades en Sonora, 1913–1939" (Tesis de doctorado, El Colegio de México, 1993), 324; Ray to SD, 8 January 1935, SD/18.

69. *Propaganda doctrinaria antidogmática para maestros rurales,* 1, 2, 3 (Magdalena, January 1936).

70. Yepis to SS, 7 August 1935, RG 84, CACG, vol. V, 800, NAW.

71. Interview, Escobosa, 21, 22 May 1992; Angel Encinas Blanco, "El movimiento cristero de Luis Ibarra en Granados" in *IX Simposio de historia de Sonora: Memoria* (Hermosillo: Instituto de Investigaciones Históricas, Universidad de Sonora, 1984), 447.

72. Corbalá, *Calles,* 154–55, 158; Ramírez to DGEF, 3 May 1935, SEP/AH 211.3.

73. Interview, Amadeo Hernández Coronado, Hermosillo, 26 May 1992.

Chapter 2, "The Calles-Cárdenas Conflict and the Anatomy of Sonoran Politics," 23–41

1. Boyle to SD, 29 February 1932; Voetter to SD, 5 September 1932; Ray to SD, 30 April 1934, 1 June 1934, 31 July 1934, 5 January 1935; Robinson to SD, 30 March 1935, 29 September 1934; Report, Ray, 4 January 1935, SD/18; Yepis to SS, 4 December 1935, SD/19.

2. Brown, "Church-State Relations," 204, 206, 209; Negrete, *Relaciones,* 97, 100, 171; Meyer, *La Cristiada,* 374–77, 384; *Boletín Desde México* 18 (4 August 1935), 19 (5 September 1935); Yepis to SD, 30 April 1935, SD/19; Cited in Bantjes, "Religión," 9.

3. Carmelo Corbello was responsible for propaganda, Luis Soria for collections. Vice-Consul, Tucson, to Ambassador, Washington, 28 October 1935, Ramo Presidentes, Fondo Lázaro Cárdenas (henceforth RP, FLC), 559.3/25, AGN; I-35 to OIPS, 30 December 1935, RG, DGG 2.384(22)3, AGN.

4. *El Imparcial,* 7 April 1959; *Album recuerdo: Homenaje de amor, gratitud y respeto al Exmo. y Romo Sr. Arzobispo Juan Navarrete y Guerrero* (1964); *Album conmemorativo de las Bodas de Oro Episcopales del Exmo. y Romo. Sr.*

Arzobispo Dr. Juan Navarrete y Guerrero (1969); Cruz Acuña Gálvez, *Juan Navarrete: Medio Siglo de Historia Sonorense* (Hermosillo: Editorial Urias, 1970), 34–35, 39.

5. Acuña, *Navarrete*, 35–38; *El Imparcial*, 7 April 1959; *Boletín Pro-Bodas de Plata Episcopales: Información mensual diocesana. Organo del Comité Central* (Cananea) 1, no. 1 (August 1942).

6. Zertuche to Múgica, 13 October 1935, Fondo Francisco J. Múgica, Archivo Francisco J. Múgica (henceforth AFJM), vol. 61, doc. 26; DEF to GS, 5 March 1935, AAGES 235"35"; Voetter to SD, 31 August 1933, SD/18; Carbajal to Higgins; Affidavit, 8 June 1935, Religious Persecution in Mexico Papers, May–July 1935, Latin American Library, Tulane University.

7. *El Sembrador: Hoja catequística* 4, no. 8, n.d.; AFJM, vol. 106, doc. 165; Robinson to SS, 29 May 1934, RG 84, CPR Nogales, CC 1936, vol. 2, Class 800, 840.4, NAW.

8. *Amanece: Organo mensual de la Parroquia de Nuestra Señora de Guadalupe* (Cananea) 2, no. 9 (October 1941).

9. *Esfuerzo* (La Parcela) 2, no. 14 (31 January 1940).

10. *Regis: Semanario catequístico* (Nogales) 1, no. 33 (8 June 1933); no. 37 (6 July 1935).

11. Hoja volante, Archivo de Fernando Torreblanca (henceforth AFT), Fondo Plutarco Elías Calles, EDUCACION SOCIALISTA, serie 12010805, exp. 21.

12. *Esfuerzo* 1, no. 6 (9 April 1939); no. 7 (1 May 1939); no. 9 (29 June 1939).

13. *Reconquista: Organo oficial de la Liga Nacional Defensora de la Libertad* (Méjico) 3, no. 5 (December 1935).

14 Cited in Brown, "Church-State Relations," 209, n.31.

15. Ray to SD, 1 November 1934, SD/18.

16. Vovelle, *Religion*, 274–75, 281–82; Meyer, *La Cristiada*, 2:198; Gerardo Cornejo, *La Sierra y el viento* (México: Leega Literaria, 1977), 125. One must add that strong male religiosity could be found among upper- and middle-class mestizos and most Indians. Erasmus, *Man Takes Control*, 250; Ignacio Almada Bay, "Conflictos y contactos del Estado y de la Iglesia en Sonora," in *Coloquio sobre las relaciones del Estado y las iglesias en Sonora y México: Memoria*, ed. Felipe Mora (Hermosillo: El Colegio de Sonora, Universidad de Hermosillo, 1992), 27–46.

17. Boyle to SD, 29 September 1934, 31 October 1934, and 31 May 1934; Ray to SD, 31 July 1934, 1 May 1935, SD/18; Brown, "Church-State Relations," 215, 217–18; Bantjes, "Religión," 22.

18. Suzanne Desan, *Reclaiming the Sacred: Lay Religion and Popular Politics in Revolutionary France* (Ithaca: Cornell University Press, 1990), 208. For a gendered analysis of anticlericalism and women's religion see Marjorie Becker, "Torching La Purísima, Dancing at the Altar: The Construction of Revolutionary Hegemony in Michoacán, 1934–1940," in *Everyday Forms*, ed. Joseph and Nugent, 247–64.

19. Corella to Women, Santa Ana, 5 July 1935, AAGES 235"35"/37; Mendívil, *Navarrete*.

20. RG, DGG 2.340(22)16688, AGN; AAGES 235"35"/37 and 46; Petitions, RG, DGG 2.340(22)299, AGN; Alphonse Aulard, *Christianity and the French Revolution* (New York: Howard Fertig, 1966), 116.

21. Petition to Secretario Gobierno, 28 August 1937 and 11 January 1938, RG, DGG 2/340(22)25891, AGN.

238 Notes to Pages 28–30

22. Petition to Cárdenas, 30 November 1937, RG, DGG 2.340(22)16688, AGN.

23. Yepis to SD, 21 January 1934, SD/18; DGEF to GS, 24 April 1935, AAGES 235"35"/29.

24. Ray to SD, 31 July 1934, SD/18; Informe, November 1934, SEP/AH 366.6.

25. Francisco Lozano to Enseñanza Rural, 25 May 1935, SEP/AH 211.2; Daniel Domínguez to DEF, 1 March 1936, Informe, SEP/AH 319.2; Informe, 1 February 1935, SEP/AH 249; Oficina de Migración to Secretaría de Gobernación (henceforth SG), 15 December 1934, RG, DGG 2.340(22)27, AGN; Boyle to SD, 31 December 1934 and 31 January 1935; Ray to SD, 1 December 1934, SD/18.

26. Corella to SG, 14 August 1935, AAGES 235"35"/33. Compare with Salvador Camacho Sandoval, *Controversia entre la ideología y la fe: La educación socialista en la historia de Aguascalientes, 1876–1940* (México: CNCA, 1991); DGEF to GS, 17 January 1935, AAGES 235"35"/17.

27. Corella to SG, 14 August 1935, AAGES 235"35"/33; Liga de Campesinos to GS, 11 August 1935, AAGES 235"35"/43; Director, Escuela, to PM, Oputo, 20, 21 November 1936, SEP/AH 297.19; Ramírez to DGEF, 3 May 1935, 29 July 1935, SEP/AH 211.3.

28. Raby, *Educación*, 191. My unsystematic research indicates that two, possibly three, teachers were assassinated during this period.

29. Ibid., 149, 164, 195, 197; Meyer, *La Cristiada*, vol. 2.

30. Casanova, *Pasos*, 63.

31. Compare Mark Wasserman, "Strategies for Survival of the Porfirian Elite in Revolutionary Mexico: Chihuahua during the 1920s," *Hispanic American Historical Review* 67, no. 1 (1987).

32. Gilberto Valenzuela ran an ice-cream parlor in Mesa, Marcelo Caraveo and Francisco Manzo ran gas stations in El Paso and San Diego. Fausto Topete operated a drugstore in Los Angeles and later joined the Lasky studios, while Manzo also considered the movies. MI-2, G-2 report, 16 April 1930.

33. Serie Sonora, 1a serie, roll no. 9.

34. Victor Manuel Reynoso, "Acción Nacional en Sonora: Notas para su historia" (paper presented at XIV Simposio de Historia y Antropología de Sonora, Hermosillo, 1989), 2–3; Almada, "La conexión."

35. Domingo Gutiérrez Mendívil, "Una rebelión Vasconcelista en Navojoa," in *Memoria: XII Simposio de Historia y Antropología de Sonora* (Hermosillo: Instituto de Investigaciones Históricas, Universidad de Sonora, 1988), 199, 203; Suárez, "Fundación," 425; José Abraham Mendívil, *Cuarenta años de política en Sonora* (Hermosillo: Publicidad Mendívil, 1965), 1:41; John Skirius, "José Vasconcelos en Sonora," in *Temas Sonorenses: A través de los simposios de historia* (Hermosillo: Gobierno del Estado de Sonora, 1984), 121–22. In 1929, Vasconcelistas and Cristeros were ready to take up arms. See Mendívil, *Medio Siglo*, 1:29, 39–41; Vasconcelos to Joaquín Cárdenas, 1 September 1935, AFJM, vol. 106, doc. 48; Yepis to SS, 17 October 1935, SD/19. Note the continuity between 1929 and 1935. Skirius, "Vasconcelos," 120, 126; *David. Organo oficial de la Legión de Cristo Rey y Santa María de Guadalupe: Veteranos de la Guardia Nacional (Cristeros)*, (México, D.F.), Año I, 2a Epoca, no. 3 (October 1952): 39–41; no. 9 (22 April 1953): 143; Año III, Tomo III, no. 29 (22 December 1954): 77.

36. José Ramírez to Cárdenas, 26 July 1935, Fondo Francisco J. Múgica, AFJM, Documentación suelta, carpeta 383, doc. 5256; Mendívil, *Medio Siglo,* 34; Robinson to SD, 30 April 1935; Boyle to SS, 17 May 1935; Yepis to SS, 17 October 1935, SD/19; *The Arizona Daily Star* (Tucson), 19 May 1935; Teléfonos Ericson, 17 December 1935, AFJM, vol. 56, doc. no. 124; R. E. Calles to Soledad [Cholita] González, n.d., APEC, ELIAS CALLES CHACON, Rodolfo, inv. 1733, exp. 4, leg. 4/24.

37. Departamento Diplomático to SG, 7 August 1935, RG, DGG 2.340(22)3.2, AGN; Robinson to SD, 1 July 1935, 31 August 1935; Ray to SD, 3 July 1935; Yepis to SS, 17 October 1935, SD/19; Corella to PMs, 4 July 1935, AAGES 231.5"35"/29; Ramos, 3 August 1935, AAGES 231.5"35"/ 30; PM, Altar, 16 August 1935; PM, Cananea, 13 August 1935; and PM, Nacozari, 17 August 1935; Amparo, Ayudante to GS, 19 August 1935, AAGES 231.5"35"/68; Canizales to GS, 5 July 1935, AAGES 231.5"35"/29; Receipt, AAGES 231.5"35"/71; Boyle to SS, 17, 18, 23, 31 December 1935, SD/18; Petition, Magdalena to Cárdenas, 29 June 1935, RG, DGG 2.317.4(22)4; *La Gaceta,* 30 July 1935.

38. FMTE to Secretario de Gobierno, 14 June 1937, RG, DGG 2/ 340(22)10816, AGN; *El Heraldo* (Magdalena), 2 August 1935.

39. Yepis to SS, 6 August 1935, 31 July 1935, SD/19; *La Gaceta,* 30 July 1935; I-35 to OIPS, 30 December 1935, RG, DGG 2/311 G(22)4674, AGN.

40. Lizárraga to Banco Nacional de Crédito Agrícola, 11 September 1935, Ramo Presidentes, Fondo Lázaro Cárdenas (henceforth RP, FLC), 544.2/25, AGN.

41. Boyle to SS, 22 April 1931, SD/18; Mendívil, *Medio Siglo,* 2:55, 3:3; Moncada, *Sucesión,* 47–48.

42. Robinson to SD, 5 September 1935, SD/19.

43. Galaz, *Desde el Cerro,* 156–57; José Dena to *El Heraldo del Yaqui,* 29 July 1935, AAGES 231.5"35"/67; RG, DGG 2.331.9(22)8; RP, FLC 544.2/25, AGN; Felizardo Frías to Múgica, 29 October 1935, FFJM, AFJM, vol. 61, doc. 34; Yepis to SS, 17 October 1935, SD/19.

44. Francisco Encinas to Luis I. Rodríguez, 21 June 1935, RG, DGG 2.311.M(22)7; I-35 to OIPS, 30 December 1935, RG, DGG 2.311.M(22)4674, AGN; Damián L. Rodríguez to Cárdenas, 18 December 1935, RG, DGG 2.316(22)2, AGN; Miguel Yocupicio to Cárdenas, 24 December 1935, RG DGG 2.317.4(22)9, AGN; Juan C. Zertuche to Múgica, 13 October 1935, FFJM, AFJM, vol. 61, doc. 26.

45. Aguilár, *La Frontera,* 39. Reynoso, "Acción," 2, stresses the continuity of the "civic-liberal" tradition from Maderismo through Vasconcelismo and anti-Callismo to Almazanismo.

46. Robinson to SS, 10 January 1934, SD/18; Ray to SD, 12 January 1934, 8 January 1935, SD/18; and 31 August 1935, SD/19; *El Heraldo del Yaqui,* 9, 11 January 1934; Larrañaga, *Navojoa,* 21–22; Mendívil, *Medio Siglo,* 1:17, 19, 34; Moncada, *Sucesión,* 34, 49; *Directorio Comercial del Estado de Sonora: 1920–1921* (Hermosillo: Healy-Genda, 1921), 366, 354; Gutiérrez, "Una rebelión," 206, 210–19; R. E. Calles to P. E. Calles, 5 January 1934, APEC, ELIAS CALLES CHACON, Rodolfo, inv. 1733, exp. 4, leg. 17/24, f. 84; Mendívil, *Cuarenta años,* 1:41; Erasmus, *Man Takes Control,* 354, n.9; Yepis to SD, 31 August 1935, SD/19.

47. Ray to SD, 31 January 1935, SD/18; Ray to Yepis, 19 January 1935, RG 84, CACG 1935, Vol V, 800, NAW. While U.S. diplomats estimated the

1935 population at 6–7,000, the 1950 census indicated the presence of 31,000 Mayo speakers in northwestern Mexico (incl. Sinaloa), while other 1963 data spoke of 15,000 in the Mayo Valley. Figures in 1935 may be low due to migration and dislocation. Crumrine, *The Mayo*, 15; Larrañaga, *Navojoa*, 21–22; Ray to SD, 8 January 1935, SD/18; Cárdenas to Tellechea, n.d., RG, DGG 544.2/25, AGN; Yepis to SD, 31 August 1935, SD/19; Mendívil, *Medio Siglo*, 1:19, 34; Corella to Cárdenas, 20 August 1935, RP, FLC 544.2/25, AGN.

48. Ray to SD, 28 February 1935, SD/18; Juan P. Pacheco to GS, 1 February 1935, AAGES 235"35"/12; Federico A. Corzo to Flores, 8 November 1935; Informe, DEF, October–November 1935, SEP/AH 249.

49. Teacher, Huatabampo, to Secretaría de Defensa, 1 November 1935, ARM/PHS 75.

50. Arturo Madrid to GS, 7 June 1935, AAGES 231.5"35"/38.

51. Edward H. Spicer, foreword to Crumrine, *The Mayo*.

52. Crumrine, *The Mayo*, 24.

53. Ibid., "Mechanisms," 34. During the 1939 rebellion the army killed three Mayos and captured thirty-four. Manuel Santiago Corbalá Acuña, *Alamos de Sonora* (México: Editorial Libros de México, 1977), 233–36; Macías to Cárdenas, 17 January 1940: Informes, General José Mendívil Talamante, 28 December 1939; Relación, 10 January 1940, RP, FLC 544.2/25, AGN.

54. Crumrine, *The Mayo*, 46, 121, 134–37, 147; Erasmus, *Man Takes Control*, 304.

55. Crumrine, *The Mayo*, 21–26; Crumrine Papers, Mayo Field Notes, Archives A-297 (1960–62), 487, 14 October 1961, ASM; Erasmus, *Man Takes Control*, 276–77.

56. Gastélum to GS, 21 August 1935, AAGES 231.5"35"/26; Yepis to SD, 30 September 1935, SD/19.

57. Crumrine Papers, Mayo Field Notes, Archives A-297 (1960–62), 487, 14 October 1961, ASM; Crumrine, *The Mayo*, 45, 149.

58. Manuel L. Carlos, "Enclavement Processes, State Policies, and Cultural Identity among the Mayo Indians of Sinaloa, Mexico," in *Ejidos*, ed. Crumrine and Weigand, 35–36; Yepis to Daniels, 22 April 1937, RG 84, General Records (henceforth GR) 1937, Guaymas Consulate (henceforth GC), Box 17, 861.1, NAW; Yepis to Bursley, Secretary, U.S. Embassy, 24 August 1937, RG 84, GR 1937, GC, Box 16, 852, NAW; Yepis to SS, 11 November 1936, RG 84, GR 1936, GC, Box 7, 852, NAW; Ramos to SG, 8 October 1935, RG, DGG 2.102.8(22)4813, AGN.

59. Yepis to SD, 30 September 1935, SD/19; PM, Navojoa, to Rafael Valdez, 10 August 1935, AAGES 231.5"35"/50; Encinas to Rodríguez, 21 June 1935, RG, DGG 2311.M(22)7, AGN; Teacher, Huatabampo, to Secretaría de Defensa Nacional, 1 November 1935; Felipe Montiel to Comandante Zona, 4 July 1936, ARM/PHS 75; PM, Huatabampo, to GS, 21 August 1935, AAGES 231.5"35"/26.

60. Ministerio Público, Navojoa, to Cárdenas, 20 September 1935, RP, FLC 359.3/25, AGN; Ramos to Secretario Presidencial, 7 September 1935, RP, FLC 544.2/25, AGN; Lombardo to Cárdenas, 14 March 1938, RG, DGG 2.012.2(22)30541, AGN; PNR, Quiriego, to PNR, 10 February 1935, RG, DGG 2.311M(22)11, AGN; Daniel Borbón to GS, 1 July 1935, AAGES 231.4"35"/4.

61. Cárdenas to Tellechea, 19 August 1935; Carlos Ma. Samaniego to Cárdenas, 2 September 1935, RP, FLC 544.2/25, AGN.

62. Yepis to SD, 30 September 1935, SD/19; Claudio Dabdoub, *Historia de El Valle del Yaqui* (México: Porrúa, 1964), 344–53; Comité Antielizondista to Cárdenas, 30 August 1935; I-125 to OIPS, 4 November 1935, RG, DGG 2.311.M(22)12, AGN.

63. Petition to Cárdenas, 29 June 1935; Petition to Florencio González, 7 September 1935; González to Cárdenas, 22 December 1935, RG, DGG 2.317.4(22)4, AGN; *Sonora y sus actividades: Directorio comercial-industrial-minero-profesional-agrícola-ganadero y de propietarios de bienes raíces* (Magdalena: Editorial Mijares Palencia e Hijos, 1947?), 159–65; I-35 to OIPS, 30 December 1935, RG, DGG 2.384(22)3; José Herrera to Cárdenas, 25 December 1935, RG, DGG 2.311.M(22)11; Encinas to Rodríguez, 21 June 1935, RG, DGG 2.311.M(22)7, AGN.

64. Voetter to SD, 5 September 1932, SD/18.

65. Spicer Papers, Archives, 505A (Pótam), Field Notes, 28 December 1941, May 1942, 9 June 1947; Duarte, "Mexican-Yaqui Relations," A-0384; Wilfred Bailey, "The Factors in Yaqui Acculturation," Spicer Papers, Archives, A-0671, ASM.

66. Dabdoub, *Historia*, 220–23; Edward H. Spicer, *The Yaquis: A Cultural History* (Tucson: University of Arizona Press, 1980), 235, 248, 329; Spicer Papers, Archives, 505A (Pótam), Field Notes, 26 January 1942, ASM.

67. Estudio, 9 April 1936; Mendívil Talamante to Comandante Zona, 5 July 1936, ARM/PHS 75.

68. Estudio, 9 April 1936, ARM/PHS 75; Informe, January–February 1936, SEP/AH 319.11.

69. Estudio, 9 April 1936, ARM/PHS 75; Ray to SD, 31 August 1934, SD/18.

70. DEF to Flores, 9 November 1935, ARM/PHS 75.

71. Spicer, *The Yaqui*, 113; Crumrine Papers, Mayo Field Notes, Archives, A-297 (1960–62), 334, ASM; Erasmus, *Man Takes Control*, 353, n.7; Bailey, "Factors," Spicer Papers, Archives, A-0671, ASM.

72. Pueblos Yaqui to Cárdenas, 5 June 1939, RP, FLC 533.11/1, AGN.

73. Spicer, *The Yaqui*, 88–89, 171–72.

74. Vice-Consul, Phoenix, to Consul, Tucson, 31 October 1935, RP, FLC 559.3/25, AGN; Ray to SS, 4 May 1935, RG 84, CACG, 1934, vol. IV, 800, NAW; Vice-Consul, Tucson, to Ramos, 8 October 1935, AAGES 214.1"35"/1; C.A. Rosas to Tribu Yaqui, 31 October 1935, RP, FLC 559.3/25, AGN; Consul, Nogales, to Jefe Zona, 22 October 1935; Report, Consul, Phoenix, 11 November 1935; Estudio, 9 April 1936, ARM/PHS 75; General Ervey González to Comandante, 32º Regimiento Caballería, 22 July 1936, ARM/PHS 75; Gutiérrez to Corella, 21 March 1935, AAGES 231.25"35"/3; Vice-Consul, Tucson, to Secretaría de Relaciones Exteriores (SRE), 27 January 1936, RP, FLC 544.1/25, AGN; Spicer, *The Yaquis*, 232; AFJM, vol. 61, doc. 38.

75. Altaffer to SD, 19 November 1930, SD/18; AAGES 214.1"35"/1; Estudio, 9 April 1936; General José Botello to Comandante Zona, 17 November 1935; Espinosa to Secretario de Guerra, 22 February 1936, ARM/PHS 75.

76. Frank Daugherty to Edward Spicer, 2 June 1949, Spicer Papers, Archives, 464, 154; and 505A (Pótam), 21 February 1942, ASM.

77. Ray to SD, 1 April 1935, SD/19.

Chapter 3, "The 1935 Revolt," 43–55

1. Boyle to SS, 28 October 1935, SD/19.
2. MI-3, Consular reports, 1931–1934; MI-4, G-2 6717, 17 December 1935; MI-2, G-2 6601, 11 November 1935.
3. Meyer, *La Cristiada*, 1:375–76.
4. Espinosa to Comandante 9a Zona, n.d.; and to Guerra, 28 March 1936; Montiel to Comandante Zona, 4 July 1936, ARM/PHS 75; Erasmus, *Man Takes Control*, 354, n.9; Corzo to Flores, 8 November 1935, SEP/AH 249; Miguel Yocupicio to Cárdenas, 24 December 1935, RG, DGG 2.317.4(22) 9, AGN.
5. Genaro Borbón to GS, 11 November 1935, AAGES 62/448, 1936; Borbón to Cárdenas, 24 December 1935, 13 February 1937; Petition, Quiriego to Cárdenas, 15 March 1937, RG, DGG 2.012.8(22)23960, AGN; Mendívil T. to Espinosa, 20 May 1936, AAGES 62/448, 1936.
6. Espinosa to P. A. Eliseo Martín del Campo, 2 November 1935; Espinosa to Guerra, 28 March 1936, 5 November 1935; Declaración, 15 November 1935, ARM/PHS 75.
7. Cited in *HCS*, 601.
8. Laureano Calvo Berber, *Nociones de historia de Sonora* (México: Porrúa, 1958), 313; DEF to Educación Primaria, 7 July 1936, SEP/AH 297.20; Circular, 18 October 1935, AFJM, vol. 106, doc. 104.
9. Yepis to SS, 17 October 1935; Robinson to SS, 21 October 1935, SD/19.
10. Memorandum, 15 April 1936, Archivo de VITA, 1936, Centro de Estudios sobre la Universidad (CESU), Universidad Nacional Autónoma de México (UNAM); Plan, 20 November 1934, RP, FLC 559.3/25, AGN.
11. *Boletín Desde México* 21 (16 October 1935).
12. Director, Bacadéhuachi, to GS, 12 January 1935, AAGES 235"35"/ 14.
13. PM, Bacadéhuachi, to GS, 16 December 1934, AAGES 235"35"; Ramos to Cárdenas, 8 October 1935, RP, FLC 559.3/25, AGN; PM, Granados, to GS, 13 May 1935, AAGES 235"35"/28; Boyle to SS, 24 October 1935, SD/19.
14. Ibarra was acquainted with Archbishop Francisco Orozco y Jiménez. *David*, Año I, 2a Epoca, no. 9 (22 April 1953), 143; *David. Revista ilustrada. Organo oficial de la Legión de Cristo Rey y Santa María de Guadalupe: Veteranos de la Guardia Nacional (Cristeros)*, (Guadalajara) III, no. 1 (April 1968): 12; Meyer, *La Cristiada*, 1:223–25; Encinas, "El movimiento," 445–46; I. S. Michel to *El Universal*, 7 October 1935; Zertuche to Cárdenas, 8 October 1935, RP, FLC 559.3/25, AGN.
15. Boyle to SD, 31 October 1935, SD/19.
16. Review, Boyle, 31 October 1935, SD/19; Esteban García de Alba to SEP, 26 June 1936, SEP/AH 297.19; Gutiérrez M., "Una rebelión," 202; "Declaración," 30 September 1935, ARM/PHS 75.
17. Acuña, *Navarrete*, 58–60; RP, FLC 559.3/25, AGN; *Douglas Daily Dispatch*, 12 October 1935; Boyle to SS, 7 October 1935, SD/19; Madera to Educación Primaria, 21 May 1936, SEP/AH 339.4. Encinas, "El movimiento," 449, places the ordainment in the United States.
18. Acuña, *Navarrete*, 60–61.
19. Boyle to SS, 7 October 1935, SD/19; *Douglas Daily Dispatch*, 12 October 1935; Zertuche to Múgica, 13 October 1935, AFJM, vol. 61, doc. 26;

Ramos to Cárdenas, 8 October 1935, RP, FLC 559.3/25, AGN. López Yescas is confused with a later incident. E. G. López, "Dislates en las nociones de historia de Sonora," *El Católico*, n.d., n.p.; Ignacio Ma. Durazo to López Yescas, 4 June 1969; Anastasio Rodríguez to Dolores Fuentes, 25 April 1936, AELY.

20. Zertuche to Cárdenas, 8 October 1935; Ramos to Cárdenas, 8 October 1935; Inspector to Telégrafos, RP, FLC 559.3/25; Telegram, October 1935, AFJM, vol. 61, doc. 23; Boyle to SS, 24 October 1935, SD/19; *El Pueblo* (Hermosillo), 7 October 1935; *Boletín Desde México* 23 (17 November 1935); Telegram, Nacozari, October 1935, AFJM, vol. 61, doc. 23; Muchel [*sic*] to *El Universal*, 7 October 1935; Inspector to Telégrafos, RP, FLC 559.3/25, AGN; Zertuche to General Anacleto Guerrero, 12 October 1935, ARM/ PHS 75; Encinas, "El movimiento," 450.

21. Teniente Coronel Francisco Saucedo to Fuentes, 4 December 1935, AELY.

22. Acuña, *Navarrete*, 61–75; *El Imparcial*, 7 April 1959.

23. Ruíz to Díaz, 4 October 1934, AFT, Secretaría Particular, Fondo Plutarco Elías Calles, Serie Conflicto Religioso, 1929–1934; *Boletín Desde México*, 16 October 1935.

24. Espinosa to Secretario de Guerra, 22 February 1936, ARM/PHS 75; García de Alba to SEP, 26 June 1936, SEP/AH 297.19; AAGES 62/213, 1936; Espinosa, 8 July 1936, AAGES 235"36"/10.

25. Almada, "La conexión," 367.

26. Luz A. de Pina to GS, 17 June 1936, AAGES 235"36"/3; AAGES 62/ 213, 1936; González to GS, 3 April 1936, Mayor Reyes Orozco to Fuentes, 25 April 1936, AELY; Montiel to GS, 20 May 1936, AAGES 235"36"/10; García de Alba to SEP, 26 June 1936, SEP/AH 297.19; Arturo Moret to Enseñanza Agrícola, 18 June 1936, SEP/AH 297.26; Informes, 11 September 1944, 4, 6 October 1944, SEP/AH 170.5.

27. Yepis to SS, 17 October 1935, SD/19; Thomas E. Sheridan, *Where the Dove Calls: The Political Ecology of a Peasant Corporate Community in Northwestern Mexico* (Tucson: University of Arizona Press, 1988), 120, 136– 37.

28. Encinas, "El movimiento," 455.

29. Sheridan, *Dove*, 149–56; Ariana Baroni B., "Productores agrope-cuarios en la cuenca media del Río Sonora entre 1900 y 1950," *Memoria: XII Simposio*, 28–29; Elsa M. Peña and J. Trinidad Chávez, "Ganadería y agricultura en la sierra, 1929–1980," *HCS*, 469–72, 501.

30. Folleto, n.d., RP, FLC 559.3/25, AGN.

31. Yepis to SS, 21 December 1935, RG 84, CACG, 1935, vol. V, 800, NAW; Robinson to SS, 22 October 1935, SD/18.

32. Comisariado, Querobabi, to Cárdenas, 27 April 1937, RG, DGG 2.384(22)23768, exp. 544.4/25, AGN.

33. *The Arizona Daily Star* (Tucson), 22 October 1935; Ramón Pesqueira to Corella, 5 July 1935, AAGES 231.5"35"/37.

34. John O'Keefe, Vice-Consul, Agua Prieta, to SS, 14 October 1935, SD/19; I-35 to OIPS, 30 December 1935, RG, DGG 2.384(22)3, AGN.

35. Report, 25 October 1935, RP, FLC 559.3/25, AGN; Pesqueira to Corella, 5 July 1935, AAGES 231.5"35"/37; Juan Caballero to Cárdenas, 18 October 1935.

36. Yepis to SS, 17 October 1935; Robinson to SS, 21 October 1935, SD/ 19; I-35 to OIPS, 30 December 1935, RG, DGG 2.384(22)3, AGN; Vice-

Consul, Tucson, to Consul, Douglas, 13 November 1935, RP, FLC 559.3/ 25, AGN.

37. Sheridan, *Dove*, 130; Moncada, *Sucesión*, 49; Encinas, "El movimiento," 455.

38. AFJM, vol. 61, doc. 38; Daniels to SS, 15 October 1935; Robinson to SS, 22 October 1935, SD/19; Report, 25 October 1935; Ramos to Cárdenas, 19 October 1935; Caballero to Cárdenas, 18 October 1935; Corresponsal to *Excélsior*, 7 October 1935, RP, FLC 559.3/25, AGN; Encinas, "El movimiento," 455; PM, Atil, to Cárdenas, 18 October 1935; PM, Oquitoa, to Cárdenas, 18, 24 October 1935; PNR, Huatabampo, to Cárdenas, 23 October 1935, RP, FLC 544.2/25, AGN; Robinson to SS, 21, 22 October 1935, SD/19; MI-2, G-2 6547, 25 October 1935; Rafael Luis Celaya to Cárdenas, 19 October 1935; Ramos to Secretario de Gobierno, 19 October 1935, RG, DGG 2.317.4(22)23596, AGN; MI-2, G-2 6547, 25 October 1935; Pascual López to DEF, 2 March 1936, SEP/AH 319.8.

39. MI-7, G-2 4947, 12 January 1934; G-2 5810, 10 January 1935; G-2 6402, 10 September 1935; MI-8, G-2 6547, 25 October 1935; Zertuche to Múgica, 13 October 1935, AFJM, vol. 61, doc. 26.

40. Celaya to Cárdenas, 19 October 1935; Ramos to SG, 19 October 1935, RG, DGG 2.317.4(22)23596, AGN; Zertuche to Múgica, 13 October 1935, AFJM, vol. 61, doc. 26; PNR, Huatabampo, to Cárdenas, 23 October 1935; Espinosa to Cárdenas, 28 October 1935, RP, FLC 559.3/25, AGN; Robinson to SS, 17, 21 October 1935; Yepis to SS, 17 October 1935, SD/19; Report, AFJM, vol. 61, doc. 38.

41. *The Arizona Daily Star* (Tucson), 25 October 1935; Yepis to SS, 17 October 1935; Summary, Robinson, 30 November 1935, SD/19.

42. Petition, Nogales, to Cárdenas, 11 January 1936, RG, DGG 2.012.8 (22)13233, AGN; Espinosa to Cárdenas, 28 October 1935; Gobernador de Sinaloa to Cárdenas, 31 December 1935, RP, FLC 559.3/25, AGN; I-35 to OIPS, 30 December 1935, RG, DGG 2/311G(22)4674, AGN; Espinosa to Quien corresponde, 13 December 1935, ARM/PHS 75; Encinas, "El movimiento," 454.

43. MI-4, G2 5617, 15 November 1935; G2 6689, 5 December 1935; MI-2, G2 6762, 3 January 1936.

44. Hernández, *La mecánica*, Anexo 2.

45. Yepis to SS, 17, 31 December 1935; Thomas M. Powell, U.S. Vice-Consul, Nogales, to SS, 17 December 1935; Summary, Robinson, 31 December 1935, SD/19; I-35 to OIPS, 30 December 1935, RG, DGG 2.384(22)3, AGN; AAGES 62/213"36".

Chapter 4, "The Sonoran Reconstruction," 59–67

1. Hamilton, *Limits*, 127–28; Shulgovski, *En la encrucijada*, 110.

2. Enriqueta de Parodi, *Sonora: Hombres y paisajes* (México: Ed. Pafim, 1941), 55–60; Francisco R. Almada, *Diccionario de historia, geografía y biografía sonorenses* (Chihuahua: n.p., 1952); Corbalá, *Alamos*, 219–24. Belloc served as Cárdenas's *oficial mayor* in Michoacán and later became his private secretary. Dudley Ankerson, *Agrarian Warlord: Saturnino Cedillo and the Mexican Revolution in San Luis Potosí* (DeKalb: Northern Illinois University Press, 1984),162, 175–76; María del Carmen Nava Nava and Alonso Torres Aburto, "La rebelión cedillista" (paper presented at the XI Jornadas de Historia de

Occidente, Jiquilpan, 6–7 October 1988), 16; Roderic Ai Camp, *Mexican Political Biographies, 1935–1975* (Tucson: University of Arizona Press, 1976), 18–19. Gonzalo N. Santos, *Memorias* (México: Grijalbo, 1986), 610–11, 625, offers a colorful description of how Cedillistas forced him to drink three bottles of *puré* from an *excusado de hoyo* at Domitila's fonda in Ciudad Valles.

3. Federación Sindicatos to Cárdenas, 28 December 1935; Partido Independiente Obrero to Cárdenas, 30 April 1936, RG, DGG 2.317.4(22)6, AGN; Boyle to SD, 18, 23, 31 December 1935, 31 January 1936; Robinson to SD, 31 December 1935, 31 January 1936, 29 February 1936, 30 April 1936; Yepis to SD, 29 February 1936, SD/19; J. M. Gibbs, U.S. Consular Agent, Cananea, to Robinson, 22 January 1936, RG 84, Nogales Consulate (henceforth NC), GR 1936, Box 5, NAW; Meneses to Gibbs, 17 September 1935; Gibbs to Carleton Hurst, U.S. Consul, Nogales, 8 January 1936, RG 84, C 8.4, CACAC, 1935–36, vol. XXVIII, NAW; Gibbs to Robinson, 22 January 1936, RG 84, C 8.4, CACAC, 1936–37, vol. XXX, NAW; and 6 February 1936, SD/124; Juan Solórzano to SG, 1 February 1936, RG, DGG 2.317.4(22)7, AGN; Jesús Ramírez to Secretario, 1 October 1936, RG, DGG 2.317(22)11, AGN; M. Yocupicio to Cárdenas, 24 December 1935; R. Yocupicio to SG, 4, 9 February 1937, Petitions to Cárdenas, 28, 29 December 1936, RG, DGG 2.317.4(22)9, AGN; Priciliano Ochoa to SG, 12 October 1936; Gutiérrez to SG, 28 October 1936, RG, DGG 2.317.4(22)12, AGN; RG, DGG 2.331.9(2)921, AGN; Dabdoub, *Historia*, 344–45; Matías Méndez to Cárdenas, 25 March 1936, RG, DGG 2.331.8(22)16768, AGN; Sindicato "El Cíbola" to Gutiérrez, 23 December 1935, AAGES 231.5"35"/116; Comité Casa de Teras to Yocupicio, 6 May 1937, RG, DGG 2/317.4(22)25329, AGN.

4. Brown, "Church-State Relations," 213–14.

5. García de Alba to GS, 12 June 1936, RG, DGG 2.340(22)29, AGN.

6. RG, DGG 2.340(22)29, AGN; Inspector to OIPS, 6 September 1936, RG, DGG 2/311 G(22)16454 I, AGN; AAGES 235"36"/7; Boyle to SD, 31 March 1936, 30 April 1936, 29 May 1936, SD/19; Madera to Mercado, 21 May 1936, SEP/AH 339.4; Almada, "La conexión," 350–51.

7. Negrete, *Relaciones*; Bantjes, "Religión."

8. Miguel Tinker Salas, "Under the Shadow," 271. According to Salas, the term "guacho" literally means "a seedling which forms without first having taken root in the soil." Today, *guachos* are still distrusted and discriminated against.

9. Moncada, *Sucesión*, 51–52.

10. *El Hombre Libre*, 10, 17 June 1936; *El Heraldo del Yaqui*, 13 February 1936.

11. *El Pueblo*, 11 February 1936; Yepis to SS, 17 February 1936, SD/19.

12. MI-8, G-2 6740, 26 December 1935; MI-7 G-2 4943, 11 January 1934; Yocupicio to Cárdenas, 5 September 1936, RG, DGG 2/311 G(22) 16454 I, AGN; *El Hombre Libre*, 16 October 1936; Méndez to OIPS, 6 September 1936, RG, DGG 2/311 G(22)16454 I, AGN; Galaz, *Desde el Cerro*, 2:182–84; Yepis to SD, 31 August 1936, SD/19.

13. RP, FLC 544.2/25; I-25 to OIPS, 18 September 1936; Méndez to OIPS, 18 September 1936; Praxedis Gastélum to SG, 26 August 1936; Federación de Uniones Nogales to SG, 30 August 1936, RG, DGG 2/311 G(22) 16454, AGN; I-55 to Ramíro Zapién, OIPS, 27 September 1936, RG, DGG 2/311 G(22)16454, AGN; Gran Sindicato, Oficios Varios, to SG, 4 November 1936, RG, DGG 2/311 G(29) 15083, AGN.

14. I-25 to OIPS, 18 September 1936, RG, DGG 2/311 G(22) 16454, AGN; MI-7, G-2 4943, 11 January 1934; MI-7, G-2 1322, 13 January 1927; MI-2, G-2 report, 2 June 1931; *El Hombre Libre*, 7, 16 October 1936; Méndez to OIPS, 6 September 1936, RG, DGG 2/311 G(22)16454 I, AGN; Mendívil, *Cuarenta años*, 2:24; Sanders to Cárdenas, 2 March 1936; Rodríguez to Cárdenas, 22 April 1936, RP, FLC 544.2/25, AGN.

15. Parodi, *Hombres*, 45–53.

16. MI-8, G-2 8274, 25 January 1938; Calzadíaz, *Dos Gigantes*, 96, 103.

17. Calzadíaz, *Dos Gigantes*, 96, 103; Suárez, "La fundación," 424, 427–28, 434; MI-8, G-2 8274, 25 January 1938.

18. Lorenzo Garibaldi, ed., *Memoria de la gestión gubernamental del C. General Román Yocupicio: Aspectos principales de su labor social y constructiva* (Hermosillo: Cruz Gálvez, 1939), 20; I-25 to OIPS, 18 September 1936, RG, DGG 2/311 G(22) 16454, AGN; Yepis to SS, 29 January 1937, SD/19; Parodi, *Hombres*, 45–53; *El Hombre Libre*, 18 November 1936; Corbalá, *Alamos*, 224–33.

19. Garibaldi, *Memoria*, 13–15; Parodi, *Hombres*, 45–53; MI-8, G-2 8274, 25 January 1938; Personal communication, Ignacio Almada, March 1989; Mendívil, *Cuarenta años*, 2:49; Almada, *Diccionario*; Ignacio Almada Bay, "Crónica de un retablo municipal: Yocupicio Alcalde," *Revista de El Colegio de Sonora* 5, no. 7(1994): 75–102; MI-7, G-2 1322, 13 January 1927; G-2 1560, 17 June 1927; MI-2, G-2 report, 21 May 1929; G-2 report, 2 June 1931, 71; Larrañaga, *Navojoa*, 89–91.

20. Suárez, "La fundación," 424, 427–28, 434; Mendívil, *Cuarenta años*, 2:23; Yepis to SD, 31 January 1936; Boyle to SS, 14 October 1936, SD/19; *Douglas Daily Dispatch*, 14 October 1936.

21. *El Hombre Libre*, 7 October 1936.

22. Ibid., 4, 18 January 1936, 7 October 1936; Hernández, *La mecánica*, 69; 69, n.76; Robinson to SD, 27 February 1937, SD/19; Méndez to OIPS, 18 September 1936, RG, DGG 2/311 G(22)16454 I, AGN.

23. Moncada, *La sucesión*, 52; Volante, 3–36, RG, DGG 2/311 G(22) 16454, AGN; Enrique Contreras, *Cosas viejas de mi tierra* (Hermosillo: Editorial Urias, n.d.), 239; Interview, Escobosa, 22 May 1992; Centro Director to SG, 31 July 1936, RG, DGG 2/311(22)16454 I, AGN; Mendívil, *Cuarenta años*, 2:23.

24. MI-8, G-2 8274, 25 January 1938.

25. I-25 to OIPS, 18 September 1936; Méndez to OIPS, 6, 18, 20 September 1936, RG, DGG 2/311 G(22)16454 I, AGN; Yepis to SD, 31 August 1936, SD/19; *El Hombre Libre*, 18 November 1936; Garrido, *El Partido*, 265; Yepis to SS, 30 September 1936, SD/19.

26. *El Hombre Libre*, 5 June 1936; Robinson to SD, 30 September 1936, SD/19; Volante, March 1936, RG, DGG 2/311 G(22) 16454, AGN.

27. Yepis to SD, 31 August 1936; Corbalá, *Alamos*, 224–33; Charles C. Gidney, Jr., Vice-Consul, Guaymas, to SD, 31 October 1936, SD/19.

28. Moncada, *La sucesión*, 57; Suárez, "La fundación," 424, 427–28, 434; Corbalá, *Alamos*, 224–33.

29. *El Hombre Libre*, 18 November 1936; Yepis to SD, 31 August 1936, 30 September 1936, SD/19.

30. MI-4, G-2 7436, 11 September 1936, G-2 6689, 5 December 1935; MI-4, Appendix to Joe N. Dalton, 2 September 1936.

31. MI-5, "Visit of Military Attaché," 1934; MI-4, G-2 5838, 19 January 1935; MI-4, G-2 6273, 12 July 1935.

32. MI-4, G-2 7731, 18 December 1936.

33. MI-2, G-2 6762, 3 January 1936; MI-8, G-2 8116, 1 October 1937.

34. FOC, Etchojoa, 19 October 1936; Rodríguez to Cárdenas, 2 September 1936, RP, FLC 544.2/25, AGN; Yepis to SS, 31 August 1936, 30 September 1936, SD/19; I-25 to OIPS, 18 September 1936, RG, DGG 2/311 G(22) 16454, AGN.

35. Dabdoub, *Historia*, 361; Almada, "La conexión," 254, 261; Raúl Montaño to Agustín Arroyo Chico, 12 April 1936; I-25 to OIPS, 18 September 1936, RG, DGG 2/311 G(22) 16454, AGN; Yepis to SS, 30 September 1936, SD/19.

36. Yepis to SD, 13 October 1936, 30 September 1936, SD/19; *El Hombre Libre*, 13 July 1936; I-25 to OIPS, 18 September 1936; Gutiérrez to SG, 15 August 1936, RG, DGG 2/311 G(22) 16454 I, AGN; Winfield Minor, U.S. Vice-Consul, Agua Prieta, to SD, 31 August 1936, SD/19.

37. I-55 to OIPS, 21 September 1936, RG, DGG 2/311 G(22) 16454, I, AGN; Boyle to SD, 30 September 1936, SD/19.

38. Moncada, *La sucesión*, 61; I-25 to OIPS, 21 September 1936, RG, DGG 2/311 G(22) 16454, AGN; *El Hombre Libre*, 7 October 1936.

39. Boyle to SS, 24 September 1936, SD/19.

40. Yepis to SD, 31 October 1936, SD/19; Almada, "La conexión," 377.

41. I-25 to OIPS, 12 October 1936, RG, DGG 2/311G(22)16454, AGN.

42. Yepis to SD, 13 October 1936; Boyle to SD, 31 October 1936, SD/19.

43. I-25 to OIPS, 5, 9 October 1936, RG, DGG 2/311G(22)16454, AGN; Robinson to SD, 30 September 1936, SD/19.

44. Calzadíaz, *Dos gigantes*, 48–49; Yepis to SS, 29 January 1937, SD/19.

45. Garibaldi, *Memoria*, 26–27, 30–32.

46. Robinson to SS, 7 January 1937, SD/19.

47. Corbalá, *Alamos*. Compare Mendívil, *Cuarenta años*, 2:44–45.

Chapter 5, "The Yocupicista Power Base and Bureaucratic Patronage," 69–85

1. Scott, "Patron-Client Politics."

2. MI-5, "Inspection Trip," 13–25 June 1930.

3. *El Imparcial*, 8 April 1959; Robinson to SS, 3 February 1938, SD/19. This was still considered true in the 1940s: Personal communication, Todd Sermon, Laramie, Wyoming, 1991.

4. Robinson to SS, 12 December 1936, SD/19; *El Intruso* (Cananea), 15 January 1937; *El Hombre Libre*, 22 January 1937; *El Imparcial*, 16 September 1938; Almada, *Diccionario*; Francisco de P. Pegueras, *Album Patria Libre* (Nogales: n.p., n.d.), 26; Yocupicio to SG, 20 September 1937; 10 October 1938, RG, DGG 2.317(22)7; *Acción* (Nogales), 24 January 1939.

5. For example, Marcos Coronado and Israel C. González. Report, 17 June 1937, RG, DGG 2.384(22)23760; *El Hombre Libre*, 19 April 1937; Mendívil, *Cuarenta años*, 2:28.

6. *Acción*, 25 October 1937; *El Imparcial*, 16 September 1938, 4 January 1938; *Aurora*, 22, 28 January 1938; Corbalá, *Alamos*, 224–33.

7. Guadarrama, "La integración," *HCS*, 240; *El Intruso*, 14 May 1937; Luis Encinas to Cárdenas, 13 July 1937; Report, 17 June 1937; Federación

de Uniones, Nogales, to Cárdenas, 29 June 1937, RG, DGG 2.384(22)23760; Camilo Gastélum to SG, 7 May 1937; Encinas, Uruchurtu, and Duarte to Cárdenas, 1 May 1937; Yocupicio to SG, 12, 13 May 1937, RG, DGG 2.315 E.J.(22)26035; Yepis to SD, 30 September 1937, SD/19; *El Hombre Libre*, 22 January 1937; *Boletín Oficial* no. 30 (12 October 1938); no. 24 (23 March 1938).

8. *El Intruso*, 11 March 1937; Boyle to SS, 14 June 1939, SD/19; Garibaldi, *Memoria*, 66, 69; AHGES, Tesorería General del Estado, Libros de Caja, 1939, vol. 48; Libro Balance General, 31 December 1941.

9. Powell to Daniels, 22 April 1938, RG 84, NC, GR 1938, Box 18, 800, NAW; Boyle to SS, 14 June 1939; Powell to de L. Boal, 20 May 1938, SD/19.

10. Yepis to SS, 29 January 1937, 3 May 1937, 30 September 1937; Robinson to SD, 31 March 1937, SD/19; Report to Cárdenas, 17 June 1937, RG, DGG 2.384(22)23760.

11. Guadarrama, "La integración," *HCS*, 241; *El Intruso*, 17 March 1937.

12. *Boletín Oficial* 40, no. 6 (14 July 1937), no. 7 (21 July 1937), no. 8 (28 July 1937); Leopoldo Ulloa to SG, 15 May 1937; Yocupicio to SG, 25 June 1937, RG, DGG 2.311.M(22)24420, AGN; *El Intruso*, 31 March 1937; *Aurora*, 22, 28 March 1938.

13. *El Intruso*, 8 April 1937, 25 March 1937; *Boletín Oficial* 39, no. 51 (22 June 1937); *Aurora*, 31 January 1938; Comité agrario to PM, Nacozari, 21 September 1937, RG, DGG 2.311.M(22)28009, AGN; FOC, Etchojoa, to SG, 28 December 1936; Sindicato de Obreros y Campesinos to Cárdenas, 29 December 1936; Yocupicio to SG, 9 February 1937, 4 February 1937, RG, DGG 2.317.4(22)9, AGN; Maldonado to SG, 17 August 1937; Unión Central to SG, 18 July 1937; Jacinto López to Cámara de Diputados, 23 July 1937, RG, DGG 2.311.M(22)27056, AGN; Robinson to SD, 30 September 1937, SD/19; Comisariado, Caborca, to Cárdenas, 19 June 1937, RG, DGG 2.317.4(22)23596, AGN.

14. *Diario de los debates de la Cámara de Diputados del Congreso de los Estados Unidos Mexicanos*, Año 1, XXXVII Legislatura, I, no. 2 (18 August 1937); Gobernación to OIPS, 17 January 1939, RG, DGG 2.384(22)23760, AGN.

15. José Abraham Mendívil, *La Democracia en Sonora* (Hermosillo: Publicidad Mendívil, 1980), 69; idem, *Cuarenta años*, 2:15–16; MI-7, G-2 8692, 11 October 1938; Guadarrama, "La integración," *HCS*, 243; AHGES, Tesorería General del Estado, Libros de Caja, 1939, vol. 48, 9, 19 May 1939; Federación de Uniones, Nogales, to Cárdenas, 29 June 1937; Quejas, RG, DGG 2.384(22)23760, AGN; Rafael Méndez to Secretario Particular, 29 August 1937, RP, FLC 543.1/8, AGN.

16. *El Hombre Libre*, 15 August 1938; Dabdoub, *Historia*, 361; Sindicato Central to Cárdenas, 21 September 1937; Comité de Defensa to Cárdenas, 4 August 1937, 2 September 1937, RG, DGG 2.384(22)23760, AGN; Comité de Defensa to Francisco Castillo Nájera, 10 November 1937, RP, FLC 543.1/8, AGN.

17. Quejas, RG, DGG 2.384(22)23760, AGN.

18. Garibaldi, *Memoria*, 26–27, 30–32.

19. RG, DGG 2.384(22)23760, AGN.

20. Garibaldi, *Memoria*, 63.

21. Yepis to SD, 31 March 1938; Robinson to SD, 31 July 1938; Boyle to SD, 31 March 1938, 30 October 1937, 30 November 1937, SD/19.

22. Yepis to SS, 29 January 1937, SD/19.

23. Painter Papers, MS 18, SG 1, Series 4, Folder 1, Field Notes, Magdalena, 1947, ASM.

24. Director, Escuela, to SG, 18 October 1937; Yocupicio to SG, 15 November 1937, RG, DGG 2.340(22)25234, AGN; *El Intruso*, 28 May 1937, 1 June 1937.

25. Yocupicio to SG, 7 June 1937, RG, DGG 2.340(22)25353, AGN; GS to SG, 14, 28 June 1937, 27 July 1937, RG, DGG 2.340(22)29, AGN.

26. R. Pérez Ayala to Yocupicio, 20 August 1937; SG to Yocupicio, 16 June 1937; Yocupicio to SG, 28 June 1937, RG, DGG 2.340(22)29, AGN; Yepis to SD, 3 May 1937, SD/19; Yepis to SS, 22 October 1937, RG 84, GC, GR 1937, Box 14, 800, NAW.

27. Brown, "Church-State Relations," 222.

28. *El Pueblo*, 15 March 1938; Director, Escuela Secundaria, to SG, 18 October 1937, RG, DGG 2.340(22)25234, AGN; Pérez to Oficina Hacienda Nogales, 19 April 1938; Yocupicio to SG, 19 May 1938, 9 August 1938, RG, DGG 2.340(22)25372, AGN; Yepis to SD, 3, 29, 31 May 1937, 30 June 1937; Robinson to SD, 31 June, 31 July, 31 August 1937, SD/19; Yocupicio to SG, 2 June 1937; Pérez to SG, 17 June 1938, RG, DGG 2.342(22)10828, AGN.

29. Liga de Comunidades Agrarias to SG, 4 June 1937; Pérez to SG, 17 July 1937; Damas Católicas, Navojoa, to SG, 4 June 1937, RG, DGG 2.340(22)25567, AGN; *El Pueblo*, 18 March 1938; Robinson to SD, 31 December 1937; Powell to SD, 31 May 1938, SD/19; *El Aurora*, 31 March 1938; Yepis to Powell, 27 May 1938, RG 84, NC, GR 1938, Box 18, 800, NAW; Secretaría Particular to SG, 28 June 1937; Pérez to SG, 21 August 1937, RG, DGG 2.342(22)13961, AGN.

30. Yepis to SD, 31 March 1937, SD/19; *Album conmemorativo*, 69, 119.

31. Robinson to SD, 30 June 1937; 30 September 1937; 30 October 1937; 31 December 1937; Yepis to SD, 31 May 1937, 30 June 1937, SD/19.

32. AAGES, 235"38"; Armstrong to SD, 1 November 1938, 1 December 1938, SD/19.

33. Cited in Almada, "La conexión," 387.

34. Alianza Obrero-Campesina, Cumpas, to SG, 26 April 1936, RG, DGG 2.340(22)25477, AGN; Educación Primaria to SG, 29 April 1938, ibid.

35. Comisariado, Ures, to Cárdenas, 23 December 1938, RG, DGG 2.342(22)13962, AGN.

36. E. R. Jesson to Yepis, 15 May 1938, RG 84, GC, GR 1938, Box 23, 350, NAW.

37. *El Popular*, 26 August 1938; *El Heraldo*, 31 May 1937; Director, Escuela, Cananea, to SG, 18 October 1937; Pérez to Oficina Hacienda Nogales, 14 July 1937, RG, DGG 2.340(22)25234, AGN.

38. Alfredo Galindo Mendoza, *Apuntes geográficos y estadísticos de la República y de la Iglesia Mexicana* (México: n.p., 1943), 15.

39. *Boletín Pro-Bodas de Plata Episcopales: Informe mensual diocesano. Organo del comité central*, I, nos. 1 (August 1942), 2 (September 1942), 3 (25 October 1942), 4 (29 November 1942), 6 (31 January 1943).

40. MI-4, G-2 5838, 19 January 1935; G-2 26273, 12 July 1935; Lorenzo Meyer, *México y los Estados Unidos en el conflicto petrolero, 1917–1942*, 2d ed. (México: El Colegio de México, 1972), 352.

41. MI-4, G-2 6857, 11 February 1936; MI-8, G-2 8116, 1 October 1937; Luis Medina, *Del Cardenismo al Avilacamachismo* (México: El Colegio de México, 1978), 101, n.150; Albert L. Michaels, "Las Elecciones de 1940," *Historia Mexicana* 21, no. 1 (July–September 1971): 104, 122.

42. *El Hombre Libre*, 26 July 1937, 24 October 1937; Boyle to SD, 30 June 1937, SD/19; *El Pueblo*, 23 February 1938.

43. Boyle to SD, 14 June 1939, 30 November 1937; Armstrong to SD, 1 February 1939, SD/19; *El Imparcial*, 19 March 1939; *Acción*, 16 March 1939, 21 January 1939; Calzadíaz, *Dos Gigantes*, 54–55.

44. José Carlos Ramírez, "El último auge," *HCS*, 48, 59; idem, "Cárdenas y las dos caras de la recuperación," *HCS*, 221, 229; Ramírez and Guadarrama, "Los resultados de la modernización en el campo," *HCS*, 320, 324. For a history of nineteenth-century U.S.-Sonoran relations, see Tinker Salas, "Under the Shadow."

45. Ramírez, "Una época," *HCS*, 104–5.

46. Robinson to SS, 23 March 1938, SD/19.

47. *El Imparcial*, 8 December 1939; Meyer, *México*, 439.

48. Netherlands Chargé d'Affaires to Ministerie van Buitenlandse Zaken, 13 September 1938, Algemeen Rijksarchief, Buitenlandse Zaken, Kabinetsarchief betreffende Politieke Raportage, Inv. No. 259; Luis González, *Los días del presidente Cárdenas* (México: El Colegio de México, 1981), 258; *KEN*, 21 April 1938; Vicente Lombardo Toledano, *Como actúan los Nazis en México* (México: Universidad Obrera, 1941); idem, *5th Column in Mexico* (New York: Council for Panamerican Democracy, [1942]).

49. Betty Kirk, *Covering the Mexican Front: The Battle of Europe versus America* (Norman: University of Oklahoma Press, 1942), 288; Virginia Prewitt, *Reportage on Mexico* (New York: Dutton, 1941), 281–312.

50. Salvador Novo, *La vida en México en el período presidencial de Lázaro Cárdenas* (México: Empresas Editoriales, 1964), 105, 205.

51. Blanca Torres Ramírez, *México en la segunda guerra mundial* (México: El Colegio de México, 1979), 22; Hugh G. Campbell, "The Radical Right in Mexico, 1929–1949" (Ph.D. diss., University of California at Los Angeles, 1968), 184.

52. MI-3, G-2 3843, 18 March 1932; Gerald A. Mokma, U.S. Consul, Ensenada, to SS, 22 November 1940, RG 84, GC, Confidential Records (henceforth CR) 1936–1941, Box 1, 862.8, NAW.

53. *El Pueblo*, 15 January 1938; *El Imparcial*, 15 April 1938; Mokma to SS, 24 January 1940; Powell to SS, 29 January 1940, RG 84, GC, CR 1936–1941, Box 1, 800, NAW.

54. Carlos Martínez Assad et al., *Revolucionarios fueron todos* (México: SEP, 1982); Mokma to SS, 22 November 1940, RG 84, GC, CR 1936–1941, Box 1, 862.8, NAW; *Sonora en los cuarentas* (Hermosillo: "La Diligencia," 1991), 82.

55. Friedrich E. Schuler, "Mexican-German Relations in the Second World War, 1939–1943" (Master's thesis, University of Texas at Austin, 1983), 104, 109; Andreas E. Winckler, "The Nazis in Mexico: Mexico and the Reich in the Prewar Period, 1936–1939" (Master's thesis, University of Texas at Austin, 1983), 121. For German-Mexican and Japanese-Mexican business relations, see Schuler, *Mexican Foreign Policy*, chaps. 4–5.

56. Boyle to Shaw, 7 February 1941, RG 84, GC, CR 1936–1941, Box 1, 820.02, NAW.

57. *El Intruso*, 30 June 1937.

58. *Hoy*, 30 July 1938; Yepis to SS, 20 June 1938, SD/19.

59. *Dr. Atl, 1875–1964: Conciencia y paisaje* (México: Museo Nacional de Arte, 1985), 64; *Timón* (México), 4 May 1940, 8 June 1940.

60. Yepis to Powell, 28 May 1938, RG 84, GC, GR 1938, Box 26, 840.1; Powell to Boal, 31 May 1938, 3 June 1938, RG 84, NC, GR 1938, Box 18, 800, NAW.

61. Campbell, "The Radical Right," 139–42, 147–48, 161; *Excélsior* (México), 11 November 1935, 21 November 1935; Ignacio González Polo, *Bibliografía general de las agrupaciones y partidos políticos mexicanos, 1900–1970* (México: Reforma Política, 1978), 60, 251; FMTE to Cárdenas, 17 June 1937; Lombardo to Cárdenas, 1 July 1937, RG, DGG 2.384(22)23760, exp. 544.4/25, AGN. RG, DGG 2.311P(22)18131, AGN. UNVR members included José R. Berlanga, Enrique Fuentes Frías, Jesús María Suárez, and Gilberto Suárez, who was reported to be a friend of Nicolás Rodríguez. UNVR to SG, 28 May 1938, RG, DGG 2.331.9(22)1, AGN; RG, DGG 2.331.9 (22)1, AGN; Robinson to SS, 22 March 1938; Memorandum, SG, n.d., SD/ 19; *El Imparcial*, 20, 26 May 1938, 21 July 1939; Report, Powell, 7 February 1939, RG 84, NC, GR 1938, Box 20, 850.4, NAW; Liga Agrónomos to Departamento Agrario (henceforth DA), 22 April 1938, Secretaría de la Reforma Agraria/Archivo General (henceforth SRA/AG) 23/4670; *El Pueblo*, 13 January 1938; UNVR to Yocupicio, 21 December 1938, AAGES 312.1"38"/39.

62. François Furet, *Interpreting the French Revolution* (Cambridge: Cambridge University Press, 1981), 58.

Chapter 6, "The Cardenista Counteroffensive," 89–107

1. Yepis to SD, 30 September 1937, 29 November 1937, SD/19; *Acción*, 2 October 1937; FOC, Alamos, to Cárdenas, 25 September 1937; Lombardo to Cárdenas, 29 September 1937; Yocupicio to Cárdenas, 24 September 1937, RP, FLC 543.1/8; *El Hombre Libre*, 29 September 1937, 1 October 1937; José Abraham Mendívil, *Batalla anti-Comunista* (Hermosillo: Publicidad Mendívil, 1966), 16.

2. Córdova, *La política*; Ianni, *El Estado*; Anguiano, *El Estado*, 54–55, 58.

3. Samuel León and Ignacio Marván, *La clase obrera en la historia de México: En el Cardenismo (1934–1940)* (México: Siglo XXI, 1985), 10; Kevin J. Middlebrook, *The Paradox of Revolution: Labor, the State, and Authoritarianism in Mexico* (Baltimore: Johns Hopkins University Press, 1995).

4. Hamilton, *The Limits*, 151; León and Marván, *La clase*, 161–66.

5. Basurto, *Cárdenas*, 170; Anguiano, *El Estado*, 51.

6. *La CTM en los Estados* (n.p.: Universidad Autónoma de Sinaloa and Centro de Estudios del Movimiento Obrero y Socialista, 1988), 69, 145; Joe Ashby, *Organized Labor and the Mexican Revolution under Lázaro Cárdenas* (Chapel Hill: University of North Carolina Press, 1964), 73–74; Hubert Carton de Grammont, *Los empresarios agrícolas y el Estado* (México: Instituto de Investigaciones Sociales, UNAM, 1990), 109.

7. Hamilton, *The Limits*, 151, 161–62.

8. *La CTM en los estados*, 11, 145; Anguiano, *El Estado*, 64.

9. Barry Carr, *El movimiento obrero y la política en México* (México: ERA, 1981), 264.

10. Aguilar, *La frontera*, 90; Estados Unidos Mexicanos, Secretaría de la Economía Nacional, Dirección General de Estadística, *Compendio*

estadístico (México: Secretaría de la Economía Nacional, Dirección General de Estadística, 1941), 13; Ramón Eduardo Ruiz, *The People of Sonora and Yankee Capitalists* (Tucson: University of Arizona Press, 1989), 100–102.

11. *Compendio estadístico*, 14–15.

12. Miguel Angel Vázquez, "Notas para una historia industrial de Sonora," in *Memoria: XII Simposio*, 1:105–21; Cynthia Radding, "Las estructuras formativas del capitalismo en Sonora (1900–1930)," in *De los Borbones a la Revolución*, ed. Mario Cerutti (Monterrey: Universidad Autónoma de Nuevo León, 1986), 229–65; Robinson to Shaw, 1 July 1938, RG 84, NC, GR 1938, Box 17, 160.1, NAW; Gracida, "Génesis," *HGS*, 4:54; idem, "El Sonora moderno," *HGS*, 4:102–3; Federico García y Alva, *México y sus progresos: "Album-Directorio del Estado de Sonora"* (Hermosillo: n.p., n.d.); *Sonora y sus Actividades; Directorio*; RG 84, NC, GR 1936, Box 3, 610.1, NAW; Tanneries, 15 July 1936, RG 84, GC, GR 1936, Box 4, 610.1, NAW; Jesús Félix Uribe García, *La historia de la industria en Hermosillo* (Hermosillo: "La Diligencia," 1991).

13. *Resumen general del censo industrial de 1935* (México: DAPP, 1941), 107, lists 2,156 workers in large factories. Wages, 24 May 1938, RG 84, NC, GR 1938, Box 20, 850.4, NAW; RG 84, NC, GR 1936, Box 3, 610.1; Sindicato Obrero to Departamento Autónomo del Trabajo (henceforth DAT), 2 September 1938; Francisco Cárdenas to DAT, 3 September 1938; Antonio Palacios to Trabajo, 22 October 1938; Yocupicio to Cárdenas, 23, 28 October 1938, C. 239, exp. 24, V/300(721.5)1-5, DAT, AGN; RG, DGG 2.331.8(22) 29316, AGN; AAGES 234.0"38"; World Trade Directory (henceforth WTD), RG 84, CACG, vol. IV, 1933, 610.1, NAW; Ernesto Truqui to Yepis, 26 May 1936, RG 84, GC, GR 1936, Box 4, 610.1, NAW; Flour Mills, 5 September 1934, RG 84, Consular Correspondence, Nogales, 1934, vol. V, 610.1, NAW; *El Heraldo del Yaqui* (Ciudad Obregón), 25 January 1939; RG 84, GC, GR 1939, Box 33, 610.1, NAW; Information, 17 October 1936, RG 84, Agua Prieta Consulate, GR 1936, Box 1, 350, NAW; RG 84, NC, GR 1937, Box 11, 610.1, NAW; RG 84, NC, GR 1936, Box 3, 610.1, NAW; WTD, RG 84, GC, GR 1937, Box 14, 610.1, NAW.

14. AAGES 234.0"38".

15. WTD, RG 84, NC, GR 1939, Box 23, 610.1, NAW; and RG 84, GC, GR 1937, Box 14, 610.1, NAW.

16. Wages, RG 84, GC, GR 1936, Box 7, 850.4, NAW; Stephen C. Worster, Vice-Consul, Guaymas, Wages, 14 July 1938, RG 84, GC, GR 1938, Box 26, NAW; Wages, 24 May 1938; Cía. Industrial del Pacífico to Robinson, 11 April 1938, RG 84, NC, GR 1938, Box 20, 850.4, NAW.

17. *Padrones*, AAGES 234.0"38".

18. Tarifas, AAGES 234"36"/196; Wages, 14 July 1938, 14 April 1938, RG 84, GC, GR 1938, Box 26, NAW; Wages, RG 84, GC, GR 1936, Box 7, 850.4, NAW.

19. *Padrones*, Sindicatos de Empacadoras, Cargadores, AAGES 234.0"38".

20. Calculated from data on 451 *peones* at thirty-six Yaqui Valley farms: AAGES 234.0"38".

21. Wages, 24 May 1938, RG 84, NC, GR 1938, Box 20, 850.4, NAW; Jorge Rodríguez to Cuerpo Nacional, SRA/AG 23/15791.

22. Resolución, Nacozari, AAGES 411.12"37"/12.

23. Dora Elvia Enríquez Licón, "Los trabajadores sonorenses y sus organizaciones (1873–1987)" (Tesis de licenciatura en Sociología, Univer-

sidad de Sonora, Departamento de Ciencias Sociales, 1988), 25, 38; José Abraham Mendívil, "La Revolución y la lucha obrero-campesina en Sonora," in *Segundo simposio de historia de Sonora: Memoria* (Hermosillo: Instituto de Investigaciones Históricas, Universidad de Sonora, 1977), 430–43.

24. SEP/ARPF, IV/161(IV-15)2462; Cristina Martínez, "Movilización y acción política, una visión retrospectiva," in *Movimientos sociales en el noroeste de México*, ed. Rubén Burgos (Culiacán: Universidad Autónoma de Sinaloa, 1985), 106; Enríquez, "Los Trabajadores," 50–57; Mendívil, *Medio siglo*, 2:19–21.

25. Martínez, "Movilización," 107.

26. Alan Knight, "Land and Society in Revolutionary Mexico: The Destruction of the Great Haciendas," *Mexican Studies/Estudios Mexicanos* 7, no. 1 (Winter 1991): 73–107.

27. Enríquez, "Los Trabajadores," 78–79; Gustavo Lorenzano Durán, "Situación agraria en los Valles del Yaqui y Mayo, 1922–1932," in *XV Simposio de Historia y Antropología de Sonora: Memoria*, vol. 1 (Hermosillo: Instituto de Investigaciones Históricas, Universidad de Sonora, 1991), 489–507.

28. Enríquez, "Los Trabajadores," 82.

29. Cristina Isabel Mártinez Rascón, "Campesinado, Estado y Capital en Sonora. 1930–1940" (Tesis de maestría en Ciencias Sociales, FLACSO, 1983), 70–71; Martínez, "Movilización," 107; Interview, Bernabé Arana León, 24 May 1992, Ciudad Obregón; Humberto Ochoa Bustamante, *Biografía de Jacinto López Moreno: Fundador y Secretario General de la Unión General de Obreros y Campesinos de México, U.G.O.C.M.* (Hermosillo: Editorial Nacional, 1992), 14–15; Carton, *Los empresarios*, 105; Murrieta and Graf, *Por el milagro*, 110–13.

30. Enríquez, "Los Trabajadores," 78–79.

31. Ibid.; Martínez, "Movilización," 107; idem, "Campesinado," 65; Carlos Siqueiros A., *Remembranzas Nogalenses* (Nogales: Editorial Privada, 1980), 23–24; Mendívil, *Medio siglo*, 2:19–21.

32. *El Hombre Libre*, 18 June 1937.

33. Dictamen, 31 July 1937; Primer Congreso, February 1938, in *CTM, 1936–1941*, vol. 1 (México: PRI, 1981); *Diario de Debates de la Cámara de Senadores*, 29 November 1938.

34. Robinson to SD, 27 February 1937, SD/19; Primer Congreso, February 1938, in *CTM, 1936–1941*, vol. 1, 487; Lombardo to Cárdenas, 1 July 1937, RG, DGG 2.384(22)23760, AGN; *Futuro* 24 (February 1938): 9; ibid., 33 (November 1938): 28–29; *El Machete*, 20 June 1937.

35. *Futuro* 29 (October 1938): 9.

36. Alianza Revolucionaria to Cárdenas, 12 June 1937; Yocupicio to SG, 17 June 1937, RG, DGG 2.384(22)23760, AGN; Comisión to Yocupicio, 17 July 1937, AFJM, vol. 61, doc. 43; Yepis to SS, 18, 30 June 1937; Robinson to SS, 22 March 1938, SD/19; *El Hombre Libre*, 8 September 1937, 26 July 1937; Yocupicio to Cárdenas, 17 June 1937, RP, FLC 543.1/8, AGN.

37. Cited in Carlos Alvear Acevedo, *Lázaro Cárdenas: El hombre y su mito* (México: Editorial Jus, 1961).

38. James W. Wilkie and Edna Monzón de Wilkie, *México visto en el siglo XX: Entrevistas de historia oral* (México: Instituto Mexicano de Investigaciones Económicas, 1969), 401.

39. *El Hombre Libre*, 10 June 1938.

40. Unión del Yaqui to DA, 7 August 1935, SRA/AG 23/760.

41. DA to Yocupicio, 24 April 1937, AAGES 411.12"37"/28; *El Intruso,* 28 February 1937; Robinson to SD, 27 February 1937; Yepis to SS, 23 February 1937, 18 June 1937, SD/19; Yocupicio to Cárdenas, 24 February 1937, RP, FLC 543.1/8, AGN.

42. Interview, Arana, 25 May 1992.

43. Censo, December 1939, SRA/AG 23/4670.

44. María del Carmen Castro Vázquez, "El conflicto agrario, la organización campesina en el Valle del Yaqui y sus principales fuentes de estudio (1940–1960)" (Tesis de licenciatura en Sociología, Escuela de Sociología, Universidad de Sonora, 1989), 23; Romana Falcón, *Revolución y caciquismo: San Luis Potosí, 1910–1928* (México: El Colegio de México, 1984), 246; *La CTM en los Estados*; Basurto, *Cárdenas,* 77; León and Marván, *La clase,* 273.

45. Yepis to SD, 31 March 1937, SD/19; Yocupicio to SG, 20 March 1937; Lombardo to Cárdenas, 1 July 1937, RG, DGG 2.384(22)23760, AGN; Sindicato de Empresa del Yaqui to Cárdenas, 24 March 1937, RG, DGG 2.311.8(22)22037, AGN.

46. Yepis to SD, 3, 31 May 1937, 18 June 1937, SD/19; Lombardo to Cárdenas, 10 May 1937, 1 July 1937; Yocupicio to SG, 13, 17 May 1937; 13, 17 June 1937; Federación de Uniones to Cárdenas, 15 May 1937; Lombardo to SG, 12 June 1937, RG, DGG 2.384(22)23760, AGN; Retamoza to Cárdenas, 10 May 1937; Yocupicio to Cárdenas, 17 May 1937, RP, FLC 543.1/8, AGN; MI-4, G-2 7964, 18 May 1937.

47. Martínez, "Campesinado," 77; SG to Secretario Particular, 12 June 1937; Lombardo to Cárdenas, 12 June 1937, 29 July 1937; Yocupicio to Cárdenas, 13 June 1937, RP, FLC 433/205, AGN; Dictamen, Comisión, 27 April 1937; Dictamen sobre el Informe, 31 July 1937, in *CTM, 1936–1941,* vol. I; *El Machete,* 20 June 1937; Murrieta and Graf, *Por el milagro,* 34.

48. Yepis to SD, 30 September 1937, 29 November 1937, SD/19; Mendívil, *Batalla,* 16; *Acción,* 2 October 1937; FOC, Alamos, to Cárdenas, 25 September 1937; Lombardo to Cárdenas, 29 September 1937, RP, FLC 543.1/8, AGN; *El Hombre Libre,* 29 September 1937, 1 October 1937.

49. *El Hombre Libre,* 27 September 1937.

50. Report, Boyle, 1 February 1939, RG 84, NC, GR 1938, Box 20, 850.4, NAW.

51. Report, Powell, 7 February 1939, ibid.; RG, DGG 2.331.9(22)921, AGN.

52. RG, DGG 2.384(22)23760; 2.331.8(22)22037; 2.331.8(22)25292, AGN; Enríquez, "Los Trabajadores," 100–103; FUSON to Cárdenas, 15 May 1937, RG, DGG 2.384(22)23760, exp. 543.1/8, AGN; *Acción,* 14 April 1939.

53. Informe, Congreso, SEP/AH 297.17; Acuerdos, SEP/AH 339.4; J. R. Velázquez to SEP, 9 September 1936, SEP/AH 297.19.

54. Unsigned acuerdo, SEP/AH 297.17; Yepis to SD, 1 June 1936, 30 September 1936, SD/19; Gustavo Rivera Rodríguez, *Breve historia de la educación en Sonora e historia de la Escuela Normal del Estado* (n.p., 1975), 105; CNTE, 31 August 1936; Lambares to SEP, 17 September 1936, SEP/AH 339.4; Ibarra and Camou, "Las instituciones educativas," *HCS,* 578–80; Circular 71–42, 16 March 1936, and Gutiérrez to Ximello, 6 May 1936, SEP/AH 297.20.

55. *El Intruso,* 12 May 1937; *Acción,* 15 October 1937; RG, DGG 2.384(22)23760, AGN; SEP/AMR IV/161(IV-15)2464.

56. Ibarra and Camou, "Las instituciones," *HCS*, 80; *El Machete*, 20 June 1937; *El Intruso*, 12 May 1937, 30 June 1937, 5 July 1938; Garibaldi, *Memoria*, 83–96; José Ma. Sotelo to Cárdenas, 23 November 1938; Andrés Ramos to Cárdenas, 26 May 1937; FOC, Mayo, to SG, 10 March 1937, RP, FLC 534.6/375; Document, Dusart, 15 July 1937; Report to Cárdenas, 17 June 1937, RG, DGG 2.384(22)23760, AGN; AHGES, Libro Balance General de 1940, Tesorería General, 31 December 1940; *Acción*, 17 October 1937.

57. Nava and Aburto, "La rebelión," 19; *La CTM en los Estados*; Mary Kay Vaughan, "El papel político del magisterio socialista de México, 1934–1940: Un estudio comparativo de los casos de Puebla y Sonora," in *Memoria: XII Simposio*, 2:190–91.

58. FEMSS to Cárdenas, 22 May 1937, 19 June 1937; Telegrams to Cárdenas, April 1938, RP, FLC 534.6/375, AGN; Yocupicio to Cárdenas, 17 June 1937; Inspector to Cárdenas, 14 June 1937, RP, FLC 433/205, AGN; Chávez to SG, 2 July 1938, RG, DGG 2.384(22)23760, AGN; Leobardo Parra y Marquina, Hoja de Servicios, SEP/AH, Personal Sobresaliente; *El Imparcial*, 25 October 1938, 4 December 1938.

59. The list also included José Bernal Rodríguez, Juan G. Oropeza, Leonardo Magaña, and Heriberto Salazar. RP, FLC 534.6/375, AGN; Memo, 14 July 1935, SEP/AH 249; *El Machete*, 27 July 1938; STERM to SG, 25 April 1938; Yocupicio to SG, 29 April 1938, RG, DGG 2.384(22)23760, AGN; *El Pueblo*, 14 March 1938; Arreola to Cárdenas, 2 May 1938, RP, FLC 543.1/8, AGN.

60. Suárez to SG, 12 December 1938, RG, DGG 2.384(22)23760, AGN; Daniel Sañudo to PM, Etchojoa, 6 March 1938, RG, DGG 2.340(22)18528, AGN; *Acción*, 8 April 1939, 11 January 1939; SUTES to Cárdenas, 28 October 1938; STERM to Cárdenas, 10 November 1938, RP, FLC 543.6/375, AGN; *El Imparcial*, 25, 28, 30 October 1938, 4 November 1938, 2 December 1938.

61. FMTE to Cárdenas, 17 June 1937, RG, DGG 2.384(22)23760, AGN; *El Pueblo*, 1, 21 October 1938; Cárdenas to Yocupicio, 20 September 1938, 11 October 1938; Yocupicio to Cárdenas, 25, 26, 28 October 1938, RP, FLC 534.6/375, AGN; Vaughan, "El papel," 289; Yepis to SD, 31 October 1938, SD/19.

62. Enrique W. Sánchez, "Apuntes históricos sobre el movimiento sindical del magisterio nacional," in Sindicato Nacional de Trabajadores de la Educación, *Conferencias regionales de orientación social: Memoria* (México: SNTE, 1966), 73–108; Valente Lozano Ceniceros, "Breve historia del movimiento sindical magisterial y comentario histórico del actual Sindicato Nacional de Trabajadores de la Educación," in ibid., 57–71.

63. *Informe al Primer Congreso del STERM: CEN* (México: FSTSE, 1940); Vaughan, "El papel," 190; Gerardo Peláez, *Historia del Sindicato de Trabajadores de la Educación* (México: Ediciones de Cultura Popular, 1984), 25, 33.

64. *El Imparcial*, 30 October 1938, 4, 16 November 1938, 20 December 1938.

65. Raby, *Educación*, 63.

66. Ray to SS, 1 April 1935, RG 84, CACG 1935, vol. V, 800, NAW; Gidney to SD, 30 November 1936, SD/19; Gidney to SS, 30 November 1936, 12 December 1936, RG 84, GC, GR 1936, Box 7, 850.32, NAW; Yocupicio to SG, 15 January 1937, RG, DGG 2.311.8(22)22037, AGN; Tercer Congreso in *CTM, 1936–1941*, 1:295.

67. SIPS to Cárdenas, 23 April 1937, RG, DGG 2.331.8(22)22037, AGN.

68. *El Intruso*, 8 January 1937; Acta, 20 April 1937; Informe, 30 April 1938; Directora to SUTES, 21 September 1938, SEP/Archivo de Rurales y Primarias Foráneas (henceforth SEP/ARPF) IV/161(IV-15)2464; Yepis to SS, 21 April 1938, 31 May 1938, 27 July 1938, 15 September 1938, RG 84, GC, GR 1938, Box 25, 800, NAW, and 21, 28 February 1936, RG 84, GC, GR 1936, Box 5, 811.11, NAW; Convenio, 20 February 1936, RG 84, GC, GR 1936, Box 7, 850.32, NAW; *El Imparcial*, 2 November 1938.

69. Yepis to SD, 31 May 1938, 31 August 1938, 30 September 1938; Powell to SD, 30 September 1938, SD/19; *El Pueblo*, 19 September 1938.

70. Armstrong to SD, 1 November 1938, 30 June 1939; Harry K. Pangburn, U.S. Consul, Agua Prieta, to SD, 30 September 1938; Yepis to SS, 13, 15 June 1938, SD/19.

71. Secretaría de la Economía Nacional, Dirección General de Estadística, *Anuario estadístico de los Estados Unidos Mexicanos, 1938* (México: DAPP, 1939), 158; Secretaría de la Economía Nacional, Dirección General de Estadística, *Anuario estadístico de los Estados Unidos Mexicanos, 1940* (México: Secretaría de la Economía Nacional, 1942).

72. Powell to SD, 31 July 1938; Yepis to SD, 31 May 1938, 31 August 1938, 30 September 1938, SD/19; *El Pueblo*, 11 March 1938; *El Imparcial*, 13 February 1938.

73. *Anuario estadístico . . . 1940*, 340, 359, 376–77, 382.

Chapter 7, "Yocupicio's Response," 109–22

1. Lombardo to Cárdenas, 15 March 1937, 8 November 1937; Federación de Uniones, Nogales, to Cárdenas; Comité de Defensa to Cárdenas, 31 July 1937; Rafael Méndez to Secretario Particular, 29 August 1937, RP, FLC 543.1/8, AGN; Lombardo to Cárdenas, 23 June 1937; Quejas Retamoza to Cárdenas, 14 October 1938, SG to Lombardo, 21 July 1938, Piña Soria to Cárdenas, 25 May 1938; Fernando Moreno to Cárdenas, 24 May 1938; Comité, Moctezuma, to Cárdenas, 11 November 1938, RG, DGG 2.384(22) 23760, AGN; *El Machete*, 28 July 1938; Lombardo to Cárdenas, 14 March 1938; Yocupicio to SG, 2 May 1938; Petition to Cárdenas, 15 August 1938, RG, DGG 2.012.2(22)30541, C. 61, AGN; *El Pueblo*, 22 January 1938, 1, 10 February 1938.

2. MI-2, G-2 8004, 2 July 1937.

3. Federación de Uniones, Nogales, to Cárdenas, 15 May 1937; Contreras to Cárdenas, 4 March 1937; Lombardo to Cárdenas, 12 March 1937, RG, DGG 2.384(22)23760, AGN.

4. Dictamen, 27 April 1937, in *CTM, 1936–1941*, vol. 1.

5. See Collier, *The New Authoritarianism*, 400.

6. *El Intruso*, 23, 26 May 1937; Telegrams, RP, FLC 543.1/8, AGN; Martínez, "Movilización," 111; Lombardo to Cárdenas, 1 July 1937; Crisóstomo Cavazos to Cárdenas, 3 January 1938, RG, DGG 2.384(22)23760, exp. 542.1/206, AGN; Lombardo to SG, 3 March 1937, RG, DGG 2.311.M(22)24420, AGN.

7. Cavazos to Cárdenas, 3 January 1938, RG, DGG 2.384(22)23760, exp. 542.1/206, AGN.

8. Interview, Escobosa, 21 May 1992; AAGES 234.0"38"/45, 234.2"38"; RG, DGG 2.33.1.9(22)33490, AGN; RG 84, NC, GR 1937, Box 13, 850.4; DAT,

Caja 269, exp. 3, V322(721.5)/1, AGN; Robinson to SS, 15 January 1938, RG 84, NC, GR 1938, Box 20, 850.4, NAW; *El Pueblo*, 30 July 1938; *El Imparcial*, 20 May 1938, 30 July 1938, 22 November 1939; Mercado to Cárdenas, 24 March 1937, RG, DGG 2.311.8(22)22037, AGN.

9. Middlebrook, *Paradox*, 98–101.

10. Federación, Santa Ana, to Cárdenas, 3 July 1937, RP, FLC 543.1/8, AGN; *Orden* of $100 by Yocupicio: AAGES 234.0"38"/48; AHGES, Tesorería, Libros de Caja, 1939, vol. 48: 13 April 1939, 14 April 1939, 19 July 1939; Libros de Caja, 1939, vol. 48, and Libro Balance General de 1940, 31 December 1940.

11. *El Imparcial*, 23 January 1938, 11 May 1938, 27, 31 August 1938, 2 December 1938; Circular, 10 June 1938; Acta, 1 December 1938, AAGES 234.0"38"/48; Dora Elvia Enríquez Licón, "Sonora, Sindicatos y participación política (1932–1951)," in *Memoria: XII Simposio*, 1:94; Informe, AAGES 234.0"39"; Federación de Uniones, Nogales, to Cárdenas, 15 May 1937; Lom-bardo to Cárdenas, 1 July 1937, RG, DGG 2.384(22)23760, AGN; *El Popular*, 4 July 1938.

12. *Acción*, 21 April 1939; Galaz, *Desde el Cerro*, 418–20; Informe, AAGES 234.0"39".

13. *Acción*, 6, 9 October 1937; Federación de Uniones, Nogales, to Cárdenas, 22 July 1937; Fidel Valenzuela to Cárdenas, 15 June 1937; Yocupicio to SG, 30 June 1937, RG, DGG 2.384(22)23760, AGN; Federación, Magdalena, to Yocupicio, 24 November 1938, AAGES 234.0"38"/45.

14. Pacto, AAGES, 411.12"38"/73.

15. Report, 10 March 1939, RG 84, NC, GR 1938, Box 20, 850.4, NAW; César Gutiérrez González, "Hegemonía, lucha sindical y movimiento obrero en Nuevo León, 1936–1938" (paper presented at the Coloquio "El Movimiento Obrero en América Latina entre las Dos Guerras Mundiales," Mexico City, September 1986); MI-5, MA 8831, 26 December 1938, MA 9685, 1 February 1941; MI-2, G-2 8772, 1 November 1938; *El Imparcial*, 25 May 1939, 13 June 1939.

16. *El Pueblo*, 29, 30 July 1938; *El Imparcial*, 31 July 1938, 4 August 1938; *El Popular*, 7 August 1938; Francisco Martínez P. to Yocupicio, 21 October 1938, AAGES 234.3"38"/101.

17. CROM to Yocupicio, 19 July 1938, AAGES 234.0"38"/21; Acta, 14 April 1938, DAT, C. 28, exp. 1, V/321(721.5)/1; Sindicato, Los Angeles, to Cárdenas, 8 November 1937, RG, DGG 2.331.8(22)29316, AGN; *El Imparcial*, 26, 28 August 1938.

18. Informe, 18 November 1939, AAGES 234.0"39"; Robinson to SS, 15 January 1938. Powell estimates 10,400 (CTS) and 19,000 (CTM). Report, 7 February 1939, RG 84, NC, GR 1938, Box 20, 850.4, NAW; *El Pueblo*, 5 August 1938; Guadarrama, "La integración," *HCS*, 262; RG 84, NC, GR 1937, Box 13, 850.4, NAW.

19. Enríquez, "Los trabajadores," 190.

20. *Padrones*, AAGES, 234.0"38"; and José Jesús R. Rios to Rodríguez, 26 November 1938, RG, DGG 2.311(22)35329, C 314, AGN. Guadarrama reached slightly different conclusions (she does not include the CTS miners): "La integración," *HCS*, 262.

21. Sindicatos de Oficios Varios were strong in Santa Ana, Magdalena, Cumpas, and, to a lesser extent, in Nogales, Navojoa, and Bácum.

22. Boyle to SD, 11 June 1938, 30 November 1937, SD/19; *El Machete*, 14 May 1938, 25 June 1938; SITMMSRM to Yocupicio, 22 November 1938,

AAGES 234.3"38"/108; Sindicato "Héroe Jesús García" to CTS, n.d. [10 October 1938?], AAGES 234.3"38"/104; *El Pueblo*, 2 February 1938.

23. *El Intruso*, 8, 9 May 1937; *El Pueblo*, 19 October 1938.

24. *El Pueblo*, 20 September 1938, 24, 26 October 1938; Yepis to SD, 30 September 1938, SD/19; Memorandum, n.d., AAGES 234.3"38"/49; CTS to Cía. Constructora, 2 December 1938; Yocupicio to Cía. Constructora, 23 December 1938, AAGES 234.0"38"/49; *El Imparcial*, 25 October 1938.

25. Oropeza to Yocupicio, 3 November 1938, AAGES 234.0"38"/50; SIPS to Yocupicio, 2 October 1938; Sindicato de Albañiles to Yocupicio, 2 October 1938; Fuentes to Secretario de Gobierno, 20 October 1938, AAGES 234.0"38"/42; Sindicato de Albañiles to Cárdenas, 22 July 1940; Macías to SG, 15 August 1940, RG, DGG 2.311.5(22)1, AGN; Sindicato de Albañiles to Yocupicio, 18 May 1937, DAT, C. 269, exp. 3, V/322(721.5)/1, AGN; Sindicato de Cargadores to Cázares, 26 October 1938; Unión de Empacadoras to GS, 26 October 1936, AAGES 234"36"/19; Yocupicio to Cárdenas, 17 March 1937; Sindicato de Cargadores to Cárdenas, 15 March 1937, RP, FLC 543.1/8, AGN; FOCSS to Cárdenas, 15 March 1937, RG, DGG 543.1/8; Lombardo to Cárdenas, 1 July 1937, RG, DGG 2.384(22)23760, AGN.

26. *El Imparcial*, 27 January 1938, 31 March 1938.

27. *Acción*, 10, 14, 19, 29 October 1937, 5 November 1937.

28. Sindicato de Panaderos to Cárdenas, 25 June 1938; Manuel Rodríguez to Sindicato, 1 June 1936; GS to SG, 27 July 1936, RG, DGG 2.331(22) 19266, AGN; *El Imparcial*, 14 July 1939; Sindicato de Yoremes to Cárdenas, 9 September 1937, RG, DGG 2.331.8(22)28093, AGN.

29. Gutiérrez to SG, 26 March 1936; Sindicato de Transportes to Cárdenas, 25 January 1936, RG, DGG 2.331.8(22)12695, AGN; Galaz, *Desde el Cerro*, 149–51.

30. SUTSEM to SG, 1 February 1939, RG, DGG 2.331.2(22)36380, AGN; *El Intruso*, 28 December 1938; *El Imparcial*, 28 January 1939, 22 December 1938.

31. Powell to Boal, 3 May 1938, RG 84, NC, GR 1938, Box 18, 800, NAW.

32. CTS to DAT, 30 June 1938, AAGES 234.0"38"/18.

33. *El Hombre Libre*, 27 June 1938.

34. *El Intruso*, 29 July 1938; *Hoy*, 30 July 1938; Méndez to García T., 29 August 1937, RP, FLC 543.1/8, AGN.

35. *El Intruso*, 21 December 1938, 24 March 1939.

36. *El Imparcial*, 4 November 1938.

37. CTS to GS, 23 August 1938; Oropeza to SG, 16 December 1938, AAGES 234.0"38"/50.

Chapter 8, "Agrarian Reform in Sonora," 123–49

1. Cited in Gilly, *Cartas*, 17, 238–39.

2. Murrieta and Graf, *Por el milagro*, 21.

3. Jesson to U.S. Consul, 5 June 1938, RG 84, GC, GR 1938, Box 23, 350, NAW.

4. Yepis to SS, 6 June 1938, ibid.

5. Jesson to Yepis, 2, 21 March 1938, 5, 12 June 1938; Yepis to SS, 3 May 1938, ibid.

6. Jesson to Yepis, 12, 29 June 1938, 24 July 1938, 26 August 1938, ibid.

7. Cynthia Hewitt de Alcántara, *La modernización de la agricultura mexicana, 1940–1970* (México: Siglo XXI, 1985); Melchor Soto Galindo, *Los pioneros del Yaqui* (México City: Editorial Libros de México, 1977); Carolina Romero Centeno and Eduardo Ibarra Thennet, "El ejido en Sonora (1920–1980)" (Tesis en antropología social, ENAH, 1984), 26.

8. Yepis to SS, 17 July 1937, RG 84, GC, GR 1937, Box 13, 350, NAW.

9. Gabriel Serrano, "El cultivo del trigo en el estado de Sonora," *Agricultura* 2, no. 14 (September–October 1939): 25, 33; José S. Silos and Donald K. Freebairn, *El Valle del Yaqui, Sonora: Su desarollo y potencial económico* (Chapingo: Escuela Nacional de Agricultura, 1970), 18–19.

10. Relación, 21 November 1935, SEP/AH 249.5; Stuart F. Voss, *On the Periphery of Nineteenth-Century Mexico: Sonora and Sinaloa, 1810–1877* (Tucson: University of Arizona Press, 1982), 29–30, 107; Aguilar, *La Frontera,* chaps. 1, 2; Ruiz, *People,* 145.

11. Voss, *On the Periphery,* 40, 92; idem, "Northwest Mexico," in Diana Balmori, Stuart F. Voss, and Miles Wortman, *Notable Family Networks in Latin America* (Chicago: University of Chicago Press, 1984), 79–128; *El Pueblo,* 14 January 1938, 16 August 1938; AAGES 411.12"37"/2; Relación, 21 November 1935, SEP/AH 249.5; Manuel Azuela to Comisión Agraria, 22 February 1936, SRA/AG 25/15822.

12. Sheridan, *Dove,* 48.

13. Romero and Ibarra, "El ejido," 55; Cynthia Radding de Murrieta and Rosa María Ruiz Murrieta, "La reconstrucción constitucionalista y las reformas en la región," *Historia general de Sonora,* 4:324–26; Radding, "Las estructuras formativas," 229–65; Sheridan, *Dove,* 489; *Historia general de Sonora,* 5:126, n.56; Relación, 21 November 1935, SEP/AH 249.5; Ruiz, *People,* 143; Hammond to Powell, RG 84, CPR, NC, CC 1919–1936, vol. II, Class 8, 820.2, NAW.

14. Ramírez, "Una época," *HCS,* 119 (figures on national exports in tons are confused with Sonoran exports by head), and "Cárdenas y las dos caras," *HCS,* 229–30; *Estadísticas históricas de México,* 2:687.

15. W. C. Greene to Robinson, 3 December 1936, RG 84, CACAC 1936, vol. XXIX; Daniels to SS, 4 August 1938, RG 84, NC, GR 1938, Box 17, 350, NAW; Investments, 19 February 1932, RG 84, CACG, vol. IV, 1933, 850.31, NAW; Expropriation, RG 84, GC, GR 1938, Box 23, 350, NAW.

16. Sheridan, *Dove,* 22–24, 45–49, 149–53; Dictamen, Opodepe, 12 January 1938; Dictamen, 26 January 1964; Manuel Alegría to Departamento de Asuntos Agrarios y de Colonización (henceforth DAAC), 12, 11, 22 October 1965, SRA/AG 23/23314; Dictamen, Arizpe, 8 January 1938; Eulalio Palacios to DA, 25 March 1937, SRA/AG 23/15295; Ejido Terrenate, AAGES 411.12"33"/93; Dictamen, Arivechi, 3 July 1936, SRA/AG 23/15786; Dictamen, Soyopa, 30 December 1936; Luis Carrasco to Comisión Agraria, 25 December 1933, SRA/AG 23/8002; Informe, 23 March 1937, SRA/AG 23/15764.

17. Dictamen, Opodepe, 12 January 1938, SRA/AG 23/23314; Jorge Rodríguez to Cuerpo Consultativo, 3 July 1937, SRA/AG 23/15791; Resolución, Nacozari, AAGES 411.12"37"/12; Emma Pérez López, "Economía y trabajo campesino en la Sierra Norte de Sonora (1900–1922)," in *XV Simposio,* 1:459–60; Ariane Baroni B., "Agricultura en el Valle de Ures de 1880 a 1910," *XV Simposio,* 1:477–79.

18. GS to Comisión Agraria, 8 October 1921, AAGES 411.12"37"/26; Madera to DEF, 25 March 1936, SEP/AH 319.7.

19. Comité, La Arizona, to Comisión Agraria, 11 March 1938; Agente Fiscal to Calles, 30 March 1933; Acta, 19 March 1933, AAGES 411.12"32"/73.

20. Knight, *Mexican Revolution*, 2:464; Héctor Aguilar Camín, "Los jefes sonorenses de la Revolución Mexicana," in *Caudillos y campesinos en la Revolución Mexicana*, ed. David Brading (México: FCE, 1985), 150, 155, 158; and *La Frontera*, 429, 434–35; Adrian A. Bantjes, "Bourgeoisie, Revolution and Reform in Mexico: The Case of Sonora" (paper presented at the 46th International Conference of Americanists, Amsterdam, 1988), 14; Hewitt, *La modernización*, 123.

21. Romero and Ibarra, "El ejido," 17–18; Sheridan, *Dove*, 149–53.

22. Steven E. Sanderson, *Agrarian Populism and Economic Growth in Post-Revolutionary Mexico: The Struggle for Land in Sonora* (Berkeley: University of California Press, 1981), 80–81, 228–31; Everardo Escárcega López and Saúl Escobar Toledo, *Historia de la cuestión agraria mexicana*. Vol. 5. *El Cardenismo: Un parteaguas en el proceso agrario nacional, 1934–1940 (Primera parte)* (México: Siglo XXI, CEHAM, 1990), 66. Compare Romero and Ibarra, "El ejido," 21.

23. Romero and Ibarra, "El ejido," 24.

24. Sanderson, *Agrarian Populism*, 235–40.

25. Address, 24 July 1933, RG 84, CACG, vol. VI, 1933, 861.3, NAW; Romana Falcón, "El surgimiento del agrarismo cardenista: Una revisión de las tesis populistas," *Historia Mexicana* 27, no. 3 (January–March 1978): 348.

26. Knight, "Land," 89, 92.

27. Cuadro, March–April 1935, SEP/AH 211.3; Plan de trabajo, 1935–36, SEP/AH 319.10.

28. Informe, 1936, SEP/AH 319.15; Informe, 25 May 1935, SEP/AH 211.2; Informe, 28 March 1936, 29 January 1936, SEP/AH 319.11; Lozano to DEF, 17 March 1936, SEP/AH 319.10; Informe, 1935–36, SEP/AH 319.9; Ximello to Educación Primaria, 7 July 1936, SEP/AH 297.20.

29. Ramírez to DGEF, 3 May 1935, SEP/AH 211.3.

30. Comisariado, Turicachi, to SEP, 4 July 1935, SEP/AH 249.17.

31. Informe, 28 March 1936, SEP/AH 319.11.

32. *Reforma Escolar. Hoja mensual de propaganda educativa de los maestros rurales federales de la primera zona escolar de Sonora* (Magdalena) 1, no. 3 (1936).

33. Romero and Ibarra, "El ejido," 27; Bantjes, "Bourgeoisie"; Ramírez, "Cárdenas," *HCS*, 215–17; Romero and Ibarra, "El ejido," 25–26, 34; Sanderson, *Agrarian Populism*, 91–94.

34. Romero and Ibarra, "El ejido," 34, 51–53; Hewitt, *La modernización*, 124.

35. Guadarrama, "La integración," *HCS*, 250–51; Acta, 11 May 1936, SRA/AG 25/20506.

36. Baroni, "Productores," 29.

37. FTS to Macías, 9 March 1940, AAGES 235"40"/4.

38. Acta, 26 April 1937, RG, DGG 2.384(22)23760, exp. 544.4/25, AGN.

39. Informe, March–April 1936, SEP/AH 319.7; Comité, Casa de Teras, to Cárdenas, 24 July 1937, RG, DGG 2.384(22)23760, exp. 543.1/8, AGN.

40. Macías to SG, 25 October 1941; GS to Comité, El Gavilán, 6 March 1942; Secretaría de Gobierno to Pérez, 28 August 1941, RG, DGG 2.012.8(22) 1, AGN.

41. DA to Gobernación, 27 July 1937, RG, DGG 2.384(22)23760, AGN; DA to GS, 10 March 1937, AAGES 411.12"32"/73; Informe, March–April 1936, SEP/AH 319.7.

42. Report, Boyle, 9 March 1938, RG 84, NC, CR 1936–1938, Box 1, NAW; Dabdoub, *Historia*, 333–34.

43. MI-8, Report on Mexican Army, 1930; MI-7, G-2 7580, 27 October 1936; G-2 7763, 18 January 1937; Interview, Arana, 24 May 1992; Wayne Cornelius, "Nation Building, Participation, and Distribution: The Politics of Social Reform under Cárdenas," in *Crisis, Choice, and Change: Historical Studies of Political Development*, ed. Gabriel A. Almond, Scott C. Flanagan, and Robert J. Mundt (Boston: Little, Brown, 1973), 458.

44. Palemón Zavala, *Perfiles de Sonora* (Hermosillo: Gobierno del Estado de Sonora, 1984); *El Pueblo*, 1 February 1938; Stocker to Yepis, 21 December 1937, RG 84, GC, GR 1937, Box 13, 350, NAW.

45. Yepis to SS, 21 December 1935, RG 84, CACG 1935, vol. V, 800.

46. Knight, "Land," 93; Falcón, "El surgimiento," 357, 362.

47. AAGES 411.12"37"/43; Comité to DA, 25 February 1936, SRA/AG 23/4670; *Album del Mayo y del Yaqui: Directorio comercial, 1933*, ed. Raúl E. Montaño and Octavio P. Gaxiola (Navojoa: Montaño, 1932), 152, 186–87, 166–73; Ramírez, "La estrategia," *HCS*, 141.

48. Sanderson, *Agrarian Populism*, 118; Yepis to SD, 31 July 1937, SD/19; *Acción*, 11 January 1939; Acreedores, 5 November 1943, AAGES 411.12"32"/71.

49. Yepis to SD, 3 May 1937, SD/19; Acta, 30 January 1936, AAGES 411.12"32"/25; Pascual V. Ayón to Felipe Chacón, 18 October 1936, SRA/AG/4670.

50. *El Heraldo del Yaqui*, 8 January 1937; Ayón to Cárdenas, 8 February 1937, RG, DGG 2.384(22)4, AGN.

51. Horatio Mooers, U.S. Consul, Mexicali, to SS, 24 July 1939, SD/19; María Isabel Verdugo Fimbres, *Frontera en el desierto: Historia de San Luis Río Colorado* (Hermosillo: Gobierno del Estado de Sonora, INAH-SEP, 1983), 80–81, 89; Ayón to Cárdenas, SRA/AG/4670; Romero and Ibarra, "El ejido," 55.

52. Yepis to SS, 10 January 1938, RG 84, GC, GR 1938, Box 26, 852, NAW: 1,085.4 hectares were divided among María Tapia Viuda de Obregón (two plots), and Cendia, Mayo, Ariel, Alba, Alvaro, and Francisco; Delegado, DA, to DA, 28 March 1938, 14 February 1939, SRA/AG 23/9940; Resolución, AAGES 411.12"37"/12.

53. Report, Yepis, 8 March 1938, RG 84, GC, GR 1938, Box 26, NAW.

54. *Acción*, 12 October 1937; Sanderson, *Agrarian Populism*, 113.

55. *El Hombre Libre*, 11 May 1938.

56. Dabdoub, *Historia*, 333–34; *El Hombre Libre*, 29 November 1937; Alberto Covarrubias, *Datos Agrícolas de Sonora*, 37–42; Hewitt, *La modernización*, 127; Murrieta and Graf, *Por el milagro*, 40, 64–65, 88, 114–15; Maren von der Borch, "Organización empresarial y desorganización campesina: La Costa de Hermosillo, 1940–1960," in *XIV Simposio*, 2:153–66.

57. Hewitt, *La modernización*, 125; Castro, "El conflicto," 37; Ramírez, "Cárdenas," *HCS*, 210, 222, 224; Banco Nacional de Crédito Ejidal (BNCE), Informe, 1947, AAGES 411.12"32"/25.

58. Romero and Ibarra, "El ejido," 49, 50–53.

59. Carton, *Los empresarios*, 109; Yepis to SD, 29 November 1937, SD/19; Henry T. Dwyer, Vice-Consul, Guaymas, to Shaw, 25 January 1941,

Expropriation, RG 84, GC, CR 1936–1941, Box 1, 300–843; RG 84, GC, GR 1936, Box 7, NAW; Memorandum, Campo 16, SRA/AG 23205; Yepis to SS, 10 January 1938, RG 84, GC, GR 1938, Box 26, 852, NAW; Expropriation, RG 84, GC, GR 1938, Box 23, 350, NAW.

60. Yepis to SS, 11 December 1936, RG 84, GC, GR 1938, Box 7, 852, NAW.

61. Worster to SD, 30 July 1938, SD/19; Jesson to Consul, 26 August 1938, RG 84, GC, GR 1938, Box 23, 350, NAW; Yepis to SS, 10 January 1938, RG 84, GC, GR 1938, Box 26, 852, NAW; Ana Ma. Alatorre to Yocupicio, 20 November 1937, RG 84, GC, GR 1939, Box 16, 852, NAW.

62. Romero and Ibarra, "El ejido," 50; Guadarrama, "La integración," *HCS*, 250–51; DEF to GS, 14 March 1938; Alonso Fernández to DEF, 17 February 1940, 27 August 1940; Fernández to Comité, 12 February 1940, SEP/ARPF IV/161 (IV-15)2470; DEF to Enseñanza Primaria, 1 September 1938, SEP/ARPF IV/161 (IV-15)2439; Ramón Méndez to Educación Primaria, 9 May 1940, SEP/ARPF IV/161 (IV-15)2417; Dictamen, Bacobampo, SRA/AG 23/20506; Fernández to Ramón Salido, 12 February 1940, SEP/ARPF IV/161 (IV-15)2416.

63. Ramírez, "Cárdenas," *HCS*, 229; Romero and Ibarra, "El ejido," 55–58; Sanderson, *Agrarian Populism*, 147, n.57; Secretaría de Agricultura to GS, 19 August 1938, AAGES, in Fichero de El Colegio de Sonora; *Informe que rinde el C. General Román Yocupicio, Gobernador Constitucional del Estado de Sonora, al H. Congreso del Estado, sobre la labor administrativa realizada durante el período comprendido del 1º de Septiembre de 1937 al 16 de Septiembre de 1938* (Hermosillo: J. Cruz Gálvez, 1938), 20; Resolución, 5 October 1938, AAGES 411.12"32"/73; Robinson to U.S. Embassy, 12 August 1938, and to Daniels, 6 November 1936, RG 84, NC, GR 1938, Box 17, 300, NAW; RG 84, GC, GR 1938, Box 26, 852, NAW; Manuel A. Machado, Jr., *The North Mexican Cattle Industry, 1910–1975: Conflict and Change* (College Station: Texas A & M Press, 1981), 54; Escárcega and Escobar, *Historia*, 206, 210.

64. Dictamen, Bavispe, SRA/AG 23/15791; Baroni, "Productores," 31–33, 36–37.

65. Ramírez, "Cárdenas," *HCS*, 215–17.

66. Hewitt, *La modernización*, 126; Miguel Angel Vázquez, *Los grupos de poder económico en Sonora* (Hermosillo: Editorial Unison, 1988), 38.

67. Alan Knight, "The Mexican Revolution: Bourgeois? Nationalist? Or just a 'Great Rebellion'?" *Bulletin of Latin American Research* 4, no. 2 (1985): 26.

68. Hamilton, *The Limits*, 84–90; Hans Werner Tobler, "La burguesía revolucionaria en México: Su origen y papel, 1915–1935," *Historia Mexicana* 34, no. 2 (1984): 217–26; John Mason Hart, *Revolutionary Mexico: The Coming and Process of the Mexican Revolution* (Berkeley: University of California Press, 1987), 373.

69. Knight, *Mexican Revolution*, 2:519; Tobler, "Burguesía," 215; Wasserman, "Strategies," 91–93.

70. Casanova, *Pasos*, 51.

71. Meyer, *Estado*, 300.

72. Alicia Hernández Chávez, "Militares y negocios en la revolución mexicana," *Historia Mexicana* 34, no. 2 (1984): 210–11.

73. Carton, *Los empresarios*, 124–26; Wasserman, "Strategies"; Menno Vellinga, *Economic Development and the Dynamics of Class: Industrialization, Power and Control in Monterrey* (Assen: Van Gorcum, 1979), 71–72; Thomas

Benjamin, *A Rich Land, A Poor People: Politics and Society in Modern Chiapas* (Albuquerque: University of New Mexico Press, 1989), xv, 223.

74. Aguilar, *La frontera*, 429; Bantjes, "Bourgeoisie," 14.

75. Peña and Chávez, "Ganadería," *HCS*, 491–94; Sheridan, *Dove*, 96, 136–37.

76. Hewitt, *La modernización*, 156, 164, 179–80; DAAC to Delegado, 4 October 1962, SRA/AG 23/4670.

77. Manuel Valenzuela Valenzuela, "Consideraciones sobre la burguesía sonorense" (Tesis de licenciatura en economía, Universidad de Sonora, 1984); Romero and Ibarra, "El ejido," 123–25; Vázquez, *Los grupos*, 21–28; Cecilio Gutiérrez Hernández, José Socorro López Quiñones, José Antonio Romero Sánchez, Juan Velasco Naranjo, "Ejido colectivo, revolución verde y lucha de clases en el sur de Sonora" (Tesis profesional, Facultad de Economía, UNAM, 1981), 101; Rubén Salmerón, *La formación regional, el mercado local y el poder de la oligarquía en Sonora: 1780–1840* (Hermosillo: Instituto de Investigaciones Históricas, Universidad de Sonora, 1990).

78. Salomon Eckstein, *El ejido colectivo en México* (México: FCE, 1966), 154–57; Sanderson, *Agrarian Populism*, 139; Hewitt, *La modernización*, 173.

79. Powell to SD, 30 December 1939, SD/19; Ejido Empalme to Secretaría de Agricultura, 24 May 1947, SRA/AG 23/15615; Ejido Piedras Verdes to GS, 13 January 1951, AAGES 411.12"37"; BNCE, Informe, 1947, AAGES 411.12"32"/25; Ejido Las Parras to DA, 22 April 1939, AAGES 411.12"37"/6; Campo 1402 to Comisión Agraria, 29 December 1949, SRA/AG 23/21049.

80. DAAC to Delegado, 4 October 1962, SRA/AG 23/4670; PM, Huatabampo, to GS, 14 January 1940, AAGES 411.12"37"/23; Comisariado, La Victoria, to Organización Agraria Ejidal, n.d.; Macías to Organización Agraria Ejidal, 8 October 1942, AAGES 411.12"37"/27.

81. Liga Agrónomos to DA, 22 April 1938, SRA/AG 23/4760; Fernández to DA, 18 November 1942, SRA/AG 25/4680; Lombardo to DA, 26 October 1938, SRA/AG 23/19158; Interview, Arana, 24 May 1992; Murrieta and Graf, *Por el milagro*, 34.

82. Murrieta and Graf, *Por el milagro*, 34, 157; Fernández to DA, 1 July 1942, 22 July 1941, SRA/AG 23/19158.

83. Ibid.; Interview, Arana, 24 May 1992.

84. Samuel L. Popkin, *The Rational Peasant: The Political Economy of Rural Society in Vietnam* (Berkeley: University of California Press, 1979); Petition to Alemán, 20 January 1950, SRA/AG 23/21049. See Murrieta and Graf, *Por el milagro*, 12, 21.

85. Acta, 13 November 1940, AAGES 411.12"37"/42.

86. Discurso, 20 February 1952, in "Obras de Vicente Lombardo Toledano," vol. 3, Biblioteca Pública Especializada Vicente Lombardo Toledano, México, D.F.

87. Manzanas 84 y 85 to Yocupicio, 23 August 1938, AAGES 411.12"37"/62.

88. CTM to DA, 16 June 1938, SRA/AG 23/15765; Comisariado, Etchojoa, to DA, 9 January 1939, SRA/AG 23/9940; *El Machete*, 1, 8 July 1938.

89. Ejido Las Parras to DA, 22 April 1939, AAGES 411.12"37"/6; Fernández to DA, 31 July 1941, SRA/AG 23/19158; Pedro Valero to CTM, 12 June 1941, SRA/AG 23/15765; Fernández to DA, 21 February 1942, 1 July 1942, SRA/AG 23/19158; BNCE, Informe, 1947, AAGES 411.12"32"/

25; Manzanas 84 y 85 to Yocupicio, 23 August 1938, AAGES 411.12"37"/62.

90. Acta, 23 May 1947, SRA/AG 23/4670; PRM Senado to SG, 18 November 1939, 22 December 1938, RG, DGG 2.311G(22), AGN; Asuntos Indígenas to SG, 12 January 1939, RG, DGG 2.317.4(22)29919, AGN.

91. Fernández to DA, 21 February 1942, 1 July 1942; Fernández to Parcelamiento Ejidal, 31 July 1941, SRA/AG 23/19158; Acuerdo, 30 April 1948, SRA/AG 23/21049.

92. Cited in Gilly, *Cartas*, 243.

93. Acuerdo, 21 October 1937; Cárdenas to Gobernadores, 10 June 1939, RP, FLC 533.11/1, AGN; Steven V. Lutes, "Yaqui Indian Enclavement: The Effects of Experimental Indian Policy in Northwest Mexico," in *Ejidos*, ed. Crumrine and Weigand, 12; Spicer, *The Yaquis*, 265; *Futuro* 22 (December 1937): 9–12.

94. Spicer Papers, Archives, 505A (Pótam), Field Notes, 24 January 1942, ASM.

95. Matus to Cárdenas, 9 June 1939; Cárdenas to Yaqui, 8 June 1939, RP, FLC 533.11/1, AGN.

96. Lutes, "Yaqui Indian Enclavement," 12.

97. Dabdoub, *Historia*, 238–39.

98. Yepis to SS, 26 June 1938, RG 84, GC, GR 1938, Box 23, 350, NAW; Cárdenas to Gobernador Pápago, 30 June 1939, RP, FLC 533.11/1, AGN; Cárdenas to Macías, 27 September 1940, AAGES 411.12"37"/62; Cárdenas to P. E. Calles, 18 September 1926, APEC, gav. 12, CARDENAS, Lázaro, inv. 820, leg. 2/9, exp. 206, APEC.

99. Alan Knight, "Racism, Revolution, and *Indigenismo*: Mexico, 1910–1940," in *The Idea of Race in Latin America*, ed. Richard Graham (Austin: University of Texas Press, 1990), 81, 106, n.51; Cárdenas to Yaqui, 12 June 1939; Cárdenas to Gobernadores, 10 June 1939; Chávez to Cárdenas, 14 June 1939; Cárdenas to Gobernadores, 10 June 1939; Cárdenas to Chávez, 12 July 1939; Cárdenas to Teófilo Alvarez, n.d.; Leonardo Velderrayn to Cárdenas, 21 October 1940; Cárdenas to Velderrayn, 12 September 1940; Presupuesto; Cárdenas to Eduardo Suárez, 7 June 1939; José Paredes to Cárdenas, 29 August 1938, RP, FLC 533.11/1, AGN.

100. Cárdenas to Yaqui, 12 June 1939; Cárdenas to Jefatura, Colonias Yaquis, 23 June 1939; Cárdenas to Guillermo de la Garza, 6 January 1939; Cárdenas to Dozal, 15 May 1939; Gutiérrez to Cárdenas, 17 August 1939, RP, FLC 533.11/1, AGN.

101. Cárdenas to Gobernadores, 10 June 1939, RP, FLC 533.11/1, AGN.

102. Pótam to Cárdenas, n.d. [1939?]; Juan Aguayo to Cárdenas, 1 December 1939; Cárdenas to Jesús A. Castro, 3 December 1939, 31 January 1940; Gobernadores to Cárdenas, 7 May 1939, 20, 21 May 1939; Cárdenas to Comisión Yaqui, 21 September 1940; Comisario to Cárdenas, 25 May 1939, RP, FLC 533.11/1, AGN; AAGES 411.12"37"/62.

103. Vícam to Cárdenas, 9 November 1938, RP, FLC 533.11/1, AGN.

104. Spicer Papers, Archives, 505A (Pótam), Field Notes, 4 February 1942, ASM.

105. Informe, 12 May 1939, RP, FLC 533.11/1, AGN.

106. Ernesto Camou H., "Yaquis y Mayos: Cultivadores de los valles," *HCS*, 526–37; Hewitt, *La modernización*, 241.

107. Relación, 1939, RG, DGG 2.311G(22)32100, AGN.

Chapter 9, "Industrial Workers and Cardenismo," 151–72

1. Daniel González Cortés, "Ta' oscuro el panorama: Relatos sobre los mineros del carbón," in *Monografías obreras*, ed. Victoria Novelo (México: CIESAS, 1987), 1:139–40.

2. Eric Hobsbawm, *Worlds of Labour: Further Studies in the History of Labour* (London: Weidenfeld and Nicholson, 1984), 227–51.

3. The title refers to the revisionist work of Royden Harrison et al., *Independent Collier: The Coal Miner as Archetypal Proletarian Reconsidered* (New York: St. Martin's, 1978).

4. Clark Kerr and Abraham Siegel, "The Interindustry Propensity to Strike—An International Comparison," in *Industrial Conflict*, ed. Arthur Kornhauser, Robert Dubin, and Arthur M. Ross (New York: McGraw-Hill, 1954), 189–205.

5. Royden Harrison, Introduction to *Independent Collier*, ed. Harrison et al.

6. Jaime Tamayo, *La clase obrera en la historia de México: En el interinato de Adolfo de la Huerta y el gobierno de Alvaro Obregón (1920–24)* (México: Siglo XXI, 1987), 218.

7. Charles W. Bergquist, *Labor in Latin America* (Stanford: Stanford University Press, 1986), 380.

8. Ruiz, *The People of Sonora*.

9. François-Xavier Guerra, "La Révolution Mexicaine: D'abord une révolution minière?" *Annales, E.S.C.* 36, no. 5 (1981): 804–5, 808–9; Alan Knight, "La Révolution Mexicaine: Révolution minière ou révolution serrano?" *Annales, E.S.C.* 38, no. 2 (1983): 453–57; Alan Knight, "The Working Class and the Mexican Revolution, c. 1900–1920," *Journal of Latin American Studies* 16 (1984): 51–79; Rodney Anderson, "Mexican Workers and the Politics of Revolution," *Hispanic American Historical Review* 54 (1970): 513–35.

10. Federico Besserer, José Díaz, Raúl Santana, "Formación y consolidación del sindicalismo minero en Cananea," *Revista Mexicana de Sociología* 42, no. 4 (1980): 1325; José Luis Trueba Lara, *Voces de la mina (Seis textos sobre Cananea)* (Hermosillo: Programa Cultural de las Fronteras, 1988), 11. Compare William Earl French, "The Inculcation of the Capitalist Work Ethic in a Mexican Mining District (Hidalgo District, Chihuahua, 1880–1920)" (Ph.D. diss., University of Texas at Austin, 1990), 54; Luis Reygadas, *Proceso de trabajo y acción obrera: Historia sindical de los mineros de Nueva Rosita, 1929–1979* (México: INAH, ENAH, 1988), 67.

11. Juan Luis Sariego Rodríguez, "Los mineros de la Real del Monte: Un proletariado en formación y transición," *Revista Mexicana de Sociología* 42, no. 4 (1980): 1398–99; Besserer, "Formación," 1325. Compare Norman Long and Bryan Roberts, eds., *Miners, Peasants and Entrepreneurs: Regional Development in the Central Highlands of Peru* (Cambridge: Cambridge University Press, 1984), 51–58; Heyman, *Life and Labor*, 111; José Carlos Ramírez, *Hipótesis acerca de la historia económica y demográfica de Sonora en el período contemporáneo (1930–1983)* (Hermosillo: El Colegio de Sonora, 1985), 46.

12. Robinson to George P. Shaw, U.S. Consul, Mexico City, 1 July 1938, RG 84, NC, GR 1938, Box 17, 610.1, NAW; Powell, "Current Wages," 3

September 1936, RC 84, NC, GR 36, Box 4, 850.4; and 24 May 1938, ibid., 1938, Box 20, 850.4, NAW.

13. Sariego, "Los mineros," 1397, n.33.

14. Ibid., 1400–1401; Marvin D. Bernstein, *The Mexican Mining Industry, 1890–1950: A Study of the Interaction of Politics, Economics, and Technology* (Albany: State University of New York, 1965), 89; Cuauhtémoc Velasco Avila, "Labour Relations in Mining: Real del Monte and Pachuca, 1824–1874," in *Miners and Mining in the Americas*, ed. Thomas Greaves and William Culver (Manchester: Manchester University Press, 1985), 64. Edward Shorter and Charles Tilly, *Strikes in France, 1830–1968* (Cambridge: Cambridge University Press, 1974), 13, call mining an "artisanal heavy industry."

15. June Nash, *We Eat the Mines and the Mines Eat Us: Dependency and Exploitation in Bolivian Tin Mines* (New York: Columbia University Press, 1979), 329.

16. Besserer, "Formación," 1330–32; Bernstein, *Mexican Mining*, 89; Sariego, "Los mineros," 1400; Heyman, *Life and Labor*, 77–78; Velasco, "Labour Relations," 63.

17. Bernstein, *Mexican Mining*, 89; Sariego, "Mineros," 1399; Ralph McA. Ingersoll, *In and Under Mexico* (New York, London: Century, 1924), 81.

18. Besserer, "Formación," 1331; Boyle to SD, n.d. (1931), SD/18.

19. Powell, "Current Wages," 3 September 1936, RG 84, NC, GR 1936, Box 4, 850.4, NAW.

20. Report, "Antimony Industry," by Paul Paddock, U.S. Vice-Consul, Mexico City, 4 February 1939, SD/124, 812.631; Cornejo, *Sierra*, 15, 143; Heyman, *Life and Labor*, 133; Pérez, "Economía," 456; Romero and López, "Crisis," 15–25.

21. Elsa M. Peña and J. Trinidad Chávez, "Aspectos de la vida en los minerales, 1929–1980," *HGS*, 437.

22. E. P. Thompson, "The Moral Economy of the English Crowd in the Eighteenth Century," *Past and Present* 50 (1971): 76–136; James C. Scott, *The Moral Economy of the Peasant: Rebellion and Subsistence in Southeast Asia* (New Haven: Yale University Press, 1976).

23. "Antimony Industry," 4 February 1939, SD/124, 812.631.

24. Ibid.

25. *Mines Register* (New York, 1942), 21:558–59; Ramírez, "Una época de crisis," *HCS*, 108.

26. Bernstein, *Mexican Mining*, 171–73, 189; Ramírez, "El último auge," *HCS*, 45; Juan Luis Sariego, Luis Reygadas, Miguel Angel Gómez, and Javier Ferrara, *El estado y la minería mexicana: Política, trabajo y sociedad durante el siglo XX* (México: Fondo de Cultura Económica, 1988), 148–50, 200, 213.

27. Ramírez, *Hipótesis*, 47, 50–51.

28. Secretaría de la Economía Nacional, Departamento de Minas, *Anuario de estadística minera: Año de 1933* (México: D.A.P.P., n.d.), 216–19.

29. Ingersoll, *In and Under*, passim; Boyle to SD, 25 September 1930, SD/18; *The Mines Handbook*, vol. 18, Part I (New York: Mines Information Bureau, 1931), 110–13, 165–68; "The Moctezuma Copper Co.," RG 84, Agua Prieta Consulate, GR 1936, Box 1, 350, NAW; Report, Robinson, 13 September 1937, RG 84, NC, GR 1936–38, Box 1, NAW; RG 84, NC, GR 37,

Box 11, 610.1, NAW; Gibbs to Robinson, 13 November 1935, RG 84, CACAC 1935–36, vol. XXVIII, 610.1, NAW; "U.S. Investments," RG 84, C 8.4, CACAC 1936–37, vol. XXX, NAW; "American Citizens," RG 84, C 8.4, CACAC 1936, vol. XXIX, NAW; Ramírez, "El último auge," *HCS*, 37; Boyle to SS, 24 March 1937, SD/124, 812.631; Agustín M. Pérez to Yocupicio, 20 March 1938, 15 April 1938, AAGES 238"38"/2; Trueba, *Voces*, 25–26; Sariego et al., *El estado*, 213; Inez Horton, *Copper's Children: The Rise and Fall of a Mexican Copper Mining Camp* (New York: Exposition Press, 1968), 25, 105; Ingersoll, *In and Under*, 25, 114–15, 146.

30. Boyle to SD, 25 September 1930, SD/18; *The Mines Handbook*, vol. 18, Part II, 2737–38; "El Tigre Mining Co.," 17 October 1936, RG 84, Agua Prieta Consulate, GR 36, Box 1, 350, NAW.

31. *The Mines Handbook* vol. 18, Part II, 2685–86, 2688, 2757–62.

32. Morris B. Parker, *Mules, Mines and Me in Mexico, 1859–1932* (Tucson: University of Arizona Press, 1979), 139; Horton, *Copper's Children*, 144.

33. H. J. Evans to DEF, 31 March 1937, SEP/ARPF, IV/161(IV-15)2483; Sonora Consolidated Mining Co. to DEF, 28 June 1939, SEP/ARPF, IV/161(IV-15)2480; Francisco F. Noguez to Educación Primaria, 10 May 1939, SEP/ARPF, IV/161(IV-15)2476

34. Horton, *Copper's Children*, 195, 202.

35. Bernstein, *Mexican Mining*, 173; Boyle to SD, 29 May 1931, 31 December 1932; Yost to SD, 31 March 1932, 30 April 1932, SD/18; Gibbs to Robinson, 8 October 1936, RG 84, CACAC, 1936–37, vol. XXX, NAW; José D. Oropeza to Procurador Local de la Defensa del Trabajo, 13 April 1938, AAGES 234.1"38"/1; *El Pueblo*, 13 August 1938; Hamilton, *The Limits*, 232–33; Junta Federal del Trabajo, Guaymas to, GS, 13 July 1938, AAGES 234.1"38"/2.

36. Rodolfo Elías Calles to Soledad (Cholita) González, 24 August 1931; and to Plutarco Elías Calles, 26 August 1931; Plutarco Elías Calles to Rodolfo Elías Calles, 26 August 1931, APEC, gav. 27, ELIAS CALLES CHACON, Rodolfo, inv. 1733, exp. 4, leg. 13/24.

37. Horton, *Copper's Children*, 186; Yepis to SS, 31 March 1938, 6, 24 August 1938, SD/124, 812.631; Bernstein, *Mexican Mining*, 173.

38. Report, "Silver Prices" by Robert G. McGregor Jr., U.S. Consul, Mexico City, 30 January 1939; Bernstein, *Mexican Mining*, 184–92. Townsend, *Lázaro Cárdenas*, 87, 263, gives a figure of 10 percent; Boyle to SD, 30 September 1937, 30 October 1937, 6 April 1938, 30 September 1938, 30 November 1939, SD/19; and 24 March 1937, SD/124, 812.631; Hamilton, *Limits*, 189–90; Howard F. Cline, *Mexico: Revolution to Evolution, 1940–1960* (New York: Oxford University Press, 1963), 249.

39. Ramírez, "Una época," *HCS*, 114; Elsa M. Peña and J. Trinidad Chávez, "Organización obrera de los minerales, 1929–1980," *HGS*, 452; Yost to SS, 24 December 1931, 31 March 1932; Hurst to SD, 1 December 1932; Yepis to SD, 29 December 1933; Robinson to SD, 31 August 1934; Boyle to SD, 16 October 1931, 31 May 1933, 31 July 1933, SD/18.

40. Report, "Placer Mining" by Powell, 15 October 1934, RG 84, CPR, Nogales 8.12, CACN 34, vol. IX, 863.4, NAW.

41. Robinson to SS, 30 July 1938, RG 84, NC, GR 38, Box 17, 300, NAW; "Placer Mining," 15 October 1934, RG 84, CPR, Nogales 8.12, CACN 34, vol. IX, 863.4, NAW; Peña and Chávez, "Organización," *HCS*, 459; Informe topográfico, 25 December 1933, 23/8002, Soyopa, SRA/AG; Peña and

Chávez, "Aspectos," *HCS*, 436–37; Powell to W. A. Coombs, 19 September 1936, RG 84, NC, GR 36, Box 6, 863, NAW; *El Imparcial*, 26 July 1939; Report, "Discovery of Gold" by Armstrong, 25 July 1939, SD/124, 812.631; Powell to Coombs, 19 September 1936, RG 84, NC, GR 36, Box 6, 863, NAW.

42. Yepis to SS, 24 August 1936, SD/124, 812.631.

43. Petition to Cárdenas, 10 February 1938; Comisario Policía to Cárdenas, 28 March 1938; Roberto Hughes to Cárdenas, 28 March 1938; Acta, 14 July 1938; Jesús Bojórquez to DAT, 30 September 1938; Hughes to Cárdenas, 30 September 1938; Ministerio Público to Procurador General, 11 October 1938; Raúl Godoy to DAT, 10 December 1938; Oficina de Inspección to DAT, n.d., DAT, Caja 240, exp. 2, V/300(721.5)/7, AGN.

44. "Antimony Industry," 4 February 1939, SD/124, 812.631.

45. Peña and Chávez, "Aspectos," *HCS*, 436.

46. Luis Emilio Giménez Cacho, "La constitución del Sindicato Industrial," in *Cuatro sindicatos nacionales de industria* (Universidad Autónoma de Sinaloa and CEMOS, 1988), 85; Sariego et al., *El estado*, 214.

47. Besserer et al., *El sindicalismo*, 25, 30–32; Giménez, "Constitución," 88–91.

48. Boyle to SD, n.d. (1931), SD/18.

49. Gibbs to Robinson, 30 June 1933, RG 84, CACAC, 1933–34, vol. XXVI, 863, NAW; Bernstein, *Mexican Mining*, 173; Federico Besserer, Victoria Novelo, Juan Luis Sariego, *El sindicalismo minero en México, 1900–1952* (México: Era, 1983), 28; Boyle to SD, 25 September 1930; Boyle to SD, n.d., SD/18; Ramírez, "Una época," *HCS*, 112–13.

50. Reygadas, *Proceso*, 44; Sariego, "Enclaves," 260–69.

51. "Agustín M. Pérez: Una vida en la vida de Cananea (1908–1935)," in Trueba, *Voces de la mina*, 43–45, 49.

52. Sariego, "Enclaves," 260, 273, 289; Peña and Chávez, "Organización," *HCS*, 451–56; Trueba, *Voces*, 43–45; Francisco Córdova Romero, *Perfíl histórico de Cananea (Ensayo)* (Hermosillo: Ed. Francisco Córdova Romero, 1980), 75–77; Besserer, "Formación," 1339, 1342.

53. Raby, *Educación*, 50, 56, 242; DEF to Educación Primaria, 1 April 1937, SEP/APRF, IV/161/(IV-15)/2460; Oropeza to DEF, March 1936, SEP/AH 319.3; Gibbs to Robinson, 30 June 1933, RG 84, CACAC, 1933–34, vol. XXVI, 863, NAW.

54. Townsend, *Lázaro Cárdenas*, 86–87.

55. "Silver Prices," 30 January 1939, SD/124, 812.631; Bernstein, *Mexican Mining*, 175–77, 182, 200–209.

56. Acta, 8 August 1939, SEP/ARPF, IV/161 (IV-15), 2426; *El Imparcial*, 13 March 1938; *El Intruso*, 8 May 1937, 9 May 1937; Clinch to DEF, 20 August 1936, SEP/AH 339.4; Madera to DEF, 25 August 1936, SEP/AH 319.7; and 25 August 1936, SEP/AH, 319.6; *El Intruso*, 8 May 1937, 9 May 1937; DEF to Enseñanza Primaria, 1 September 1939, SEP/ARPF IV/161 (IV-15), 2426.

57. Inspector Federal to Trabajo, 15 August 1938; Section 87 to DAT, 12 August 1938; Acta, 24 October 1938, DAT, Caja 269, exp. 17, V/341(721.5)/1; Pangburn to SD, 30 September 1938, 31 October 1938; Boyle to SD, 30 November 1938, 31 December 1938, SD/19; *El Popular*, 28 August 1938; Heyman, *Life and Labor*, 132.

58. Bernstein, *Mexican Mining*, 192–98.

59. Sariego, "Enclaves," 286; "Collective Contract . . . 1932," RG 84, CPR Nogales 8.12, CACN 1934, vol. IX, 850.4, NAW.

60. Peña and Chávez, "Organización," *HCS*, 456–57; Bernstein, *Mexican Mining*, 192–98; Pérez in Trueba, *Voces*, 45–46; Giménez, "Constitución," 90; Besserer, "Formación," 1344–45.

61. Gibbs to Robinson, 23, 25, 26 October 1935, RG 84, C 8.4, CACAC 1935–36, vol. XXVIII, 850.4, NAW; Circular, 30 December 1936, RG, DGG 2.331.8(22)13402, AGN; Sariego, "Enclaves," 306–8; Thomas D. Bowman, U.S. Consul General, Mexico City, to SS, 28 January 1936, SD/124, 812.631.

62. Bowman to SS, 28 January 1936, SD/124, 812.631.

63. Córdova, *Perfíl histórico*, 78; Boyle to SD, 31 January 1936; Robinson to SD, 31 January 1936, 29 February 1936; Yepis to SD, 29 February 1936, SD/19; Sariego, "Enclaves," 309; Gibbs to Robinson, 22 January 1936, RG 84, NC, GR 1936, Box 5, NAW; Meneses to Gibbs, 17 September 1935, RG 84, C 8.4, CACAC 1935–36, vol. XXVIII, NAW; Gibbs to Hurst, 8 January 1933, RG 84, C 8.4, CACAC 1935–36, vol. XXVII, NAW; Gibbs to Robinson, 22 January 1936, RG 84, C 8.4, CACAC 1936–37, vol. XXX, NAW; "Collective Contract . . . 1932," RG 84, CPR Nogales 8.12, CACN 1934, vol. IX, 850.4, NAW; Gibbs to Robinson, 6 February 1936, SD/124, 812.631.

64. Bowman to SS, 28 January 1936, SD/124, 812.631.

65. Robinson to SD, 31 March 1936, SD/19; Sariego, "Enclaves," 311–12; Peña and Chávez, "Organización," *HCS*, 458.

66. Sariego, "Enclaves," 322.

67. *El Machete*, 27 June 1938, 7 September 1938; A. Mendelsohn to Armstrong, 27 October 1938, RG 84, NC GR 1938, Box 17, 300, NAW; Córdova, *Perfíl histórico*, 78; Yocupicio to Cárdenas, 4 May 1938; Oficina Federal del Trabajo to DAT, 28 July 1938; OIPS to DAT, 12 September 1938, DAT, Caja 173, exp. 10, V/211.2 (721.5)/1, AGN; Powell to SD, 30 September 1938, SD/19; *El Imparcial*, 9 July 1938; Robinson to SS, 12 September 1938, SD/124, 812.631; *El Intruso*, 6 July 1938; Powell to Boal, 17 May 1938, RG 84, NC, GR 1938, Box 18, 800, NAW; Sariego, "Enclaves," 329.

68. MA 9747, 19 March 1941, MI-5; Córdova, *Perfíl histórico*, 78; Acta, 12 September 1940; STMMSRM to Mendelsohn, 25 March 1940, DAT, Caja 219, exp. 9, 4.1/300(22)/1, AGN; Sariego, "Enclaves," 341; Peña and Chávez, "Organización," *HCS*, 460; *El Intruso*, 1 June 1940.

69. Peña and Chávez, "Organización," *HCS*, 451.

70. Oficina Federal del Trabajo to DAT, 28 July 1938; Wenceslao Muñoz to Oficina de Inspección, 4 October 1938; Departamento Diplomático to DAT, 4 November 1938; Cámara Minera to Cárdenas, 29 October 1938; Inspector Federal to DAT, 23 December 1938; Departamento de Minas to DAT, 4 March 1939; Investigación, DAT, Caja 173, exp. 10, V/211.2 (721.5)/1, AGN; Armstrong to SD, 1 November 1938, SD/19; *El Imparcial*, 25 October 1938, 28 November 1939; Trueba, *Voces*, 43.

71. MA 9747, 19 March 1941, MI-5; G-2 304, 18 August 1930, MI-2; "Informe que rinde el ejecutivo . . .," 1 April 1937, Serie Sonora, 1a serie, vol. XVIII, 1924–40; Bowman to SS, 28 January 1936, SD/124, 812.631; Gibbs to Robinson, 23 October 1935, 25 October 1935, 26 October 1935, RG 84, C 8.4, CACAC 1935–36, vol. XXVIII, 850.4, NAW.

72. Boyle to SD, 30 September 1937, 30 October 1937, 6 April 1938, 30 September 1938, 30 November 1939, SD/19; Boyle to SS, 24 March 1937; "Silver Prices," 30 January 1939, SD/124, 812.631; MA 9588, 8 November 1940, MI-5.

73. Sariego et al., *El estado*, 222–26.

74. SITMMSRM to Yocupicio, 22 November 1938, AAGES 234.3"38"/ 108; Sindicato Minero "Héroe Jesús García" to CTS, AAGES 234.2"38"/ 104; AAGES 234.2"38"/3; *El Machete*, 14 May 1938, 25 June 1938; "Labor in Industry" by Boyle, 1 February 1939, RG 84, Agua Prieta Consulate, GR 1936, Box 1, 350, NAW; Yocupicio to PM, Nacozari, 9 November 1938; DAT to Thais García, 17 November 1938, AAGES 234.3"38"/108; Boyle to SS, 11 June 1938, 30 November 1937, SD/19; Inspector Federal to Trabajo 5, 27 June 1938; Sección 114 to SITMMSRM, 5 July 1938, DAT, Caja 269, exp. 3, V/322(721.5)/1, AGN; *El Popular*, 7 July 1938.

75. Feliciano Rodríguez to DAT, 9 February 1938, DAT, Caja 269, exp. 3, V/332(721.5)/1, AGN; Boyle to SD, 30 September 1937, 30 October 1937, 6 April 1938, 30 September 1938, 30 November 1939, SD/19; Boyle to SS, 24 March 1937, SD/124, 812.631.

76. *Contrato colectivo de trabajo celebrado entre The Moctezuma Copper Company y el Sindicato Minero "Héroe Jesús García"* (Pilares de Nacozari, 1940).

77. Acta, 8 August 1939, SEP/ARPF, IV/161 (IV-15), 2426; *El Imparcial*, 13 March 1938; *El Intruso*, 8, 9 May 1937; Clinch to DEF, 20 August 1936, SEP/AH; Madera to DEF, 25 August 1936, SEP/AH 319.7.

Chapter 10, "Cardenista Politics and the Mexican Right," 175–86

1. The term "Thermidor" is not used to argue that all revolutions necessarily pass through similar phases.

2. *El Imparcial*, 4 January 1938; Smith to Assistant Chief of Staff, G-2, 2 October 1937; Robinson to SD, 30 October 1937, SD/19.

3. Yepis to SS, 10 November 1937, SD/19.

4. Boyle to SD, 30 November 1937, SD/19.

5. Ibid., 6 April 1938.

6. Yepis to SD, 30 April 1938, SD/19.

7. Robinson to SS, 3 February 1938, SD/19.

8. *El Imparcial*, 28, 29 January 1938; Yepis to SS, 31 January 1938, 20 June 1938, SD/19; Ibarra to Yocupicio, 18 April 1938, AAGES 234.2"38"/2.

9. *El Imparcial*, 16 June 1938, 28 January 1938, 29 November 1938; *El Pueblo*, 20 July 1938; *El Machete*, 23 July 1938; Yepis to SS, 13 October 1938; Robinson to SD, 30 April 1938, SD/19.

10. MI-4, G-2 Memorandum, 17 May 1938.

11. MI-4, G-2 7973, 1 June 1937.

12. Carlos Martínez Assad, "La rebelión cedillista o el ocaso del poder tradicional," *Revista Mexicana de Sociología* 41, no. 3 (1979): 709–29.

13. Ankerson, *Agrarian Warlord*, 212–16.

14. MI-4, Anon. Report, 2 September 1936; G-2 Resumé, 20 October 1937; G-2 7436, 11 September 1936; Meyer, *México*, 437.

15. Santos, *Memorias*, 588.

16. Nava and Aburto, "La rebelión," 20; Confidencial, 17 June 1938, AFJM, vol. 107, doc. 462; Ankerson, *Agrarian Warlord*, 188–89; MI-9, G-2 8216, 27 December 1937; MI-4, G-2 Resumé, 20 November 1937; Manuel Fernández Boyoli and Eustaquio Marrón de Angelis, *Lo que no se sabe de la rebelión Cedillista* (México: Grafi-Art, 1938), 123, 181, 195–96.

17. Falcón, *Revolución*, 236.

18. *Acción*, 12 October 1937; Méndez to Secretario Particular, 29 August 1937, RP, FLC 543.1/8, AGN; *El Pueblo*, 3 March 1938; *El Hombre Libre*, 14 March 1938; *El Machete*, 7 May 1938, 12 March 1938, 12 February 1938; Powell to Boal, 25, 28 May 1938, RG 84, NC, GR 1938, Box 18, 800, NAW; Ankerson, *Agrarian Warlord*, 182.

19. MI-4, G-2 Memorandum, 17 May 1938; MI-9, G-2 8216, 27 December 1937.

20. Informe, 4 March 1938, AFJM, vol. 107, doc. 578; Informe, September 1937, RP, FLC 559.1/53, AGN.

21. Schuler, *Mexican Foreign Policy*, chap. 4.

22. Ankerson, *Agrarian Warlord*, 180; Carlos Martínez Assad, *Los rebeldes vencidos: Cedillo contra el Estado Cardenista* (México: FCE/UNAM, 1990), 146.

23. Alejandro Peña to Policía Militar, AFJM, vol. 107, doc. 462.

24. Informe, AFJM, vol. 106, doc. 165.

25. *El Imparcial*, 22 May 1938; Fernández and Marrón, *Lo que no se sabe*, 123, 181, 195–96.

26. MI-2, G-2 8721, 21 October 1938.

27. Robinson to SS, 13 August 1938, SD/19; Ankerson, *Agrarian Warlord*, 189, 215.

28. Interview, Arana, 24 May 1992.

29. Ankerson, *Agrarian Warlord*, 190.

30. Stephen R. Niblo, *War, Diplomacy, and Development: The United States and Mexico, 1938–1954* (Wilmington, DE: SR Books, 1995), 41.

31 Negrete, *Relaciones*, 18.

32. González, *Los Días*, 178–81; Alan Knight, "The Politics of Expropriation," in *The Mexican Petroleum Industry in the Twentieth Century*, ed. Jonathan C. Brown and Alan Knight (Austin: University of Texas Press, 1992), 111–16.

33. AAGES 234.2"38"/3; *El Imparcial*, 10, 20, 23 March 1938, 9 April 1938; Robinson to SD, 23, 31 March 1938; Yepis to SS, 23 March 1938, SD/19.

34. Robinson to SD, 23, 31 March 1938; Yepis to SS, 23 March 1938, SD/19.

35. Boyle to SD, 31 March 1938, SD/19.

36. Cámara de Comercio Mayo to Cámara Nacional, 21 April 1938; Cárdenas to Yocupicio, 14 April 1938, AAGES 234.2"38"/3; AAGES 234.2"38"/2; *El Imparcial*, 10, 20, 22, 23 March 1938, 9 April 1938, 20/21 May 1938.

37. Ibarra to Yocupicio, 18 April 1938, AAGES 234.2"38"/2.

38. Nava and Aburto, "La rebelión," 11–11a.

39. Pansters, *Politics*, 48–69; MI-5, MA 11179, 9 June 1941; MI-2, G-2 7154, 19 May 1936; *El Imparcial*, 19 January 1939; Camp, *Political Biographies*, 23–24; Weyl, *The Reconquest*, 239; Prewitt, *Reportage*, 155, 175; Novo, *La vida*, 395; Wilkie and Monzón, *México visto*, 336; *La CTM en los Estados*, 108.

40. Heather Fowler Salamini, *Movilización campesina en Veracruz (1920–1938)* (México: Siglo XXI, 1979), 164–72; Weyl, *The Reconquest*, 150, 215, 238; Prewitt, *Reportage*, 150, 259; Ankerson, *Agrarian Warlord*, 170, 183–85; Basurto, *Cárdenas*, 113–15, 157; J. H. Plenn, *Mexico Marches* (Indianapolis: Bobbs-Merrill, 1939), 259, 270; Medina, *Del cardenismo*, 23, 58, 74; Raymond

Buve, "Los Gobernadores de estado y la movilización de los campesinos en Tlaxcala," in *Caudillos*, ed. D. A. Brading, 298–303.

41. Benjamin, *A Rich Land*, 188–219; MI-5, MA 9571, 25 October 1940.

42. Santos, *Memorias*, 603, 584, 648.

43. *El Intruso*, 26 July 1938; Fernández and Marrón, *Lo que no se sabe*, 320–24; Michaels, "The Crisis," 61; Moisés González Navarro, *La CNC en la reforma agraria*, 3d ed. (México: El Día, 1985), 103–4; *El Nacional*, 24 August 1939.

44. Fernández and Marrón, *Lo que no se sabe*, 320–24; Basurto, *Cárdenas*, 113–17; *La CTM en los estados*; MI-2, G-2 8536, 19 July 1938; *El Hombre Libre*, 3 March 1937; *El Imparcial*, 1, 22 April 1938.

45. *El Imparcial*, 30 March 1938, 13 April 1938, 3 May 1938; González Navarro, *La CNC*, 102; Document, Liga de Comunidades Agrarias, 15 April 1938; SUTES to Cárdenas, 14 April 1938, RP, FLC 534.6/375, AGN; RP, FLC 543.1/8, AGN.

46. *Hoy*, 23 July 1938; *El Popular*, 13, 14, 19 July 1938; *El Imparcial*, 23 July 1938, 3 September 1938; *Diario de los Debates de la Cámara de Diputados del Congreso de los Estados Unidos Mexicanos*, 6 July 1938.

47. Santos, *Memorias*, 583–87, 647.

48. Ibid., 648–49; Hernández, *La mecánica*, 199–201; Arnulfo Ferreiro to Yocupicio, 17 May 1939, AAGES 221.1"37"/1; Ariel Contreras, *México, 1940: Industrialización y crisis política* (México: Siglo XXI, 1977), 16.

Chapter 11, "From Polarization to *Continuismo*, 1938–39," 187–203

1. Cited in Gustavo Gordillo, *Campesinos al asalto del cielo: Una reforma agraria con autonomía* (México: Siglo XXI, 1988), 88.

2. *El Popular*, 16 July 1938; Yepis to SD, 31 May 1938, 30 April 1938; Powell to SD, 31 May 1938, SD/19.

3. Comisariado, Palos Chinos, to Cárdenas, 29 April 1938, RP, FLC 543.1/8, AGN.

4. Interview, Arana, 24 May 1992.

5. Policía, Huatabampo, to Yocupicio, 7 February 1937; PNR, Huatabampo, to Cázares, 24 October 1936; Federación Mexicana de la Enseñanza to Secretario de Gobierno, 15 March 1937, AAGES 234.3"36"/196; Lombardo to SG, 15, 17 March 1937, RG, DGG 2.384(22)23760, AGN; Lombardo to Procurador General, 3 January 1938; Comité, Bacobampo, to Cárdenas, 7 December 1938; Godofredo Beltrán to SG, 2 April 1938; GS to SG, 24 January 1938; Yocupicio to SG, 26 August 1938, RG, DGG 2.317.4(22)29919, C 61, AGN; *El Pueblo*, 2 April 1938; *El Imparcial*, 4 January 1938; UNVR to Yocupicio, 20 January 1938, RG, DGG 2.317.4(22)30648, AGN; Córdova, *Perfil*, 72.

6. MI-2, G-2 8545, 10 May 1938; Yocupicio to SG, 5 April 1938; Morentín to SG, 7 May 1938; Yocupicio to SG, 11, 12 June 1938; Oficina Postal to SG, 28 August 1938, RG, DGG 2.317.4(22)31533, AGN; *El Hombre Libre*, 28 March 1938, 13 May 1938; *El Imparcial*, 11, 25 March 1938, 14 September 1938, 14 October 1938; *El Pueblo*, 4, 28, 30 March 1938, 26 April 1938, 7, 9, 10 May 1938, 7 August 1938, 13, 15 October 1938; MI-2, G-2 8545, 10 May 1938; M. Sandomingo, *Historia de Agua Prieta: En su primer cincuentenario* (n.p., n.d.),

242–44; Pangburn to SD, 30 September 1938, SD/19; Yocupicio to Cárdenas, 16 October 1938, RG, DGG 2.384(22)23760, AGN.
7. Ceceña to Cárdenas, 27 October 1937, RG, DGG 2.012.8(22)28811, AGN; Yocupicio to FOCSS, 5 March 1937; Lombardo to SG, 23 February 1937; Gastélum to Cárdenas, 5 December 1937; SIPS to Cárdenas, 4 November 1937; Félix to SG, 18 September 1939, 13 November 1939; Macías to Cárdenas, 16, 18 September 1939; López to Cárdenas, 18 September 1939; Félix Verduzco to Cárdenas, 25 March 1938; Lombardo to Cárdenas, 24 March 1938, RG, DGG 2.317.4(22)3, AGN; Sindicato Oriental del Valle to Cárdenas, 15 April 1937; Yocupicio to SG, 27 May 1937, 12 November 1937, RG, DGG 2.012.8(22)25292, AGN; Yocupicio to SG, 9 March 1937, RG, DGG 2.384(22)23760, AGN; Dabdoub, *Historia*, 344–53; *El Imparcial*, 15, 25 March 1938; *El Pueblo*, 7, 8, 9, 12, 30 March 1938, 19 April 1938, 9, 26 July 1939.
8. Yepis to SD, 23 March 1938, SD/19; Dabdoub, *Historia*, 344–53; *El Pueblo*, 22, 26, 29 March 1938, 9, 20 April 1938, 9 May 1938; *El Hombre Libre*, 27 April 1938; *El Imparcial*, 30 March 1938; *Aurora*, 20 August 1939; Secretaría de Gobernación and Gobierno del Estado de Sonora, *Los municipios de Sonora* (México: Talleres Gráficos de la Nación, 1988), 102.
9. Report, Powell, 18 October 1938, RG 84, NC, GR 1938, Box 18, 800, NAW.
10. Powell to SD, 31 May 1938; Yepis to SD, 31 May 1938; Boyle to SD, 30 April 1937, 31 July 1937; Robinson to SD, 30 June 1938, SD/19; Nava and Aburto, "La rebelión," 22; MI-7, G-2 8974, 24 March 1939; MI-8, G-2 8975, 24 March 1939; Camp, *Political Biographies*, 161.
11. MI-8, G-2 6149, 7 May 1935; MI-7, G-2 8375, 22 March 1938; *El Popular*, 20 August 1938.
12. *El Machete*, 24 October 1938; *El Popular*, 24 August 1938.
13. *El Hombre Libre*, 22, 24 August 1938, 17 October 1938.
14. Yepis to SS, 30 September 1938, 13 October 1938, SD/19; MI-7, G-2 8692, 11 October 1938; G-2 8587, 24 August 1938.
15. Luis Rivas to SG, 11 October 1938, RG, DGG 2.384.(22)23760, AGN; Informe, 18 November 1939, AAGES 234.0"39"; Moncada, *La sucesión*, 69–71; *El Pueblo*, 10, 18 October 1938; *El Imparcial*, 13, 15, 16, 20, 29 October 1938.
16. Yepis to SS, 17 October 1938, SD/19; *El Popular*, 2 August 1938; *El Machete*, 21 July 1938; Lombardo to Cárdenas, 7 November 1938, RG, DGG 2.384(22)23760, AGN; *El Pueblo*, 1 February 1938, 14 October 1938; *El Imparcial*, 14 October 1938.
17. *El Imparcial*, 15 October 1938; *El Pueblo*, 15 October 1938; Yepis to SS, 18 October 1938, SD/19; *Hoy*, 20 October 1938; Yocupicio to Cárdenas, 16 October 1938, RG, DGG 2.384(22)23760, AGN; *El Pueblo*, 15 October 1938.
18. *El Pueblo*, 15 October 1938; *El Imparcial*, 18 October 1938; Moncada, *La sucesión*, 71; Armstrong to SS, 20 October 1938; Yepis to SS, 21 October 1938; Daniels to SS, 17 October 1938, 21 October 1938, SD/19; *El Hombre Libre*, 24 October 1938.
19. MI-2, G-2 8772, 1 November 1938; G-2 8778, 4 November 1938; *Hoy*, 29 October 1938; *El Pueblo*, 19 October 1938; Yepis to SS, 17, 21 October 1938; Armstrong to SD, 1 November 1938, 1 December 1938, 2 May 1939, SD/19; MI-7, G-2 8772, 21 October 1938; G-2 9119, 11 July 1939; G-2 9725, 1 March 1940.
20. Garrido, *El Partido*, 328–29.

21. Córdova, *La política*, 173.

22. Yepis to SD, 31 May 1938, SD/19.

23. Armstrong to SD, 1 December 1938, SD/19; *El Imparcial*, 12 May 1938, 16 September 1938; Moncada, *La Sucesión*, 67, 73–74.

24. RG, DGG 2.311G(22), AGN; Moncada, *La Sucesión*, 67; Corbalá, *Alamos*, 233–36; Yepis to SD, 30 April 1938, SD/19; Boyle to SD, 31 December 1938, 28 February 1939, SD/19; *El Hombre Libre*, 20 July 1938; *El Imparcial*, 8 July 1938.

25. *El Pueblo*, 16 May 1938; Powell to Boal, 20 May 1938; Yepis to SD, 31 May 1938, SD/19; FTS to Cárdenas, 14 June 1938; Beltrán to SG, 16 June 1938, RG, DGG 2.311G(22)32100, AGN; Moncada, *La Sucesión*, 64–65, 72; Powell to Boal, n.d. [June 1938], 15 June 1938, RG 84, NC, GR 1938, Box 18, 800, NAW; *El Imparcial*, 15 June 1938, 12 July 1938; *El Pueblo*, 14 October 1938; Liga to SG, 19 December 1938; Unión de Obreros y Campesinos Yaqui to SG, n.d., RG, DGG 2.311G(22), AGN.

26. *El Hombre Libre*, 22 July 1938.

27. Manifiesto, 20 June 1938, RG, DGG 2.311G(22)32100, AGN.

28. Méndez to Cárdenas, 20 October 1938, RG, DGG 2.311G(22), AGN; *El Hombre Libre*, 24 March 1938, 19 April 1938; Yepis to SS, 29 January 1937, SD/19; Moncada, *La Sucesión*, 64–65; *El Pueblo*, 14 August 1938; *Acción*, 28 February 1939; Eugenio Guerrero to OIPS, 17 January 1939, RG, DGG 2.384(22)23760, AGN; *El Imparcial*, 12 May 1937, 27 June 1938; *Aurora*, 20 June 1938; *El Intruso*, 4 March 1937, 12 May 1937; *El Noroeste*, 6 March 1937.

29. De Parodi, *Sonora*, 37–43; Moncada, *La Sucesión*, 66; MI-8, G-2 7476, [9 February 1936?]; Corbalá, *Alamos*, 233–36; MI-7, G-2 2277, 7 September 1928; G-2 4947, 12 January 1934; MI-5, Visit, Military Attaché, 1934.

30. Wilkie and Monzón, *México visto*, 592; Hernández, *La mecánica*, 69–70, 201, 201, n.16; *El Imparcial*, 14 June 1938.

31. Beltrán to SG, 1 August 1938; CTS to SG, 2 August 1938; Peralta to SG, 22 June 1938; Asuntos Indígenas to SG, 2 July 1928, RG, DGG 2.311G(22)32100, AGN; *El Machete*, 15 June 1938, 2 July 1938; *El Intruso*, 8 January 1937; *El Pueblo*, 7 October 1938; AHGES, Tesorería, Libro Balance General de 1940, 31 December 1940; Biographic Data, Armstrong, 7 October 1939, RG 84, NC, CR 1939–41, Box 2, NAW.

32. Moncada, *La Sucesión*, 66, 80, 92; *El Imparcial*, 12, 19 June 1938, 14 December 1938; *El Noroeste*, 8 March 1937; Alejo Bay to Comité Pro-Macías, 13 October 1938, RG, DGG 2.311G(22)32100, AGN; Otero to Cárdenas, 30 December 1938; Macías to Cárdenas, 18, 31 December 1938, RP, FLC 544.2/25, AGN; Petition, STERM, RP, FLC 543.6/375, AGN.

33. *Acción*, 18 March 1939; Armstrong to SD, 30 September 1939, SD/19.

34. Moncada, *La Sucesión*, 67; Corbalá, *Alamos*, 233–36; *El Hombre Libre*, 26 March 1939, 7 April 1939.

35. Boyle to SD, 30 January 1938, SD/19; Discurso, Padrés, 27 December 1938, RP, FLC 544.2/25, AGN; Genaro Velázquez to Cárdenas, 6 December 1938, RG, DGG 2.311G(22)32100, AGN; Letter to Cárdenas, 6 December 1938; Campos Yaqui to Cárdenas, 9 December 1938, RG, DGG 2.311G(22), AGN.

36. *El Machete*, 8 August 1938; RG, DGG 2.311G(22), AGN.

37. *El Imparcial*, 8 January 1939.

38. Ibid., 12 September 1939, 26 October 1938, 23 November 1938; *El Pueblo*, 2 March 1938.

39. Powell to SD, 31 January 1939, SD/19.

40. *El Machete*, 20 July 1938; Worster to SD, 30 July 1938; Robinson to Boal, 21 June 1938, SD/19; Moncada, *La Sucesión*, 66.

41. *El Imparcial*, 29 November 1938; Padrés to Cárdenas, 21 January 1939, RG, DGG 2.311G(22), AGN; *El Machete*, 8 August 1938; Robinson to SD, 30 July 1938, SD/19; Moncada, *La Sucesión*, 71, 73; Peña to Cárdenas, 13 October 1938; Yocupicio to SG, 1 October 1938, RG, DGG 2.311G(22) 32100, AGN; Comité Pro-Otero to Cárdenas, 14 October 1938, RG, DGG 2.384(22)23760, AGN.

42. Moncada, *La Sucesión*, 72; *Acción*, 3 January 1939; PS-7 to OIPS, 19 December 1938, RG, DGG 2.311G(22), AGN.

43. *El Imparcial*, 31 December 1939; Francisco Figueroa to Enrique Romero, 5, 6 December 1938; Padristas to Cárdenas, 23 January 1939; PS-7 to OIPS, 19 December 1938; Bórquez to Cárdenas, 13 February 1939, RG, DGG 2.311G(22), AGN; Padrés to PRM, n.d. (1939); Padrés to Cárdenas, 3/5 January 1939, 19 February 1939, RP, FLC 544.2/25, AGN; *El Hombre Libre*, 30 April 1939, 19 May 1939.

44. Macías to Cárdenas, 18, 31 December 1938, RP, FLC 544.2/25, AGN; Beltrán to SG, 19 December 1938, RG, DGG 2.311G(22), AGN.

45. Yocupicio to SG, 1 February 1939, RG, DGG 2.311M(22)35656, AGN; Figueroa to Romero, 5, 6 December 1938; PS-7 to OIPS, 19 December 1938; Padristas to Cárdenas, 23 January 1939; Liga Femenil, San José, to SG, 19 December 1938; Unión de Obreros y Campesinos Yaqui to Delegado, PRM, n.d.; Bórquez to Cárdenas, 13 February 1939; Mendoza to Romero, 5, 6 December 1938; Padrés to Cárdenas, 5 January 1939, RG, DGG 2.311G(22), C 314, AGN; Padrés to PRM, n.d. [1939]; and idem to Cárdenas, 3 January 1939, 19 February 1939, RP, FLC 544.2/25, AGN.

46. Padrés to PRM, n.d. [1939]; and idem to Cárdenas, 3 January 1939, 19 February 1939, RP, FLC 544.2/25, AGN.

47. *El Imparcial*, 24 January 1939, 7 February 1939; Bórquez to Cárdenas, 13 February 1939, RG, DGG 2.311G(22), AGN.

48. *El Imparcial*, 6, 8, 10 December 1938.

49. *Acción*, 5, 11 January 1939; *El Imparcial*, 14 December 1939, 3, 4, 6, 7–14, 17, 18, 20 January 1939.

50. *El Imparcial*, 22, 24, 25, 27–30 December 1938.

51. PS-7 to OIPS, 19 December 1938; Voting lists, DGG 2.311G(22)22, AGN.

52. Corbalá, *Alamos*, 233–36; Padrés to SG, 6 February 1939; Peralta to Cárdenas, 24 February 1939, RG, DGG 2.311G(22), AGN; Report, Armstrong, 7 October 1939, RG 84, NC, CR 1939–1941, Box 2, NAW; *Acción*, 7, 28 February 1939, 8 March 1939; *El Hombre Libre*, 14, 24 March 1939; Boyle to SD, 28 February 1939; Powell to SD, 1 March 1939, SD/19.

53. *El Imparcial*, 14 June 1939; RG, DGG 2.317.1(22)39292, AGN; *Boletín Oficial* no. 13 (12 August 1939); *Acción*, 2 February 1939.

54. *El Imparcial*, 7, 12, 14, 19, 20 March 1939; 1, 4, 12, 18, 23, 25, 30 April 1939; 9, 13 May 1939; 22 June 1939; 8, 15 July 1939; 14 September 1939; 4, 13, 18 October 1939; 1 November 1939; 2 December 1939; Juan Gallardo to SG, 8 June 1939; Yocupicio to SG, 2 June 1939, RG, DGG 2.311M(22)37396, AGN; *Boletín Oficial* no. 13 (12 August 1939); Soto to Congreso, 30 May

1939, RG, DGG 2.311M(22)38311, AGN; Comisariados Arizpe, Bamori, Sinoquipe to Cárdenas, 9 April 1939; Comisariado, Bacanuchi, to Cárdenas, 22 May 1939; Comité, PRM, to SG, 28 June 1939; ibid. to PRM, 28 June 1939, RG, DGG 2.311M(22)37425, AGN; Powell to SD, 30 September 1939, SD/19.

Epilogue, "The Accommodation," 205–12

1. Yepis to SS, 11 June 1938, RG 84, GC, GR 1938, Box 23, 350, NAW; Sanderson, *Agrarian Populism*, 125; *El Hombre Libre*, 10, 29 December 1939, 14 January 1939; Calzadíaz, *Dos Gigantes*, 117–21; Boyle to SS, 24 May 1939; Memorandum, GC, 27 June 1939, SD/19.
2. *El Hombre Libre*, 19 May 1939; *El Imparcial*, 21, 25 May 1939, 6 June 1939; Powell to SS, 3 June 1939; Armstrong to SD, 31 May 1939, 30 June 1939, SD/19; Calzadíaz, *Dos Gigantes*, 117–21.
3. Memorandum, GC, 27 June 1939, SD/19; *El Imparcial*, 6 June 1939; *El Heraldo del Yaqui*, 15, 18 June 1939.
4. Peter H. Smith, *Labyrinths of Power: Political Recruitment in Twentieth Century Mexico* (Princeton: Princeton University Press, 1979).
5. *El Nacional*, 2 September 1939; Moncada, *La sucesión*, 86–88, 97; *El Imparcial*, 16 August 1939, 3 September 1939.
6. *El Imparcial*, 5, 8 September 1939; Armstrong to SD, 30 September 1939, SD/19; DGG 2.317(22)38829, AGN; Felipe Mora and Gabriela González Barragán, "La representación política de los trabajadores en Sonora (1937–1988)," in *XIV Simposio*, 3:215; Corbalá, *Alamos*, 233–36; Almada, "La conexión," 468, 747.
7. Lombardo to Cárdenas, 22 September 1939, RP, FLC 544.2/25, AGN.
8. MI-5, MA 9747, 19 March 1941; MA 9587, 7 November 1940, MA 9861, 28 May 1941; Dwyer to Shaw, 25 January 1941, RG 84, GC, CR 1936–41, Box 1, 300–843, NAW; Powell to SD, 1 April 1939, 1 September 1939; Armstrong to SD, 30 September 1939, SD/19; *El Imparcial*, 9, 12 March 1939, 24 January 1939, 11, 12, 14, 18, 23, 30 July 1939, 2, 4 August 1939, 17, 24 October 1939, 20, 21, 24 September 1939.
9. Powell to SD, 30 September 1939, SD/19; MI-7, G-2 9498, 6 September 1940; 9378, 4 June 1940.
10. Boyle to SD, 31 March 1939, 31 October 1939, 30 November 1939; Powell to Armstrong, 6 November 1939, RG 84, GC, GR 1939, Box 34, 800, NAW; Dwyer to SD, 10 May 1939, SD/19; Contreras, *México, 1940*, 81; Galaz, *Desde el Cerro*, 241–43; Luis López Alvarez, *Aquellos tiempos anchos* (Hermosillo: Talleres Gráficos y Editoriales Pitíc, 1983), 67–68; *El Imparcial*, 26 September 1938; C. W. Adair, U.S. Vice-Consul, Nogales, to Shaw, 13 November 1940, RG 84, NC, CR 1939–41, Box 2, NAW.
11. *El Imparcial*, 22 January 1939; *Acción*, 25 January 1939; Informe, 18 November 1939, AAGES 234.0"39"; Report, Powell, 7 February 1939, RG 84, NC, GR 1938, Box 20, 850.4, NAW; Robinson to SS, 13 August 1938; Dwyer to SD, 31 August 1939; Boyle to SD, 28 February 1939, 31 October 1939, 30 November 1939; Armstrong to SD, 31 October 1939; Powell to SD, 30 November 1939, SD/19; Boyle to SS, 3, 10 June 1940, RG 84, Agua Prieta Consulate, CR 1926–40, Box 1, NAW.
12. F. A. Byerly to Pangburn, 6 April 1940, RG 84, GC, GR 1940, Box 42, 800, NAW; Larrañaga, *Navojoa*, 71.

13. López, *Aquellos tiempos*, 67–69; Galaz, *Desde el Cerro*, 242; *El Intruso*, 8 June 1940.

14. *El Imparcial*, 23 September 1939, 15, 23, 31 August 1939, 13 September 1939.

15. *El Nacional*, 3 September 1939; *El Imparcial*, 9, 12 July 1939; *Acción*, 29 March 1939; Armstrong to SD, 30 September 1939, SD/19; RP, FLC 556.2/70, 111/3674, 135.2/146, 556.64/428, 702.2/12556, AGN; Lázaro Cárdenas, *Obras*. Vol. 1. *Apuntes 1941/1956* (México: UNAM, 1973), 2:24; Calzadíaz, *Dos Gigantes*, 90–92; Moncada, *La sucesión*, 74.

16. Ramírez and Guadarrama, "Los resultados," *HCS*, 344; Enríquez, "Los Trabajadores," 123–24.

17. Antonio Rivera Flores, "Unión General de Obreros y Campesinos de México," in *Las Derrotas obreras, 1946–1952*, ed. Víctor M. Durand Ponte (México: UNAM, 1984), 50.

18. Ramírez and Guadarrama, "Los resultados," *HCS*, 347; Enríquez, "Los trabajadores," 135.

Conclusion, 213–26

1. Sanderson, *Agrarian Populism*, 111, n.74.

2. Knight, "Cardenismo," 73, 77.

3. Alejandra Lajous, *Los orígenes del partido único en México* (México: UNAM, 1979), 184; Córdova, *La política*, 41–44, 173, 180; Tzvi Medin, *Ideología y praxis política de Lázaro Cárdenas* (México: Era, 1981), 230; Falcón, *Revolución*, 235.

4. Hernández, *La mecánica*; Falcón, *Revolución*.

5. Martínez, *El laboratorio*, 233.

6. Paul Friedrich, *The Princes of Naranja: An Essay in Anthrohistorical Method* (Austin: University of Texas Press, 1986), 150, 156–59.

7. Charles Tilly, *From Mobilization to Revolution* (Reading, MA: Addison-Wesley, 1978).

8. Lorenzo Meyer, *La segunda muerte de la Revolución Mexicana* (México: Cal y Arena, 1992), 272, 274.

Selected Bibliography

Archives and Special Collections

Mexico

Archivo General de la Nación, Mexico City
  Ramo Departamento Autónomo del Trabajo
  Ramo Gobernación, Dirección General de Gobierno
  Ramo Presidentes, Fondo Lázaro Cárdenas
Archivo del Gobierno del Estado de Sonora, Hermosillo
  Archivo Administrativo del Gobierno del Estado de Sonora
  Archivo Histórico del Gobierno del Estado de Sonora
Instituto Nacional de Antropología e Historia, Mexico City
  Archivo de la Revolución Mexicana/Patronato de Historia de
    Sonora (microfilm)
  Serie Sonora, 1a serie, Vol. XVIII, 1924–1940 (microfilm)
Secretaría de Educación Pública, Mexico City
  Archivo Histórico
  Archivo de Rurales y Primarias Foráneas
Secretaría de la Reforma Agraria, Mexico City
  Archivo General
Archivo Francisco J. Múgica, Jiquilpán de Juárez
  Fondo Francisco J. Múgica
    Archivo Francisco J. Múgica
Archivos Plutarco Elías Calles y Fernando Torreblanca,
    Mexico City
  Archivo de Plutarco Elías Calles
  Archivo de Fernando Torreblanca
Universidad Nacional Autónoma de México, Mexico City
  Archivo de VITA
El Colegio de Sonora, Hermosillo
  Fichero de El Colegio de Sonora
Archivo de Ernesto López Yescas, Bácum, Sonora
Biblioteca Pública Especializada Vicente Lombardo Toledano,
    Mexico City

Other

National Archives, Washington, D.C./Suitland, Maryland

279

Records Relating to the Internal Affairs of Mexico, U.S. State
	Department, 1929–1940 (812.00, 812.631) (microfilm)
	Record Group 84, Consular Post Records
General Records
	Agua Prieta, Cananea, Guaymas, Nogales
Confidential Records
	Agua Prieta, Guaymas, Nogales
U.S. Military Intelligence Reports, Mexico, 1919–1940 (microfilm)
Arizona State Museum, University of Arizona, Tucson
	N. Ross Crumrine Papers
	Edward Spicer Papers
	Muriel Thayer Painter Papers
Latin American Library, Tulane University, New Orleans
	Religious Persecution in Mexico Papers
Algemeen Rijksarchief, The Hague, The Netherlands
	Buitenlandse Zaken, Kabinetsarchief betreffende
		Politieke Raportage

Interviews

Bernabé Arana León, Ciudad Obregón, May 24, 1992
Gilberto Escobosa Gámez, Hermosillo, May 21, 22, 1992
Profesor Amadeo Hernández Coronado, Hermosillo, May 26, 1992
Padre Ernesto López Yescas, Bácum, May 24, 1992

Periodicals

Acción (Nogales)
*Alma Sonorense. Organo mensual de la Federación de Maestros del
	Estado de Sonora* (Ures)
*Amanece. Organo mensual de la Parroquia de Nuestra Señora de Guada-
	lupe* (Cananea)
The Arizona Daily Star (Tucson)
Aurora (Cananea)
Boletín Desde México (Mexico City)
*Boletín Oficial. Organo del gobierno constitucional del estado de
	Sonora* (Hermosillo)
*Boletín Pro-Bodas de Plata Episcopales. Informe mensual diocesano.
	Organo del comité central* (Hermosillo)
Criterio. Semanario de orientación social
CROM. Organo oficial de la C.R.O.M. (Mexico City)
*David. Organo oficial de la Legión de Cristo Rey y Santa María de Guada-
	lupe: Veteranos de la Guardia Nacional (Cristeros)* (Mexico City)
El Diario (Guaymas)
*Diario de los Debates de la Cámara de Diputados del Congreso de los
	Estados Unidos Mexicanos* (Mexico City)
*Diario de Debates de la Cámara de Senadores del Congreso de los
	Estados Unidos Mexicanos* (Mexico City)

Douglas Daily Dispatch (Douglas, Arizona)
Esfuerzo (La Parcela, Sonora)
Excélsior (Mexico City)
Futuro (Mexico City)
La Gaceta (Guaymas)
El Heraldo (Magdalena)
El Heraldo del Yaqui (Ciudad Obregón)
El Hombre Libre (Mexico City)
Hoy (Mexico City)
El Imparcial (Hermosillo)
El Intruso (Cananea)
El Machete (Mexico City)
El Nacional (Mexico City)
Nacozari al Día (Nacozari)
El Noroeste (Nogales)
El Popular (Mexico City)
Propaganda Doctrinaria Antidogmática Para Maestros Rurales
    (Magdalena)
El Pueblo (Hermosillo)
*Reconquista. Organo oficial de la Liga Nacional Defensora de la
    Libertad* (Mexico City)
*Reforma Escolar. Hoja mensual de propaganda educativa de los mae-
    stros rurales federales de la primera zona escolar de Sonora*
    (Magdalena)
Regis. Semanario catequístico (Nogales)
El Sembrador. Hoja catequística
Timón (Mexico City)
El Universal (Mexico City)

Printed Contemporary Sources

Cárdenas, Lázaro. *Obras*. Vol. 1. *Apuntes 1941/1956*. México: Uni-
    versidad Nacional Autónoma de México, 1973.
*Contrato colectivo de trabajo celebrado entre The Moctezuma Copper
    Company y el Sindicato Minero "Héroe Jesús García."* Pilares de
    Nacozari, 1940.
C.T.M., 1936–1941. Vol. 1. México: Partido Revolucionario Institu-
    cional, 1981.
Directorio comercial del Estado de Sonora, 1920–1921. Hermosillo:
    Healy-Genda Editores, 1921.
Estados Unidos Mexicanos, Secretaría de la Economía Nacional,
    Dirección General de Estadística. *Compendio estadístico*. México:
    Secretaría de la Economía Nacional, Dirección General de Esta-
    dística, 1941.
Excitiva para fundar la Confederación Obrera-Campesina. México:
    Talleres Gráficos Marte, 1932.
Fernández Boyoli, Manuel, and Eustaquio Marrón de Angelis. *Lo
    que no se sabe de la rebelión Cedillista*. México: Grafi-Art, 1938.

García y Alva, Federico. *México y sus progresos: "Album-Directorio del Estado de Sonora."* Hermosillo: N.p., n.d.

García Fomenti, Arturo. *Desde la tribuna revolucionaria de Sonora (Escuela socialista y otros temas).* México, 1935.

Garibaldi, Lorenzo, ed. *Memoria de la gestión gubernamental del C. General Román Yocupicio: Aspectos principales de su labor social y constructiva.* Hermosillo: Imprenta José Cruz Gálvez, 1939.

Horton, Inez. *Copper's Children: The Rise and Fall of a Mexican Copper Mining Camp.* New York: Exposition Press, 1968.

Informe al Primer Congreso del STERM: CEN. México: FSTSE, 1940.

Informe que rinde el C. General Román Yocupicio, Gobernador Constitucional del Estado de Sonora, al H. Congreso del Estado, sobre la labor administrativa realizada durante el período comprendido del 1o de Septiembre de 1937 al 16 de Septiembre de 1938. Hermosillo: Imprenta J. Cruz Gálvez, 1938.

Ingersoll, Ralph McA. *In and Under Mexico.* New York, London: Century, 1924.

Lombardo Toledano, Vicente. *Como actúan los Nazis en México.* México: Universidad Obrera de México, 1941.

———. *5th Column in Mexico.* New York: Council for Panamerican Democracy, [1942].

Memoria General: Informe rendido por el C. Rodolfo Elías Calles, Gobernador Constitucional del Estado, ante la H. XXXII Legislatura local, el 16 de Septiembre de 1934. Hermosillo: Imprenta Cruz Gálvez, 1934.

The Mines Handbook. New York: Mines Information Bureau, 1931.

Mines Register: Successor to the Mines Handbook. New York: Mines Information Bureau, 1942.

Montaño, Raúl E., and Octavio P. Gaxiola, eds. *Album del Mayo y del Yaqui: Directorio comercial, 1933.* Navojoa: Imprenta Montaño, 1932.

Parker, Morris B. *Mules, Mines, and Me in Mexico, 1895–1932.* Tucson: University of Arizona Press, 1979.

Partido Nacional Revolucionario. *La gira del General Lázaro Cárdenas.* México: Partido Revolucionario Institucional, 1989.

Pegueras, Francisco de P. *Album Patria Libre.* Nogales: N.p., n.d.

Resumen general del censo industrial de 1935. México: Departamento Autónomo de Prensa y Publicidad, 1941.

Secretaría de la Economía Nacional. Departamento de Minas. *Anuario de estadística minera: Año de 1933.* México: Departamento Autónomo de Prensa y Publicidad, n.d.

———. Dirección General de Estadística. *Anuario estadístico de los Estados Unidos Mexicanos, 1938.* México: Departamento Autónomo de Prensa y Publicidad, 1939.

———. Dirección General de Estadística. *Anuario estadístico de los Estados Unidos Mexicanos, 1940.* México: Secretaría de la Economía Nacional, 1942.

Sonora en los cuarentas. Hermosillo: Editora "La Diligencia," 1991.

Sonora y sus actividades: Directorio comercial-industrial-minero-profesional-agrícola-ganadero y de propietarios de bienes raíces. Magdalena: Ediciones Mijares Palencia e Hijos, [1947?].

Uribe García, Jesús Félix. *La historia de la industria en Hermosillo.* Hermosillo: Publicaciones "La Diligencia," 1991.

Secondary Works

Abascal, Salvador. *Lázaro Cárdenas: Presidente Comunista.* 2 vols. México: Editorial Tradición, 1988–89.

Acción y pensamiento vivos de Lázaro Cárdenas. México: Federación Editorial Mexicana, 1973.

Acuña Gálvez, Cruz. *Juan Navarrete: Medio siglo de historia sonorense.* Hermosillo: Editorial Urias, 1970.

Aguilar Camín, Héctor. "Los jefes sonorenses de la Revolución Mexicana." In *Caudillos y campesinos en la Revolución Mexicana,* edited by D. A. Brading. México: Fondo de Cultura Económica, 1985.

―――. *La frontera nómada: Sonora y la Revolución Mexicana.* México: Secretaría de Educación Pública, 1985.

Album conmemorativo de las Bodas de Oro Episcopales del Exmo. y Romo. Sr. Arzobispo Dr. Juan Navarrete y Guerrero. N.p., [1969].

Album recuerdo: Homenaje de amor, gratitud y respeto al Exmo. y Romo. Sr. Arzobispo Juan Navarrete y Guerrero. N.p., 1964.

Almada, Francisco R. *Diccionario de historia, geografía y biografía sonorenses.* Chihuahua: N.p., 1952.

Almada Bay, Ignacio. "La conexión Yocupicio: Soberanía estatal, tradición cívico-liberal y resistencia al reemplazo de las lealtades en Sonora, 1913–1939." Tesis de doctorado, El Colegio de México, 1992.

―――. "Conflictos y contactos del Estado y de la Iglesia en Sonora." In *Coloquio sobre las relaciones del Estado y las iglesias en Sonora y México. Memoria,* edited by Felipe Mora A. Hermosillo: El Colegio de Sonora, Universidad de Hermosillo, 1993.

―――. "Crónica de un retablo municipal: Yocupicio Alcalde." *Revista de El Colegio de Sonora* 5:7 (1994): 75–102.

Alonso, Ana María. *Thread of Blood. Colonialism, Revolution, and Gender on Mexico's Northern Frontier.* Tucson: University of Arizona Press, 1995.

Alvear Acevedo, Carlos. *Lázaro Cárdenas: El hombre y su mito.* México: Editorial Jus, 1961.

Anderson, Rodney. "Mexican Workers and the Politics of Revolution." *Hispanic American Historical Review* 54 (1970): 513–35.

Anguiano, Arturo. *El Estado y la política obrera del Cardenismo.* México: Era, 1975.

Ankerson, Dudley. *Agrarian Warlord: Saturnino Cedillo and the Mexican Revolution in San Luis Potosí.* DeKalb: Northern Illinois University Press, 1984.

Ashby, Joe. *Organized Labor and the Mexican Revolution under Lázaro Cárdenas.* Chapel Hill: University of North Carolina Press, 1964.

Aulard, Alphonse. *Christianity and the French Revolution.* New York: Howard Fertig, 1966.

Bantjes, Adrian A. "Bourgeoisie, Revolution and Reform in Mexico: The Case of Sonora." Paper presented at the 46th International Conference of Americanists, Amsterdam, 1988.

———. "Política nacional y regional en el México post-revolucionario: Lázaro Cárdenas y la revuelta sonorense de 1935." In *XIV Simposio de Historia y Antropología de Sonora: Memoria,* 2:101–19. Hermosillo: Instituto de Investigaciones Históricas, Universidad de Sonora, 1990.

———. "Politics, Class and Culture in Post-Revolutionary Mexico: Cardenismo and Sonora, 1929–1940." Ph.D. diss., University of Texas at Austin, 1991.

———. "Religión y Revolución en México, 1929–1940." *Boletín* 15 (1994).

———. "Burning Saints, Molding Minds: Iconoclasm, Civic Ritual, and the Failed Cultural Revolution." In *Rituals of Rule, Rituals of Resistance: Public Celebrations and Popular Culture in Mexico,* edited by William H. Beezley, Cheryl English Martin, and William E. French, 261–84. Wilmington, DE: SR Books, 1994.

———. "Idolatry and Iconoclasm in Revolutionary Mexico: The Dechristianization Campaigns, 1929–1940." *Mexican Studies/ Estudios Mexicanos* 13:1 (Winter 1997): 87–120.

Baroni B., Ariane. "Productores agropecuarios en la cuenca media del Río Sonora entre 1900 y 1950." In *Memoria: XII Simposio de Historia y Antropología de Sonora,* 2:25–46. Hermosillo: Instituto de Investigaciones Históricas, Universidad de Sonora, 1988.

———. "Agricultura en el Valle de Ures de 1880 a 1910." *XV Simposio de Historia e Antropología de Sonora: Memoria,* 1:477–79. Hermosillo: Instituto de Investigaciones Históricas, Universidad de Sonora, 1991.

Bartolini Verdugo, Hector Rubén. *Monografía de Aconchi (Acontzi).* Hermosillo: N.p., 1983.

Basurto, Jorge. *Cárdenas y el poder sindical.* México: Era, 1983.

Becker, Marjorie. "Black and White and Color: *Cardenismo* and the Search for a Campesino Ideology." *Comparative Studies in Society and History* 29:3 (July 1987): 453–65.

———. "Lázaro Cárdenas and the Mexican Counter-Revolution: The Struggle over Culture in Michoacán, 1934–1940." Ph.D. diss., Yale University, 1988.

———. "Torching La Purísima, Dancing at the Altar: The Construction of Revolutionary Hegemony in Michoacán, 1934–1940." In *Everyday Forms of State Formation: Revolution and the Negotiation of Rule in Modern Mexico,* edited by Gilbert M. Joseph and Daniel Nugent, 247–64. Durham: Duke University Press, 1994.

————. *Setting the Virgin on Fire: Lázaro Cárdenas and the Redemption of the Mexican Revolution.* Berkeley: University of California Press, 1995.

Bellah, R. N. *Beyond Belief.* New York: Harper and Row, 1970.

Benjamin, Thomas. "The Leviathan on the Zócalo: Recent Historiography of the Postrevolutionary Mexican State." *Latin American Research Review* 20:3 (1985): 195–217.

————. *A Rich Land, A Poor People: Politics and Society in Modern Chiapas.* Albuquerque: University of New Mexico Press, 1989.

Benjamin, Thomas, and Mark Wasserman, eds. *Provinces of the Revolution: Essays on Regional Mexican History, 1910–1929.* Albuquerque: University of New Mexico Press, 1990.

Bergquist, Charles W. *Labor in Latin America.* Stanford: Stanford University Press, 1986.

Bernstein, Marvin D. *The Mexican Mining Industry, 1890–1950: A Study of the Interaction of Politics, Economics, and Technology.* Albany: State University of New York, 1965.

Besserer, Federico, José Díaz, and Raúl Santana. "Formación y consolidación del sindicalismo minero en Cananea." *Revista Mexicana de Sociología* 42:4 (1980): 1321–53.

Besserer, Federico, Victoria Novelo, and Juan Luis Sariego. *El sindicalismo minero en México, 1900–1952.* México: Era, 1983.

Blanco Moheno, Roberto. *Tata Lázaro: Vida, obra y muerte de Cárdenas, Múgica y Carrillo Puerto.* México: Editorial Diana, 1972.

Brandenburg, Frank. *The Making of Modern Mexico.* Englewood Cliffs: Prentice Hall, 1964.

Brown, Jonathan C., and Alan Knight, eds. *The Mexican Petroleum Industry in the Twentieth Century.* Austin: University of Texas Press, 1992.

Brown, Lyle. "Mexican Church-State Relations, 1933–1940." *A Journal of Church and State* 7 (1964): 202–22.

Buve, Raymond. "Los Gobernadores de estado y la movilización de los campesinos en Tlaxcala." In *Caudillos y campesinos en la Revolución Mexicana,* edited by D. A. Brading. México: Fondo de Cultura Económica, 1985.

Calvo Berber, Laureano. *Nociones de historia de Sonora.* México: Porrúa, Publicaciones del Gobierno del Estado de Sonora, 1958.

Calzadíaz Barrera, Alberto. *Dos Gigantes: Sonora y Chihuahua.* Hermosillo: Escritores Asociados del Norte, 1964.

Camacho Sandoval, Salvador. *Controversia entre la ideología y la fe: La educación socialista en la historia de Aguascalientes, 1876–1940.* México: Consejo Nacional para la Cultura y las Artes, 1991.

Camou H., Ernesto. "Yaquis y Mayos: Cultivadores de los valles." In *Historia general de Sonora: Historia contemporánea de Sonora, 1929–1984.* Hermosillo: El Colegio de Sonora, 1988.

Camp, Roderic Ai. *Mexican Political Biographies, 1935–1975.* Tucson: University of Arizona Press, 1976.

Campbell, Hugh G. "The Radical Right in Mexico, 1929–1949." Ph.D.
diss., University of California at Los Angeles, 1968.
Carlos, Manuel L. "Enclavement Processes, State Policies, and Cul-
tural Identity among the Mayo Indians of Sinaloa, Mexico." In
Ejidos and Regions of Refuge in Northwestern Mexico, edited by N.
Ross Crumrine and Phil C. Weigand, 33–37. Anthropological Pa-
pers of the University of Arizona, No. 46. Tucson: University of
Arizona Press, 1987.
Carr, Barry. *The Peculiarities of the Mexican North, 1880–1928: An Essay
in Interpretation*. Occasional Papers, No. 4. Glasgow: Institute of
Latin American Studies, University of Glasgow, 1971.
———. *El movimiento obrero y la política en México*. México: Era, 1981.
Carton de Grammont, Hubert. *Los empresarios agrícolas y el Estado*.
México: Instituto de Investigaciones Sociales, Universidad
Nacional Autónoma de México, 1990.
Casanova, Abelardo. *Pasos perdidos*. Hermosillo: Grupo Editorial
Imágen, 1986.
Castro Vázquez, María del Carmen. "El conflicto agrario, la organi-
zación campesina en el Valle del Yaqui y sus principales fuentes
de estudio (1940–1960)." Tesis de licenciatura en sociología,
Escuela de Sociología, Universidad de Sonora, 1989.
Cline, Howard F. *Mexico: Revolution to Evolution, 1940–1960*. New
York: Oxford University Press, 1963.
Collier, David, ed. *The New Authoritarianism in Latin America*.
Princeton: Princeton University Press, 1979.
Collier, Ruth Berins, and David Collier. *Shaping the Political Arena:
Critical Junctures, the Labor Movement, and Regime Dynamics in
Latin America*. Princeton: Princeton University Press, 1991.
Contreras, Ariel José. *México, 1940: Industrialización y crisis política*.
México: Siglo XXI, 1977.
Contreras, Enrique. *Cosas viejas de mi tierra*. Hermosillo: Editorial
Urias, n.d.
Corbalá, Manuel S. *Rodolfo Elías Calles: Perfiles de un sonorense*.
Hermosillo: N.p., 1970.
Corbalá Acuña, Manuel Santiago. *Alamos de Sonora*. México: Edito-
rial Libros de México, 1977.
Córdova, Arnaldo. *La política de masas del cardenismo*. México: Era,
1974.
Córdova Romero, Francisco. *Perfil histórico de Cananea (Ensayo)*.
Hermosillo: Edición prop. del Lic. Francisco Córdova Romero,
1980.
Cornejo, Gerardo. *La sierra y el viento*. México: Leega Literaria, 1977.
———, ed. *Historia general de Sonora: Historia Contemporánea de
Sonora, 1929–1984*. Hermosillo: El Colegio de Sonora, 1988.
Cornelius, Wayne. "Nation Building, Participation, and Distribu-
tion: The Politics of Social Reform under Cárdenas." In *Crisis,
Choice, and Change: Historical Studies of Political Development*, ed-

ited by Gabriel A. Almond, Scott C. Flanagan, and Robert J. Mundt, 392–498. Boston: Little, Brown, 1973.

Crumrine, N. Ross. *The Mayo Indians of Sonora: A People Who Refuse to Die.* Tucson: University of Arizona Press, 1977.

———. "Mechanisms of Enclavement Maintenance and Sociocultural Blocking of Modernization among the Mayo of Southern Sonora." In *Ejidos and Regions of Refuge in Northwestern Mexico,* edited by N. Ross Crumrine and Phil C. Weigand, 22–31. Anthropological Papers of the University of Arizona, No. 46. Tucson: University of Arizona Press, 1987.

Dabdoub, Claudio. *Historia de El Valle del Yaqui.* México: Porrúa, 1964.

De Parodi, Enriqueta. *Sonora: Hombres y paisajes.* México: Editorial Pafim, 1941.

Desan, Suzanne. *Reclaiming the Sacred: Lay Religion and Popular Politics in Revolutionary France.* Ithaca: Cornell University Press, 1990.

Dr. Atl, 1875–1964: Conciencia y paisaje. Museo Nacional de Arte, Palacio de Minería, Diciembre 1984–Marzo 1985. México: Museo Nacional de Arte, 1985.

Eckstein, Salomon. *El ejido colectivo en México.* México: Fondo de Cultura Económica, 1966.

Encinas Blanco, Angel. "El movimiento cristero de Luis Ibarra en Granados." In *Memoria del IX Simposio de Historia de Sonora,* 445–56. Hermosillo: Instituto de Investigaciones Históricas, Universidad de Sonora, 1984.

Enríquez Licón, Dora Elvia. "Sonora, Sindicatos y participación política (1932–1951)." In *Memoria: XII Simposio de Historia y Antropología de Sonora,* 1:86–103. Hermosillo: Instituto de Investigaciones Históricas, Universidad de Sonora, 1988.

———. "Los trabajadores sonorenses y sus organizaciones (1873–1987)." Tesis de licenciatura en sociología, Departamento de Ciencias Sociales, Universidad de Sonora, 1988.

Erasmus, Charles J. *Man Takes Control: Cultural Development and American Aid.* Minneapolis: University of Minnesota Press, 1961.

———. "Cultural Change in Northwest Mexico." In Charles J. Erasmus, Solomon Miller, and Louis C. Faron, *Contemporary Change in Traditional Communities of Mexico and Peru,* 1–132. Urbana: University of Illinois Press, 1978.

Escárcega López, Everardo, and Saúl Escobar Toledo. *Historia de la cuestión agraria mexicana.* Vol. 5. *El Cardenismo: Un parteaguas en el proceso agrario nacional, 1934–1940 (Primera parte).* México: Siglo XXI, CEHAM, 1990.

Estadísticas históricas de México. 2 vols. México: Instituto Nacional de Estadística, Geografía y Informatica, 1985.

Falcón, Romana. "El surgimiento del agrarismo cardenista: Una revisión de las tesis populistas." *Historia Mexicana* 27:3 (January–March 1978): 333–86.

————. *Revolución y caciquismo: San Luís Potosí, 1910–1938*. México: El Colegio de México, 1984.

Fowler Salamini, Heather. *Movilización campesina en Veracruz (1920–1938)*. México: Siglo XXI, 1979.

Freedberg, David. *Iconoclasts and Their Motives*. Maarsen, The Netherlands: Gary Schwartz, 1985.

French, William Earl. "The Inculcation of the Capitalist Work Ethic in a Mexican Mining District (Hidalgo District, Chihuahua, 1880–1920)." Ph.D. diss., University of Texas at Austin, 1990.

Friedrich, Paul. *The Princes of Naranja: An Essay in Anthrohistorical Method*. Austin: University of Texas Press, 1986.

Furet, François. *Interpreting the French Revolution*. Cambridge: Cambridge University Press, 1981.

Galaz, Fernando A. *Desde el Cerro de la Campana: Relatos*. 2 vols. Hermosillo: Editorial Urias, 1964.

Galindo Mendoza, Alfredo. *Apuntes geográficos y estadísticos de la República y de la Iglesia Mexicana*. México: N.p., 1943.

Gall, Olivia. *Trotsky en México y la vida política en el periodo de Cárdenas, 1937–1940*. México: Era, 1991.

Garrido, Luis Javier. *El Partido de la Revolución Institucionalizada: Medio siglo de poder político en México. La formación del nuevo estado (1928–1945)*. México: Secretaría de Educación Pública, 1986.

Gilly, Adolfo, ed. *Cartas a Cuauhtémoc Cárdenas*. México: Era, 1989.

————. *El cardenismo, una utopía mexicana*. México: Cal y Arena, 1994.

Giménez Cacho, Luis Emilio. "La constitución del Sindicato Industrial." In *Cuatro sindicatos nacionales de industria*. N.p.: Universidad Autónoma de Sinaloa and Centro de Estudios del Movimiento Obrero y Socialista, 1988.

Gledhill, John. *Casi Nada: A Study of Agrarian Reform in the Homeland of Cardenismo*. Albany: Institute for Mesoamerican Studies, University at Albany, State University of New York, 1991.

González, Luis. *Los días del presidente Cárdenas*. México: El Colegio de México, 1981.

González Cortés, Daniel. "Ta' oscuro el panorama: Relatos sobre los mineros del carbón." In *Monografías obreras*. Vol. 1, edited by Victoria Novelo. México: Centro de Investigaciones y Estudios Superiores en Antropología Social, 1987.

González Navarro, Moisés. *La CNC en la reforma agraria*. 3d ed. México: El Día en Libros, 1985.

González Polo, Ignacio. *Bibliografía general de las agrupaciones y partidos políticos mexicanos: 1900–1970*. México: Reforma Política, 1978.

Gordillo, Gustavo. *Campesinos al asalto del cielo: Una reforma agraria con autonomía*. México: Siglo XXI, 1988.

Gracida Romo, Juan José. "Génesis y consolidación del Porfiriato en Sonora (1883–1895)." In *Historia general de Sonora*. Vol. 4. *Sonora moderno: 1880–1929*, edited by Cynthia Radding de Murrieta. Hermosillo: Gobierno del Estado de Sonora, 1985.

————. "El Sonora moderno (1892–1910)." In *Historia general de Sonora*. Vol. 4. *Sonora moderno: 1880–1929*, edited by Cynthia Radding de Murrieta. Hermosillo: Gobierno del Estado de Sonora, 1985.

Greaves, Thomas, and William Culver, eds. *Miners and Mining in the Americas*. Manchester: Manchester University Press, 1985.

Griffith, James S. *Beliefs and Holy Places: A Spiritual Geography of the Pimería Alta*. Tucson: University of Arizona Press, 1992.

Guadarrama, Rocío. "Las alianzas políticas." In *Historia general de Sonora: Historia contemporánea de Sonora, 1929–1984*, edited by Gerardo Cornejo Murrieta. Hermosillo: El Colegio de Sonora, 1988.

————. "La reorganización social." In *Historia general de Sonora: Historia contemporánea de Sonora, 1929–1984*, edited by Gerardo Cornejo Murrieta. Hermosillo: El Colegio de Sonora, 1988.

————. "Los cambios en la política." In *Historia general de Sonora: Historia contemporánea de Sonora, 1929–1984*, edited by Gerardo Cornejo Murrieta. Hermosillo: El Colegio de Sonora, 1988.

————. "La integración institucional." In *Historia general de Sonora: Historia contemporánea de Sonora, 1929–1984*, edited by Gerardo Cornejo Murrieta. Hermosillo: El Colegio de Sonora, 1988.

Guerra, François-Xavier. "La Révolution Mexicaine: D'abord une révolution minière?" *Annales, E.S.C.* 36:5 (1981): 785–812.

————. "Réponse de François-Xavier Guerra." *Annales, E.S.C.* 38:2 (1983): 460–69.

————. *Le Mexique: De l'ancien regime à la révolution*. 2 vols. Paris: l'Harmattan, 1985.

Gutiérrez González, César. "Hegemonía, lucha sindical y movimiento obrero en Nuevo León, 1936–1938." Paper presented at the Coloquio "El Movimiento Obrero en América Latina entre las Dos Guerras Mundiales." Mexico City, September 1986.

Gutiérrez Hernández, Cecilio, José Socorro López Quiñones, José Antonio Romero Sánchez, and Juan Velasco Naranjo. "Ejido colectivo, revolución verde y lucha de clases en el sur de Sonora." Tesis profesional, Facultad de Economía, Universidad Nacional Autónoma de México, 1981.

Gutiérrez Mendívil, Domingo. "Una rebelión Vasconcelista en Navojoa." In *Memoria: XII Simposio de Historia y Antropología de Sonora*, 198–220. Hermosillo: Instituto de Investigaciones Históricas, Universidad de Sonora, 1988.

Hamilton, Nora. *The Limits of State Autonomy*. Princeton: Princeton University Press, 1982.

Harrison, Royden, et al. *Independent Collier: The Coal Miner as Archetypal Proletarian Reconsidered*. New York: St. Martin's, 1978.

Hart, John Mason. *Revolutionary Mexico: The Coming and Process of the Mexican Revolution*. Berkeley: University of California Press, 1987.

Hernández, Manuel Diego, and Alejo Maldonado Gallardo. "En torno a la historia de la Confederación Revolucionaria Michoacana del Trabajo." In *Jornadas de historia de occidente: Movimientos populares en el occidente de México, siglos XIX y XX*. Jiquilpán de Juárez: Centro de Estudios de la Revolución Mexicana "Lázaro Cárdenas." A.C., 1980: 128–29.

Hernández Chávez, Alicia. *La mecánica cardenista*. México: El Colegio de México, 1979.

———. "Militares y negocios en la revolución mexicana." *Historia Mexicana* 34:2 (1984).

Hewitt de Alcántara, Cynthia. *La modernización de la agricultura mexicana, 1940–1970*. México: Siglo XXI, 1985.

Heyman, Josiah McC. *Life and Labor on the Border: Working People of Northeastern Sonora, Mexico, 1886–1986*. Tucson: University of Arizona Press, 1991.

Historia general de Sonora. 5 vols. Hermosillo: Gobierno del Estado de Sonora, 1985.

Hobsbawm, Eric. *Worlds of Labour: Further Studies in the History of Labour*. London: Weidenfeld and Nicholson, 1984.

Hu-DeHart, Evelyn. "Racism and Anti-Chinese Persecution in Sonora, Mexico, 1876–1932." *Amerasia* 9:2 (1982): 1–28.

———. *Yaqui Resistance and Survival: The Struggle for Land and Autonomy, 1821–1910*. Madison: University of Wisconsin Press, 1984.

Hunt, Lynn. *Politics, Culture, and Class in the French Revolution*. Berkeley: University of California Press, 1984.

Ianni, Octavio. *El Estado capitalista en la época de Cárdenas*. México: Era, 1977.

Ibarra, Eduardo, and Ernesto Camou Healy. "Las instituciones educativas." In *Historia general de Sonora: Historia contemporánea de Sonora, 1929–1984*, edited by Gerardo Cornejo Murrieta. Hermosillo: El Colegio de Sonora, 1988.

Joseph, Gilbert M. *Revolution from Without: Yucatán, Mexico, and the United States, 1880–1924*. 2d. ed. Durham: Duke University Press, 1988.

Joseph, Gilbert M., and Daniel Nugent, eds. *Everyday Forms of State Formation: Revolution and the Negotiation of Rule in Modern Mexico*. Durham: Duke University Press, 1994.

Katz, Friedrich. *The Secret War in Mexico: Europe, the United States, and the Mexican Revolution*. Chicago: University of Chicago Press, 1981.

Kaufman, Robert. "Industrial Change and Authoritarian Rule in Latin America: A Concrete Review of the Bureaucratic-Authoritarian Model." In *The New Authoritarianism in Latin America*, edited by David Collier. Princeton: Princeton University Press, 1979.

Kerr, Clark, and Abraham Siegel. "The Interindustry Propensity to Strike–An International Comparison." In *Industrial Conflict*, edited by Arthur Kornhauser, Robert Dubin, and Arthur M. Ross, 189–205. New York: McGraw-Hill, 1954.

Kirk, Betty. *Covering the Mexican Front: The Battle of Europe versus America.* Norman: University of Oklahoma Press, 1942.

Knight, Alan. "La Révolution Mexicaine: Révolution minière ou révolution serrano?" *Annales, E.S.C.* 38:2 (1983): 449–59.

———. "The Working Class and the Mexican Revolution, c. 1900–1920." *Journal of Latin American Studies* 16 (1984): 51–79.

———. "Caudillos y campesinos en el México revolucionario, 1910–1917." In *Caudillos y campesinos en la Revolución Mexicana*, edited by D. A. Brading, 32–85. México: Fondo de Cultura Económica, 1985.

———. "El liberalismo mexicano desde la Reforma hasta la Revolución (una interpretación)." *Historia Mexicana* 35:1 (1985): 59–91.

———. "The Mexican Revolution: Bourgeois? Nationalist? Or just a 'Great Rebellion'?" *Bulletin of Latin American Research* 4:2 (1985): 1–37.

———. *The Mexican Revolution.* 2 vols. Cambridge: Cambridge University Press, 1986.

———. "Revolutionary Project, Recalcitrant People." In *The Revolutionary Process in Mexico: Essays on Political and Social Change, 1880–1940*, edited by Jaime E. Rodríguez O., 227–64. Los Angeles, Irvine: UCLA Latin American Center and the Mexico/Chicano Project, University of California, Irvine, 1990.

———. "Racism, Revolution, and *Indigenismo*: Mexico, 1910–1940." In *The Idea of Race in Latin America*, edited by Richard Graham, 71–113. Austin: University of Texas Press, 1990.

———. "Land and Society in Revolutionary Mexico: The Destruction of the Great Haciendas." *Mexican Studies/Estudios Mexicanos* 7:1 (Winter 1991): 73–107.

———. "The Rise and Fall of Cardenismo, c. 1930–c. 1946." In *Mexico since Independence*, edited by Leslie Bethell, 241–320. Cambridge: Cambridge University Press, 1991.

———. "The Politics of Expropriation." In *The Mexican Petroleum Industry in the Twentieth Century*, edited by Jonathan C. Brown and Alan Knight. Austin: University of Texas Press, 1992.

———. "Cardenismo: Juggernaut or Jalopy?" *Journal of Latin American Studies* 26:1 (February 1994): 73–107.

Krauze, Enrique. *General misionero: Lázaro Cárdenas.* México: Fondo de Cultura Económica, 1987.

———. *Reformar desde el orígen: Plutarco Elías Calles.* México: Fondo de Cultura Económica, 1987.

La CTM en los estados. N.p.: Universidad Autónoma de Sinaloa and Centro de Estudios del Movimiento Obrero y Socialista, 1988.

Lajous, Alejandra. *Los orígenes del partido único en México.* México: Universidad Nacional Autónoma de México, 1979.

Larrañaga Robles, Francisco Alfredo. *Monografía de la Ciudad de Navojoa.* N.p., 1971.

———. *Monografía del Municipio de Navojoa, 1982.* Navojoa: N.p., [1985].

León, Samuel, and Ignacio Marván. *La clase obrera en la historia de México: En el Cardenismo (1934–1940).* México: Siglo XXI, 1985.

Lerner, Victoria. *La educación socialista.* México: El Colegio de México, 1979.

Long, Norman, and Bryan Roberts, eds. *Miners, Peasants and Entrepreneurs: Regional Development in the Central Highlands of Peru.* Cambridge: Cambridge University Press, 1984.

López Alvarez, Luis. *Aquellos tiempos anchos.* Hermosillo: Talleres Gráficos y Editoriales Pitíc, 1983.

Lorenzano Durán, Gustavo. "Situación agraria en los Valles del Yaqui y Mayo, 1922–1932." In *XV Simposio de Historia y Antropología de Sonora: Memoria,* 1:489–507. Hermosillo: Instituto de Investigaciones Históricas, Universidad de Sonora, 1991.

Lozano Ceniceros, Valente. "Breve historia del movimiento magisterial y comentario histórico del actual SNTE." In Sindicato Nacional de Trabajadores de la Enseñanza, *Conferencias regionales de orientación social: Memoria.* México: SNTE, 1966.

Lutes, Steven V. "Yaqui Indian Enclavement: The Effects of Experimental Indian Policy in Northwest Mexico." In *Ejidos and Regions of Refuge in Northwestern Mexico,* edited by N. Ross Crumrine and Phil C. Weigand, 11–20. Anthropological Papers of the University of Arizona, No. 46. Tucson: University of Arizona Press, 1987.

Machado, Manuel A., Jr. *The North Mexican Cattle Industry, 1910–1975: Conflict and Change.* College Station: Texas A & M Press, 1981.

Martínez Assad, Carlos. "La rebelión cedillista o el ocaso del poder tradicional." *Revista Mexicana de Sociología* 41:3 (1979): 709–29.

———. *El laboratorio de la revolución: El Tabasco garridista.* México: Siglo XXI, 1979.

———. *Los rebeldes vencidos: Cedillo contra el Estado Cardenista.* México: Fondo de Cultura Económica, Universidad Nacional Autónoma de México, 1990.

Martínez Assad, Carlos, Ricardo Pozas Horcasitas, and Mario Ramírez Rancano. *Revolucionarios fueron todos.* México: Secretaría de Educación Pública, 1982.

Martínez Rascón, Cristina Isabel. "Campesinado, estado y capital en Sonora, 1930–1940." Tesis de maestría en ciencias sociales, Facultad Latinoamericana de Ciencias Sociales, 1983.

———. "Movilización y acción política, una visión retrospectiva." In *Movimientos sociales en el noroeste de México,* edited by Rubén Burgos, 103–24. Culiacán: Universidad Autónoma de Sinaloa, 1985.

Medin, Tzvi. *Ideología y praxis política de Lázaro Cárdenas.* México: Era, 1981.

Medina, Luis. *Del Cardenismo al Avilacamachismo.* México: El Colegio de México, 1978.

Mendívil, José Abraham. *Cuarenta años de política en Sonora.* 2 vols. Hermosillo: Publicidad Mendívil, 1965.

———. *Batalla anti-Comunista.* Hermosillo: Publicidad Mendívil, 1966.

———. *Medio siglo de lucha (social y política).* 2 vols. Hermosillo: Publicidad Mendívil, n.d.

———. *Don Juan Navarrete y Guerrero: Como pastor y como hombre.* Hermosillo: Publicaciones Mendívil, 1975.

———. "La Revolución y la lucha obrero-campesina en Sonora." In *Segundo Simposio de Historia de Sonora: Memoria,* 430–43. Hermosillo: Instituto de Investigaciones Históricas, Universidad de Sonora, 1977.

———. *La Democracia en Sonora.* Hermosillo: Publicidad Mendívil, 1980.

Meyer, Jean. *La Cristiada.* 3 vols. México: Siglo XXI, 1973.

———. "Mexico: Revolution and Reconstruction in the 1920s." In *Cambridge History of Latin America,* Vol. 5 *(1870–1930),* edited by Leslie Bethell, 155–94. Cambridge: Cambridge University Press, 1986.

Meyer, Jean, Enrique Krauze, and Cayetano Reyes. *Estado y sociedad con Calles.* México: El Colegio de México, 1977.

Meyer, Lorenzo. *México y los Estados Unidos en el conflicto petrolero, 1917–1942.* 2d ed. México: El Colegio de México, 1972.

———. *La segunda muerte de la Revolución Mexicana.* México: Cal y Arena, 1992.

Michaels, Albert L. "The Crisis of Cardenismo." *Journal of Latin American Studies* 2:1 (1970): 51–79.

———. "Las Elecciones de 1940." *Historia Mexicana* 21:1 (July–September 1971): 80–135.

Middlebrook, Kevin J. *The Paradox of Revolution: Labor, the State, and Authoritarianism in Mexico.* Baltimore: Johns Hopkins University Press, 1995.

Moisés, Rosalío, Jane Holden Kelley, and William Curry Holden. *A Yaqui Life: The Personal Chronicle of a Yaqui Indian.* Lincoln: University of Nebraska Press, 1971.

Moncada O., Carlos. "El escenario político de Sonora." In *Municipios en conflicto,* edited by Carlos Martínez Assad, 27–54. México: Instituto de Investigaciones Sociales, Universidad Nacional Autónoma de México, 1985.

———. *La sucesión política en Sonora (1917–1985).* Hermosillo: Editorial Latinoamericana, 1988.

Mora, Felipe, and Gabriela González Barragán. "La representación política de los trabajadores en Sonora (1937–1988)." In *XIV*

Simposio de Historia e Antropología de Sonora: Memoria. Vol. 3. Hermosillo: Instituto de Investigaciones Históricas, Universidad de Sonora, 1990.

Muñoz, Hilda. *Lázaro Cárdenas: Síntesis ideológica de su campaña presidencial*. México: Fondo de Cultura Económica, 1976.

Murrieta, Mayo, and Ma. Eugenia Graf. *Por el milagro de aferrarse: Tierra y vecindad en el Valle del Yaqui*. Hermosillo: El Colegio de Sonora, Instituto Tecnológico de Sonora, Instituto Sonorense de Cultura, 1991.

Naranjo, Francisco. *Diccionario biográfico revolucionario*. [1st ed. 1935]. México: Instituto Nacional de Estudios Históricos de la Revolución, 1985.

Nash, June. *We Eat the Mines and the Mines Eat Us: Dependency and Exploitation in Bolivian Tin Mines*. New York: Columbia University Press, 1979.

Nava Nava, María del Carmen, and Alonso Torres Aburto. "La rebelión cedillista." Paper presented at the XI Jornadas de Historia de Occidente, Jiquilpán, 6–7 October 1988.

Negrete, Martaelena. *Relaciones entre la Iglesia y el Estado en México, 1930–1940*. México: Universidad Iberoamericana, 1988.

Niblo, Stephen R. *War, Diplomacy, and Development: The United States and Mexico, 1938–1954*. Wilmington, DE: SR Books, 1995.

Novo, Salvador. *La vida en México en el período presidencial de Lázaro Cárdenas*. México: Empresas Editoriales, 1964.

Nugent, Daniel. *Spent Cartridges of Revolution: An Anthropological History of Namiquipa, Chihuahua*. Chicago: University of Chicago Press, 1993.

Ochoa Bustamante, Humberto. *Biografía de Jacinto López Moreno: Fundador y Secretario General de la Unión General de Obreros y Campesinos de México, U.G.O.C.M.* Hermosillo: Editorial Nacional, 1992.

Ozouf, Mona. *La fête révolutionnaire, 1789–1799*. Paris: Gallimard, 1976.

Pansters, Wil G. *Politics and Power in Puebla: The Political History of a Mexican State, 1937–1987*. Amsterdam: CEDLA, 1990.

Peláez, Gerardo. *Historia del Sindicato de Trabajadores de la Educación*. México: Ediciones de Cultura Popular, 1984.

Peña, Elsa M., and J. Trinidad Chávez. "Ganadería y agricultura en la sierra, 1929–1980." In *Historia general de Sonora: Historia contemporánea de Sonora, 1929–1984*, edited by Gerardo Cornejo Murrieta. Hermosillo: El Colegio de Sonora, 1988.

———. "Aspectos de la vida en los minerales, 1929–1980." In *Historia general de Sonora: Historia contemporánea de Sonora, 1929–1984*, edited by Gerardo Cornejo Murrieta. Hermosillo: El Colegio de Sonora, 1988.

———. "Organización obrera de los minerales, 1929–1980." In *Historia general de Sonora: Historia contemporánea de Sonora, 1929–1984*, edited by Gerardo Cornejo Murrieta. Hermosillo: El Colegio de Sonora, 1988.

Pérez López, Emma. "Economía y trabajo campesino en la Sierra Norte de Sonora (1900–1922)." In *XV Simposio de Historia y Antropología de Sonora: Memoria*. Vol. 1. Hermosillo: Instituto de Investigaciones Históricas, Universidad de Sonora, 1991.

Plenn, J. H. *Mexico Marches*. Indianapolis: Bobbs-Merrill, 1939.

Popkin, Samuel L. *The Rational Peasant: The Political Economy of Rural Society in Vietnam*. Berkeley: University of California Press, 1979.

Prewitt, Virginia. *Reportage on Mexico*. New York: Dutton, 1941.

Raby, David L. *Educación y revolución social en México (1921–1940)*. México: Secretaría de Educación Pública, 1974.

Radding, Cynthia. "Las estructuras formativas del capitalismo en Sonora (1900–1930)." In *De los Borbones a la Revolución: Ocho estudios regionales*, edited by Mario Cerutti, 229–65. Monterrey: Universidad Autónoma de Nuevo León, 1986.

Radding de Murrieta, Cynthia, and Rosa María Ruiz Murrieta. "La reconstrucción constitucionalista y las reformas en la región." In *Historia general de Sonora*. Vol. 4. *Sonora Moderno: 1880–1929*. Hermosillo: Gobierno del Estado de Sonora, 1985.

Ramírez, José Carlos. *Hipótesis acerca de la historia económica y demográfica de Sonora en el período contemporáneo (1930–1983)*. Cuadernos del Viejo Pitic No. 1. Hermosillo: El Colegio de Sonora, 1985.

———. "La estrategia económica de los Callistas." In *Historia general de Sonora: Historia contemporánea de Sonora, 1929–1984*, edited by Gerardo Cornejo Murrieta. Hermosillo: El Colegio de Sonora, 1988.

———. "El último auge." In *Historia general de Sonora: Historia contemporánea de Sonora, 1929–1984*, edited by Gerardo Cornejo Murrieta. Hermosillo: El Colegio de Sonora, 1988.

———. "Cárdenas y las dos caras de la recuperación." In *Historia general de Sonora: Historia contemporánea de Sonora, 1929–1984*, edited by Gerardo Cornejo Murrieta. Hermosillo: El Colegio de Sonora, 1988.

———. "Una época de crisis económica." In *Historia general de Sonora: Historia contemporánea de Sonora, 1929–1984*, edited by Gerardo Cornejo Murrieta. Hermosillo: El Colegio de Sonora, 1988.

Ramírez, José Carlos, and Rocío Guadarrama. "Los resultados de la modernización en el campo." In *Historia general de Sonora: Historia contemporánea de Sonora, 1929–1984*, edited by Gerardo Cornejo Murrieta. Hermosillo: El Colegio de Sonora, 1988.

Reygadas, Luis. *Proceso de trabajo y acción obrera: Historia sindical de los mineros de Nueva Rosita, 1929–1979*. México: Instituto Nacional de Antropología e Historia, Escuela Nacional de Antropología e Historia, 1988.

Reynoso, Victor Manuel. "Acción Nacional en Sonora: Notas para su historia." Paper presented at the XIV Simposio de Historia y Antropología de Sonora, Hermosillo, 1989.

Rivera Flores, Antonio. "Unión General de Obreros y Campesinos de México." In *Las Derrotas Obreras, 1946–1952*, edited by Víctor M. Durand Ponte, 25–57. México: Universidad Nacional Autónoma de México, 1984.

Rivera Rodríguez, Gustavo. *Breve historia de la educación en Sonora e historia de la Escuela Normal del Estado.* N.p., 1975.

Roberts, Bryan. "The Place of Regions in Mexico." In *Mexico's Regions: Comparative History and Development,* edited by Eric Van Young, 227–45. San Diego: Center for U.S.-Mexican Studies, 1992.

Romero Centeno, Carolina, and Eduardo Ibarra Thennet. "El ejido en Sonora (1920–1980)." Tesis en antropología social, Escuela Nacional de Antropología e Historia, 1984.

Romero Gil, Juan Manuel, and José Carlos López Romero. "Crisis y resistencia comunitaria (1929–1934): Tercer acto." In *XIV Simposio de Historia y Antropología de Sonora: Memoria,* 2:15–26. Hermosillo: Instituto de Investigaciones Históricas, Universidad de Sonora, 1990.

Ruíz, Ramón Eduardo. *The Great Rebellion: Mexico, 1905–1924.* New York: Norton, 1980.

———. *The People of Sonora and Yankee Capitalists.* Tucson: University of Arizona Press, 1989.

Salmerón, Rubén. *La formación regional, el mercado local y el poder de la oligarquía en Sonora: 1780–1840.* Hermosillo: Instituto de Investigaciones Históricas, Universidad de Sonora, 1990.

Sánchez, Enrique W. "Apuntes históricos sobre el movimiento sindical del magisterio nacional." In Sindicato Nacional de Trabajadores de la Educación, *Conferencias regionales de orientación social: Memoria.* México: SNTE, 1966.

Sanderson, Steven E. *Agrarian Populism and Economic Growth in Post-Revolutionary Mexico: The Struggle for Land in Sonora.* Berkeley: University of California Press, 1981.

Sandomingo, M. *Historia de Agua Prieta: En su primer cincuentenario.* N.p., n.d.

Santos, Gonzalo N. *Memorias.* México: Grijalbo, 1986.

Sariego, Juan Luis. "Los mineros de la Real del Monte: Un proletariado en formación y transición." *Revista Mexicana de Sociología* 42:4 (1980): 1379–1403.

Sariego, Juan Luis, Luis Reygadas, Miguel Angel Gómez, and Javier Ferrara. *El estado y la minería mexicana: Política, trabajo y sociedad durante el siglo XX.* México: Fondo de Cultura Económica, 1988.

Sariego Rodríguez, Juan Luis. "Enclaves y minerales en el norte de México: Historia social de los mineros de Cananea y Nueva Rosita." Tesis de maestría en antropología social, Universidad Iberoamericana, 1986.

Schuler, Friedrich Engelbert. "Mexican-German Relations in the Second World War, 1939–1943." Master's thesis, University of Texas at Austin, 1983.

———. *Mexican Foreign Policy in the Age of Lázaro Cárdenas.* Albuquerque: University of New Mexico Press, 1998.

Scott, James C. "Patron-Client Politics and Political Change in Southeast Asia." *American Political Science Review* 66 (March 1972): 91–113.

———. *The Moral Economy of the Peasant: Rebellion and Subsistence in Southeast Asia.* New Haven: Yale University Press, 1976.

Secretaría de Gobernación and Gobierno del Estado de Sonora. *Los municipios de Sonora.* México: Talleres Gráficos de la Nación, 1988.

Serrano, Gabriel. "El cultivo del trigo en el estado de Sonora." *Agricultura* 2:14 (September–October 1939).

Sheridan, Thomas E. *Where the Dove Calls: The Political Ecology of a Peasant Corporate Community in Northwestern Mexico.* Tucson: University of Arizona Press, 1988.

Shorter, Edward, and Charles Tilly. *Strikes in France, 1830–1968.* Cambridge: Cambridge University Press, 1974.

Shulgovski, Anatol. *México en la encrucijada de su historia.* México: Fondo de Cultura Económica, 1972.

Silos, José S., and Donald K. Freebairn. *El Valle del Yaqui, Sonora: Su desarollo y potencial económico.* Chapingo: Escuela Nacional de Agricultura, 1970.

Simpson, Eyler N. *The Ejido: Mexico's Way Out.* Chapel Hill: University of North Carolina Press, 1937.

Sindicato Nacional de Trabajadores de la Educación. *Conferencias regionales de orientación social: Memoria.* México: SNTE, 1966.

Siqueiros, Carlos A. *Remembranzas nogalenses.* Nogales: Edición Privada, 1980.

Skirius, John. "José Vasconcelos en Sonora." In *Temas sonorenses: A través de los Simposios de Historia.* Hermosillo: Gobierno del Estado de Sonora, 1984.

Smith, Peter H. *Labyrinths of Power: Political Recruitment in Twentieth-Century Mexico.* Princeton: Princeton University Press, 1979.

Soto Galindo, Melchor. *Los pioneros del Yaqui.* México: Editorial Libros de México, 1977.

Spicer, Edward H. *The Yaquis: A Cultural History.* Tucson: University of Arizona Press, 1980.

Suárez Arvizu, Gilberto. "La fundación de la Universidad de Sonora." In *VII Simposio de Historia de Sonora: Memoria*, 424–34. Hermosillo: Instituto de Investigaciones Históricas, Universidad de Sonora, 1982.

Tamayo, Jaime. *La clase obrera en la historia de México: En el interinato de Adolfo de la Huerta y el gobierno de Alvaro Obregón (1920–24).* México: Siglo XXI, 1987.

Thayer Painter, Muriel. *With Good Heart: Yaqui Beliefs and Ceremonies in Pascua Village*. Tucson: University of Arizona Press, 1986.

Thompson, E. P. "The Moral Economy of the English Crowd in the Eighteenth Century." *Past and Present* 50 (1971): 76–136.

Tilly, Charles. *From Mobilization to Revolution*. Reading, MA: Addison-Wesley, 1978.

Tinker Salas, Miguel. "Under the Shadow of the Eagle: Sonora, the Making of a Norteño Culture, 1850–1910." Ph.D. diss., University of California, San Diego, 1989.

Tobler, Hans Werner. "La burguesía revolucionaria en México: Su origen y papel, 1915–1935." *Historia Mexicana* 34:2 (1984): 217–26.

Torres Ramírez, Blanca. *México en la segunda guerra mundial*. México: El Colegio de México, 1979.

Townsend, William Cameron. *Lazaro Cardenas: Mexican Democrat*. Ann Arbor: George Wahr, 1952.

Trueba Lara, José Luis. *Voces de la mina (Seis textos sobre Cananea)*. Hermosillo: Programa Cultural de las Fronteras, 1988.

Valadés, José C. *Historia general de la Revolución Mexicana: Un presidente substituto*. México: Secretaría de Educación Pública, Ediciones Gernika, Dirección General de Publicaciones, 1985.

Valenzuela Valenzuela, Manuel. "Consideraciones sobre la burguesía sonorense." Tesis de licenciatura en economía, Universidad de Sonora, 1984.

Vanderwood, Paul. "Building Blocks but not yet Building: Regional History and the Mexican Revolution." *Mexican Studies/Estudios Mexicanos* 3:2 (1987): 421–32.

Van Young, Eric. "Introduction: Are Regions Good to Think?" In *Mexico's Regions: Comparative History and Development*, edited by Eric Van Young. San Diego: Center for U.S.-Mexican Studies, 1992.

Vaughan, Mary Kay. *Estado, clases sociales y educación en México*. 2 vols. México: Secretaría de Educación Pública, 1982.

———. "El papel político del magisterio socialista de México, 1934–1940: Un estudio comparativo de los casos de Puebla y Sonora." In *Memoria: XII Simposio de Historia y Antropología de Sonora*, 2:175–97. Hermosillo: Instituto de Investigaciones Históricas, Universidad de Sonora, 1988.

Vázquez Ruiz, Miguel Angel. *Los grupos de poder económico en Sonora*. Hermosillo: Editorial Unison, 1988.

———. "Notas para una historia industrial de Sonora." In *Memoria: XII Simposio de Historia y Antropología de Sonora*, 1:105–21. Hermosillo: Instituto de Investigaciones Históricas, Universidad de Sonora, 1988.

Velasco Avila, Cuauhtémoc. "Labor Relations in Mining: Real del Monte and Pachuca, 1824–1874." In *Miners and Mining in the Americas*, edited by Thomas Greaves and William Culver. Manchester: Manchester University Press, 1985.

Vellinga, Menno. *Economic Development and the Dynamics of Class: Industrialization, Power, and Control in Monterrey*. Assen: Van Gorcum, 1979.

Verdugo Fimbres, María Isabel. *Frontera en el desierto: Historia de San Luis Río Colorado*. Hermosillo: Gobierno del Estado de Sonora, Instituto Nacional de Antropología e Historia, Secretaría de Educación Pública, 1983.

Von der Borch, Maren. "Organización empresarial y desorganización campesina: La Costa de Hermosillo, 1940–1960." In *Simposio de Historia y Antropología de Sonora: Memoria*, 2: 153–66. Hermosillo: Instituto de Investigaciones Históricas, Universidad de Sonora, 1990.

Voss, Stuart F. *On the Periphery of Nineteenth-Century Mexico: Sonora and Sinaloa, 1810–1877*. Tucson: University of Arizona Press, 1982.

———. "Northwest Mexico." In Diana Balmori, Stuart F. Voss, and Miles Wortman, *Notable Family Networks in Latin America*. Chicago: University of Chicago Press, 1984.

Vovelle, Michel. *Religion et Révolution: La déchristianisation de l'an II*. Paris: Hachette, 1976.

Warnke, Martin. "Bilderstürme." In *Bildersturm: Die Zerstörung des Kunstwerks*, edited by Martin Warnke. Munich: Carl Hanser Verlag, 1973.

Wasserman, Mark. "Strategies for Survival of the Porfirian Elite in Revolutionary Mexico: Chihuahua during the 1920s." *Hispanic American Historical Review* 67:1 (1987): 87–107.

———. *Persistent Oligarchs: Elites and Politics in Chihuahua, Mexico, 1910–1940*. Durham: Duke University Press, 1993.

Weyl, Nathaniel, and Sylvia Weyl. *The Reconquest of Mexico: The Years of Lázaro Cárdenas*. London, New York, Toronto: Oxford University Press, 1939.

Wilkie, James W., and Edna Monzón de Wilkie. *México visto en el siglo XX: Entrevistas de historia oral*. México: Instituto Mexicano de Investigaciones Económicas, 1969.

Winckler, Andreas Eberhard. "The Nazis in Mexico: Mexico and the Reich in the Prewar Period, 1936–1939." Master's thesis, University of Texas at Austin, 1983.

Zavala, Palemón. *Perfiles de Sonora*. Hermosillo: Gobierno del Estado de Sonora, 1984.

Index

Acción Mexicanista, 83, 178
Acerba Animi (papal encyclical), 24
Agraristas: arming of, 223 (*see also* Reserves); and Cardenista power base, 121, 140, 144, 148–49, 219, 222; criticize Yocupicio, 99; and CTM, 99, 107; early, 123–24, 127–31; excluded from Yocupicista base, 84; failed unification, 98–99; in Mayo Valley politics, 35; and municipal politics, 71–72; 1976 mobilization, 149, 212; receive land, 215; in Sierra, 131–32, 137; support Callismo, 32; threaten landowners, 123; in Yaqui Valley, 134–35. *See also* Land reform
Agriculture, commercial: 94, 107, 125, 225; crops, 125–26; exports to U.S., 80; R. E. Calles and, 6
Agua Prieta: CTM in, 101; municipal politics, 71, 188; support for Yocupicio, 66; uprising, 187, 222
Aguascalientes (state): Catholic resistance in, 28
Alamos: backs Otero, 66; churches reopen, 77; labor federation, 95, 100
Alcohol, 30, 33, 147, 155, 159, 198, 206
Alemán, Miguel: and agrarian reform, 99; faction, 184–85; governor of Veracruz, 183; opposes labor, 183
Almada, Ignacio, 30
Almazán, General Juan Andreu: miners' support, 172; opposes Cárdenas, 64; presidential

campaign, 208–10; support for, 209; visits Hermosillo, 210
Altar (city): municipal politics, 36, 202; 1935 revolt in, 51–52
Altar (district): agriculture, 138, 140; 1935 revolt in, 51–52
Alvarado, General Salvador: developmentalism of, 7–8
Amaro, General Joaquín: conspires against Cárdenas, 64
Americanization: of *norteños*, 8
Anarchism: of Cananea miners, 164
Anti-Americanism, 80–81; of miners, 170, 181. *See also* Xenophobia
Anticlericalism: curbed in Puebla, 183; and education, 18–21; legislation, 11; Liga Anticlerical, 15; of males, 24, 26; popular, 21, 23–24; and Sonoran politics, 31, 44; of teachers, 102. *See also* Iconoclasm; Jacobinism
Anti-communism, 26, 47, 120–21, 178, 183–84, 223, 225
Anti-Semitism, 82–84
Arana, Bernabé, 180, 187
Arellano Belloc, Francisco, 59–61
Arizona: arms purchases in, 41; Catholic schools, 19, 28; relations with Sonora, 79–80; and Yaquis, 37
Arizpe: municipal politics, 202; ejido, 127
Artisans, 93–94, 214; in CTS, 111, 116–17; in mining, 154
Assassination: of union leaders, 109, 212
Astiazarán family, 126, 130, 140
Atl, Dr.: anti-Semitism of, 82
Authoritarianism, 217, 220, 225

Latin American Silhouettes
Studies in History and Culture

William H. Beezley and
Judith Ewell
Editors

Volumes Published

William H. Beezley and Judith Ewell, eds., *The Human Tradition in Latin America: The Twentieth Century* (1987). Cloth ISBN 0-8420-2283-X Paper ISBN 0-8420-2284-8

Judith Ewell and William H. Beezley, eds., *The Human Tradition in Latin America: The Nineteenth Century* (1989). Cloth ISBN 0-8420-2331-3 Paper ISBN 0-8420-2332-1

David G. LaFrance, *The Mexican Revolution in Puebla, 1908–1913: The Maderista Movement and the Failure of Liberal Reform* (1989). ISBN 0-8420-2293-7

Mark A. Burkholder, *Politics of a Colonial Career: José Baquíjano and the Audiencia of Lima*, 2d ed. (1990). Cloth ISBN 0-8420-2353-4 Paper ISBN 0-8420-2352-6

Carlos B. Gil, ed., *Hope and Frustration: Interviews with Leaders of Mexico's Political Opposition* (1992). Cloth ISBN 0-8420-2395-X Paper ISBN 0-8420-2396-8

Heidi Zogbaum, *B. Traven: A Vision of Mexico* (1992). ISBN 0-8420-2392-5

Jaime E. Rodríguez O., ed., *Patterns of Contention in Mexican History* (1992). ISBN 0-8420-2399-2

Louis A. Pérez, Jr., ed., *Slaves, Sugar, and Colonial Society: Travel Accounts of Cuba, 1801–1899* (1992). Cloth ISBN 0-8420-2354-2 Paper ISBN 0-8420-2415-8

Peter Blanchard, *Slavery and Abolition in Early Republican Peru* (1992). Cloth ISBN 0-8420-2400-X Paper ISBN 0-8420-2429-8

Paul J. Vanderwood, *Disorder and Progress: Bandits, Police, and Mexican Development*, revised and enlarged edition (1992). Cloth ISBN 0-8420-2438-7 Paper ISBN 0-8420-2439-5

Sandra McGee Deutsch and Ronald H. Dolkart, eds., *The Argentine Right: Its History and Intellectual Origins, 1910 to the Present* (1993). Cloth ISBN 0-8420-2418-2 Paper ISBN 0-8420-2419-0

Steve Ellner, *Organized Labor in Venezuela, 1958–1991: Behavior and Concerns in a Democratic Setting* (1993). ISBN 0-8420-2443-3

Paul J. Dosal, *Doing Business with the Dictators: A Political History of United Fruit in Guatemala, 1899–1944* (1993). Cloth ISBN 0-8420-2475-1 Paper ISBN 0-8420-2590-1

Marquis James, *Merchant Adventurer: The Story of W. R. Grace* (1993). ISBN 0-8420-2444-1

John Charles Chasteen and Joseph S. Tulchin, eds., *Problems in Modern Latin American History: A Reader* (1994). Cloth ISBN 0-8420-2327-5 Paper ISBN 0-8420-2328-3

Marguerite Guzmán Bouvard, *Revolutionizing Motherhood: The Mothers of the Plaza de Mayo* (1994). Cloth ISBN 0-8420-2486-7 Paper ISBN 0-8420-2487-5

William H. Beezley, Cheryl English Martin, and William E. French, eds., *Rituals of Rule, Rituals of Resistance: Public Celebrations and Popular Culture in Mexico* (1994). Cloth ISBN 0-8420-2416-6 Paper ISBN 0-8420-2417-4

Stephen R. Niblo, *War, Diplomacy, and Development: The United States and Mexico, 1938–1954* (1995). ISBN 0-8420-2550-2

G. Harvey Summ, ed., *Brazilian Mosaic: Portraits of a Diverse People and Culture* (1995). Cloth ISBN 0-8420-2491-3 Paper ISBN 0-8420-2492-1

N. Patrick Peritore and Ana Karina Galve-Peritore, eds., *Biotechnology in Latin America: Politics, Impacts, and Risks*

(1995). Cloth ISBN 0-8420-2556-1 Paper ISBN 0-8420-2557-X

Silvia Marina Arrom and Servando Ortoll, eds., *Riots in the Cities: Popular Politics and the Urban Poor in Latin America, 1765–1910* (1996). Cloth ISBN 0-8420-2580-4 Paper ISBN 0-8420-2581-2

Roderic Ai Camp, ed., *Polling for Democracy: Public Opinion and Political Liberalization in Mexico* (1996). ISBN 0-8420-2583-9

Brian Loveman and Thomas M. Davies, Jr., eds., *The Politics of Antipolitics: The Military in Latin America*, 3d ed., revised and updated (1996). Cloth ISBN 0-8420-2609-6 Paper ISBN 0-8420-2611-8

Joseph S. Tulchin, Andrés Serbín, and Rafael Hernández, eds., *Cuba and the Caribbean: Regional Issues and Trends in the Post-Cold War Era* (1997). ISBN 0-8420-2652-5

Thomas W. Walker, ed., *Nicaragua without Illusions: Regime Transition and Structural Adjustment in the 1990s* (1997). Cloth ISBN 0-8420-2578-2 Paper ISBN 0-8420-2579-0

Dianne Walta Hart, *Undocumented in L.A.: An Immigrant's Story* (1997). Cloth ISBN 0-8420-2648-7 Paper ISBN 0-8420-2649-5

Jaime E. Rodríguez O. and Kathryn Vincent, eds., *Myths, Misdeeds, and Misunderstandings: The Roots of Conflict in U.S.-Mexican Relations* (1997). ISBN 0-8420-2662-2

Jaime E. Rodríguez O. and Kathryn Vincent, eds., *Common Border, Uncommon Paths: Race, Culture, and National Identity in U.S.-Mexican Relations* (1997). ISBN 0-8420-2673-8

William H. Beezley and Judith Ewell, eds., *The Human Tradition in Modern Latin America* (1997). Cloth ISBN 0-8420-2612-6 Paper ISBN 0-8420-2613-4

Donald F. Stevens, ed., *Based on a True Story: Latin American History at the Movies* (1997). ISBN 0-8420-2582-0

Jaime E. Rodríguez O., ed., *The Origins of Mexican National Politics, 1808–1847* (1997). Paper ISBN 0-8420-2723-8

Che Guevara, *Guerrilla Warfare*, with revised and updated introduction and case studies by Brian Loveman and Thomas M. Davies, Jr., 3d ed. (1997). Cloth ISBN 0-8420-2677-0 Paper ISBN 0-8420-2678-9

Adrian A. Bantjes, *As If Jesus Walked on Earth: Cardenismo, Sonora, and the Mexican Revolution* (1998). ISBN 0-8420-2653-3

Henry A. Dietz and Gil Shidlo, eds., *Urban Elections in Democratic Latin America* (1998). Cloth ISBN 0-8420-2627-4 Paper ISBN 0-8420-2628-2

A. Kim Clark, *The Redemptive Work: Railway and Nation in Ecuador, 1895–1930* (1998). ISBN 0-8420-2674-6

Joseph S. Tulchin, ed., with Allison M. Garland, *Argentina: The Challenges of Modernization* (1998). ISBN 0-8420-2721-1

Louis A. Pérez, Jr., ed., *Impressions of Cuba in the Nineteenth Century: The Travel Diary of Joseph J. Dimock* (1998). Cloth ISBN 0-8420-2657-6 Paper ISBN 0-8420-2658-4

Guy P. C. Thomson, *Patriotism, Politics, and Popular Liberalism in Nineteenth-Century Mexico: Juan Francisco Lucas and the Puebla Sierra* (1998). ISBN 0-8420-2683-5

June E. Hahner, ed., *Women through Women's Eyes: Latin American Women in Nineteenth-Century Travel Accounts* (1998). Cloth ISBN 0-8420-2633-9 Paper ISBN 0-8420-2634-7

James P. Brennan, ed., *Peronism and Argentina* (1998). ISBN 0-8420-2706-8